Tianxia in Comparative Perspectives

CONFUCIAN CULTURES
Roger T. Ames and Peter D. Hershock, series editors

Confucianism: Its Roots and Global Significance
Ming-huei Lee, edited by David Jones

Confucianisms for a Changing World Cultural Order
Edited by Roger T. Ames and Peter D. Hershock

Li Zehou and Confucian Philosophy
Edited by Roger T. Ames and Jia Jinhua

Xu Fuguan in the Context of East Asian Confucianisms
Chun-chieh Huang, translated by Diana Arghirescu

Confucianism and Deweyan Pragmatism: Resources for a New Geopolitics of Interdependence
Edited by Roger T. Ames, Chen Yajun, and Peter D. Hershock

Tianxia in Comparative Perspectives: Alternative Models for a Possible Planetary Order
Edited by Roger T. Ames, Sor-hoon Tan, and Steven Y. H. Yang

Tianxia in Comparative Perspectives

Alternative Models for a Possible Planetary Order

EDITED BY ROGER T. AMES,
SOR-HOON TAN,
and STEVEN Y. H. YANG

University of Hawai'i Press
Honolulu

East-West Center
Honolulu

© 2023 University of Hawai'i Press
All rights reserved
Printed in the United States of America

First printed, 2023

Library of Congress Cataloging-in-Publication Data

Names: Ames, Roger T., editor. | Tan, Sor-hoon, editor. | Yang, Steven Y. H., editor.
Title: Tianxia in comparative perspectives : alternative models for a possible planetary order / edited by Roger T. Ames, Sor-hoon Tan, and Steven Y.H. Yang.
Other titles: Confucian cultures.
Description: Honolulu : University of Hawai'i Press ; East-West Center, [2023] | Series: Confucian cultures | Includes bibliographical references and index.
Identifiers: LCCN 2023024902 (print) | LCCN 2023024903 (ebook) | ISBN 9780824895174 (hardback) | ISBN 9780824896034 (epub) | ISBN 9780824896041 (kindle edition) | ISBN 9780824896027 (pdf)
Subjects: LCSH: Cosmopolitanism. | Internationalism. | International relations—Philosophy. | Social justice. | Cosmology, Chinese.
Classification: LCC JZ1308 .T53 2023 (print) | LCC JZ1308 (ebook) | DDC 306.01—dc23/eng/20230608
LC record available at https://lccn.loc.gov/2023024902
LC ebook record available at https://lccn.loc.gov/2023024903

Calligraphy by Peimin Ni

University of Hawai'i Press books are printed on acid-free paper and meet the guidelines for permanence and durability of the Council on Library Resources.

Contents

Acknowledgments		vii
Introduction		1
Roger T. AMES, Sor-hoon TAN, and Steven Y. H. YANG		

Part I Challenging Hegemony and Global Capitalism   19

1. Relationality without Hierarchy: Hong Daeyong's Reappraisal of *Tianxia*   21
Jun-Hyeok KWAK

2. *Tianxia* as Anticosmopolitan and Protoracial: A Case Study of Late Imperial Vietnam   39
Liam C. KELLEY

3. "We Choose to Go to the Moon" for Truth, Justice, and Peace on Earth: A Dialogue for Socioeconomic Justice between *Ubu-ntu* and *Buren*   68
Mogobe B. RAMOSE

4. Ideology, Quixotism, or Enabling Utopia? The Notion of *Tianxia* as a Model for a New Form of Global Governance and Coexistence, Seen in the Light of the Japanese Experience   97
Christian UHL

5. Toward a New World Order: Reading *Tianxia* with Marx and Hegel   118
Viren MURTHY

Part II From Nation-States to a Relational Ecology   153

6. Why Does *Tianxia* Need a Nation-State? Nation and *Tianxia* in Modern China   155
Ban WANG

7	Comparing the Ancient Chinese *Tianxia* Order and the Postwar UN-Centric International Order Qingxin K. WANG	174
8	*Tianxia* and Islam Mustapha Kamal PASHA	198
9	*Tianxia:* A Process of Relations QIN Yaqing	221
10	Universalizing *Tianxia* in an East Asian Context Takahiro NAKAJIMA	236
11	Virtuosic Relationality and Ethical Diversity: A Buddhist Revisioning of International Relations beyond Anarchy and Hierarchy Peter D. HERSHOCK	250
Part III A Minimalist Morality for Solidarity and Mutual Critique		**267**
12	Spheres of Global Justice and *Tianxia* Theory Binfan WANG	269
13	*Tianxia* and Global Distributive Justice Sor-hoon TAN	289
14	Heavenly Governing All-under-Heaven: Reconceptualizing the Confucian *Daren* 大人 Idea for the *Tianxia* 天下 Leadership Xinfeng KONG	308
15	Without War or Conquest: The Idea of a Global Political Order in Asoka's *Dhamma* Rajeev BHARGAVA	322
16	From John Dewey to the Confucian "Idea" of Internationalism Roger T. AMES	345
	Contributors	371
	Index	377

Acknowledgments

We are grateful for the generous support and guidance offered by Song Bing and Liu Zhe, co-directors of the Peking University Berggruen Research Center, as well as the dedication and professionalism of its staff, Li Xiaojiao, Shelley Hu, Tian Xinyuan, and Zhan Yiwen. This *tianxia* project has been an inspiring example of team effort. All of us at the Berggruen China Center have the same purpose in cultivating a hub for East-West research and dialogue. We are committed to the cross-cultural and interdisciplinary study of the grand transformations that are affecting humanity. We are hopeful that this *tianxia* project will bring our world closer to global peace and harmony.

Introduction

Roger T. AMES, Sor-hoon TAN, and Steven Y. H. YANG

OVER THE FIRST two decades of the twenty-first century, the rise of East Asia, and of China in particular, has occasioned a seismic sea change in the economic and political order of the world. And add to this that China is more than just a country. With a population larger than Africa, it is a diverse and yet continuous civilization on a continental scale. Given the differential effects of the COVID-19 pandemic on global business and trade, it is now estimated by some that China will become the world's largest economy before the end of the 2020s. Like it or hate it, friend or foe, China's trajectory is upward, and it is not going away anytime soon. And if the anxiety conveyed through the popular media is any indication, the exponential ascent of what has been happily ignored over the past few centuries as the Chinatown of the world has startled the once-unchallenged liberal West and shaken it to its very core.

The tremors emanating from this newly emerging world order are testing the resilience of the modern system of sovereign and equal nation-states ushered in by the Treaty of Westphalia more than three and a half centuries ago. This Westphalian model institutionalizing the principle of state sovereignty parallels the values of individual autonomy and equality in liberal individualism. To the extent that such a system of single actors at the international level, each playing to win, has pitted the interests of each state against all others, it has drawn the world toward a politics of anarchism. And as a zero-sum game of winners and losers, it has proven at the global level to be wholly ineffective in addressing the pressing issues of our times, with the COVID-19 pandemic being only the first and most immediate crisis among many more in the mix. The compounding, irreversible problems defining our human predicament—climate warming, environmental degradation, continental refugee migration, income inequities, food and water shortages, mass species extinction, proxy wars, global hunger, and so on—are themselves organically interrelated, and unless they are addressed in a

1

wholesale manner, there can be no effective resolution. Traversing any and all national, ethnic, and religious boundaries, this gathering storm can only be confronted and weathered effectively by a global village working collaboratively for the good of the world community as a whole.

It was under these pressing conditions that the Peking University Berggruen Research Center organized a conference series to quarry world cultures for novel ideas that can be activated in formulating a new planetary order. What inspiration can the wisdom of the ages sedimented into our alternative world cultures—European, Confucian, Buddhist, Islam, Hindu, African—provide for anticipating an evolving concept of a new global order and guiding it toward a shared human flourishing? In 2018, the Berggruen China Center responded to the lack of a "planetary vision" of governance by initiating a program under the rubric *tianxia* or "All-under-Heaven" in search of a strategy for "taking the world as the world."

Zhao Tingyang 趙汀陽 and the *Tianxia* Conference Series

In order to build upon the theoretical foundation of the *tianxia system* (*tianxiatixi* 天下體系) first proposed by prominent contemporary philosopher Zhao Tingyang in 2005, the Berggruen China Center in June 2018 initiated the first installment of its continuing *tianxia* program. Since this inaugural conference, the program has gathered leading thinkers to discuss and debate how the theory of *tianxia* can serve as an inspiration for rethinking global governance and rebuilding trust in the shared future of humanity. True to the Center's dedication to the cross-cultural and interdisciplinary research into the transformations affecting humanity at a planetary scale, its *tianxia* program has brought together ideas from across a wide spectrum of cultural and intellectual terrain.

The purpose of the first conference of the *tianxia* program was to ask the question "What is *tianxia?*" as it is used in the East Asian sinic languages in order to set a context for the ensuing discussions on Zhao Tingyang's *tianxia* theory. *Tianxia* (天下)—conventionally translated as "All-under-Heaven"—is a familiar term in everyday Chinese parlance that simply means "the world." But *tianxia* is also a geopolitical term found throughout the canonical literature that has a deeper historical and philosophical significance. Over the past few decades, the meaning of this technical term, often referred to as the "All-under-Heaven System," has been much debated, primarily but not only in the Chinese literature, as a possible planetary framework for thinking about a new and evolving world order and a new model of world governance.

Although there are many understandings of *tianxia,* these interpretations within the Chinese process cosmology generally begin from an ecological understanding of *intra*-national relations that acknowledge the mutuality and interdependence of all economic and political activity. Within this cosmology as it is made explicit in the *Yijing* 易經 or *Book of Changes,* a *tianxia* understanding of "the world" begins from the primacy of relationality, thus redefining the nation-state as a second-order abstraction from the organic relations that constitute it. The twentieth-century philosopher Tang Junyi 唐君毅 underscores this organic aspect of Confucian natural cosmology in which there is only "worlding" or "world-making." We are all living interdependently within an unbounded ecology that has no external perspective, no view from nowhere. Tang would insist that

> when Chinese philosophers speak of the world, they are thinking of the world we are living in. There is no world beyond or outside of the one we are experiencing.... They are not referencing "a world" or "the world," but are simply saying "worlding," where the fact that "world as such" does not have a definite or indefinite article in front of it is really significant.[1]

And the dynamics of the flux and flow of such "worlding" are integral to itself without the need to appeal to something foundational and causal:

> In the minds of Chinese people, the cosmos has always been nothing more than a continuous stream, a kind of flow; all of the things and events of the cosmos are just a continuing process. And beyond this process there is not some other fixed substratum that supports it.[2]

Zhao Tingyang has captured this vision of a "vital inside without an outside" in his concept *wuwai* (無外): "no outside."[3] This notion of "no outside" is important because it obviates the familiar charge made against Zhao's theory that because he uses the Chinese term *tianxia* rather than "global order," and because he appeals to a historical event in the early Zhou dynasty as his example, he is in fact advocating for a Chinese hegemony rather than a new world order. *Tianxia* as "taking the world as the world" assumes the primacy of vital relationality, thus relegating the nation-state as a discrete, sovereign entity to the status of a second-order abstraction from the unbounded organic economic, political, and geographical relations that define it. When applied to the relations that obtain among nation-states, *intra*-national relations within the ecology of a global whole references a radical contextuality that might be characterized in Confucian language as the inseparability of the many focal aspects within their holographic fields (*yiduobufen* 一多不分). It describes a manifold of unique nation-states within the political organism, each construing the *intra*-national order from its own particular perspective, with China being only one among them. The one is many, the many one. The dynamic of this global ecology then is the emergence of an always provisional and resolutely unsummed totality of all orders. Said another way, absent in this model is any single, privileged, and dominant order that would override its others. This same continuing reformist dynamic is captured in the basic postulate in Confucian process cosmology of the symbiotic relationship between "forming and functioning" (*tiyong* 體用). The identity of each focal, holographic state emerges from its unique pattern of relations within the vital functioning of the world organism. This living planetary ecology itself is a holistic and inclusive pluralistic order (rather than a reductionistic, rationalized, and thus unitary order) engendered by the mutual accommodation among these unique focal states as this shared order is construed from the alternative perspective of each one of them.

Where did China as an early iteration of an ecological *tianxia* world order come from? Over the past few decades, this is a question that has absorbed the thoughts of many of China's best historians and has also been engaged over the past several decades by philosophers such as Zhao Tingyang. In his philosophical reading of *tianxia,* Zhao, keenly aware of the persistent and pernicious asymmetry in the prevailing way we have gone about theorizing China according to Western concepts and categories, has tasked Chinese and Western scholars alike to "rethink China" (*chongsi Zhongguo* 重思中國), where "rethinking China" thus conceived is relational.[4] For those outside, it is "thinking *with* China" by trying to take China on its own terms. And for China itself, it is "thinking *with* the world community," thereby trying to accommodate the world's many different perspectives. Taking on this revisionist task himself, Zhao provides a profoundly original philosophical interpretation of China's story that he insists has a contemporary relevance beyond the Chinese narrative. Indeed, Zhao's declared motivation in formulating his *tianxia* theory is that it be for the benefit of a world community in search of a new world order. Zhao asks: When the Central Plain (*Zhongyuan* 中原) was perceived by its inhabitants as the center of the world, what were the causes, the forces, and the destiny that coalesced across its four-millennia-long narrative to sustain the vital and generative unity of China as a state, as a civilization, and as a history? In telling this story, Zhao is advancing a novel and compelling thesis on not only how we should understand China, but also how, until recently, China has understood itself.

Zhao introduces what he terms a distinctively Chinese centripetal "whirlpool" model of world order on the Central Plain to interpret the historical progression of *tianxia* identity construction. This process of identity formation was driven over time by a series of interrelated "cultural attractors" with perhaps the most significant among them being the Chinese written character. This writing system as a political and spiritual attractor includes by extension the canonical texts it has engendered that perpetuate a shared cultural identity and a political theology integral to it. These attractors from earliest times have drawn the many disparate populations on the Central Plain and the expanding circle of its surrounding territories, into a political and cultural whirlpool. This vortex was already taking shape thousands of years ago during the Xia, Shang, and Zhou dynasties, and has continued in protean form down to the fall of the Qing dynasty in the early twentieth century.

Zhao argues that the expansion of China was due not merely to the interchange among the disparate civilizations or to the lure of expansionist behavior in the form of military conquest. Rather China's growth was the result of the fusion over time of the distinctive contributions of the many contenders for political control as they were constantly being pulled into the swirls and eddies of the whirlpool. Being drawn into this whirlpool of growth and amalgamation, the peoples surrounding the plains on all four sides sought to win the greatest material benefits and greatest spiritual resources by shaping their ways of thinking and living around the evolving core spiritual culture of the Central Plain. This *tianxia* vision of world order was able to transform the fierce currents of contention within the whirlpool itself into a shared identity that brought a significant degree of unity to the disparate cultures and peoples with their many different ways of living and forms of governance. The values that emerged in this "worlding" process within the political organism were relational equity that respects and accommodates the differences among the various cultures, and an achieved diversity that arose out of activating these differences in service to a shared well-being.

Objections to Zhao Tingyang's *Tianxia* System as a Planetary Model

We can identify three prominent concerns in the literature as scholars have responded to Zhao Tingyang's *tianxia* theory. First, there is the familiar criticism that while Zhao's account of the whirlpool formation of the Chinese state and its identity over its long history is compelling, it is also a rather idealized, romantic account of a historical process that occasioned much warfare and carnage. A closer look at this story would certainly reveal that as the whirlpool turned, there was much blood in the water. But more concerning is the criticism that the intention of this utopian story is to promote a distinctively Chinese version of world hegemony, that is, a Pax Sinica to replace the Pax Americana as it prevails today. In Wang Ban's introduction to *Chinese Visions of World Order: Tianxia, Culture, and World Politics,* for example, he points out that

> as a body of thought and practice, *tianxia* has wavered between the normative claim to values and culture on the one hand, and coercive mechanisms of domination on the other. The concept has played out between an impulse towards universal principles and an ideological cover for power

politics. In its modern avatars, the fault line parallels the divide between cosmopolitanism and interstate geopolitics.[5]

Indeed, this interpretation of *tianxia* as "an ideological cover for power politics" constitutes one of the major lines of argument against it. On this point, Wang insists that

> the talk of *tianxia* is increasingly perceived as an ideology behind China's soft power offensive on the global stage.... The political practice of *tianxia* evinces the entwined operation of consent and coercion. Instead of cosmopolitanism, critics see the rise of *tianxia* as the official ideology behind China's aggressive push into the murky waters of global competition and world politics. A looming Pax Sinica rivaling the Pax Americana, China is projecting its soft power and brandishing its culture around the world.[6]

The first prominent scholar to press this "Chinese hegemony" line of argument was William Callahan, who as early as 2008 contended that "rather than guide us toward a post-hegemonic world order, *tianxia* presents a new hegemony where imperial China's hierarchical governance is updated for the twenty-first century."[7] Callahan reminds observers in this debate that not all nations will want to be included in Zhao's *tianxia* system.

From the beginning, however, and continuing in his direct response to Callahan's complaint, Zhao argues that "although the concept of *tianxia* comes from China, its significance belongs to the entire world. Callahan seems to have conflated the *tianxia* system with China in our present world. His judgment that many nation states do not want to be ruled by China is of course true, but it misses the point. Today's China is a sovereign state and not *tianxia*. Doubts with respect to contemporary China should not be used as an argument against the *tianxia* system."[8] Zhao's repeated attempts to respond to this issue have resonated with scholars who adopt a more charitable interpretation of his *tianxia* system. For instance, Zhang Feng 張鋒 accepts and supports Zhao's clarification that the *tianxia* system is not an ideological cover for Pax Sinica. Zhang reiterates the point being made by Zhao himself in saying that

> it is a common impression that by employing the idea of *tianxia*, Zhao is trying to revive the old hierarchical, Sino-centric system of pre-modern East Asia, which, at least to some foreign observers, suggests that China has hegemonic ambitions. This is a fundamental misunderstanding. Zhao has pointed out clearly in several places that he is not simply recycling the old concept of *tianxia*; rather, he is trying to renew it and give it fresh meaning within the realities of world politics in the 21st century. His

understanding of *tianxia* is, therefore, different from the imperial Chinese view (indeed, from any other scholar's view).⁹

A second, perhaps more daunting challenge to Zhao's *tianxia* system arises from this same attempt to dehistoricize *tianxia* with game theory, and in so doing, to make it into a purely rational and thus universalizable theoretical model. This line of criticism questions the feasibility of his system in our contemporary context. Even if the ideal of *tianxia* can be justified in theory, to what extent can it be implemented on the political level? That is, what is the possibility of setting up a world institution based on this theoretical model? While generally positive in his response to Zhao's *tianxia* theory, Zhang Feng insists that

> the critical flaw of Zhao's thesis . . . is his failure to outline any clear pathway that might lead to the creation of the world institution of *tianxia* system—something on which he places so much emphasis. . . . "Common imitation" may fail because there may not be any common knowledge of the best strategy, or the best strategy is simply not recognized. As for "Confucian improvement," it may not be possible to reach conceptual agreement on the common interests that are perceived to be greater than individual interests. In any case, the relative gain of interests is most likely to be proven ex post facto.¹⁰

Zhang's criticism focuses not simply on Zhao's theoretical and philosophical assertions about his *tianxia* system but perhaps more importantly on the possibility of its implementation. To this challenge, Zhao simply replies that as a political philosopher he is only responsible for research on the concepts and principles of the *tianxia* system, and that the specific ways to achieve it should be left for political scientists to figure out.¹¹

A third criticism of Zhao's *tianxia* theory emerges from a decidedly Confucian perspective. Zhao Tingyang's centripetal whirlpool metaphor tells the story of an evolving Chinese *tianxia* system of global order pursued over the millennia among so many disparate peoples, languages, ways of life, modes of governance, and so on. While this diversity is truly profound, there would seem to have been enough of a shared morality within this diversity to hold it together as a continuous civilization and history for four thousand years and counting. Zhao argues that the shared identity that has provided the "continuity in change" (*biantong* 變通) over time lies in the written Chinese character and the classics born of this writing system. But what is missing in Zhao's story of what he takes to be a specifically political concept is an account of the minimalist morality that has been made explicit in these same canonical texts. While Zhao offers a normative political theory, he self-consciously rejects the relevance of Confucian morality when in this tradition the concept of the political as a symbiosis between family, state, and world is understood as an extension of what are fundamentally ethical concerns.[12]

Comparing Zhao's *Tianxia* Theory with Alternative Models of Global Governance

Having sought in the first meeting to bring the notion of *tianxia* into clearer focus within the East Asian cultural narrative itself, over two weekends in April 2021 the Berggruen China Center hosted a second conference in the *tianxia* program on the theme of "*Tianxia* in Comparative Perspectives: Alternative Models of Geopolitical Order." For this event, the initial cadre of primarily East Asia scholars were complemented by a chorus of international voices representing different cultural traditions: Buddhist, Islamic, Indian, African, Confucian, and European as well. The goal was to contextualize the *tianxia* vision of world order within alternative strategies drawn from a broad spectrum of the world's cultures and peoples. The participants in this second chapter of the conference series were guided by the following central questions:

1. Is *tianxia* only one Chinese model of cosmopolitanism among others?
2. What are the comparable ideas and ideals to *tianxia* within the context of other major cultural traditions?
3. What are the alternative visions of global justice that have inspired these Western, Indian, Islamic, Buddhist, and African cultural traditions?

The discussion began where the first iteration of the conference series left off. First, as we saw above, Zhao Tingyang's *tianxia* theory has lent itself to being perceived as a veiled strategy for justifying a Chinese hegemony. In the present volume, Jun-Hyeok Kwak (chapter 1) insists the "Heaven" of *tianxia* as "All-under-Heaven" must give us a firmament in which there is no center and no domination. In his analysis of the Chinese-style cosmopolitanism espoused under the rubric of *tianxia,* he finds the same fallacy found in the Eurocentric or Westphalian views of world politics where the notion of "relationality" fails to provide the regulative ideal needed to guarantee equality in the discourse among diverse states. He appeals to the *Dialogue on Mount Uisan* 醫山問答 of eighteenth-century Korean Silhak or Practical Learning scholar Hong Daeyong 洪大容 for an alternative conception of *tianxia* in which all states are placed on an equal footing rather than in a hierarchy. In explicating Hong's antihierarchical no-centrism, Kwak argues that Hong's notion of nondomination is precisely what is needed to supplement Chinese-style cosmopolitanism to preclude the emergence of a central hegemon.

Liam C. Kelley (chapter 2) suggests that Zhao's theory dovetails with themes in a field of scholarship known as "decoloniality." The argument is that the West, in conquering much of the world during the age of imperialism and imposing their divisive ideas concerning nations, races, and gender, also exerted a form of epistemic violence and injustice. Decoloniality scholars argue that prior to contact with the Western world, various peoples around the globe possessed visions of society that were more inclusive and accepting of diversity than in the West. But these cultures having been "invisabilized" now need to "decolonize" themselves from the forms of knowledge imposed upon them by the West. In this same vein but with some irony, the term *tianxia* appears frequently in premodern Vietnamese sources written in classical Chinese and is appropriated by Vietnam in the expression of its own colonizing attitudes. When it is used, it refers not to China, but to a more specific Vietnamese *"tianxia"* as the universe of the Vietnamese with the same elitist connotations as in China at that time. The history of Vietnamese expansion toward the south and interactions with people of different ethnicities, especially the Cham and Khmer, influenced the perceptions of the Vietnamese elite with their own sense of civilizational superiority.

Mogobe B. Ramose (chapter 3) joins Kelley in the decoloniality discourse as well as in Christian Uhl's (chapter 4) plea for a global structure that will overcome the existing capitalist order. From the perspective of several different episodes in recent human history, Ramose provides an account of the underlying source of the contemporary global human condition. At its core is an epistemic absolutism that negates the possibility of justice through a tenacious commitment to sustain the prevailing order of international politics dominated by an economic fundamentalism. This tendency toward absolutism is the affirmation of a dogmatism that for Ramose is the antichrist of philosophical thinking. Resistance is the only appropriate response to it. Ramose finds this resistance in a dialogue between *ubu-ntu,* an African philopraxical concept meaning "humaneness," and *buren* 不忍, a Chinese philosophical concept meaning "a heart that cannot bear suffering." The concern is with not only Africa and China but the rest of the peoples of the world with the ethical imperative to pursue and establish justice in human and interstate relations through the eradication of the injustice that lies at the root of capitalism. The ethical dimension of both *ubu-ntu* and *buren* demands an alternative model of global human relations in the pursuit of truth, justice, and peace in the world. The convergence between the ethics of *buren* and *ubu-ntu* is used to question the apparent dogma of the inalienability of sovereign statehood and the false belief in the immortality of a fundamentally immoral capitalism. Ramose's discussion on the ethics of *buren* and *ubu-ntu* certainly sheds light on the potential of cross-cultural philosophical dialogues in constructing alternative models of global governance.

These possibilities will ultimately enrich and broaden our ongoing theory-building process on *tianxia*.

Uhl joins Kwak in his concern about hegemony, arguing that oscillating between nationalism and cosmopolitanism, the debate on Confucian relational ethics as a foundation for an alternative world order risks reproducing rather than overcoming the contradictions and conflicts of a global capitalist modernity. He asks the question of what must happen to really unleash the critical potentials of *tianxia* and to prevent models such as Zhao Tingyang's "All-under-Heaven System" (*tianxiatixi*) from remaining a mere expression of the alienated conditions suffered under global capitalism. How is the rhetoric of Zhao and others different from the earlier discourse in wartime Japan? Uhl invokes for comparison the Japanese philosopher Nishida Kitarō and his students, who were able to interpret Japan's war effort to bring "the world under a single roof" (*hakkō ichiu*) as an attempt to build a harmonious and cooperative "new world order" (*sekai shinchitsujo*) based on "Eastern values." What is needed more than the mere evocation of Confucian values is the creation of concrete social and political institutions and economic conditions that will allow such values to be lived and acted upon in overcoming of the existing capitalist order.

Viren Murthy (chapter 5) responds to the different ways in which the problems of capitalism have been invoked to confront *tianxia* theory, and Zhao Tingyang's interpretation of *tianxia* theory in particular. Murthy argues that by putting Marxism and *tianxia* theory into conversation, he can show that *tianxia* theory must confront the problem of a postcapitalist world order. He begins by insisting any discussion of a new world order must acknowledge the contemporary expansion of Chinese capital. By invoking a comparison with Hegel on the one-many problem, Murthy examines the philosophical basis of Zhao's *tianxia* theory and argues that Zhao conceives of the one as an amorphous unity capable of enveloping infinite multiplicity without negating particularity. This, then, is the philosophical ground on which Zhao constructs his conception of internationalism. As we have seen in Uhl's chapter, a historical reading of Zhao's *tianxia* theory brings to mind the attempt of the Japanese to legitimize their imperial expansion during the interwar period. While Zhao has been criticized for being too nationalistic and also for proposing a world-state, Murthy suggests that Zhao could respond to such concerns effectively by drawing on early debates concerning Third World anti-imperialist nationalism. By bringing a Marxist critique into the discussion, Zhao's theory could be reworked in such a way as to take the otherwise suppressed problem of capitalism seriously.

Again, in the conference deliberations it was argued an alternative planetary order cannot simply be substituted for the existing one, but rather a process of reform needs to be initiated that begins by not underestimating the importance of the nation-state itself. Indeed, Ban Wang (chapter 6) takes as his basic question: Why does *tianxia* theory need the nation-state? In the *tianxia* discourse the modern nation-state system has always been targeted as the stumbling block to the peace and unity of the world. Yet thrust into the midst of clashing nation-states, China in modern times has had no choice but to engage the Western model of the sovereign state. In the wake of the fall of the Qing empire, Chinese reformers and revolutionaries alike devoted themselves to building a modern nation-state to enable China to survive as a polity and culture. Liang Qichao, Sun Yat-sen, Mao Zedong, and others were certainly nationalist thinkers, but in the process of nation-building they also had an internationalist *tianxia* vision that extended beyond the nation-state. In his chapter Wang focuses and elaborates on how Liang, Sun, and Mao invested in nation-building as a necessary and powerful means of realizing their cosmopolitan and internationalist visions of a world order. With the nation-state being reconceived in terms of Zhao's notion of *tianxia* as an organic political ecology with "no outside," the family and kinship with their private morality are the indispensable basis of social welfare and security within the various nation-states. And beyond the nation-state, an interdependent socioeconomic and normative infrastructure is needed to secure the planetary commons.

Qingxin K. Wang (chapter 7) argues we do not need a world government to effect *tianxia* as a planetary world order. Wang argues that in moving from idea to implementation, an analogy can be drawn between the Zhou-dynasty *tianxia* order and its modern iteration as the United Nations with the Security Council sitting at the top of the hierarchy. It is an appropriately weak nominal power that can function effectively under specified conditions: the notion of limited sovereignty, the conception of just war, the obligation of states to exercise self-restraint in the use of force, the obligation of states to protect human dignity and human rights, the legitimacy of humanitarian intervention, and the role and responsibility of the dominant states in the maintenance of international peace. Wang brings into focus important similarities between these two international orders—the Zhou dynasty and the United Nations—to draw some implications for the future of the international order in light of China's rise as a global power. Such similarities suggest the differences between the UN-centric postwar international order and the future international order that draws upon the ancient Chinese *tianxia* order may not be as great as are commonly assumed and that the two international orders might complement each other rather than being exclusive or conflicted.

Mustapha Kamal Pasha (chapter 8) asks and answers the question: How can a pluralistic global order be reconciled with Abrahamic religions such as Islam that begin from the exclusive universalism of a self-sufficient, transcendent deity? It would seem the registers of *tianxia* and Islam present opposing horizons. But Pasha would argue that such apparent divergences often conceal latent points of contact, dialogue, and convergence. While *tianxia* is based upon an immanentist cosmological postulate devoid of theological pretensions, the Islamic appeal to the Transcendent offers an alternative picture. Pasha visualizes an intimate connection between the universalisms produced within *tianxia* and Islam. Their expansive understandings of imagined community both challenge the nation-state as primary affiliation. The universal community promised in *tianxia* avoids parochial attachments to Westphalia, nation, or tribe. Islam too offers a horizontal nexus to humankind secured by a vertical relation to the One. While *tianxia* and Islam affirm ontological parity, they both depend upon a cosmological hierarchy to instantiate their universalisms. The basic problem for both *tianxia* and Islam is the challenge of reconciling inclusion with otherness. While conquest and conversion are familiar modalities of addressing Otherness, there are alternate pathways that can affirm universalism within *tianxia* and Islam. For Islam, the notion of *Ummah* as "the community of the faithful" is rooted within the Islamic cosmology in a more fundamental universal community of humankind in which there is the possibility of absorbing difference without erasure or marginalization. This elementary intuition directs inquiry into the spiritual edifice of Islam rather than its political expression.

Tianxia is often taken as a spatial structure where substantial entities exist and coexist. Consistent with the idea of a living political ecology, Qin Yaqing (chapter 9) rejects the default assumption regarding nation-states as atomistic entities and argues *tianxia* must instead be understood as a vital, temporal-spatial process of fluid, dynamic, and complex relations. Since *tianxia* is irreducibly relational, it is necessary to understand the nature of such relations in their original state of harmony, defined in terms of maximum cooperation and characterized by immanent inclusivity and mutual complementarity. Consistent with this *zhongyong* 中庸 logic, conflict is fundamentally resolvable and harmony achievable. Qin uses the goal of planetary order as an example to illustrate how relational governance can be an important complement to rule-based governance for cooperation and harmony in international society.

Again, for scholars such as Takahiro Nakajima (chapter 10), as important as the nation-state is in the world order, we must acknowledge the fact that more fundamental than the notion of the formal nation-state are the informal and shared lives of the world's people, imbricated as they are ecologically and concretely in all of their various interpenetrating activities: politics, economics, culture, environment, religion, security, health, and so on. Taking the historical perspective of "order as process" further, Nakajima argues *tianxia* must be reconceived as a pluralistic *praxis* rather than as an abstract theory taking the totality as its ideal. The "place" of *tianxia* is worlds nested within worlds with a constant redrawing of the boundaries "taking place" in the continuing process of formulating an always-emerging world order.

Peter D. Hershock's (chapter 11) Buddhist perspective shares Qin's assumption that relationality is ontologically more basic than individuality and Nakajima's emphasis on the emergent nature of an always-changing global order. He insists that, while new technologies and artificial intelligence can contribute to the emergence of a new world order, the human predicament today is fundamentally an ethical issue. For this reason, reorienting global values, intentions, and practices requires a sharp methodological turn from instrumental to moral reasoning. The global human condition can only be addressed by promoting an "ethical ecology" in which differences in ethical perspectives can be activated to contribute to realizing globally shared values. For Hershock, the therapeutic strategy of the Buddhist "middle path" has the proximal aim of engaging in international "relational therapy" and the reality of healing relations that will redress the historical wounds caused by states acting in their own self-interest. Buddhism thus points to the possibility of a truly ecological world order realized by valuing relational equity and an achieved diversity in the global commons.

A Minimalist Morality for Solidarity and Critique in a New World Order

The success of any conference series is not determined as much by providing answers to a given question as it is by clarifying the further direction of the discussion. The two most important lines of critique that have emerged have been (1) that Zhao's *tianxia* system is a purely rational endeavor lacking any vision for its practical implementation in the real world and (2) that as a political economy it conspicuously avoids any engagement with nonutilitarian ethics. With this critique in mind, the next conference of Berggruen China Center's *tianxia* program shall set as its primary objective the search for possible practical and ethical dimensions that can be built upon Zhao's theoretical work. The fundamental premise here is that in order for the *tianxia* system to remain relevant and significant in our world today and in our vision for the future, it must at once acknowledge the plurality of moral ideals defining the world's cultures and at the same time seek practical ways to formulate a minimalist morality that provides the limited solidarity needed to bring the world's people together.

Michael Walzer, in his *Thick and Thin: Moral Argument at Home and Abroad,* wants "to endorse the politics of difference and, at the same time, to describe and defend a certain sort of universalism."[13] Walzer claims that "there are the makings of a thin and universalist morality inside every thick and particularist morality" and that "minimalist meanings are embedded in the maximal morality, expressed in the same idiom, sharing the same (historical / cultural / religious / political) orientation."[14] And as for the substance of thin morality, for Walzer such minimalism does not mean minor or emotionally shallow morality; on the contrary, thin and intensity come together as "morality close to the bone."[15] Indeed, what Walzer wants from this minimalism is nothing less than "a certain limited, though important and heartening, solidarity" that can bring the people of the world together.[16] For Walzer himself, his candidate for this thin morality would be "a common, garden variety kind of justice." Other philosophers within the "thick" liberal morality would undoubtedly appeal to the Universal Declaration of Human Rights as their universalist ethic. Several of the essays presented at the second conference anticipate the direction of this further inquiry by suggesting their own answers to the question of the minimalist morality needed for human solidarity.

Binfan Wang (chapter 12) endorses Walzer's political pluralism. In his book *Spheres of Justice,* Walzer argues that "the deepest assumption of most of the philosophers who have written about justice, from Plato onward, is that there is one, and only one, distributive system that philosophy can rightly encompass."[17] For Walzer and Wang, too, this assumption ignores the different cultural backgrounds of political communities in which theories of justice are put into practice. In advancing his argument, Walzer claims that any formulation of a theory of distributive justice must have room for cultural diversity and political preferences. Wang insists that following this logic, the just principle of equal distribution in society in respecting the diverse cultural backgrounds of political theories must be complex rather than simple. Wang captures this symbiotic relationship between statism and cosmopolitanism with Fei Xiaotong's political aestheticism: "Each tradition celebrates the beauty of its own culture as well as the beauty of others, and by bringing this beauty into a shared diversity, the world achieves its inclusive unity."[18]

In our developing and increasingly affluent world, legions of the hopeless poor have still been left behind. In response to modern tragedies such as this, Sor-hoon Tan (chapter 13) looks to Confucian philosophy and ethics in particular as a resource for reflecting on the pressing issue of global distributive justice. While Zhao's *tianxia* theory as an ideal political concept is clearly normative in recommending a model that would encourage a commitment to a salutary planetary order, Zhao specifically rejects the idea that the early Zhou dynasty as his historical example embraced "government by virtue" and instead states that it advanced "fairness in benefit distribution" as a "concept of political economics." Given the premise that everyone, not just governments, has a responsibility to promote a global justice grounded in ethical values, a theory of global justice based on his rational model of *tianxia* philosophy that neither recognizes nor draws upon the primacy of the ethical in Confucian philosophy is not a compelling model. Central to Confucian teachings is a relational ethics that is applicable in all situations in which humans interact. This means that while political systems and institutions are certainly important, the primary ethically significant relationships in Confucian ethics are those between persons, not those between nation-states or other groups, and as such, they provide a standard for diagnosing failings in the existing institutional order.

Xinfeng Kong (chapter 14) follows Tan in insisting that morality must be at the center of the kind of global governance inspired by the *tianxia* model. To this end, he surveys the best of contemporary scholarship and brings clarity to the cluster of traditional terms that best express the notion of virtuous governance within the *tianxia* system. Kong tells the story of the awakening of humanism and the replacement of religion by moral education in the transition from the Shang dynasty to the Zhou. This movement from religion to education was vital in extending and consolidating *tianxia* and in pre-empting violent interethnic conflict, Again, it was also the way to cultivate the moral rulership of *daren*s who could govern *tianxia* effectively. Kong takes the model of ancient China as a diffused, pluralistic, and inclusive subject with an identity defined by a minimalist civilizational order, and by analogy he argues the modern world as a community could also be understood as a scaled-up political subject that can be shaped into a shared world community through an evolving pluralistic unity.

Exploring conceptual resources beyond the academic terrain of *tianxia,* Rajeev Bhargava (chapter 15) finds another model of global ethical leadership in Asoka, who lived in the third century BCE. Asoka inherited the warrior ethic of military prowess and territorial expansion from his ancestors and lived his political life in conformity with it during his early rule, but over time, he began to see the futility of warfare and the human cost of territorial conquest. As a result, he began to develop a new political ethic for rulers. He proposed the idea that rulership should be based on and guided by a new political morality for which he used the Indic term *dhamma*. Both ruler and subjects were to submit to this higher ethic. In order that political violence and conquest be minimized, kings had to rule less by force and more by persuasion. Officials were to be appointed not only to instruct people within the territory of the king but also to spread *dhamma* as a moral minimalism promoted assiduously through a regimen of international education. Physical conquest was to be replaced by moral conquest, brute power by moral hegemony. Thus, Asoka envisaged a new global order grounded largely in nonviolence and noninjury toward others. The parallel between *dhamma*'s advocacy for moral persuasion and *tianxia*'s mechanism of *hua* 化, a transformation that "works by winning over the hearts of others instead of subduing them by force," strengthens the argument that a minimalist morality transcends cultural boundaries.[19]

Roger T. Ames (chapter 16) answers Walzer's search for a minimalist morality by bringing in a Confucian perspective. In so doing, he echoes the insistence of Tan and Kong that morality must be at the center of any proposed planetary order. It is the cluster of terms surrounding "family reverence" (*xiao* 孝) as the prime moral imperative in the Confucian tradition that has made family feelings the root and the substance of a continuing Confucian social, political, and global order. Ames insists it is family feeling that is the most basic shared value universally understood and thus has the potential of bringing all people together past the "us" and "them" binary. The institution of family has always been indispensable in providing a basic level of social welfare and security in all dimensions of the human experience that is not and can never be provided by the nation-state or other such formal entities. Family teaches the wisdom of interdependence, and by underscoring the inseparability of privilege and responsibility, of entitlements and obligations, it is the model of human organization that can most effectively challenge the prevailing ideology of individualism and the pernicious effects of justified self-interest.

One conclusion that has emerged from this *tianxia* series is that in our search for a minimalist morality needed for human solidarity, the Chinese experience must be included in the discussion. If we begin from the fact that China, even with a population almost twice that of a combined eastern and western Europe, has persisted as a continuous civilization for some four thousand years and counting, we can appreciate the scale of the diversity that has been pursued over the millennia among so many disparate peoples, languages, ways of life, modes of governance, and so on. While this diversity is truly profound, at the same time there has been enough of a shared minimalist morality to hold it together as a cultural and political entity. But perhaps even more immediate than the historical example of China itself is the response of the various sinic East Asian nations to the COVID-19 pandemic. All of these political entities have very different forms of governance, and yet with their different but overlapping Confucian cultures, their populations' sense of community and willingness to restrain themselves out of consideration for the well-being of others—instead of rejecting all restrictions to curb the spread of the pandemic as infringements on their autonomy—have been critical to their success in minimizing the human cost of the disease.

Notes

1. Tang Junyi 唐君毅, *Complete Works of Tang Junyi* 唐君毅全集 (Taipei: Xuesheng shuju, 1991), vol. 11, pp. 101–103.

2. Ibid. 中國人心目中之宇宙恆只為一種流行，一種動態；一切宇宙中之事物均只為一種過程，此過程以外別無固定之體以為其支持者 (substratum).

3. Zhao Tingyang 趙汀陽, 天下的當代性：世界秩序的實踐與想象 (A possible world of All-under-Heaven system: The world order in the past and for the future) (Beijing: China CITIC Press, 2016), pp. 75–79.

4. Zhao Tingyang 趙汀陽, 天下體系: 世界制度哲學導論 (The *tianxia* system: An introduction to the philosophy of world institutions) (Beijing: People's University Press, 2011), p. 1.

5. Ban Wang, "Introduction," in *Chinese Visions of World Order: Tianxia, Culture, and World Politics*, ed. Ban Wang (Durham, NC: Duke University Press, 2017), p. 5.

6. Wang, "Introduction," pp. 18–19.

7. William A. Callahan, "Chinese Visions of World Order: Post-Hegemonic or a New Hegemony?," *International Studies Review* 10, no. 4 (December 1, 2008): 749–761.

8. 趙汀陽. 天下的當代性: 世界秩序的實踐與想象 (All-under-Heaven: The *tianxia* system for a possible world order), 1st ed., trans. Steven Y. H. Yang (Beijing: CITIC Press, 2016), pp. 278–279.

9. Zhang Feng, "The Tianxia System: World Order in a Chinese Utopia," *Global Asia* 4, no. 4 (Winter 2010): 110.

10. Ibid., pp. 111–112.

11. Zhao Tingyang, "Some Questions Regarding the 'Tianxia System,'" April 16, 2020. Unpublished WeChat interview with Steve Yang.

12. This organic symbiosis is described in the *Mencius* 4A5:

人有恆言，皆曰『天下國家』。天下之本在國，國之本在家，家之本在身。

There is a popular adage heard among the people who all say: "The world, the state, the family." The world is rooted in the state, the state in the family, and the family in one's own person.

13. Michael Walzer, *Thick and Thin: Moral Argument at Home and Abroad* (Notre Dame, IN: University of Notre Dame Press, 1994), p. x.

14. Walzer, *Thick and Thin,* pp. xi, 3.

15. Walzer, *Thick and Thin,* pp. 4–15.

16. Walzer, *Thick and Thin,* p. 11.

17. Michael Walzer, *Spheres of Justice: A Defense of Pluralism and Equality* (Oxford: Robertson, 1983), p. 5.

18. 各美其美，美人之美，美美與共，天下大同。

19. 趙汀陽. 天下體系—世界制度哲學導論 (The *tianxia* system: An introduction to the philosophy of world institutions), 1st ed., trans. Steven Y. H. Yang (Nanjing: Jiangsu Educational Press, 2005), p. 33.

PART I

Challenging Hegemony and Global Capitalism

CHAPTER 1

Relationality without Hierarchy

Hong Daeyong's Reappraisal of *Tianxia*

Jun-Hyeok KWAK

WITHIN THE CONFINES of Chinese political philosophy, *tianxia* (天下 "All-under-Heaven") has been frequently regarded as an alternative to the Eurocentric set of rules governing international relations (Li 2002; Carlson 2011; Zhang 2011). This way of understanding the notion of *tianxia* is not limited to those scholars who wish to place China at the center of world politics. More and more intellectuals have written about *tianxia* as a way of overcoming the world problems that are situated in the very nature of the nation-state system since the Westphalian treaties (Tong 2006; Zhao 2009a, 2011, 2013, 2015; Yan 2011; Gan 2012; Wu 2013; Wang 2017). And the recent debates on "Chinese-style" hegemony in the field of international relations have become inextricably entangled with the ideas of *tianxia* codified in tributary relationships and inescapably focused on their pivotal roles in the justification of a China-led hierarchical order during periods of its dominance in East Asia (Hua 2005; Callahan 2008; Zhang 2009, 2015; Han 2012; Kang 2012; Bell 2017; Bell and Wang 2020).

One of the striking features of these current debates on *tianxia* is that they assume that governing principles of peaceful coexistence should operate with a "morally" or "practically" justifiable inequality between sovereign states. Instead of emphasizing a formal equality between states, the rules of which directly or indirectly relate to the Westphalian nation-state system, the most imperative reference point of *tianxia* for peaceful coexistence is a hierarchy in which a hegemonic state acquires its authority by realizing a moral community or a diplomatic framework within which states work together for negotiating the common good.

At this juncture, the notion of *tianxia* is suggested as another cosmopolitanism, the backdrop of which does not lie at the crossroads between liberal democracy and Eurocentric universalism—one that conceives people everywhere as being the same (Zhao 2009a; Yan 2011; Gan 2012; Wu 2013; Wang 2017). Concomitantly, the practices of *tianxia* through the tributary system in Chinese history are redeployed as the very rationale for building up a Chinese-style peaceful coexistence as opposed to the post–Cold War world in which major powers compete for hegemony in world politics (Hua 2005; Zhang 2011, 2015, pp. 20–46; Han 2012; Kang 2012, pp. 1–24; Bell and Wang 2020, pp. 106–142).

Specifically, on the one hand, the advocates of Chinese-style cosmopolitanism seek to find a universal system the normative foundations of which can be accepted universally as a set of regulative principles that guide all states into a harmonious relationship. They are very confident of the probability that the traditional notion of *tianxia* exhorts all states to pursue the common good of the world rather than their national interests. At this juncture, the notion of *tianxia* is taken to signify a world institution embracing a normative principle with which all states voluntarily work together to transform the world. For instance, Gan Chunsong believes that a return to the principle of *tianxia,* originating in Chinese philosophy three thousand years ago, will replace the order of relentless competition by force in international relations with that of a "family" conceptualized through Confucian virtues such as "benevolence" and "harmony" (Gan 2012, pp. 139–145). In similar vein, Zhao Tingyang trusts that the world institution espoused by the notion of *tianxia* will benefit the people of all nations (Zhao 2009b, pp. 93–94).

At first sight, such advocacy of Chinese-style cosmopolitanism appears to be egalitarian in the sense that it is concerned with diverse or plural voices in international relations. However, it can hardly be denied that the advocates of Chinese-style cosmopolitanism do not pay appropriate attention to the problem of domination in the historical practices of *tianxia* in which China was placed at the center of a hierarchical world while neighboring countries were nothing but tributary states. The narratives of Chinese-style cosmopolitanism about the Sino-centric tributary system eventually end up with China's exceptional civilization. In their conceptual and institutional elaborations of the Chinese tributary order, they do not answer the serious question of the extent to which autonomy was given to neighboring states under China's historical empires. The result is that they fall prey to the dangers of exaggeration regarding the voluntary subjugation of neighboring states to the central hegemon, while they underappreciate the possibility of resistance by the subordinate states against that hegemony.

On the other hand, the Chinese-style international relations (IR) theory, which evolved through the surge of scholarly interest in searching for an alternative to Eurocentric IR theories, places heavy emphasis on inequality between states.

For instance, analyzing the sustaining mode of stability under the hegemony of the Ming and Qing dynasties from 1368 to 1841 in East Asia, David Kang sets up the ordering principles of Chinese-style IR theory: A hierarchy ranked by military and cultural achievements, an aristocratic society across countries sharing Confucian ideas, and the tributary system institutionalized as its rules and norms (Kang 2012, pp. 8–11). In a similar vein, and despite some differences in their emphasis on the role of culture in consolidating the tributary system, Zhang Feng suggests "a relational theory" in which the course of relational interaction between states is determined not solely by the "instrumentality" of mutual gains or realpolitik but by the "expressivity" of ideational affections (Zhang 2015, pp. 26–28).

It is undeniable that the turn led by the Chinese-style IR theory is valuable. The Chinese-style IR theories offer a new perspective that challenges the dominant view of IR theory based on Eurocentric notions such as "balance of power" and the Westphalian ideas such as "national sovereignty." The new perspective appears to be a development at first glance from within the attempts to promote China's soft power in the contemporary world, but it goes beyond that since it does aim to find a set of ordering principles that can replace the Westphalian international system. However, such an interpretation of the tributary system is extracted chiefly from the traditional doctrine of Sino-centrism in light of modern understanding. As Daniel Bell and Wang Pei point out, the revival of the China-led tributary system is incompatible with the idea of the equality of sovereign states in the contemporary world (2020, pp. 129–131). More importantly, the Chinese-style IR theory displays a pervasive negligence of voices from peripheral states against the hegemonic state in the China-led tributary system throughout the history of East Asia, and thereby it ultimately fails to charge the central hegemon with the task of constraining its own excess of domination within the hierarchy.

This chapter tackles the theories of global justice that seek an alternative to Eurocentric or Westphalian views of world politics. Specifically, first, I examine the Chinese-style cosmopolitanism whose alternative vision of peaceful coexistence is espoused by the notion of *tianxia*. In doing so, I claim that it retains the very fallacy that can be found in the Eurocentric or Westphalian views of world politics. Particularly, I will put forward its notion of "relationality" in the sense that the Chinese-style cosmopolitanism fails to provide us with a regulative ideal through which different justifications for justice can be steered toward an equal discursive stance between states. Second, through analyzing *Dialogue on Mount Uisan*, which was written by Hong Daeyong (1731–1783), I explore an alternative conception of *tianxia* in which all states are placed on an equal footing rather than in a hierarchy. At this juncture, explicating his antihierarchical no-centrism, I will suggest his notion of nondomination as a guide with which to supplement

Chinese-style cosmopolitanism in favor of making a discursive stance between states without a central hegemon.

Tianxia in Sino-centric Cosmopolitanism

Chinese-style cosmopolitans believe that the political ideals of *tianxia* will attract other states or peoples through their moral and political realization in any given country (Gan 2009; Wu 2013, pp. 26–38, 335–338). Surely, the mere fact that the notion of *tianxia* emerged in Chinese contexts does not render it parochial. Nevertheless, we can hardly deny that a Chinese style of cosmopolitanism can be parochial. It is not because the world institution espoused through the notion of *tianxia* implicitly represents China as a new hegemon in world politics (Ge 2011, pp. 91–131). It is because Chinese-style cosmopolitans do not provide us with a regulative principle with which we can guard ourselves against the cultural as well as political domination of one state over other states. Rather than criticizing the distinction between *hua* (civilized 華) and *yi* (uncivilized 夷), which was employed explicitly to justify the tributary order in Chinese history, they espouse the world of *tianxia* as a hierarchical order in which barbarian states as well as tributary states should become enlightened through their competition with one another to resemble the superior state (Zhao 2009b, pp. 53–54; Gan 2012, pp. 12–13). Briefly, Sino-centrism is part of the Chinese style of cosmopolitanism, given the tributary hierarchical order in Chinese history the normative justification of which played the pivotal role in assimilating neighboring states to Chinese civilization while preventing those states from achieving full dignity in its actualization.

Zhao's "compatible cosmopolitanism" is exemplary in this regard (2013, pp. 62–64; 2015, pp. 20–21). Firstly, drawing on the geographical notion of *tianxia*, he contrasts the rules of the Westphalian international system with the traditional Chinese senses of universal relationship. He praises the latter for the political circumstances in which all states voluntarily promote universal well-being, while he expresses his dissatisfaction with the former that enhances international conflicts (2009a, pp. 5–7). Secondly, he brings Confucianism to the psychological notion of *tianxia* as its ideal consequence and concludes that Confucianism has developed a cosmopolitan ideal that embraces "a compatible multiverse united by universal relationship" (2013, p. 63). It is more idealistic than other Chinese-style cosmopolitanisms in turning the Confucian ethics of harmonious relationship toward the possibility of spontaneous order in which all states find the rules of coexistence through mutual adjustment (2013, pp. 47–52). Finally, identifying the ideal of *tianxia* with the transition of utilitarian cooperation into moral harmony, he maintains that a world-system governed by the notion of *tianxia* is held to be better because of the moral goods it will produce, such as reciprocity, autonomy, and the inclusion of all citizens. At this juncture, he invites us to praise the traditional senses of *tianxia* from the point of view of a relationship that is not solely political but also moral (2015, pp. 19–20).

Zhao's cosmopolitan rendering of *tianxia* is attractive, though idiosyncratically idealistic. What makes his Chinese-style cosmopolitanism distinctively idealistic is its emphasis on "compatibility" as a supreme value to be pursued through world politics. Distinguishing "compatibility" (*he* 和) indispensable for peaceful coexistence from "universality" (*tong* 同) inherently entangled with restless domination, he argues that "while the former encourages states to attain reciprocal knowledge through deliberation, the latter stimulates them to strive for superiority through competition" (2015, p. 12). And, throughout his characterization of cosmopolitanism, a harmonious relationality between states is always presupposed:

> Based on the ontology of coexistence, methodological relationism focuses on reliable interests by means of *relational rationality,* or relational calculation, considering that relations are the limits of accessible interest, instead of the aggressive pursuit of the maximization of self-interests, as *individual rationality* encourages. (Zhao 2013, p. 50)

As we can see above, his conception of relational rationality precludes the maximization of self-interest, and by the same token, the core of relational rationality presupposes the consideration of others in the pursuit of self-interest. The relational rationality he uses here is not at all new. He adopts the traditional notion of "harmonization" (*he* 和) in Confucianism, which indicates "the action of the gentleman in harmony with others," that is, "compatibility" in his term, as opposed to "conformity" or "mere bargaining" (*Analects* 13.23). In similar vein, his conception of relational rationality is construed through a realization of natural hierarchy, and its paradigmatic actualization spells out the possibility of conflict in actual relationships. Although "toleration of different forms of life for others" is suggested as one of the basic principles, his compatible cosmopolitan view does not embrace "value pluralism" in that there is a recognition of irreconcilable conflicts (Berlin 2013 [2000], pp. 14–17; Zhao 2013, pp. 62–63). Furthermore, the priority of commonality or family-ship over individuality differentiates his compatible cosmopolitanism from Rawlsian reasonable pluralism in that the different justifications for goodness and justice require a discursive stance that is indispensable for reaching good judgment (Rawls 1993, pp. 133–172; 1999, pp. 11–23; Zhao 2015, pp. 11–13). In his cosmopolitanism, a universal political system of family-ship should be made in advance and simultaneously conflict needs to be minimized by virtue of "compatibility"

(Zhao 2013, p. 51), while democratic deliberation between persons or states is not necessarily given as a basic structure.

Certainly, differing from those liberal cosmopolitan theorists who attempt to extend liberal principles to the global realm, his compatible cosmopolitanism does not impose any ideological principle as a supreme value. Nevertheless, if Zhao is proposing the notion of *tianxia* as a regulative ideal that would guide deliberation between states about what global justice requires in particular cases, he needs to explain more clearly a feasible way through which the discursive stance in which states can be treated equally is to be built into the global system. Otherwise, the notion of *tianxia* would just be another normatively parochial value into which substantially "Chinese" cultural components are smuggled. At this juncture, it is worth considering a report about the Korean tribute mission during the Ming dynasty:

> The Emperor of Ming should treat us as equal persons (一視同仁). And he shouldn't be suspicious and disdainful of us. But the Emperor treats our country rather differently. (requoted from Fuma 2015, pp. 154, 640)

As we can see above, Huh Bong, who led the tribute mission of the Joseon dynasty to the Ming in 1574, recorded his disappointment in the "Confucian relational justification" that had been his moral and political compass before the mission. And, criticizing the Ming's unfair treatment of Joseon, he expressed his experience of the Ming dynasty with the phrase "nominally China [中國] but actually nothing but barbarian [達子: literally 'the Mongols']" (Fuma 2015, pp. 151, 639). This shows that while the world system of *tianxia* might have been able to sustain peaceful coexistence, it could not be just permissively and admittedly a harmonious relationship in which each state could have equal access to justification. Briefly, without an equal discursive stance, a co-operative relationship or a normative Confucian justification of compatible relationality can easily degenerate into domination.

Furthermore, there is nothing we can find in Zhao's compatible cosmopolitanism that can be applied to the weaker states to give them a voice against or resist the strongest state whose benevolent governance does not meet their general demands for harmonious relationship. What Zhao aims to offer with Laozi's notion of nonstance is not a discursive stance but more or less a self-cultivation for obtaining a commonality that would return to harmony, as we can see from his statement that "the best way for human action is to do things in harmony with nature" (2013, p. 48). Put another way, alongside the nonstance analysis of diverse perspectives between states, there is the moral justification of harmonious relationship producing a hierarchy between states. The former aims at establishing coexistence by reducing the asymmetrical relationships between states, while the latter aspires to the higher ethical qualification of the world-system by justifying asymmetrical distinctions between states. This double standard is the result of his concern to ensure a spontaneous order in which all states voluntarily promote universal well-being without a comprehensive principle. But he does not keep up with this initial concern with spontaneity in his final reflection on *tianxia* as the world-system. When he conducts the inquiry into the feasibility of *tianxia* that begins with the ethical justification of the world-system, the former evaluation of diverse perspectives with "nonstance" is unduly switched to the latter aspiration for harmonious consensus with "holism." For instance, juxtaposing the Daoist notion of "things themselves" with the Confucian pursuit of "virtuous order" through self-cultivation, Zhao sees the Daoist nonstance or nonaction as an ontological condition for realizing the Confucian harmonious relationship (2013, pp. 48–49).

It is certain that Zhao peculiarly detests imperial domination between states (2013, pp. 6–7; 2015, pp. 7–9). In addition, he emphasizes that the world-system conceptualized by the notion of *tianxia* aims not to realize peaceful coexistence under another imperialistic hegemony but rather to provide a referential blueprint for realizing a discursive stance that embraces diverse voices regardless of the asymmetrical relations according to military and economic power (2013, pp. 56–58; 2015, pp. 20–21). However, he does not show how a co-operative relationship should be or can be constructed despite the asymmetrical power relations between states in the current global realm. Instead, he suggests a "Confucian relational justification" that is different from what he calls "the Western modern political justification" elaborated by him as "self-referential" and "democratic" (2013, p. 61). What is still missing in his renewal of *tianxia* is, then, a discursive stance through which the different views of the appropriate relationship between states can be justified. In other words, Zhao's compatible cosmopolitanism might be able to vindicate the moral significance of the superior state with the notion of *tianxia,* but abiding by it would not suffice to render its governance democratically permissive or politically acceptable.

Hong Daeyong's Transvaluation of Confucianism

Shocked by the emergence of the Manchuria-based Qing dynasty in 1644, the seventeenth-century Korean Confucians questioned the Sino-centric view of *tianxia,* whose validity was severely damaged by the replacement of the Ming dynasty with the Manchurian empire. And some of them openly strove to place Korea at the center of the world, calling the Qing dynasty a barbarian empire while rendering Korea as an alternative center. For these proponents of the mentality of "little China," the highest duty was to respect the moral superiority of the Ming dynasty. And the denunciation of the Qing dynasty became a scholarly vogue among intellectuals in the late seventeenth century (Cho 1996; Park 2013, pp. 229–366; Fuma 2015, pp. 118–171). At this juncture, no substantial difference in the presupposition of a hierarchical system can be found between the Sino-centric view of *tianxia* in China and the "little Sino-centrism" in Korea.

In the meantime, there was a group of scholars in Korea who aimed to overcome both Sino-centrism and little Sino-centrism altogether. This group was called Silhak (Practical Learning), and its frequent encounters with Western disciplines of learning in the eighteenth century garnered an unprecedented interest in Korean history. Western astronomical science ushered in the reevaluation of the Sino-centric view of *tianxia,* and subsequently the traditional notion of *tianxia* in which one state was placed at the center of the world started to be dismantled. For them, the little Sino-centrism that came to the fore in Korea after the emergence of the Manchuria-based Qing dynasty was not so very different from the Sino-centric view of *tianxia* that relegated all China's neighboring countries to the periphery.

Hong Daeyong (1731–1783) was a Silhak scholar in the Joseon dynasty of Korea. Like his contemporary Silhak scholars, he did not rest satisfied with the Confucian criticism of the Manchuria-based Qing dynasty. He also acknowledged the problem of the Confucian senses of *tianxia,* and he tackled the nature of "little Sino-centrism," particularly as postulated by the Neo-Confucian scholars in his time:

> "I am going to ask again. What do you mean by the 'wise man (賢者)'?" Heoja (虛子) replies. "Esteem the achievements of the Duke of Zhou (周公) and Confucius (孔子) and learn the words of the Cheng brothers (程顥, 程頤) and Zhu Xi (朱熹), keep the *Great Learning,* drive out a false teaching, save the world through benevolence, and practice self-discipline with sagacity. This is what the Confucians call the 'wise man.'" Silong (實翁) raises his head and talks with a smile. "I come to see that you are really infatuated with inappropriate learning and studies. After the death of Confucius, his disciples messed up his true teachings, and the school of Zhu Xi was disrupted by the Confucians at the end. They esteemed Confucius, but they lost his true teachings. And all learned his words without knowing their true meanings." (Hong 2011, pp. 26–27; my translation)

In *Dialogue on Mount Uisan* (醫山問答, hereafter *Dialogue*), Hong substantiates the fallacies of the "little Sino-centrism" through the mouth of Silong (an old man of practicality). Silong proclaims first that Heoja should have abandoned the central neo-Confucian virtues and practices in the first place, including "the *Great Learning,*" "benevolence," and "self-discipline." And then he criticizes the moral and political orthodoxies made by the neo-Confucians at that time. The critical point of the passage above is that any Confucian teaching like Zhu Xi's that posits an undisputable opposition between "right" and "wrong" only serves to disguise selfish "minds." For him, the neo-Confucian visionaries based themselves on the delusion that through the learning of the neo-Confucian moral and political doctrines, each man can be or will suddenly become benevolent and wise.

At first glance, Hong appears to be sympathetic to the Confucianism of his time, since he does not challenge directly the teachings of Confucius or Zhu Xi themselves. However, he has no intention to renew their original teachings. As we can see below, he ultimately transvalues the Confucian views of world order by his own view of *tianxia* that is grounded rather in Mozi and Zhuangzi (Song 1999; Park 2013, pp. 67–83; Sea-Jeong Kim 2016; Yu-jin Kim 2017). Particularly with Mozi, he repudiates the Confucian visionary of the Golden Age and informs us that the Zhou dynasty is not in any way to be conceived as an ideal state.

> The Xia (夏) dynasty treated people right (忠) and the Shang (商) dynasty revered natural value (質), but compared with the periods of the sage kings Yao (堯) and Shun (舜), they were pompous. The Zhou dynasty pursued nothing but magnificence and sumptuousness. The disciplines of its rulers were already on the decline at the times of King Zhao (昭) and King Mu (穆), so that the helm of governance was in the hands of feudal lords. (Hong 2011, p. 139; my translation)

Hong specifies that the Zhou dynasty was deprived of righteousness from its very beginning. And he declares that because of the lavish way of life, any righteousness was not actualized in the Zhou dynasty. In this way, he directly contrasts his view of the three dynasties with what Confucius says in the *Analects:* "The Zhou dynasty gazes down upon the two dynasties [the Xia and Shang dynasties]. How brilliant in culture (文) it is! I follow the Zhou" (3.14, 23). Surely, at this juncture, what he seeks to undermine is not only the neo-Confucian doctrinaire ethics in which the vision of the consummate life was grounded in their reverence for the Zhou dynasty, but also the Confucian orthodoxy itself that the Zhou dynasty is the ideal one that is always righteous. For Hong, a virtuous life does not consist in having a civilized way of life, as for Confucius.

Hong's transvaluation of the Zhou dynasty in the Confucian view of world order is firmly anchored in his adaptation of the Mohist criticism of Confucianism. On the one hand, he accepts the Mohist view of frugality in his depreciation of the Zhou dynasty (Mozi 2010, pp. 25, 211–231). Criticizing the extravagance of the funerals and burials in his time, he proclaims through the mouth of Silong, "revere frugality (崇其儉) and moderate ornaments (節其文)" (Hong 2011, p. 126). Along the same line, he criticizes the Zhou dynasty for its luxurious culture, and he juxtaposes Mozi with Mengzi as a way of explicating the fallacies of the latter. More importantly, on the other hand, he appropriates the Mohist doctrine of "inclusiveness" in his statements of the relationality of the Zhou dynasty with neighboring states. Some scholars identify his advocacy of indiscriminate love with Mozi's doctrine of "universal love" (Park 2013, pp. 74–83, 189–192). But, while agreeing with Mozi in spirit, he directs his contemporaries to pay more attention to Mozi's criticism of Confucianism than the Mohist view of "care" or "concern." At least in *Dialogue*, the need for an impartial attitude in relationality with others is taken not in terms of "care" or "concern" but in terms of challenging the Confucian imaginary of the Zhou dynasty. For instance, Silong declares that the replacement of the Zhou dynasty with the Yin dynasty was driven by the selfish avarice of the former to seize *tianxia* (Hong 2011, p. 141). Briefly, he does not fully accept Mozi's doctrine of "universal love" that cannot reach an account of antihierarchical no-centrism. Consider the following three statements in this regard:

1. From the Heaven's-eye view, humans (人) and things (物) are all equal (Hong 2011, p. 36; my translation).
2. All are the same in the sense that each feels close to his own compatriots (Hong 2011, p. 149; my translation).
3. If Confucius floated out on the sea and lived in the lands of the Eastern barbarians, he would have set up the Way of Zhou there by cultivating those barbarians with Chinese things (customs and laws). Then he would have written *Spring and Autumn* outside China (域外春秋), taking into account its own distinction between inside and outside and its own way of revering the king and expelling the barbarians. This is why he has been called a sage (Hong 2011, p. 151; my translation).

Hong's notion of equality between men and things in statement (1) sheds light on the impact of Mozi's teaching on his thought about an impartial attitude, even more so when we see that Mozi's doctrine of universal love is grounded in Mozi's antithetical view against the Confucian notion of humanity (*ren* 仁) that requires a discriminating love centered in a particular belongingness (Loy 2013; Thompson 2014; Zhang 2016, pp. 143–162). As the notion of "the Heaven's-eye view" as an identifiable expression of "the will of Heaven" indicates, Hong appears to inherit from Mohism the key tendency of reducing distinctions by upholding the need for treating everything equally. However, the underlying Mohist conjectures in (1) cannot be automatically consistent with his explications of no-centrism with "things themselves" in (2) and (3). In fact, the latter statements show that his ideal of equality is owed not so much to Mohism but to something else, because he even appears to endorse Confucianism in the sense that he puts forward discriminating love as what things themselves show in (2). And in (3), he enjoins Confucius to convince us of the inevitability of natural affection to particularistic attachments. The contradictions among these three statements signify that we need something other than Mozi's notion of universal love to appreciate his view of *tianxia* with antihierarchical no-centrism.

Hong's Alternative View of *Tianxia*

Hong's transvaluation of the Confucian view of world order relates to his avowed purpose in *Dialogue* that he will give an alternative view of world order through the eyes of Heaven (天視) (Hong 2011, p. 39). But what precisely he means by "seen from Heaven (天)" is not clear if we try to grasp it with Mozi's doctrine of universal love that imposes the will of Heaven as a guiding principle for the sake of reducing social inequalities and equalizing subordinate relationships. To the extent that the Mohist view of world order remains elusive because of its agreement with the Confucian visionary of just hierarchy, the subversive character of Hong's alternative view of *tianxia* will remain unrecognized.

Through the eyes of Heaven, Hong ultimately aims to abolish any views of world order in which a hierarchy can be justified as a practice of education and cultivation. At this juncture, he takes Zhuangzi rather than Mozi. Although he does not accept Zhuangzi's individualistic notion of spiritual freedom, his cosmology of "seen from Heaven" is firmly grounded in the Zhuangzian vision of returning to a primitive society in which all peoples can live as the Way (道) moves. Briefly, through his eclectic readings of Mozi and Zhuangzi, which are named the way of "learning different views with impartiality" (公觀併受), he suggests his own view of *tianxia,* the essential feature of which can be found in its construction of the relationality between states with nondomination.

NO-CENTRISM WITHOUT HIERARCHY

After explicating the origins of men and things in terms of the nature of Heaven and Earth (天地之性), Silong answers the question of whether the Earth is the center of the universe. At this juncture, using his knowledge of Western astronomical science, Hong declares that in the world of *tianxia,* there is no center:

> Of all the stars in the heavens, there is no star that does not have a world unto itself. If we look from the view of other heavenly stars, the Earth is nothing but a star. An unlimited number of worlds are spread out across the universe, and thereby saying that peculiarly the Earth is the center of the universe is not appropriate. (Hong 2011, p. 61; my translation)

As we can see above, Hong urges that any sort of centrism strays from the Way of *tianxia*. Here he accepts Zhuangzian naturalism, namely, a spontaneous natural movement in which all myriad things (萬物) live in their own way as a part of *tianxia*. But while he admits that *tianxia* as the relational whole is there because of all things and the myriad things are there because of *tianxia*, he also believes that these two views should be taken differently. For him, the latter view is recognizably natural in scientific observation, but the former view is problematic when each part wishes to place itself at the center of *tianxia*. In other words, to say that there is a center in the world of *tianxia* is to make a justification of hierarchy between states in the former sense. He refuses to do this, and he goes further to suggest that all countries are equal in *tianxia*:

> Seen from Heaven (天), how can there be any distinction between "in" and "out"? Thus China (華) and barbarians (夷) are all the same in the sense that each feels close to his own compatriots, each respects his own ruler, each defends his own country, and each finds comfort in his own customs. (Hong 2011, pp. 148–149; my translation)

At first glance, the quote above appears to state something similar to the Mohist notion of universal love. However, if we look carefully, we can see that Silong neither attempts to elaborate the will of Heaven nor aims to suggest the highest overall principle governing the world order. Rather he simply portrays a feature in which all, including China and its neighboring countries, dwell. In this feature, equality between states, or at least an equal cause for justification between states, is concretized as a condition through which the Way of *tianxia* that all can be included is actualized. By the same token, the distinction between China and barbarians is discarded, and any centrism that places one's country at the center is rejected.

There is no doubt that Hong's antihierarchical no-centrism was influenced by Zhuangzi's cosmology of spontaneity. But even if we grant Hong's application of Zhuangzi's criticism of Confucianism as a rhetorical tool to dismantle the Sino-centrism of Neo-Confucianism and thus grant that there are some purposes aimed at by using Zhuangzi's relativistic attitude, it certainly does not follow that his cosmology of spontaneity ends up with a relativistic view of what is right and what is wrong. He does not leave his no-centrism undecided as to how one can weigh a universally acceptable justification of coexistence against particular rationales with which each state pursues its own interest. What he maintains is that all states, whether civilized or uncivilized, are identical to each other in their nature and thereby each state should be considered as just one among many states existing in the world of *tianxia* (Hong 2011, p. 150). He no longer views the world of *tianxia* as embodying a hierarchy the Neo-Confucians considered essential, and he suggests instead an equal stance between states in which all the different voices should be respected equally.

SPONTANEITY WITH NONDOMINATION

Hong's eclectic reading of the *Zhuangzi* does not unavoidably qualify his reconciliation with Zhu Xi's theory of moral self-cultivation. The most convincing textual evidence in this regard can be found in Silong's laments over contemporary Confucianism in *Dialogue:*

> Their maintaining the *Great Learning* actually comes from their hubris (矜心). Their ostracizing a false teaching really comes from their longing for mastery (勝心). Their benevolence with which they seek to save the world actually originates from their lust for power (權心). Their ethical justification of self-discipline is grounded in their selfish avarice (利心). (Hong 2011, p. 27; my translation)

Shirking Zhu Xi's aesthetic theory of moral cultivation in which all things are predisposed and structured by *li* (propriety 禮) for objective learning, Hong urges instead that the way of the past or the dominant view of what is just in a particular time cannot be utilized for coping with a problem at our disposal in the present:

> Adapting to customs in accordance with the times is the art of rule by the sages. They do not detest harmony and generosity. But if times go by and new customs arise, there is no way to prevent new trends. Anyone who goes against them will make the turmoil greater. Even the sages are not able to prohibit them. Thus it is said that anyone who lives in the present but wishes to return to the way of the past will end up with disaster. (Hong 2011, p. 136; my translation)

As we can see above, Hong uses Zhuangzi's relativism not only to transvalue the dogmatic view of neo-Confucianism but to suggest an alternative perspective that enables people to be free from the blind practice of the rituals canonized by Zhu Xi's emphasis on the immutability of *li*. The upshot is that the knowledge of things is different in accordance with times and places and thereby no state can claim moral or epistemological superiority over the others (Hong 2011, pp. 147–151).

Given that Hong does not seek a single ethical scheme inherent in things themselves, we need to see carefully what would be his guiding principle with which the different voices of each state are treated equally in his view of *tianxia*. His contemporary Confucians postulated the model of "familyhood" as a regulative direction aimed at rectifying an imperfect relationship, and in the neo-Confucian doctrines, the ideal of familyhood can be actualized through a learning process by family members in their interactions with one another. What is imperative in this regard is his appropriation of the spontaneity of vital energy (氣) with which he criticizes the Confucian ideal of familyhood. His elaboration of the origin of evil minds serves to negate the validity of the Confucian ideal of familyhood and make it undesirable:

> The sun's heat and light reached the earth, and all myriad things flourished. Their bodies copulated with one another and gave birth to babies. Then, heavenly wisdom (神智) got blocked day by day, shifting knacks (小慧) grew day by day. Selfish cupidity (利慾) became so immoderate, life and death became trivial. This is the situation of the earth, and that is what you know. (Hong 2011, p. 70; my translation)

The passage above indicates the reason why the Confucian ideal of familyhood is not implausible. For Hong, it constitutes obstacles to the natural flow of vital energy that runs freely within and without human bodies. Particularly, he stresses the ways in which the selfish desires of humans prevailed through familyhood in the earth. Juxtaposing the emergence of family with the evil minds of his contemporary Confucians—"hubris (矜心)," "longing for mastery (勝心)," "lust for power (權心)," "selfish cupidity (利心)"—he hints that the appropriate model of morally justifiable order in the world of *tianxia* cannot be analogically identical with the ideal of the good parent in neo-Confucianism that "the rulers serve for the people." In this regard, consider this passage about natural hierarchy: "The greedy men of courage and wisdom (勇智多欲者) came out and gathered their followers who agreed with them. They occupied lands and became the leaders. Then the weaker men were obliged to labor, the stronger men enjoyed all benefits" (Hong 2011, p. 134: my translation).

In the light of the Daoist view of "noncoercive actions" (*wuwei* 無爲), he rejects the Confucian ideal of familyhood that puts forward the mutual commitment of the ruler and the ruled. Instead, illustrating that natural hierarchy is nothing but blind obedience to abusive rulers, he warns that any simplistic idealization of familyhood as a guiding direction in the world of *tianxia* is not appropriate. At this juncture, he goes further to set up nondomination as a guiding direction in the world of *tianxia*: "Should it be measured from the Earth, it is right to say that the Earth is the center of the seven stars 七政: the Sun, the Moon, Mercury, Venus, Mars, Jupiter, and Saturn as it is encircled by them. But saying that the Earth is the center of all stars in the universe is just like the view of a babe in the woods [literally 'a frog in the well']" (Hong 2011, p. 61; my translation).

Hong's no-centrism reaches an account of the coexistence of different views in which deliberation with equal stance becomes a condition for coming together without imposing the structure of hierarchy between them. Interlacing Zhuangzi's relativism with his no-centrism, Hong praises difference opposing commonality with a single ethical scheme. He even states: "If things are seen from a human point of view, humans are noble and things are ignoble. If humans are observed according to the point of view of things, things are noble and humans are ignoble" (Hong 2011, p. 36). At this juncture, if "equal concern for everyone" or "impartial caring" is taken as the governing principle, it is difficult to explain his emphasis on the equal worth of different perspectives in the eyes of Heaven. His vision of indiscriminate love is certainly inclusive, but it rules out the possibility of equalizing different views with a hierarchy of knowledge or a monolithic ethical scheme.

In his alternative view of *tianxia,* Hong puts forward the problem of the unequal discursive stance in the traditional Chinese senses of *tianxia.* As we can see from the previous quote, switching the Confucian "doctrine" to an "assertion" of centrality, he claims that any assertion should be approved within relationality with others in the sense that no one is able to place oneself at the center of the world of *tianxia.* At this juncture, it is particularly the question of domination that leads Hong to be concerned about the asymmetrical relationship between states and to distinguish between authority (*wangdao* 王道) and domination (*badao* 霸道) as well as between the eyes of Heaven and the point of view of earthly politics (Hong 2011, pp. 38–39, 90, 142–143). More importantly, he maintains that harmonious coexistence in the world of *tianxia* is guaranteed not through mutual benefit but through establishing a relationality in which different justifications of justice are taken equally in deliberation between states (Hong 2011, pp. 130–141). For him, only such a concern with the domination of a hegemonic state allows for both relationality without hierarchy and spontaneity with nondomination. At this juncture, the tributary order in which China was placed at the center is rejected not only in view of no-centrism but in view of the plurality of ethical justification in the world of *tianxia.*

Conclusion

Hong's view of *tianxia* reveals what the Chinese-style cosmopolitans miss in their interpretations of *tianxia.* First, they fail to suggest a set of conditions in which all states whose powers are asymmetrical can be embraced. Describing the order of *tianxia* as a historical experience, they instead depict the Chinese tributary system as a paradigmatic example for coming close to the ideal of *tianxia.* Second, they do not show us clearly how an effective discursive stance between states can be established. A deliberative stance and diverse voices among states are emphasized, but their visions of peaceful coexistence neglect the need for the discursive stance of states with equal status. In contrast, Hong portrays *tianxia* as a world order without a center in which all states enjoy relationality with equality, at least in their basic claims to exist together with the others and seek justice between them. In this portrayal, the view of *tianxia* itself constitutes the very condition under which a discursive stance between states can be established.

Hong's reappraisal of *tianxia* indicates the problem of asymmetrical justificatory power between states in the global realm. The inequality of the justificatory power in question is constantly being captured at the very moment that a coexistence of diverse views requires a democratic deliberative stance in the global realm. But this unease with asymmetrical justificatory power does not direct us sufficiently to go beyond the liberal cosmopolitanism emphasizing a formal equality between states or the Chinese-style cosmopolitanism putting forward a shared ethical commonality under a central hegemon. In this sense, by elaborating Hong's antihierarchical no-centrism with nondomination, I propose an alternative view of *tianxia* through which "coexercisable" and "coenjoyable" rules can help better regulate competing justifications between states. The best way to overcome asymmetrical power relations between states is not only to establish a discursive stance in which each state has an equal access to justification but to actualize the requirements of nondomination with which a hegemonic state can be constrained by subordinate states from its potential excess of domination. At this juncture, relationality with nondomination as a guiding principle can form a ground for democratic deliberation on which various political and cultural calls for justice can be coordinated in a nondominating way.

Note

This chapter is a slight adaptation of the author's article "Global Justice without Self-centrism: *Tianxia* in *Dialogue on Mount Uisan*," *Dao* 20, no. 2 (2021): 289–307.

References

Bell, Daniel. 2017. "Realizing *Tianxia:* Traditional Values and China's Foreign Policy." In *Chinese Visions of World Order:* Tianxia, *Culture, and World Politics,* edited by Ban Wang, pp. 129–146. Durham, NC: Duke University Press.
Bell, Daniel, and Wang Pei. (2020). *Just Hierarchy*. Princeton, NJ: Princeton University Press.
Berlin, Isaiah. 2013 [2000]. *Power of Ideas*. Edited by Henry Hardy. Princeton, NJ: Princeton University Press.
Callahan, A. William. 2008. "Chinese Visions of World Order: Post-hegemonic or a New Hegemony?" *International Studies Review* 10, no. 4: 749–761.
Carlson, Allen. 2011. "Moving beyond Sovereignty? A Brief Consideration of Recent Changes in China's Approach to International Order and the Emergence of the Tianxia Concept." *Journal of Contemporary China* 20, no. 68: 89–102.
Cho, Youngrok [曺永祿]. 1996. 朝鮮의 小中華觀-明淸交替期 東亞三國의 天下觀의 變化를 中心으로 (A study on Chosun's self-consciousness of "So-Junghwa": In compari-

son with Chinese and Japanese scholars' view of *tianxia* in Late Ming and Early Qing Period). 『歷史學報』(*Journal of the Korean Historical Association*) 149: 105–138.
Confucius. 2003. *The Analects*. Translated by Edward Slingerland. Indianapolis, IN: Hackett.
Fuma, Susumu [夫馬進]. 2015. 『朝鮮燕行使と朝鮮通信使』(Korean embassies to Beijing and Korean embassies to Japan). 名古屋Nagoya: 名古屋大学出版会 Nagoya Daigaku Shuppankai.
Gan, Chunsong [干春松]. 2009. 王道與天下國家: 從儒家王道政治重思天下國家觀念 (*Wangdao* and *Tianxia* state: Reconsideration of the idea of *Tianxia* state from the perspective of Confucian *Wangdao* politics). 紀念孔子誕辰2560週年國際學術研討會暨國際儒聯會員大會 Paper presented at the International Conference in Honor of the 2560th Anniversary of Confucius and Congress of the International Confucian Association.
Gan, Chunsong [干春松]. 2012. 『重回王道 — 儒家與世界秩序』(Back to Wangdao: Confucianism and the world order). 上海 Shanghai: 華東師範大學出版社 Huadong Shifan Daxue Chubanshe.
Ge, Zhaoguang [葛兆光]. 2011. 『宅兹中國』(Here in "China" I dwell). 北京 Beijing: 中華書局 Zhonghua Shuju.
Han, Yuhai [韩毓海]. 2012. 『天下: 包納四夷的中國』(Under the Heaven: An all-inclusive China). 北京 Beijing: 九州出版社Jiuzhou Chubanshe.
Hong, Daeyong [洪大容]. 2011. 『醫醫山問答』(Dialogue on Mount Uisan). 서울 Seoul: 지식을만드는지식Jisigeul Mandeuneun Jisik.
Hua, Shiping. 2005. "A Perfect World." *The Wilson Quarterly,* Autumn, 62–67.
Kang, David. 2012. *East Asia before the West*. New York: Columbia University Press.
Kim, Sea-Jeong [김세정]. 2016. 『『의산문답』에 나타난 홍대용의 공생의 생태주의』 (Ecological philosophy in Hong Daeyong's *Dialogue on Mount Uisan*) 『儒學研究』 (*Studies in Confucianism*) 35: 125–152.
Kim, Yu-jin [김유진]. 2017. 『담헌 홍대용의 '천(天)' 관념』 (A study on Hong Daeyong's *Notion of the Heaven*) 『국문학연구』 (*Journal of Korean Literature*) 36: 65–90.
Laozi [老子]. 2008. *Annotations of Laozi's* Daodejing 『老子道德經注校釋』. With annotations by Wang Bi 王弼注. Interpretations by Lou Yulie 樓宇烈校釋. Beijing 北京: Zhonghua Shuju 中華書局.
Li, Yangfan [李扬帆]. 2002. 天下觀念考 (On the idea of *tianxia*). 『國際政治研究』(*Studies of International Politics*) 1: 105–114.
Loy, Hui-chieh. 2013. "On the Argument for *Jian'ai*." *Dao* 12: 487–504.
Mozi. 2010. *The Mozi: A Compete Translation*. Translated and annotated by Ian Johnston. Hong Kong: Chinese University of Hong Kong.
Park, Heebyung [박희병]. 2013. 『범애와 평등-홍대용의 사회사상』(Universal love and equality: Social thoughts of Hong Daeyong). 파주Paju: 돌베게Dolbege.
Rawls, John. 1993. *Political Liberalism*. New York: Columbia University Press.
Rawls, John. 1999. *The Law of Peoples*. Cambridge, MA: Harvard University Press.
Song, Yong-bae. 1999. "Countering Sinocentrism in Eighteenth-Century Korea: Hong Tae-Yong's Vision of "Relativism" and Iconoclasm for Reform." *Philosophy East and West* 49, no. 3: 278–297.
Thompson, Kirill O. 2014. "Mozi's Teaching of 'Jianai'" (Impartial Regard): A Lesson for the Twenty-First Century?" *Philosophy East and West* 64, no. 4: 838–855.

Tong, Shijun. 2006. "Chinese Thought and Dialogical Universalism." In *Europe and Asia beyond East and West,* edited by Gerald Delanty, pp. 305–315. London: Routledge.

Wang, Ban. 2017. "The Moral Vision in Kang Youwei's Book of the Great Community." In *Chinese Visions of World Order:* Tianxia, *Culture, and World Politics,* edited by Ban Wang, pp. 87–105. Durham, NC: Duke University Press.

Wu, Jiaxiang [吳稼祥]. 2013. 『公天下: 多中心治理與雙主體法權』 (Tianxia for all: Polycentric governance and rights of dual-subject). 桂林 Guilin: 廣西師範大學出版社 Guangxi Shifan Daxue Chubanshe.

Yan, Xuetong. 2011. *Ancient Chinese Thought, Modern Chinese Power.* Edited by Daniel Bell and Sun Zhe. Translated by Edmund Ryden. Princeton, NJ: Princeton University Press.

Zhang, Feng. 2009. "Rethinking the 'Tribute System': Broadening the Conceptual Horizon of Historical East Asian Politics." *Chinese Journal of International Politics* 2: 545–574.

Zhang, Feng [张锋]. 2011. 天下體系: 一個中國式烏托邦中的世界秩序 (The *tianxia* system: A world order in a Chinese utopian style). 『復旦國際關係評論』 (*Fudan International Studies Review*) 1: 87–92.

Zhang, Feng [张锋]. 2015. *Chinese Hegemony.* Stanford, CA: Stanford University Press.

Zhang, Qianfan. 2016. *Human Dignity in Classical Chinese Philosophy, Confucianism, Mohism, and Daoism.* New York: Palgrave Macmillan.

Zhao, Tingyang [趙汀陽]. 2009a. "A Political World Philosophy in Terms of All-under-Heaven (Tian-xia)." *Diogenes* 56, no. 1: 5–18.

Zhao, Tingyang [趙汀陽]. 2009b. 『壞世界研究: 作為第一哲學的政治哲學』 (Investigations of the bad world: Political philosophy as first philosophy). 北京 Beijing: 中國人民大學出版社 Zhongguo Renmin Daxue Chubanshe.

Zhao, Tingyang [趙汀陽]. 2010. 天下體系的現代啟示 (Modern revelation of the *tianxia* system). 『文化縱橫』 (*Beijing Cultural Review*) 6: 34–41.

Zhao, Tingyang [趙汀陽]. 2011. 『天下體系: 世界制度哲學導論』 (The *tianxia* system: An introduction to the philosophy of world institution). 北京Beijing: 中國人民大學出版社 Zhongguo Renmin Daxue Chubanshe.

Zhao, Tingyang [趙汀陽]. 2012. "The Ontology of Coexistence: From *Cogito* to *Facio.*" *Diogenes* 57, no. 4: 27–36.

Zhao, Tingyang [趙汀陽]. 2013. "All-under-Heaven and Methodological Relationism: An Old Story and New World Peace." In *Contemporary Chinese Political Thought: Debates and Perspectives,* edited by Fred Dallmayr and Zhao Tingyang, pp. 46–66. Lexington: University of Kentucky Press.

Zhao, Tingyang [趙汀陽]. 2015. "天下秩序的未來性" (Prospect of the *tianxia* system). 『探索與爭鳴』 (*Exploration and Free Views*) 1, no. 11: 7–21.

Zhuangzi. 1995. *Commentaries on the Zhuangzi* 『莊子集釋』. With annotations by Guo Qingfan 郭慶藩 (選). Punctuation by Wang Xiaoyu 王孝魚 (點校). Beijing 北京: Zhonghua Shuju 中華書局.

CHAPTER 2

Tianxia as Anticosmopolitan and Protoracial
A Case Study of Late Imperial Vietnam

Liam C. KELLEY

IN RECENT YEARS, the increasing presence and influence of the People's Republic of China on the world stage has led some scholars to seek to develop new theories about international relations. Under the assumption that there is a dichotomy in the world between "Western" and "non-Western" societies, some scholars see China as "non-Western," and as such, view its rise to prominence as potentially offering an alternative to the Western-dominated world order that over the past few centuries has overseen not only competition between nation-states but also imperialism, colonialism, and world wars. While there are numerous scholars who have written on this matter, the work of Chinese philosopher Zhao Tingyang 趙汀陽 has been particularly influential. Through a monograph and a series of articles in both Chinese and English, Zhao Tingyang has argued that within the Chinese intellectual tradition are sufficient concepts to develop a new theory for international relations and world governance, one that he calls the "*tianxia* system" (*Tianxia tixi* 天下體系).[1]

Central to Zhao's ideas is the concept of "*tianxia*" 天下. Often translated into English as "All-under-Heaven," *tianxia* is a term that one can find used frequently throughout Chinese history to refer to something like "the known world." For Zhao, this term points to a critical distinction between Chinese and Western traditions. Western ideas about the world, according to Zhao, begin with the nation, and as such, the post-Westphalian international order that the Western world created in modern times is not a true "world order" but instead is a global system of competing nation-states in which some nations dominate others, and where that domination is enabled and exacerbated by

39

perspectives that this division of the world into nations generates, namely nationalism and racism. By contrast, Zhao argues, the starting point for thinking about the world in the Chinese tradition is "*tianxia*," again, a term that he sees as signifying the entire world. Therefore, Zhao believes that by conceptualizing international relations from the perspective of *tianxia*, we can develop a sense of "worldness" instead of "internationality," and that this can lead to a less divisive world order.[2]

To be clear, Zhao does not argue that the *tianxia* system ever actually existed in the past and that we can resurrect it. Instead, his argument is that ideas about *tianxia* that we can find in historical sources can provide us today with the intellectual foundation to imagine a new world order. The key ideas for doing this are inherent in the very term *tianxia*, which Zhao argues has three meanings. First, it can refer to "the earth, or the whole world under Heaven." Second, it can also signify "the 'hearts of all peoples' (*minxin* 民心), or the 'general will of the people.'" Third, Zhao claims that *tianxia* is "a world institution, or a universal system for the world, a utopia of the world-as-one-family."[3] Again, Zhao does not argue that such a world institution that governed the earth and was sympathetic to the hearts of all peoples ever existed. Instead, he is taking inspiration from what he sees in the idea of *tianxia* and its associated concepts to propose a new world system.

While not claiming the historical existence of the *tianxia* system, Zhao nonetheless relies on historical information to support his proposal for such a future system. This is where Zhao's position breaks down, as we will see below, but it is also where it will appeal to certain readers. Zhao's ideas dovetail nicely with the ideas in a field of scholarship known as decoloniality.[4] According to scholars in this field, not only did the West conquer much of the rest of the world during the age of high imperialism, but it also exerted a form of epistemic violence against the world by imposing divisive ideas, particularly its ideas concerning nations, races, and gender. Decoloniality scholars argue that prior to contact with the Western world, various peoples around the globe possessed visions of society that were more inclusive and accepting of diversity than we can find in the West, and that those societies now need to "decolonize" or "decolonialize" themselves from the forms of knowledge that were imposed on them by the West. This is where Zhao's ideas can find a receptive audience, as he places the *tianxia* system in opposition to the Western-created international world order and its underlying worldview and argues that ancient Chinese ideas point to a superior alternative.

Zhao's theory of the *tianxia* system therefore fits well with the position of decoloniality scholars. Zhao's work, however, also suffers from the same weakness as decoloniality scholarship, in that both approaches posit an idealized "non-West" but do so largely through imagination rather than by attempting to document reality in the non-Western past prior to contact and engagement with the West. We can see this, for instance, in the way that Zhao selectively quotes from ancient texts. In arguing for the "worldness" of the concept of *tianxia*, for instance, Zhao discusses a concept that he sees as related to *tianxia*, the concept of *wuwai* 無外, and in the process, distorts the meaning of this term. Literally meaning "nothing outside" or "no outside," in Zhao's rendering, *wuwai* refers to the "worldness" of the concept of *tianxia* in that it indicates to him that there is "nothing outside" of *tianxia*, because *tianxia* is "the world" and nothing can be conceptually larger than the world (short of thinking in terms of the universe). Zhao argues that it is very likely that this perspective prevented China from developing what he considers to be the Western perspective of viewing certain peoples as "heretics," and that it also did not allow for the development of a clear-cut sense of nationalism, which Zhao also says is distinctly Western.[5]

To make this point, Zhao states that "*tianxia* is a family, and nothing is outside of it" (*Tianxia wei jia er wuwai* 天下爲家而無外), and to support this explanation, he cites in a footnote information from two ancient texts: from Cai Yong's 蔡邕 (133–192) *Solitary Decisions* (*Duduan* 獨斷) Zhao cites the phrase "[For] the Son of Heaven there is no outside, and he takes *tianxia* as [his] family" (*Tianzi wuwai, yi tianxia wei jia* 天子無外, 以天下為家); and from the *History of the Han* (*Hanshu* 漢書) he cites the phrase "The Son of Heaven takes the four seas as [his] family" (*Tianzi yi sihai wei jia* 天子以四海為家).[6] In Zhao's rendering, *tianxia* is the subject, and it is explained as a family with nothing outside of it. However, in the texts that he cites, the Son of Heaven, or emperor, is the subject, and it is the emperor's view or perspective that is presented. What is it that the emperor sees? It is not *tianxia* in the sense of "the world" as a geographic space. Instead, it is the important people in his world, those who govern over his empire. Zhao cites only a selection from the passage in the *Solitary Decisions*. When we look at the passage in its entirety, we can see more clearly what *wuwai* refers to. It appears in a passage where the term "Heavenly family" is defined, and that passage is as follows: "*Tianjia, baiguan xiaoli zhi suo cheng, tianzi wuwai, yi tianxia wei jia, gu cheng tianjia* 天家, 百官小吏之所稱, 天子無外, 以天下為家, 故稱天家. Heavenly family: a name for the officials and clerks. [For] the Son of Heaven there is no outside, and he takes *tianxia* as [his] family. This is therefore called the Heavenly family."[7]

This passage does not say that there is "nothing outside" of *tianxia*, and it does not see *tianxia* as "the world." Instead, it is about the important people under the emperor's control, the officials who staff his imperial bureaucracy. The emperor, or Son of Heaven, views all of these people as members of his family. He does not discriminate and see some as "outside" of the "Heavenly family" of his bureaucracy regardless of where they are in *tianxia*, which in this context, can only signify the empire, for it is only men in the empire who staff the emperor's bureaucracy.

As for the phrase in the *History of the Han*, "The Son of Heaven takes the four seas as [his] family," this also refers to the important people in the empire. It appears in a passage about the construction of palace buildings during the early years of Han dynasty rule. When Emperor Gao (Gaodi 高帝; r. 202–195 BCE) saw that grand-looking (*zhuangli* 壯麗) palaces were being built at his capital, he got angry, saying that *tianxia* was still in a state of unrest, as there were still people who had not submitted to his rule, and that therefore, there were more important matters to attend to. The official in charge of the palace construction, however, countered that with *tianxia* still unpacified it was precisely the time to build such palaces because "the Son of Heaven takes the four seas as [his] family; if [his] palaces are not grand looking, then the opportunity will be lost to demonstrate might [*zhongwei* 重威]."[8]

What we can see from these two passages are two important points. First is that in each of these texts, *tianxia* clearly refers to the empire rather than "the world." Second, we can also see that of critical importance to the ruler of the empire, the Son of Heaven or emperor, was his control over the officials who governed over the empire on his behalf, as well as potential rivals in "the four seas," meaning the various regions of the empire. The emperor could at times embrace officials and powerful local rulers as members of his family so that they did not feel left "outside." However, if they resisted joining the "Heavenly family," the emperor could demonstrate his might. In other words, what we see here are clear signs of power politics and domination, precisely the elements that Zhao Tingyang attributes to the Western world order.

In what follows, we will challenge Zhao Tingyang's claim that the concept of *tianxia* that we find in the historical record can provide us with the intellectual tools to develop a new philosophy for world governance. We will do so by examining what we can see of the *tianxia* system in late imperial Vietnam. What we will find is that the conditions that prevailed in nineteenth-century Vietnam were strikingly similar to what was documented some two thousand years earlier in the *Solitary Decisions* and the *History of the Han*, namely, a world of power politics and attempts at domination. We will also find evidence that the Vietnamese ruling elite had a clear sense of difference between themselves and "others." What we will argue is that many elements that Zhao Tingyang and decoloniality scholars attribute to the West are in fact universal and can easily be found in the "*tianxia* system" of late imperial Vietnam.

Possessing *Tianxia* in Late Imperial Vietnam

The term and concept of "*tianxia*" (*Thiên hạ* in Vietnamese) is one that has historically been as important in Vietnam as it has been in China. In searching through the premodern Vietnamese dynastic chronicles, one will encounter hundreds of instances in which this term was used. However, as one does so, one will also detect a semantic pattern, as the term was invariably used to indicate the empire rather than "the world"; and when the emperor spoke to *tianxia,* we can understand that to signify that he was communicating with the important people in the empire—his officials—who were then tasked, if necessary, with transmitting that information to common people in their jurisdiction. We can thus find examples of emperors issuing edits to *tianxia* (*dụ Thiên hạ* 諭天下) and making pronouncements to *tianxia* (*cáo Thiên hạ* 誥天下), and when they were pleased about something, they would grant amnesty to *tianxia* (*đại xá Thiên hạ* 大赦天下). Emperors were able to do all of this because they possessed *tianxia* (*hữu Thiên hạ* 有天下). However, in governing their possessions, they required the assistance of others, and that is why one can repeatedly find in the chronicles that in certain years there were exams to test the scholars of *tianxia* (*hội thí Thiên hạ sĩ nhân* 會試天下士人) so that these men could be recruited into government service to assist the emperor.

As such, although on one level *tianxia* denotes a geographic space, historically it was a space that belonged to a single person—the emperor—and at a larger level, to his family. The emperor, meanwhile, could only possess that space with the assistance of others, but there were many who were willing to offer their services. The men who did so were members of the educated elite, men who had risen to prominence by gaining mastery of the knowledge in the Confucian classics and by passing the civil service exams. Where exactly in *tianxia* these men came from did not matter, as their adherence to the larger ideals of serving the emperor and morally transforming (*giáo hóa* 教化) the people trumped any sense of local identification that they might have harbored. This is what enabled *tianxia* to exist, and emperors knew that, none more so than Emperor Gia Long 嘉隆 (1762–1820), the founder of the last Vietnamese dynasty, the Nguyễn dynasty (*Nguyễn triều* 阮朝; 1802–1945).

The Nguyễn dynasty was preceded by another dynasty, one that Gia Long and his ancestors theoretically served, the Lê dynasty (*Lê triều* 黎朝; 1428–1788), founded in 1428, with its capital located at what is today Hanoi. Over time the Lê emperors gradually lost their full control over their empire, and by the seventeenth century, they relied on two powerful families to control the northern and southern halves of the realm: the Trịnh 鄭 in the north and the Nguyễn 阮, Gia Long's family, in the south. Over the course of the seventeenth and eighteenth centuries, the Trịnh and Nguyễn occasionally fought with each other, as the Trịnh sought, unsuccessfully, to bring the Nguyễn more directly back under Lê-dynasty control. Meanwhile the Nguyễn gradually expanded the region they controlled southward into the Mekong delta.

In the 1770s, however, this entire world was turned upside down when an uprising, known as the Tây Sơn Rebellion (1771–1802), began in the area that the Nguyễn controlled. The Trịnh took advantage of the unrest caused by the Tây Sơn 西山 to invade the region in hopes of defeating their nemesis, the Nguyễn, only to be defeated themselves by the Tây Sơn. In the decades of warfare that followed, the Lê sought assistance from the Qing dynasty (1644–1912), but the army sent to protect the Lê was defeated by the Tây Sơn, and Emperor Qianlong 乾隆 ended up officially recognizing the Tây Sơn ruler. Meanwhile, all but one member of the Nguyễn family—Nguyễn Phúc Ánh 阮福暎—died in the fighting of that period. This lone survivor put together a multiethnic army of Vietnamese, Khmer, Cham, Chinese, Siamese, and some Europeans and continued to fight, eventually capturing Saigon in 1788 and Hue, which had previously served as the Nguyễn clan's capital in the south, in 1802. Nguyễn Phúc Ánh then launched a successful campaign to defeat the remaining Tây Sơn forces in the north. With their defeat, the Nguyễn dynasty was established, and Nguyễn Phúc Ánh became its first emperor, Emperor Gia Long.

While it is customary for modern historians to say that Gia Long (the name I will use throughout the rest of this chapter) established a dynasty, in the dynastic chronicles one can find other terms that describe this event, such as that Gia Long "possessed *tianxia*" (*hữu Thiên hạ* 有天下). Indeed, the events surrounding Gia Long's possession of *tianxia* provide us with ample material from which we can gain a sense of what *tianxia* was, particularly in the eyes of people like Gia Long and his officials. In doing so, what we will find is that their understanding of *tianxia* was precisely as I have described it above. It was a personal, or family, possession that was maintained by members of an elite class from across the realm who shared a common idea that their role was to preserve order by, among other means, morally transforming the people. There was also a clear sense among the ruling elite that *tianxia* should be culturally homogenous, and efforts were made to "transform" (*hóa* 化) not only the moral behavior of people in the empire, but also the language, dress, and customs of people who were ethnically distinct from the dominant population—the ethnic Vietnamese—as they were politically incorporated into the expanding empire. Let us now look at these issues in more detail.

Obtaining and Administering *Tianxia*: Morally Transforming the People

Gia Long's fight with the Tây Sơn began in 1777, when he was forced to flee from the area around what is now the city of Hue in central Vietnam, and came to an end in 1802 when he defeated the final Tây Sơn forces in the northern part of Vietnam. A couple of important mileposts along the way came in 1788, when Gia Long captured Saigon and built a base there, and in 1802, when he retook his family's old capital of Hue. In capturing Hue, Gia Long urged his officials to recommend men of talent in order to start to fill positions in government ministries and in the Hàn Lâm Academy, an institution in charge of scribal and scholarly affairs. He ordered his officials to look for people they knew from among the ranks of talented students and "surrendered officials" (*hàng quan* 降官).⁹ This term appears to have referred to Tây Sơn officials who had surrendered to the Nguyễn. Indeed, after Hue was captured, most of the initial civil officials who were recruited to work in the capital were selected from surrendered Tây Sơn officials. This bothered one of Gia Long's officials, a man from the north and the descendent of a Lê-dynasty official, so much that he submitted a memorial to the emperor to protest the presence at the capital of these men, but to no avail.¹⁰

The former Tây Sơn officials who served Gia Long were soon joined by officials from the north, for in 1802 Gia Long launched a successful military campaign to bring that region under his control. There he succeeded in recruiting former Lê-dynasty officials who had refused to serve the Tây Sơn as well as former Lê-dynasty officials who had agreed to serve the Tây Sơn. Gia Long did so after issuing an edict that was directed at such men in which he encouraged them to join the fledgling Nguyễn administration by appealing to their ambition to "morally transform" (*hóa* 化) the people. To quote, "Recently when the Tây [Sơn] bandits offended the norms of Heaven and Earth and brought darkness to all in between, there were many who hid their ambitions, avoided the contamination of serving as illegitimate officials, and upheld their morals and talent, believing that their time would come. Now the gang of bandits has been pacified, the military campaign has achieved its goals, and it is the most appropriate time to give rise to moral transformation [*hưng hóa* 興化]. How can a generation of talents bear to rot together with the weeds?"¹¹ Gia Long then urged these men to report to the top Nguyễn officials in the north, and he indicated that he would examine their words and deeds and employ them based on their talent so that "the wise will have positions and the capable will have posts, and so that all can work together to achieve the proper way of administering [*chính đạo* 政道]." The chronicles report that following this call many "scholars in recluse" (*ẩn dật giả* 隱逸者) came out and contended with each other to seek employment.¹²

Having thus appealed to everyone except the Tây Sơn leaders (the final Tây Sơn leader was captured and quartered by elephants), Gia Long then appointed military and civil officials to take control of the administrative units in and around the Red River Plain. The men who filled these positions came from a diverse range of political backgrounds and geographic locations. Longtime southern supporters of Gia Long (including northerers who had earlier gone south) were mixed together with the likes of former Lê-dynasty officials and recent recruits. This act of appointing officials to rule over the north completed the staffing of the empire, as Gia Long had appointed officials in the south and center as those regions came under his control. The north was the final region to be incorporated into his empire, and once it had been, he discussed with his officials the next essential task—morally transforming the people. In the first lunar month of 1804 Gia Long issued an edict that called for the establishment of new village regulations for the northern half of the kingdom. To quote,

> A kingdom is an accumulation of village communities. From the village to the kingdom, morally transforming the people and creating [good] customs [hóa dân thành tục 化民成俗] is a monarch's first task. In recent years, teaching has been neglected and administration has deteriorated. Villages do not have good customs, and the longer such customs have been carried on, the deeper they have sunk. The festivals for holding banquets, the rituals for performing weddings, the ceremonies for funerals, and the worshipping of spirits and the Buddha all overstep the [moral] bounds of ritual propriety. Local powers use these events to fleece the poor. The accumulation [of debts leading to] vagrancy is because of this reason. We have now examined the necessary donations and eliminated their excesses to create village regulations in the hope of reforming these aberrations at their source so that all can return to the correct path [đại đạo 大道].[13]

This document then discusses in detail the various village practices in need of transformation. In each instance, the Confucian classics are first cited to provide a moral guidepost from which to critique the bad practices in the village. The edict then goes on to discuss and provide specific recommendations for each bad practice. In the case of banquets, the edict states that people have been holding banquets that they cannot afford and have been pawning their belongings to the village head. When these people cannot pay back the village head, he taxes them extra, thereby creating extra hardship. To reduce expenses for banquets so that such instances of indebtedness would no longer occur, Gia Long's edict called for a ban on alcohol and meat at banquets. Two years earlier Gia Long had banned alcohol in Saigon. Hence, we can see here an effort to create a standard social life across the realm, one that was morally upright and that was supported by the Confucian classics.

Were we to only examine the period of Gia Long's rule, we could craft a positive depiction of *tianxia*. While the Nguyễn dynasty's realm stretched from the southern border of the Qing empire down to the Mekong delta, Gia Long's administration did not directly rule over that entire territory. Instead, the emperor delegated oversight of the administration of the Red River and Mekong deltas to two military generals who were granted a good deal of autonomy. Meanwhile, in the mountainous regions of the north, people whom we would now refer to as ethnic minorities were likewise granted the autonomy to rule over their own lands. Finally, beyond his own kingdom, Gia Long had established sovereign-vassal relations over Cambodia, but as was the case with these relations in the Chinese world, the Cambodian ruler continued to have autonomy over his realm.

Tianxia under Gia Long was thus cosmopolitan to a degree, and as we have seen above, it was also meritocratic to some extent, as Gia Long recruited men to serve in his administration from a diverse range of prior political affiliations. Finally, one could also make the claim that Gia Long's rule was benevolent in that he sought to transform some of the population under his control in ways that were intended to make their lives more stable and prosperous. This positive view of governance over *tianxia,* however, becomes much more difficult to sustain when we examine the rule of Gia Long's successor, his son, Emperor Minh Mạng 明命 (r. 1820–1841).

Imperial Expansion: Using *Xia* to Transform the Barbarians

Having inherited a decentralized empire from his father, Emperor Minh Mạng went to great efforts to bring the realm under the direct control of the Central Court. This was done by eliminating the practice of having the two deltas overseen by military commanders and by extending direct imperial rule not only into those two areas but also into the mountainous regions of the north, as well as into Cambodia. These latter two locations were inhabited by non-Vietnamese peoples, and in examining the ideas of Minh Mạng and his officials about how to govern over these areas, we can see an approach that was clearly not cosmopolitan. Instead, the extension of Vietnamese imperial rule to areas inhabited by non-Vietnamese peoples was intimately tied to efforts to assimilate those populations.

In the language of nineteenth-century Nguyễn-dynasty sources, these non-Vietnamese people were referred to as "savages" (*Man* 蠻), or sometimes as "barbarians" (*Di* 夷). As for the Vietnamese, they are referred to in these documents as "Hán" 漢, the same term that we now use to refer to the Han Chinese. As for actual ethnic Chinese, in Nguyễn-dynasty chronicles they are usually referred to as "Qing people" (*Thanh nhân* 清人). However, in other nineteenth-century Vietnamese documents one can also find the term *Minh hương* 明香 to indicate the descendants of Ming loyalist refugees who fled to the area of what is now Vietnam during the period of the Ming-Qing transition in the seventeenth century. This term literally means "Ming incense" and was meant to indicate that these people continued to make ritual offerings to the Ming dynasty. And finally, some sources also refer to ethnic Chinese as *Đường nhân* 唐人 (literally "Tang people").

As such, in Nguyễn dynasty sources, the expansion of imperial rule into mountainous regions and into Cambodia under the orders of Minh Mạng is depicted in terms of contact not between "Vietnamese" and "non-Vietnamese," but instead between "Hán" and "savages." Further, as these names suggest, there was a belief among the Nguyễn-dynasty elite that these two groups were culturally distinct and unequal. There was also a clear sense that the cultural distinctions between these groups should be eliminated. This anticosmopolitan objective was to be attained through a process of getting savages to follow Hán ways or mores (*Hán phong* 漢風) and by "using *xia* to transform the barbarians" (*dụng Hạ biến Di* 用夏變夷). "*Xia*" here is not the "*xia*" of "*tianxia*," but instead is the name of the earliest Chinese dynasty, the Xia dynasty, and a term that was used here to essentially refer to what we can think of as classical Sinitic culture, that is, the culture that the Nguyễn-dynasty elite participated in and revered.

Many attempts to use *xia* to transform the barbarians took place during the 1830s, when Emperor Minh Mạng made a significant effort to expand imperial control. By examining the communications between the emperor and the officials in charge of extending dynastic rule into areas inhabited by non-Vietnamese peoples, we can get a sense of what following Hán ways and "using *xia* to transform the barbarians" entailed.

One area in the north that Minh Mạng sought to control more directly was a place called Tuyên Quang 宣光 Province. In 1834, an official by the name of Nguyễn Công Trứ 阮公著 submitted a memorial to the throne in which he recommended that the capital of Tuyên Quang be moved to a new location that would facilitate the expansion of imperial control over the province. This province was sparsely inhabited and was inland from the main areas of the Red River delta. There were Chinese miners who had taken up residence in the area, and there were various non-Vietnamese people living there as well. This was an area that was not firmly under Nguyễn-dynasty control, and Nguyễn Công Trứ described the site that he argued would be more suitable for the provincial capital in bluntly strategic terms. It could defend against (*chế ngự* 制禦) areas to the west, and it could suppress (*trấn áp* 鎮壓) areas to the east, including a place called Đại Man, or "Great Savage," subprefecture (*Đại Man châu* 大蠻州).

Given the strategic importance of this location, Nguyễn Công Trứ argued that from this new capital, it would be easy to nip disturbances in the province in the bud and eliminate any unrest. Finally, he argued that if officials were put in place who could bring the people into submission and get them to follow rules, in three years' time the people in the province would automatically "transform their savage customs into Hán ways" (*biến man tập vi Hán phong* 變蠻習為漢風) and border problems could be permanently eliminated. The emperor agreed with Nguyễn Công Trứ's assessment but felt the task of relocating the provincial capital was too difficult, and he decided to wait on the matter.[14]

Three years later, in 1837, Ngô Dưỡng Cáo 吳養告, the provincial administration commissioner of Hưng Hóa 興化 Province, a mountainous region on the southwestern edge of the Red River delta, submitted a memorial to the emperor in which he noted that three prefectures had been established the previous year, but that no officials had been assigned to govern over them yet, and that they therefore literally existed in name only. Ngô Dưỡng Cáo thereupon requested that the emperor assign officials to these new prefectures. In his response, Emperor Minh Mạng stated that one of the main purposes of establishing "circulating officials" (*lưu quan* 流官), meaning bureaucratic officials whom the court could assign throughout the empire, was to use *xia* to transform the barbarians, but that this had to be done gradually and only when the occasion was right. If it was forced, then people might react adversely and then it would be difficult to transform such people. Further, the emperor also noted that it was costly to station and provision officials. He therefore encouraged Ngô Dưỡng Cáo to do what he could on his own, and in particular, to make known the court's moral benevolence (*đức ý* 德意), to get the savages to recognize (gratitude) and be moved (by benevolence) (*tri cảm* 知感), to get the local headman to fear the court's might, and to start to restrain the people from following their old habits, so that they could collectively be infused with Hán mores (*cộng nghiễm ư Hán phong* 共染於漢風). This was also a way, the emperor argued, to eradicate (bad) customs (*cách tục* 革俗), and he encouraged Ngô Dưỡng Cáo for now to follow this approach.[15]

While Emperor Minh Mạng urged his officials to move slowly in extending imperial control into the mountainous regions around the Red River Plain, we can nonetheless see that imperial expension was their goal and that a key technique in this enterprise was "using *xia* to transform the barbarians." In that same decade of the 1830s, Minh Mạng and his officials also sought to expand imperial control into Cambodia by annexing that kingdom into the empire. By the 1830s, the Nguyễn had long been in contact with Khmer peoples, as the Nguyễn officials who had ruled over the southern half of the Lê dynasty realm in the seventeenth and eighteenth centuries had expanded their control into the Mekong delta. Then after the establishment of the Nguyễn dynasty in 1802, the Cambodian monarch became a vassal of this new Vietnamese empire. Perhaps due to that familiarity, Minh Mạng and his officials took a more aggressive approach toward "using *xia* to transform the barbarians" in Cambodia in the 1830s, or what they referred to at that time as Trấn Tây 鎮西 ("the Suppressed West").

We can get a sense of the Nguyễn approach to Cambodia from an edict that Emperor Minh Mạng issued in the twelfth lunar month of 1835 to General Trương Minh Giảng 張明講 and Grand Adjutant Lê Đại Cương 黎大綱, the two main officials in charge of the annexation. There is much of interest in this document, and therefore, I will quote from it at length.

The Trấn Tây citadel is a vital location on the frontier. Having just been established, although it is of the utmost importance to build defenses, this savage land has long belonged to our territory, and the savage people are my children. It is necessary to encourage and induce them, and to get them to be daily imbued with Hán mores [*nhật nhiễm Hán phong* 日染漢風].

What is more, agriculture, sericulture, teaching, and nurturing truly are the starting point for royal governance [*vương chánh* 王政]. Recently I have heard that this area's land is vast and fertile, and that there are many oxen and that cultivation is easy, but that the [local] customs for working the land are to only dig open the land with shovels, and that people are not familiar with using oxen to plow. They grow rice only for their own consumption, and do not accumulate and store it. As for silk cloth, ducks, pigs, and other common necessities for the people, these are too expensive. A bolt of silk is as much as five or six strings of cash, and a single duck is as much as two strings of cash. In sum, their not knowing how to be diligent and to grow excess crops is the result of their savage customs and ignorant nature.

In your free time from military training to defend the frontier, I authorize you to transform the people. Teach them to plow with an ox and to plant a lot of rice, so that there is no land that does not bring benefit, and so that each household has excess wealth. Let the people also extensively plant mulberry trees to produce silk cloth, and to raise many pigs and ducks to provide food. For everything that is needed, they must study the Hán people's diligence in pursuing a livelihood.

As for language, let them gradually learn the Hán language, and for food and clothing, get them to also gradually follow Hán customs [*Hán tục* 漢俗]. Beyond this, if there are other bad habits that should be eradicated to facilitate a change of behavior, I leave that to you to enlighten [the people] as you see fit.

Although they are savages, they nonetheless have intelligence [*tri năng* 知能]. What is more, our troops have established agrocolonies [*đồn điền* 屯田] in their midst. As they see each other and get along, this is an opportunity to influence them to reform [*cảm hóa* 感化]. But eradicate customs gradually. It is critical to do this slowly. In teaching conduct, do not go overboard in supervising their progress. Carry things out in a progression, from one matter to the next. Get them to follow [Shang] di's precepts without consciousness of their effort [*bất thức bất tri, thuận Đế zhi tắc* 不識不知, 順帝之則]. Through gradual seeping influence [*huân đào tẩm nhiễm* 熏陶浸染], use *xia* to transform the barbarians. This is also a way of altering mores and changing customs [*di phong dịch tục* 移風易俗之道].[16]

On the one hand, one could argue that the Nguyễn sought to genuinely benefit the people in the area of the Trấn Tây citadel by improving their knowledge about agriculture and hopefully enabling them to live more productive and stable lives. On the other hand, however, this positive development was accompanied by a parallel vision that hoped for the gradual elimination of the cultural differences between Khmer and Vietnamese by getting the Khmer to assimilate to Vietnamese culture. This hope was based on clear ideas of cultural superiority. As expressed here by Emperor Minh Mạng, simply by having Khmer peoples live in proximity with Nguyễn-dynasty soldiers, "Hán ways" would gradually seep into the Khmer and they would "follow Shangdi's precepts without consciousness of their effort." This last phrase comes from the ancient *Classic of Poetry* (*Shijing* 詩經).[17] Shangdi is an early Chinese deity that later came to be replaced by the concept of *tian*, or "Heaven." Saying that the Khmer would "follow Shangdi's precepts without consciousness of their effort" was another way of saying the superiority of Hán ways would automatically lead the Khmer to emulate them, without the need to order or force them to do so.

Bureaucratic Incorporation: There Is No Outside

In extending imperial rule into the mountains around the Red River Plain and into Cambodia, the Nguyễn dynasty showed a clear desire to transform these areas to create a homogenous culture across the expanding empire. As such, at the core of the *tianxia* system in late imperial Vietnam was a definite anticosmopolitan impulse. That said, we can also see from the repeated appeals from Emperor Minh Mạng to his officials that they proceed slowly and gradually in "using *xia* to transform the barbarians," that cultural homogeneity was a distant goal, and that in reality, a great deal of cultural diversity continued to exist in the Nguyễn realm. That diversity, however, existed by default and was counter to the ultimate objective of the dynasty.

Meanwhile, from other examples we can get a sense of how areas and peoples who had once been on the periphery of the empire were incorporated and assimilated into the Nguyễn bureaucracy and culture. We can see this clearly, for instance, in the case of a military outpost in the Mekong delta. In 1787, during the Tây Sơn Rebellion, the future emperor Gia Long left Bangkok where he had been living in exile and began an effort to retake control of the Mekong delta from the Tây Sơn forces. He quickly established an outpost in the area of what is now Trà Vinh and Vĩnh Long provinces. Gia Long ordered a Khmer (*Lạp nhân* 臘人) officer under his authority by the name of Nguyễn Văn Tồn 阮文存 to recruit a few thousand "frontier people" (*phiên dân* 番民) to man the outpost.[18]

This outpost was initially called the Siamese Soldiers Outpost (*Xiêm Binh đồn* 暹兵屯). It is not clear why this name was chosen. Perhaps some of the officers in charge at the time were Siamese, as there were Siamese soldiers who served Gia Long. Certainly the "frontier people" were not Vietnamese, as this term was used to refer to people of other ethnicities in the Mekong delta, such as Khmer and Cham. In 1810 the name of this base was changed to the Uy Viễn Outpost (*Uy Viễn đồn* 威遠屯), roughly meaning the outpost that was "overpowering distant [regions]."[19] Throughout this time period, the soldiers of this outpost loyally supported Gia Long, and when peace finally came to the region in the early nineteenth century, they continued to support the Nguyễn dynasty that Gia Long established. Further, they did so under the command of Nguyễn Văn Tồn, who served as commander in chief (*thống quản* 統管) of the Uy Viễn Outpost until his death in 1820.[20]

Nguyễn Văn Tồn was not this man's original name. There is an entry about Nguyễn Văn Tồn in an official Nguyễn-dynasty collection of biographies that states that this man was originally known simply as "Duyên" 沿; that he was orginally from the area of Trà Vinh, the region where he later recruited men to serve at the outpost; and that at some point early in his life he became a palace slave. When the Tây Sơn Rebellion broke out, however, he took up arms in service of Gia Long, and in time he was rewarded for his loyal service by being granted the name "Nguyễn Văn Tồn."[21] In a statement that he made to officials in the Ministry of Rites after Nguyễn Văn Tồn had passed away, Emperor Minh Mạng stated that "although Nguyễn Văn Tồn was outside [the sphere of moral] transformation [*hóa ngoại* 化外], nonetheless for years he made every effort to serve the previous emperor with an unwavering moral heart, and deserves our extreme compassion."[22] He later stated that "although Tồn was a captured slave [*nô lỗ* 奴虜], he was by nature loyal and curageous" and that "Midi of the Han probably had nothing to surpass him."[23]

"Midi of the Han" refers to Jin Midi 金日磾 (134–86 BCE), a "barbarian" Xiongnu man who loyally served the Han dynasty. In the worldview of men like Emperor Minh Mạng, such men were exceptions. Barbarians who lived outside the sphere of moral transformation were not seen as capable of loyally following an emperor from the imperial center. The only way that this could happen, again according to Emperor Minh Mạng, was if Heaven endowed such a barbarian with a sufficient sense of loyalty and courage to do so. This is what Minh Mạng felt had happened with Nguyễn Văn Tồn. However, such a barbarian who loyally served an emperor was nonetheless still an anomaly, and to rectify the contradictions between Nguyễn Văn Tồn's status and his actions, Gia Long had earlier granted him a full name so that he could more logically fit into the *xia* cultural world of the empire.

After Nguyễn Văn Tồn died, some of the savage officers at the Uy Viễn Outpost apparently decided that they too wanted to attain a similar status to the one that Nguyễn Văn Tồn had possessed. In the fourth lunar month of 1823,

Lê Văn Duyệt 黎文悅, the top official in the southern third of the kingdom, submitted a memorial to the throne in which he stated that the cohort colonels (*chi hiệu* 支校), squadron majors (*cai đội* 該隊), and squadron captains (*đội trưởng* 隊長) of the Uy Viễn Outpost, all of whom were savages, had requested that they be granted surnames "in order to transform [their] barbarian customs" (*dĩ biến di tập* 以變夷習). Emperor Minh Mạnh replied that, "Although they are Savage Lao [*Man Lao* 蠻獠], early during the restoration [of our dynasty] they rendered service to our troops. Once conditions had become pacified, they expressed admiration for Hán ways [*mộ Hán phong* 慕漢風] and got rid of barbarian customs [*cách trừ di tục* 革除夷俗]. I specially grant them caps and robes to provide them with the proper appearance."[24]

Two years later, in the third month of 1825, the military structure of the Uy Viễn Outpost was reformed. Here the most important changes were that the largest military units were changed from cohorts (*chi* 支) to battalions (*cơ* 奇) and that the officers at the outpost were, for the first time, granted official ranks, thereby incorporating these men into the hierarchy of the Nguyễn-dynasty bureaucracy. Each battalion was now led by a battalion commander (*quản cơ* 管奇) holding an upper fourth rank and a lieutenant colonel holding a lower fourth rank. Below the battalions were squadrons, each of which was led by a squadron major holding an upper fifth rank, a squadron captain holding an upper sixth rank, and a deputy squadron captain carrying an upper seventh rank. Finally, all of these officers were ordered to bring their troops in succession to the capital to officially greet the emperor.[25]

Emperor Minh Mạng issued an edict at this time in which he made the following comments about the officers at the Uy Viễn Outpost:

> From the time that our dynasty first restored itself, they have been filial and loyal, and have contributed to great accomplishments. After the realm was pacified, we honored them with official positions, and glorified them with robes; using *xia* to transform the barbarians and extending charity equally to all [*nhân đồng nhất thị* 仁同一視]. Now we have additionally granted them with surnames and established their ranks in order to demonstrate that there is no outside [*vô ngoại* 無外].
>
> Now, considering that they have long lived on the frontier and have yet to know about the Central Court's cultural splendor [*văn vật chi thịnh* 文物之盛], have those from the position of squadron commandant and above divide into three groups and have one group visit the capital each year for a royal audience.[26]

From these developments we can see that Emperor Minh Mạng employed the term "no outside" in the same way that it was used roughly two millenia earlier in the *Solitary Decisions*. By granting savage officials surnames and ranks, the emperor sought to bring these men into the "Heavenly family" of the bureaucracy. However, just as the effort to extend imperial control into the mountainous regions of the north during this period encountered obstacles, so did this attempt to incorporate the officials from the Uy Viễn Outpost into the bureaucracy reveal limitations as well. In the fifth lunar month of 1825, Lê Văn Duyệt reported to the emperor that, having been granted surnames and official titles, the men at the Uy Viễn Outpost were willing to also change their style of dress and to wear the robes of Hán people. The emperor approved, but before long there was trouble. According to the dynastic chronicles, a savage officer by the name of Kiên Xác 堅推 took advantage of this situation to swindle the frontier people. It appears that Kiên Xác must have reported to common people that they were going to be ordered to change their clothing style, and he went about collecting money from them, saying that he needed eight hundred strings of coins to make a request that they be exempt from this new rule. Eventually Kiên Xác learned that Lê Văn Duyệt had caught wind of what he was doing and was investigating the matter. Xác feared that he would be punished and had one thousand in cash delivered to Lê Văn Duyệt to smooth matters over.

This plan, however, backfired and Lê Văn Duyệt requested approval from the emperor to execute Xác. He noted that the issue of requesting to change clothing styles was the idea of other officers and that Kiên Xác had spread rumors among the ignorant people (*ngu dân* 愚民) for his own benefit. Such disregard for the law, Lê Văn Duyệt argued, deserved nothing less than a death sentence. This was particularly important, he noted, given the specific conditions in this distant frontier region. The people there, according to Duyệt, knew how to receive favors (*mông ân* 蒙恩) but they did not yet know to fear the law (*úy pháp* 畏法). Lê Văn Duyệt noted further that Kiên Xác had been granted an official position, and yet he had still engaged in bribery. Those who had not yet received such a favor from the Central Court would therefore fear the law even less. Duyệt therefore argued that Kiên Xác should be beheaded in order to warn the people (*cảnh chúng* 警眾). The emperor agreed.[27]

Alongside seeking to bring savage officials into the bureaucracy, Emperor Minh Mạng also employed techniques to bring people into submission by demonstrating the might of the dynasty. One technique was to execute officials who disobeyed orders, like Kiên Xác. Another technique, however, was to follow the example of Emperor Gao of the Han and to use the might of the grand-looking palaces at the capital to awe officials into submission. Following Emperor Minh Mạng's order that officials from the Uy Viễn Outpost visit the capital to view its "cultural splendor," in 1836 the first group of officers made the journey to the capital. Considering how arduous this journey was, the emperor ordered that these men be provided with adequate provisions. However, some officials in the Ministry of Revenue strictly adhered to certain rules and refused to provide these men with provisions for their return journey, as the number of soldiers was below one hundred, the requisite number to warrant financial support. The returning soldiers apparently suffered from hunger. The emperor learned about this and ordered that the men be provided with provisions, but by that point they had already reached their destination, so the emperor ordered that they be given five hundred strings of cash instead. The stickler for rules in the Ministry of Revenue, meanwhile, was punished.[28]

As such, it is unclear what kind of impression the soldiers obtained, but Emperor Minh Mạnh's intent is clear. Like the official who oversaw palace construction in the early Han period, the emperor believed that it was possible to awe people in the empire into submission, and that this technique could be used in tandem with the granting of surnames and ranks, so that no officials were left "outside" of the imperial bureaucracy.

From Hoa to Hán: Protoracial Consciousness

At the same time that the Nguyễn officials sought to entice and awe savage officials into the bureaucracy, they also reported instances in which such officials continued to follow their own cultural practices. In 1839, for instance, Emperor Minh Mạng reported to the members of his privy council that the "frontiers headmen" (*phiên mục* 藩目), meaning Khmer officials, in Trấn Tây had accepted official positions in the bureaucracy, but that in their interactions, they continued to refer to each other by their Khmer titles. The emperor thereupon ordered his officials to convince the Khmer officials that it was an honor to have official Nguyễn-dynasty titles, and that in addressing each other, they should employ those titles rather than Khmer ones.[29]

Such instances point to a tension in the interactions between Nguyễn officials and savage peoples. On the one hand, the Nguyễn felt that their Hán culture would automatically be followed by savages once they became aware of it, for as Emperor Minh Mạng noted above, "Although they are savages, they nonetheless have intelligence," and it was assumed that such intelligence would lead to an appreciation of Hán ways. This, however, did not always happen, and the Nguyễn elite had to find a way to rationalize this fact.

In many periods and places in East Asian history we can find reference to a dichotomy between *hua* 華 and *yi* 夷 (*hoa* and *di* in Vietnamese), or what I like to translate as "efflorescents" and "barbarians." This term, *hua*, has essentially the same meaning as *xia*. It refers to a cultural world and tradition, that of the Middle Kingdom, and the two terms can be combined to refer to this culture as *huaxia* culture. As such, this *hua-yi* dichotomy is usually viewed as indicating a cultural or civilizational difference between those who uphold the cultural practices of the Middle Kingdom, the efflorescents, and those who do not, the barbarians. Indeed, scholars like Zhao Tingyang have argued this point and have strongly rejected the possibility that there were racial distinctions in the *tianxia* world, arguing that such ideas are Western.

In the case of Nguyễn Vietnam, however, I would argue that something akin to a "protoracial" sense of difference emerged among the Nguyễn-dynasty elite in the nineteenth century, and that the use of the term "Hán" points to this new development. The use of this term as a self-referent was a new practice and is one that we only find recorded in Nguyễn-dynasty documents. If we look at materials that were compiled independently of the dynasty, such as a gazetteer of the Mekong delta region that was compiled in the early 1820s, we find that the efflorescent-barbarian dichotomy was used to refer to the difference between people whom we would now refer to as Vietnamese and Khmer, respectively, and that ethnic Chinese were referred to as "Tang people" (*Đường nhân* 唐人).³⁰ There is also a well-known instance in which a Vietnamese official on a mission to the Qing empire in 1831 was asked to stay at a hostel in the area of what is now Fujian Province that had a sign outside that read "Barbarian Guesthouse." This official was offended by this name, and thereupon wrote an angry diatribe entitled the "Discourse on Efflorescents and Barbarians" in which he laid out a long list of cultural practices that he upheld, from following the moral teachings of Confucius and Mencius to wearing caps and robes following the styles of the Han and Ming dynasties, and asked how he could possibly be considered a "barbarian."³¹

From these sources we can see that in the early nineteenth century there were educated Vietnamese who saw themselves as *hoa* and that this pointed primarily to a cultural difference. However, slightly later, in the 1830s and 1840s, we can find Emperor Minh Mạng and his successor making comments about the Qing that seem to point to a sense of difference that was more than cultural. In 1830, for instance, Emperor Minh Mạng had a discussion with his officials about armor to protect soldiers. He stated that while the kingdom was not facing any imminent danger at that time, he wanted to make the best preparations possible to ensure the long-term security of his descendents, as well as of the officials and the people. With this in mind, the emperor examined a compendium of Qing-dynasty governmental institutions and found the armor there to be "soiled by the kingdom's customs" (*nê quốc tục* 泥國俗), and as a result, exceedingly unattractive. By the "kingdom's customs," Emperor Minh Mạng was referring to the specific customs of the Manchu rulers of the Qing dynasty, and went on to make this point more explicitly in noting of Qing-dynasty court robes and caps that "they all follow barbarian customs" (*giai tòng Di tập* 皆從夷習) and did not accord with the system of attire of the ancients (*cổ nhân phục sức chi chế* 古人服飾之制). As such, they were definitely not to be emulated.³²

The fact that the Middle Kingdom was ruled by Manchus, that is, by people who came from a barbarian land that was outside of the *xia/hua* cultural world, created a problem for the Nguyễn. While the Middle Kingdom was the fount of the culture that they upheld, the Manchus were barbarians, and it appears that no matter how much they may have adopted *xia/hua* ways, there was something beyond culture that prevented them from being fully accepted by the Nguyễn rulers.

We can see this in other comments that Emperor Minh Mạng made. In the tenth lunar month of 1834, for instance, the emperor issued an edict on the occasion of a bumper harvest in Nam Định Province, a province in the Red River Plain. Essentially what Emperor Minh Mạng argued was that this bumper harvest was Heaven's reward for the Nguyễn's legitimacy, and in making this point he contrasted the accomplishments of his father, Emperor Gia Long, with the actions of the first two Qing emperors to rule over the main area of China, emperors Shunzhi 順治 (r. 1644–1661) and Kangxi 康熙 (r. 1661–1722). To quote, Emperor Minh Mạng stated that

> The Qing obtained the Ming [empire] by entering the Middle Kingdom as Xiongnu and using barbarians to transform *xia*. That put them in a very difficult position. Shunzhi was a child emperor and his uncle served as regent, calling himself the imperial father. This was truly a contravention of the proper principles. However, by relying on this technique, peace was maintained. When Kangxi came to power he was only eight years old, and there was the Revolt of the Three Feudatories. The situation became dangerous, however before long he was able to pacify it. Could this have happened without Heaven's assistance?
>
> My father obtained the Northern Region from the Tây Sơn, not from the Lê family. [His] legitimacy probably exceeded that of the Qing.
>
> I came to rule over *tianxia* as an adult. I had some understanding of worldly affairs and human sentiments. The issuing of each policy and the implementation of each order invariably accorded with Heaven's intent above and satisfied people's hopes below, such as changing clothing styles. This was a case of using *xia* to transform barbarians and was truly easy to carry out. If one relies on Heaven's intent, there will be bumper crops year after year, and one can naturally enjoy eternal peace.[33]

According to Emperor Minh Mạng, that the Qing ruled over the Middle Kingdom was because Heaven granted its assistance, and therefore, they had to be accepted as legitimate rulers. Nonetheless, the fact that they were "Xiongnu," a term that Minh Mạng employed here to refer in a general sense to barbarians from the area to the north of the Middle Kingdom, detracted from their status in Emperor Minh Mạng's eyes, and it explained why some of the actions of Qing rulers were improper, because as barbarians they had tried to transform Xia.

By contrast, Minh Mạng felt that there was nothing that detracted from his father's status as a legitimate ruler who had gained Heaven's support. We can see this in his explanation of how his father had established the dynasty. Just as the Qing came to power following centuries of Ming-dynasty rule, so did the Nguyễn come to power following centuries of Lê-dynasty rule. According to Emperor Minh Mạng, however, there was a distinction. Whereas the Qing had overthrown a legitimate dynasty, the Ming, Emperor Gia Long had defeated the Tây Sơn rebels who had earlier overthrown a legitimate dynasty, the Lê. He did not therefore overthrow a legitimate dynasty, but instead had righteously defeated rebels. As such, again according to Minh Mạng, his "legitimacy probably exceeded that of the Qing."

That Gia Long was not a barbarian likewise meant that he surpassed his Qing counterparts. In other words, from Minh Mạng's perspective there were various interconnected factors that made the Nguyễn in some ways superior to the Qing. Minh Mạng's son and successor, Emperor Thiệu Trị 紹治 (r. 1841–1847), agreed with his father. In 1842, Thiệu Trị made similar comments as the ones above by Minh Mạng. The occasion for his remarks came during a trip to Hanoi to receive a Qing envoy. While he was there, Emperor Thiệu Trị commented about how the clothing styles of people in the north had now changed due to a policy that his father had first implemented in the 1820s to unify clothing styles, and he praised the fact that this policy had been carried out gradually.

Emperor Thiệu Trị stated that it would have been easy for his grandfather, Emperor Gia Long, to issue an order to change clothing styles; however, he argued that changing customs is something that has to be carried out gradually. He therefore praised the approach of his father, Emperor Minh Mạng, who had issued an order for clothing styles in the north to change but allowed several years for the transformation to take place, particularly so that people who did not have the financial means to purchase new robes immediately could do so over time. The result, Emperor Thiệu Trị stated, was that clothing styles in the kingdom were now uniform, or as he stated it, "North and south are of the same style, blended together with no differing customs" (*nam bắc đồng phong, hỗn vô di tục* 南北同風, 混無異俗).[34]

Emperor Thiệu Trị then contrasted the approach of his father and grandfather with that of the early Qing rulers. In his comments, it is clear that the emperor wished to emphasize that the Qing were barbarians, and that their alienness made them incapable of appreciating the culture of the *xia/hua* world.

Thiệu Trị makes this point, for instance, by talking about Nurhaci (1559–1626), the progenitor of the Qing dynasty. In the early seventeenth century, Nurhaci unified the various tribes to the north of the Middle Kingdom and led them to attack the Ming empire. After conquering Ming territory, Emperor Thiệu Trị claims that Nurhaci stated, "We obtained *tianxia* on horseback, what need do we have for robes and sashes?" To Thiệu Trị, such a comment explicity revealed how barbarian the Qing were, for nothing was more important to *huaxia* culture than the propriety associated with the wearing of caps and robes.[35]

Thiệu Trị noted further that during the rule of the first Qing emperor, Shunzhi, men were told to shave their foreheads and grow the rest of their hair in a queue in the style of the Manchus, and that those who did not comply would be executed. This order was succinctly summarized in a saying that Emperor Thiệu Trị quotes that went, "If you want to keep your head, then lose your hair; if you want to keep your hair, then you will lose your head." The emperor then made the following points:

> To get people who had passed through centuries of Han, Tang, Song, and Ming rule to suddenly change and fully follow the order of the Manchus, how rash this was!
>
> What is more, to possess the Middle Kingdom, and to not possess the ways of the Middle Kingdom [*Trung Quốc chi phong* 中國之風], then how can barbarians be transformed into *xia*? It is thus no wonder that the world of northern barbarians [*Di dịch* 夷狄] is a world of calamities.
>
> [Confucian] scholars argue that "The temperament of a king is to be lenient; the temperament of a hegemon is to be hasty." That applies to this case.[36]

From these comments we can see that Nguyễn-dynasty emperors possessed a healthy dose of self-confidence, such that at times they could view themselves as superior to their Qing-dynasty counterparts. Such expressions of self-importance, however, point to something more significant than hubris, because in subtle ways we can see that people like emperors Minh Mạng and Thiệu Trị felt that the Qing were inhibited by their barbarian origins, and that this barbarian-ness obstructed their ability to fully participate in the *huaxia* world. That the Nguyễn were able to do this, they felt, was because they were not barbarian. They saw themselves as Hán. As such, beyond the sense of cultural difference between efflorescents and barbarians, one can sense that members of the Nguyễn elite were aware of other types of distinctions, particularly ones that either enabled or prevented one from fully adopting *huaxia* culture, and that distinction, I would argue, was what we can think of as a protoracial distinction.

Race and Social Darwinism

While it is difficult to differentiate between cultural and perhaps protoracial ideas in the ideas about the Hán / savage and Hán / Qing-barbarian binaries that we can find documented in nineteenth-century Nguyễn-dynasty sources, once members of the Vietnamese educated elite became exposed to ideas about race around the turn of the twentieth century, they were able to adapt their knowledge to these new concepts with great ease. By that time, the Nguyễn dynasty had come under French "protection," and while a minority of Nguyễn-dynasty officials knew French, many turned to reformist writings coming from China to learn about the Western world, and in such works these scholars were exposed to the concept of race.

In 1906, the French launched an initiative to reform the educational system in Nguyễn-dynasty Vietnam. While still allowing students to learn classical Chinese and study for the civil service examinations as they had done for centuries, French administrators worked with reformist Nguyễn-dynasty officials to transform the exam curriculum. Instead of focusing solely on the Confucian classics, students now had to study about the history of Vietnam and about the geography and peoples of French Indochina. As part of this transformation, textbooks were created to introduce this new knowledge, and one of the first, the *Summary of Việt History for Secondary Schools* (*Trung học Việt sử toát yếu* 中學越史撮要), taught students about race.

This textbook was written by a Nguyễn-dynasty official by the name of Ngô Giáp Dậu 吳甲酉 (1853–1929) and published in 1911. In the early twentieth century, a common term for race had yet to be established in Chinese, and therefore, in this and other texts we can find a variety of terms used to denote this concept, terms that refer to such related concepts as "lineage" or "clan" (*tộc* 族), "type" (*chủng* 種), and "kind" (*loại* 類). Ngô Giáp Dậu begins this textbook on Vietnamese history with a brief section on geography, followed by a section on race, or what he literally referred to as "lineage types" (*tộc loại* 族類). He argues that originally there were various nationalities (*dân tộc* 民族) in the region, and then he documents well-known historical cases of people migrating from the area of what is today China into the Red River Plain, from convicts exiled to the region during the Qin and Han dynasties to scholars and officials who fled unrest at the end of the Han-dynasty period and Song and Ming loyalists who sought refuge during periods of dynastic change. He argues that these people pushed the original inhabitants up into the mountains where they organized themselves into tribes (*bộ lạc* 部落).[37] That said, Ngô Giáp Dậu does not argue that all of the people whom we would today label "Vietnamese" are descendants of people who had earlier migrated into the region from China. However, he does explicitly state that the elite class has such roots. He states, for instance, that "in examining those who have the ability to demonstrate their greatness in the kingdom by means of literary matters and martial achievements, they are generally *hoa* descendants [*Hoa duệ* 華裔]."³⁸

This term "*hoa*" here is the term that I translated above as "efflorescent" and that in earlier texts often signifies a cultural counterpart to barbarians. Here it likewise signifies a cultural group, the classically educated elite, but Ngô Giáp Dậu has explained this group's distinctness in terms of race. They are distinct because they are the descendants of people who migrated into the region from the area of what is now China. Finally, while I argued above that the Nguyễn elite may have started to use the term "Hán" in the nineteenth century to indicate such a racial distinction, Ngô Giáp Dậu did not use that term here. However, a few years later, in 1918, a reformist scholar by the name of Dương Bá Trạc (1884–1944) wrote an article on this same topic where he did refer to the Vietnamese as "Hán."

Dương Bá Trạc's article was entitled "An Examination of Việt History" and it appeared in classical Chinese and vernacular Vietnamese in the same issue of a new journal called *Southern Mores* (*Nam phong* 南風). This journal was a forum for reformist ideas and reached a diverse audience as it contained sections in classical Chinese, vernacular Vietnamese, and French. Early in his article on Việt history, Dương Bá Trạc has a section on "human types" (*nhân chủng* 人種). Like Ngô Giáp Dậu's use of the term "lineage type," this appears to be Dương Bá Trạc's term of choice to designate the Western concept of "race." He argues in the classical Chinese version of his article that there was an original type (*chủng* 種) of people in the Red River Plain, one that he calls the Giao Chỉ 交趾 type, using an ancient Chinese term for the area of what is now northern Vietnam. In the Vietnamese version, Dương Bá Trạc uses a Vietnamese term, *giống*, that can denote "breed," or now, "race," to refer to the Giao Chỉ people. Making the same argument as Ngô Giáp Dậu, Dương Bá Trạc argues that this original Giao Chỉ type or breed later interacted with a new type / breed that arrived from the north as first the Qin and then the Han dynasty extended their control across the region. Dương Bá Trạc refers to this new type / breed in both versions of the article as the "Hán lineage" (*Hán tộc* 漢族).³⁹

Although at one point, Dương Bá Trạc says that the mixing of the Hán and Giao Chỉ types / breeds created a new type / breed, later in the essay he indicates that this was more of a process of assimilation of the Giao Chỉ type / breed by the Hán lineage. In the Vietnamese version of this essay, the author states that "one can see that the current breed of Vietnamese people [*giống người Việt Nam*] are largely from the Han lineage [*Hán tộc*]," while in the classical Chinese version the same sentence is "there is no doubt but that our country's type [*Ngã quốc chủng* 我國種] was assimilated into the Hán lineage [*Hán tộc* 漢族]."⁴⁰

Dương Bá Trạc then concludes this section by offering some social Darwinist words of praise for his people. Referring to "our Hán lineage" (*Hán tộc ta*) in the Vietnamese version and "the glorious Hán lineage" (*đường đường Hán tộc* 堂堂漢族) in the classical Chinese version, Dương Bá Trạc says that the fact that it was able to expand southward through history, driving away other peoples along the way, until it finally reached what Dương Bá Trạc refers to as "our country" (*nước ta*) in the Vietnamese version and "this land" (*tư thổ* 斯土) in the classical Chinese text, is evidence of the civilized character and competitive power of the lineage. Further, it is this power of the Hán lineage, Dương Bá Trạc tells us, which enabled it to occupy Cambodia, to conquer all of the other old breeds or types in the area, and to become the master (*chủ nhân ông* 主人翁) of the land.[41]

In their efforts to write about race, we can see that Ngô Giáp Dậu and Dương Bá Trạc employed a variety of terms, as a set expression for race had yet to be established. Nonetheless, in the midst of the confusion of terms that appear in their writings, a relatively clear sense of race emerges. These men may have struggled to find the words to explain a new concept, but the idea that this new concept denoted was not new to them. As we have seen above, Nguyễn-dynasty emperors and officials had long seen themselves as distinct from the peoples who lived in the mountainous regions of the kingdom as well as from the people who lived in separate polities like Cambodia, and they had also long recognized that they shared similarities with the educated elite in the area of what is now China. While these distinctions were often depicted in cultural terms, as I have attempted to demonstrate above, in the nineteenth century something resembling a sense of racial difference appears to have emerged as well, and it is this sense, I argue, that men like Ngô Giáp Dậu and Dương Bá Trạc easily expressed through the concept of race when they were exposed to that concept in the early twentieth century.

Finally, at the same time that reformist scholars came to explain who the Vietnamese were in racial terms, they also produced new depictions of the groups of people in their land who had long been referred to simply as "savages." Ngô Giáp Dậu's *Summary of Việt History for Secondary Schools* was paired in the new reformed curriculum with a textbook on the geography of Vietnam that contained a section on such peoples. This book was written by reformist scholar Lương Trúc Đàm 梁竹潭 (1876–1908) and published in 1908. Entitled *The Land and Territory of the Southern Kingdom* (*Nam quốc địa dư* 南國地輿), this text covered basic information about the geography of Vietnam, its natural resources, and its administration. At the end it then contained a section on "savage and aboriginal human types" (*man thổ nhân chủng* 蠻土人種). The purpose of this section was to educate readers about the people who lived in the kingdom. As the title of the section indicates, the descriptions of the "savage and aboriginal types" were quite derogatory. Nonetheless, that Lương Trúc Đàm sought to identify different groups and describe them was something new, and this was likely influenced by the Western practice of identifying races or nationalities.

The section lists forty-five different groups: twenty-two in the north, fifteen in the center, and eight in the south. Each group is named and described, and information is provided about where the members of each group reside. The descriptions at times cover defining features such as hairstyles and types of clothing, and at other times they offer assessments of the character or behavior of the members of certain groups. These assessments are invariably negative.

In particular, a common theme that runs through the descriptions of the various savage groups is the idea that these people are dangerous. So, for instance, the text says of a people in the north simply referred to as "savages" (*Man nhân* 蠻人) that the men are treacherous and deceitful. Meanwhile it says of a group called the Mường (*Mường nhân* 人 / 芒人) that the men are fond of killing people and eating their livers and gallbladders while the women can trick people and steal their belongings.[42] In describing the Lao people (*Lao nhân* 佬人) of the northern region, the text states that "the faces of men and women are like indigo. If they come across a person, they kill him with a poisoned arrow and steal his goods. They also cut off the person's hair and use it to make women's clothing."[43] Among the Thoa Châm savages (*Thoa châm man nhân* 釵針蠻人) in the central region, the women would warmly welcome outsiders as if they were old friends but would then secretly poison them.[44] Also in the central region of the kingdom were a group that we can roughly translate as the "Blood-Sucking savages" (*Châm huyết man nhân* 針血蠻人). Whenever someone had an injury, these people would transform into demons at night, and would suck the blood of the injured person until he or she died.[45] Even more gruesome were the Cam Nanh Bỉ people (*Cam nanh bỉ nhân* 甘獰彼人), who also resided in the central region. When a man died these people would cut the eyes, tongue, and penis from his corpse and eat these body parts in snake soup.[46]

Another common characteristic of the various groups of savages, according to *The Land and Territory of the Southern Kingdom,* was their use of black magic. For instance, the text states of a people in the north called the Xá (*Xá nhân* 佘人) that "women are the leaders of the *động* [洞, i.e., the name of an administrative unit in a minority area]. They wear a tricolored turban on their heads and a tricolored belt around their waists. They carry bows and daggers like men. They often harm people with demonic magic [*yêu thuật* 妖術]."[47] The readers of this text are also told that they should be careful should they ever enter a village in the central region occupied by the Cam Môn aborigines (*Cam Môn thổ nhân* 甘門土人). To protect themselves from harm, they were to avoid eating chicken, to not laugh at anything strange or to spit, and to cover their urine and feces with soil when they relieved themselves. If they failed to do these things, then it would be difficult to avoid calamity.⁴⁸ Less dangerous but equally mysterious were the Hàm Ngài Xá (*Hàm Ngài Xá nhân* 含艾倮人). At night, these people would place artemisia in their mouths and enter the forest. There they would obtain the *Neocinnamomum* plant (*bạch quế* 白桂) and sell it to someone. Later, that person would transform into a tiger.⁴⁹ Finally, the Mãnh people (*Mãnh nhân* 猛人) in the north were evil by nature and could place a curse on people, and the Dao (*Dao nhân* 搖人) were wicked by nature and would use poisonous plants and opium to harm people.⁵⁰

Seeing the world in terms of nations, races, and ethnic groups demonstrates precisely the type of divisive mental categories that Zhao and scholars in the field of decoloniality argue originated in the West. This is true. Indeed, we can see such concepts appear for the first time in writings in Vietnam in the early twentieth century, such as the ones discussed above, and from the way in which these authors employed these concepts, we can sense that they were grappling with new ways of expressing their ideas. At the same time, however, the ideas that these men expressed through these new concepts were clearly not new. They were concepts that had emerged in the *tianxia* system of Nguyễn-dynasty Vietnam, before the educated elite had been exposed to Western ideas.

Conclusion

On August 16, 1945, one day after Japan surrendered in World War II and two weeks before Hồ Chí Minh declared Vietnam's independence, someone in Hanoi, writing under the name "Quốc Thụy," completed writing a booklet entitled *The National Question* (*Vấn đề dân tộc*). Published later that year by The Masses Publishing House, this book sought to teach students about nations, races, minorities, and national liberation movements. It was a text that was clearly intended to prepare young people to understand and support the struggle for independence from France that would soon get underway.

In the booklet there is a section on race, or what the author labels as "human types" (*nhân chủng*), the same term that Dương Bá Trạc employed in his 1918 bilingual essay. This is a Sinitic term and Quốc Thụy glosses it with a Vietnamese expression, "human breeds" (*giống người*), that was apparently now more familiar to students, given that the study of classical Chinese had been replaced with education in Vietnamese and French since the early 1920s. Quốc Thụy states in this section that "in terms of physiology and culture, the imperialists divide the breeds / races of people into two categories: the civilized and the savage. They label themselves as civilized and consider the breeds / races of people in colonies and semicolonies to be savages. As such, they take the position that the civilized breeds / races must govern over the savage breeds / races, and must control the weak."⁵¹

If Quốc Thụy had written these lines a century earlier, in 1845, the wording would have been unfamiliar to the educated elite at that time, but the concepts would have made complete sense. Nguyễn-dynasty officials, for instance, would not have understood what "imperialists" were yet, and they did not have a term to convey the concept of "race," but they nonetheless would have completely agreed that the world was divided into two groups, the civilized and the savage. Further, as the self-proclaimed leaders of the civilized half of humanity, these men also would have agreed that it was their duty to not only rule over savages but to transform them until they also became civilized, and to incorporate savage leaders who had been civilized into the Heavenly family of the imperial bureaucracy so that there would be "no outside."

Zhao's effort to promote the "*tianxia* system" as a new philosophy for world governance is based on the idea that a *tianxia* view of the world would be different from, and superior to, the current Western-established global order. However, in this chapter we have attempted to demonstrate that the *tianxia* world of late imperial Vietnam was also divisive and oppressive toward Others, and that as a result, we cannot find the intellectual resources in the historical record from that time period to make the claim for an alternative approach to world governance. Nineteenth-century Vietnam is of course just one case. However, we argue that if scholars take the approach of this chapter, which is to read historical sources in their original contexts, then the same conclusions will be reached in examining other places and time periods as well.

Notes

1. Zhao Tingyang, "Rethinking Empire from a Chinese Concept 'All-under-Heaven' (Tian-xia)," *Social Identities* 12, no. 1 (2006): 29–41; "A Political World Philosophy in Terms of All-under-Heaven (Tian-xia)," *Diogenes*, no. 221 (2009): 5–18; *Tianxia tixi: Shijie zhidu zhexue daolun* 天下體系：世界制度哲學導論 (The *tianxia* system: An introduction to the philosophy of a world institution) (Beijing: Renmin daxue chubanshe, 2011); and *All under Heaven: The Tianxia System for a Possible World Order*, trans. Joseph E. Harroff (Berkeley: University of California Press, 2021).

2. Zhao, "Political World Philosophy," p. 221.

3. Zhao, "Rethinking Empire," p. 30.

4. For an overview, see Walter D. Mignolo and Catherine E. Walsh, *On Decoloniality: Concepts, Analytics, Praxis* (Durham, NC: Duke University Press, 2018).

5. Zhao, *Tianxia tixi*, p. 34.

6. Zhao, *Tianxia tixi*, p. 34.

7. Cai Yong 蔡邕, *Duduan* 獨斷 (Solitary decisions) (2nd cent. AD), Juanshang 卷上 (my translation).

8. Ban Gu 班固, *Hanshu* 漢書 (History of the Han) (92 AD), Juan yi 卷一, Gaodi jixia 高帝紀下 (my translation).

9. *Đại Nam thực lục chính biên đệ nhất kỷ* 大南寔錄編第一紀 (Veritable records of Đại Nam, first compilation) (1848), 17/6a (hereafter ĐNTL 1).

10. See the entry for Nguyễn Viên 阮王 / 員 in *Đại Nam liệt truyện tiền biên* 大南列傳前編 (Arrayed biographies of Đại Nam, preliminary compilation) (1852), 20/18a–21b (hereafter ĐNLTTB).

11. ĐNTL 1, 18/1a–1b.

12. ĐNTL 1, 18/1a–1b.

13. ĐNTL 1, 23/7b.

14. *Đại Nam thực lục chính biên đệ nhị kỷ* 大南寔錄編第二紀 (Veritable records of Đại Nam, second compilation) (1861), 121/10b (hereafter ĐNTL 2).

15. ĐNTL 2, 184/6b–7a.

16. ĐNTL 2, 163/10a–11b.

17. *Shijing* 詩經 (Classic of poetry), Daya 大雅, Huangyi 皇矣 (my translation).

18. ĐNTL 1, 3/6a–6b. For reference to Nguyễn Văn Tồn as a Khmer, see ĐNTL 1, 2/10b.

19. ĐNTL 1, 3/6b.

20. ĐNTL 2, 1/22b.

21. ĐNTL 2, 28/3a.

22. ĐNTL 2, 1/22b.

23. ĐNTL 2, 51/28a; ĐNLTTB, 28/4a.

24. ĐNTL 2, 19/17b–18a.

25. ĐNTL 2, 32/22a.

26. ĐNTL 2, 22b–23a.

27. ĐNTL 2, 33/23b–24b.

28. ĐNTL 2, 41/2b–3a.

29. ĐNTL 2, 207/14a.

30. Trịnh Hoài Đức 鄭懷德, *Gia Định thành thông chí* 嘉定城通志 (Comprehensive gazetteer of Gia Định Citadel) (1820), Société Asiatique manuscript, 2/42a and 43b.

31. Liam C. Kelley, "'Confucianism' in Vietnam: A State of the Field Essay," *Journal of Vietnamese Studies* 1, no. 1–2 (2006): 314–370.

32. ĐNTL 2, 70/2a.

33. ĐNTL 2, 137/15b–16b.

34. *Đại Nam thực lục chính biên đệ tam kỷ* 大南寔錄編第三紀 (Veritable records of Đại Nam, third compilation) (1877), 17/25a–25b (hereafter ĐNTL 3).

35. ĐNTL 3, 17/25b.

36. ĐNTL 3, 17/25b–26a.

37. Ngô Giáp Dậu 吳甲酉, *Trung học Việt sử toát yếu* 中學越史撮要 (Summary of Việt history for secondary schools), vol. 1 (1911), National Library of Vietnam manuscript R.1342, 7a–8a.

38. Ngô Giáp Dậu, 8a–8b.

39. Dương Bá Trạc 楊伯濯, "Việt sử khảo" 越史考 (An examination of Việt history), *Nam phong* 南風 (Southern mores) 15 (2018): 129 (hereafter "Chinese version"); and Dương

Bá Trạc "Việt sử khảo" (An examination of Việt history), *Nam phong* (Southern mores)15 (2018): 143 (hereafter "Vietnamese version").

40. Dương Bá Trạc, Chinese version, 129; Vietnamese version, 143.

41. Dương Bá Trạc, Chinese version, 130; Vietnamese version, 143.

42. Lương Trúc Đàm 梁竹潭, *Nam quốc địa dư* 南國地輿 (The land and territory of the Southern Kingdom) (1908), National Library of Vietnam manuscript R.1424, 73a.

43. Lương Trúc Đàm, 73a–73b.

44. Lương Trúc Đàm, 77a.

45. Lương Trúc Đàm, 75b.

46. Lương Trúc Đàm, 76a–76b.

47. Lương Trúc Đàm, 73b.

48. Lương Trúc Đàm, 76b.

49. Lương Trúc Đàm, 76a.

50. Lương Trúc Đàm, 73a.

51. Quốc Thụy, *Vấn đề dân tộc* (The national question) (Hà Nội: Nhà sách Đại chúng, 1945), 14–15.

CHAPTER 3

"We Choose to Go to the Moon" for Truth, Justice, and Peace on Earth

A Dialogue for Socioeconomic Justice between *Ubu-ntu* and *Buren*

Mogobe B. RAMOSE

AT THE CORE of our contemporary global human condition is an epistemic absolutism that negates the possibility of justice through a tenacious commitment to sustain the prevailing order of international politics dominated by an economic fundamentalism. This tendency toward absolutism is the affirmation of a dogmatism that is the antichrist of philosophical thinking. Resistance is the only appropriate response to it. We can find this resistance in a dialogue between *ubu-ntu,* an African philopraxical concept meaning "humaneness," and *buren* 不忍, a Chinese philosophical concept meaning "a heart that cannot bear suffering." The concern is not only with Africa and China, but the rest of the peoples of the world with the ethical imperative to pursue and establish justice in human and interstate relations through the eradication of the injustice that lies at the root of capitalism. The ethical dimension of both *ubu-ntu* and *buren* demands an alternative model of global human relations in the pursuit of truth, justice, and peace in the world. The ethical convergence between *buren*'s and *ubu-ntu*'s ethics is used to question the apparent dogma of the inalienability of sovereign statehood and the false belief in the immortality of a fundamentally immoral capitalism. Our discussion on *buren*'s and *ubu-ntu*'s ethics will certainly shed light on the potential of cross-cultural philosophical dialogues in constructing alternative models of global governance. These possibilities will ultimately enrich and broaden our ongoing theory-building process on *tianxia*.

First, why should we focus on dialogue? Philosophy as experience and concept presupposes dialogue. The concept of philosophy without dialogue is dogmatism. Dogmatism is against philosophy because it is tyranny suppressing freedom of thought and action. In this chapter we adopt the understanding of philosophy as freedom from dogmatism. It is from this perspective that we will give an exposition of the dialogue between *ubu-ntu* and *buren* in the quest for a socioeconomic model consistent with the ethical imperative to pursue truth, justice, and peace in human relations. The quest for such a model is based on the recognition that the injustice at the root of capitalism renders it ethically indefensible. We recognize that for some readers "peace on Earth" might evoke reminiscences of Pope John XXIII's 1963 encyclical known by the same name conveyed in Latin as *Pacem in Terris*. The recollection is in order as it reveals a common interest in the quest for truth, justice, and peace on Earth. We now turn to the context within which the dialogue will be conducted.

History and His-story: The Complex Matrix in the Search for Truth

Truthfulness is related conceptually to truth.[1] In practice, one ought to be true to oneself as the first step of enunciating and acting truth. The minimum expectation here is that the others will either recognize one's truth, understanding it to be theirs as well, or dispute it. The bases of dispute are potentially multiple and, sometimes even incompatible. An integral part of the acceptability of truth is that it may never be imposed upon others. "Nobody is entitled to enforce by compulsion his own truth on other individuals."[2] This prohibition applies even to the scientific endeavor, which ought to engage in the pursuit of more and more critical reasoning in the search for truth instead of resorting to either physical force or coercion under the guise of persuasion.[3] Science ought not to compel "reason to abdicate its critical function and become a mere instrument of the system."[4] On this reasoning, truth is inextricably linked with justice. "Justice in its concrete realization never suffices. It has constant need of review, reform and improvement. It also does not suffice that the socio-political structures are 'possessed' by the face-a-face. Alone, this would leave them undisturbed, unmoved to constant reform. It is necessary for them to always submit themselves to new critique in order to remain certain that they still answer to the ethical and just intentions at their origin."[5]

Justice is the guarantor of peace only if it recognizes the challenge of the truth at a given historical moment and responds accordingly. The refusal to respond accordingly is the destruction of the peacefulness that was prevailing prior to the emergence of the new elements of "disturbance." The pursuit of truth in the broad context of human relations and in science for the sake of justice and peace is the exercise of epistemic and political love.[6] Thus if the scientific endeavor insists upon turning critical reason into "a mere instrument of the system," it provides no other alternative than "a person must die for the sake of truth."[7]

The Context of the Contemporary Global Historical Condition

Under the prism of truth, justice, and peace presented in the preceding paragraphs, we now turn to the contextualization of the contemporary global historical condition. Our contextualization includes the injustice of the Western colonization of "the New World" but without going into elaborate details about this experience. The colonial wars were ethically unjust because they were the violation of the indigenous peoples' right to their land and the abrogation of their right to freedom. The inextricable connection between land and life means that the injustice of Western colonial conquest was at the same time the violation of the indigenous peoples' right to life. This injustice is plain even according to the Western colonizer's own just war doctrine.[8] The following is what we should like to underline with regard to the injustice of Western colonial conquest.

1. The "voyages of discovery" were not pleasure trips undertaken by West European countries. The concept of "discovery" acquired a technical meaning referring to the regulation of relations among and between the West European countries (England is included in this context).[9] According to Palmer, "Spain and Portugal took the lead in these early voyages of discovery, though they were soon followed by England and Holland, which towards the close of the sixteenth century freed herself from Spanish rule, and early in the seventeenth began to build up a colonial empire of her own."[10]

Among the colonial conquerors from the West, "Spain alone had the courage to hold a comprehensive debate on the ethics and morality of European presence in the Indies. In the other countries of the world, the right to occupy these lands was regarded as too obvious to be questioned."[11] We extend this observation to Africa, Australia, New Zealand, and all the other countries in which the indigenous peoples, being the rightful owners of those countries from time immemorial, lost sovereign title to their territories as a result of the injustice of Western colonial conquest.

2. Our interest in the problem of conquest in the unjust wars of colonization is linked directly to the ethics of war on the one hand and the question of economic inequality on the other. Epistemic justice is an integral part of our concern and focus upon the problem of conquest in the unjust wars of colonization. For us there is a link between the ethics of war and the problem of economic inequality and social injustice. We will explore this link in our search for a socioeconomic model responsive to the question of truth, justice, and peace on Earth.

3. In 2002, Sampie Terreblanche, a professor of economic history in Stellenbosch University in conqueror South Africa, published the book *A History of Inequality in South Africa 1652–2002*.[12] The historical period covered in this book, particularly the start date of 1652, recognizes conquest of the indigenous peoples by the Dutch in the unjust war of the colonization of the land of the indigenous peoples.[13] In terms of the doctrine of "discovery" the Dutch, in the name of Jan van Riebeeck, claimed the exercise of the ethically questionable "right of conquest." By virtue of this "right" they instituted economic inequality and epistemic injustice between the colonial conqueror and the conquered indigenous peoples of the country.

Terreblanche recognizes this situation, although he does not state directly and explicitly "the right of conquest." In effect, he sets aside the ethical question of whether or not the colonial war waged by the Dutch against the indigenous peoples was morally justified. This is the crucial and primary question for us. But his exposition of the economic history of conqueror South Africa evidently upholds the original injustice of conquest in the unjust wars of the colonization of the country subsequently named "South Africa" by the colonial conqueror. Terreblanche avers that he narrates this history from the position of "the left of the ideological spectrum."[14] "We cannot properly interpret the special relationship between power, land, and labour in South African history without focusing on the power of the colonial masters *vis-à-vis* the powerlessness of the indigenous people. It would not have been possible for white colonists to become landowners if they did not have the power to turn the Khoisan and the Africans into a subservient labour force. The political, economic, and military nature of the white master class has determined the nature and course of South Africa's history for almost 350 years."[15]

4. Twelve years later, Thomas Piketty, a professor of economics at the Paris School of Economics, published *Capital in the Twenty-First Century*. The book is focused on "understanding the historical dynamics of wealth and income."[16] Piketty describes his book as a "Francocentric project" studying "inequality in France."[17] Both Terreblanche's and Piketty's books share a focus on the historical dynamics of economic inequality. The former is studying the history of "inequality" in conqueror South Africa and the latter is doing the same with regard to France. That both Terreblanche and Piketty are focused on the question of inequality is aptly emphasized, though with no apparent intention to do so, by the editors of *After Piketty: The Agenda for Economics and Inequality*.[18] We take special note of the word "inequality" in the subtitle of this book.

It is interesting that the first sentence in the first chapter of Piketty's book—a "Francocentric project"—is a statement on the strike by the miners working for Lonmin in Marikana, situated near the town of Rustenburg in conqueror South

Africa. This shows that Piketty's "Francocentric project" will extend beyond France. He states explicitly that "this book relies primarily on the historical experience of the leading developed countries: the United States, Japan, Germany, France and Great Britain."[19] We read in the same page that it will "proceed by extrapolation to poor and emerging countries." Piketty's term "extrapolation" suggests that these countries are marginal. Yet his project extends to them to the extent that it is an attempt to construct hypotheses applicable at the global level. It is certain that Piketty or anyone else may not be saddled with the impossible task of covering the whole world. So words such as "global" and "world" should be understood as the local seeking to extend its experience beyond its confines. The attempt at universalizability—in this essay the preferred concept is "pluriversality"—is legitimate provided it does not impose itself onto others by force.

5. Our criticism of Piketty's research is predicated on the unreserved acceptance of his direct and robust declaration that the "answers contained" in his book "are imperfect and incomplete." We commend Piketty's openness to the possibility to "perfect" and "complement" his answers through ongoing scientific research. We also accept unreservedly his observation that, "Given the dialogue of the deaf, in which each camp justifies its own intellectual laziness by pointing to the laziness of the other, there is a role for research that is at least systematic and methodical if not fully scientific. *Expert analysis will never put an end to the violent political conflict that inequality inevitably instigates.*"[20] Furthermore, we acknowledge his caveat, relating to one of the conclusions of his research, that "one should be wary of any economic determinism in regard to inequalities of wealth and income. The history of the distribution of wealth has always been deeply political, and it cannot be reduced to purely economic mechanisms."[21] Finally, we accept his openness to the possibility that "one can imagine other forms of organization" different from the prevailing global model of economic organization.[22]

"EXTRAPOLATION"

What we find somewhat problematic about Piketty's "extrapolation" is that it refers to the "social democratic gains" after World War II in Western Europe in laudatory terms but seems virtually silent about the contribution of its former colonies to those gains. H. M. Lange breaks the silence in this way:

> Another respect in which Western Europe today differs strikingly from the Atlantic seaboard colonies in North America in the late eighteenth century is that . . . Western Europe has strictly limited resources and a very large population. It moreover is rapidly losing its grip on the colonial empires which, during the nineteenth century, made up its deficiencies. . . .

the emancipation of former colonial peoples may involve ... a very serious loss of resources on the part of West European nations. We are faced with an increasing pressure of population against limited natural resources.[23]

He is followed by E. C. Djamson making the following observations. Already at the birth of the Treaty of Rome, colonial relations and thus colonial interests had to be included. The First Yaoundé Convention, which was concluded on July 20, 1963, and came into force on June 1, 1964, became the substantive instrument to preserve and protect the economic interests of the colonizing powers. This was followed by the Yaoundé II Convention, which came into force on January 1, 1971. Even regional economic integration organizations in Africa, such as the former East African Community comprising Kenya, Tanzania, and Uganda, were also brought into the orbit of the preservation and protection of the economic interests of the European Economic Community (EEC) in the former colonies. Thus the Arusha Convention was signed on July 26, 1966, and was to run for five years. The intention to protect and preserve EEC economic interests beyond decolonization was not restricted to Africa. This was made concrete by the introduction of successive conventions with African, Caribbean, and Pacific countries (ACP) between the EEC and its former colonies. These conventions, sometimes referred to as the Lomé Conventions, are formally known, for example, as the Second ACP-EEC Convention, signed at Lomé, Togo, on October 31, 1979. There is also the Fourth ACP-EEC Convention signed at Lomé on December 15, 1989.[24]

D. K. Fieldhouse does not provide the same details given by Djamson. However, he examines the thesis of the preservation of colonial economic interests in the concession to grant only political independence to the colonized states in Africa. In this respect there is convergence between Djamson and Fieldhouse. The examination of Fieldhouse is historically grounded, appropriately nuanced, and carefully elaborated. The thesis is that, "Historically the main function of colonialism was to restructure the economies of the Third World countries so that they would fit into their allotted slots in the newly emergent world system.... it was necessary to create physical, political and juridical structures which were well adapted to the needs of foreign capital; that is, so that capitalism could operate as efficiently in Africa as it could in Europe or North America."[25]

Fieldhouse ends with a carefully nuanced conclusion of his examination, stating that "there were important economic elements in the process of decolonization; but the colonies were not set free simply because continued political control by Britain, France or Belgium offered them no economic advantages, or even because the difference was not thought important."[26]

Fieldhouse's and Djamson's arguments are an important challenge to Piketty's "extrapolation" to Africa.

PIKETTY'S STANDPOINT TOWARD CAPITALISM

Like Terreblanche, Piketty also defines the position from which he conducts his project: "I was vaccinated for life against the conventional but lazy rhetoric of anticapitalism.... I have no interest in denouncing inequality or capitalism per se—especially since social inequalities are not in themselves a problem as long as they are justified, that is, founded only upon common utility."[27] The historic "Declaration of the Rights of Woman and Citizen" (*Déclaration des droits de la femme et de la citoyenne*) (1790), spearheaded by Olympe de Gouges in France, "was modelled on the 'Declaration of the Rights of Man and Citizen' of 1789."[28] This modelling contained elements of epistemic imitation even if it advocated for the rights of women from a specifically woman's experience. In what way and to what extent did such epistemic imitation reflect epistemological dependency? Despite this apparent epistemic dependency, "the woman's question" inaugurated by this Declaration was a direct challenge, epistemologically and historically, to the 1789 "Declaration of the Rights of Man and Citizen." Epistemic equality is undermined by the preservation of the dominance of the male epistemological paradigm. Epistemicide is not the exclusive province of the injustice of Western colonization. It belongs also to the sphere of female-male relations. Gender equality consists in actually taking into account the epistemologies of being-a-woman-in-the-world in the search for gender truth, justice, and peace. Olympe de Gouges "went to the guillotine in November 1793 for her open opposition to Robespierre and the Jacobins."[29]

It is somewhat odd that Piketty seems to have not been sensitized by the Declaration of the Rights of Woman and Citizen to the woman's question in his "historical" investigation of the question of economic inequality. The women's Declaration was a direct challenge to the relevance and "universal" applicability, even within France, of the Declaration of the Rights of Man and Citizen. Piketty applies this apparent insensitivity by "extrapolation," extending the findings of his research to the "poor and emerging" economies in the world. This extension is tenuous in terms of relevance and dubious in terms of its claim to be "universal."

Even the United Nations Universal Declaration of Human Rights is not by ethical or historical necessity relevant to and applicable to all human historical conditions. It was born out of the historical experience of the primary belligerents in World War II.[30] The epistemologies of the Global South were not party to its conception and affirmation. As such the Declaration is the reflection of the historical experience of one segment of the human family. If the Declaration were valid for all historical conditions, why then the proliferation of new and other human rights perspectives such as the American Convention on Human Rights, the European Convention on Human Rights, and the African Charter on Human and Peoples' Rights? The relevance and universal applicability of the Declaration are not a foregone conclusion. The economic history of Piketty is silent on the absence of the epistemologies of the Global South, but his findings from the history of one segment of the human family are to be "extrapolated" to the Global South. Why?

PIKETTY AND THE MORALITY OF CAPITALISM

We concur with Piketty that even the best economic blueprint is not necessarily the solution to the problem of economic inequality, because "the history of inequality is shaped by the way economic, social, and political actors view what is just and what is not, as well as by the relative power of those actors and the collective choices that result. It is the joint product of all relevant actors combined."[31] He repeats this point at pages 35 and 40 of his book, respectively.

What we find puzzling—insofar as it may be construed as Piketty's sensitivity to injustice—is that he makes one of his characters declare: "And why behave morally at all? Since social inequality was in itself immoral and unjustified, why not be thoroughly immoral and appropriate capital by whatever means are available?"[32] The apparent permissibility of "the end justifies the means" is often practiced in the name of "pragmatism." At times, the pragmatism is flavored with the taste of "realism." In practice, the protagonists of pragmatism often turn out to be consenting conformists willing to enjoy the comfort and convenience gained from capitalism at the expense of justice to the other. Being the keeper of one's sister and brother is replaced with deadly individualist egoism indifferent to the exigency of justice with and to the other.[33] In this frame of mind charity serves as the palliative to prolong injustice and suppresses the realization of justice that is due to the other.

Is it so that the best option is necessarily to condone immorality? The point of this rhetorical question is to suggest that to challenge immorality is also open to choice for Piketty's character. This choice means that it is ethically questionable to discard the examination of the moral foundations, in this case, of capitalism. For us this examination is prior to the construction of economic models. Our choice of ethics as the platform from which we will examine the problem of economic inequality and epistemic injustice emanating from Western colonization and the emergence of capitalism is at odds with Piketty's disregard for the morality of capitalism. "The end justifies the means" is countered by the ethical principle that "the end does not justify the means." This is the task we set ourselves in one of the subsequent sections.

Terreblanche and Piketty: Members of the Epistemologies of the North

Sampie Terreblanche is thirty-eight years older than Piketty. He is also geographically apart from him because his habitual residence is in conqueror South Africa while that of Piketty is France. Despite these differences, the two authors are characterized by epistemological affinity and methodological kinship. With regard to the former, they drink from the same epistemological well of the Western paradigm of scientific knowledge, in particular, economics.

Terreblanche leaves no doubt about his ideological orientation: "My ideological orientation has always been the social democratic approach of continental Europe as distinct from the narrow liberal and neoclassical approach of the Anglo-American world."[34] Given his ideological identity with Piketty, Terreblanche could as well have written "continental Europe, particularly France where Piketty lives." Piketty himself leaves no doubt about his assessment of "the Anglo-American world":

> I wanted to return to France and Europe, which I did when I was twenty-five.... One important reason for my choice has a direct bearing on this book: I did not find the work of US economists entirely convincing.... I was only too aware of the fact that I knew nothing at all about the world's economic problems.... I quickly realized that there had been no significant effort to collect historical data on the dynamics of inequality since Kuznets, yet the profession continued to churn out purely theoretical results without even knowing what facts needed to be explained. And it expected me to do the same. When I returned to France, I set out to collect the missing data.[35]

Piketty's option for "continental Europe" coincides with that of Terreblanche. His "modernizing rather than dismantling the social state" is consistent with "the social democratic approach" chosen by Terreblanche.[36]

The methodological kinship between the two economists is reflected by their pairing of economics and history explaining the problem of economic inequality primarily through the use of statistics. They are thus a pair espousing one of the epistemologies of the Global North, preserving capitalism by doing some carpentry on it. They are surely not the only carpenters of capitalism preferring to disregard its roots and the soil in which they are anchored.[37] There are also those who focus on the roots of capitalism and the soil in which it is anchored.[38] In his encyclical *Evangelii Gaudium* 2013, paragraph 59, Pope Francis describes capitalism as a socioeconomic system that is "unjust at its root." "Competition" is the leitmotif of this socioeconomic system permitting the employer either to kill other employers or to merge with them. It also allows the employer to kill the employees on the one hand and the employees to kill one another on the other.[39]

Jane Kelsey is also critical of the "economic fundamentalism" upheld by capitalism.[40] She argues that TAMA (there are many alternatives) is the counter to the prevailing dogma of TINA (there are no alternatives [to capitalism]). Holloway also moves in the same direction as Kelsey.[41] The global dominance of the epistemologies of the Global North may no longer be taken for granted. In fact, they are currently under critical scrutiny by the epistemologies of the South.[42] The aim of the latter is to abolish epistemicide and to bring about "the end of the cognitive empire."[43]

CRITIQUE OF TERREBLANCHE AND PIKETTY

Third, the concession to political independence at decolonization did not restore sovereign title to territory to the conquered of the Earth.[44] The ensuing result is limping sovereignty burdened with bondage to economic dependency and foreign debt. To this structural, systemic, and continual systematic material impoverishment must be added intellectual poverty on the part of the multitude of the conquered of the Earth, insofar as they have not acquired the education imposed by the Western colonial conqueror. From the point of view of the conquered of the Earth, the foreign debt burden is an escape from the ethical duty to pay reparations as well as compensation for the quadruple injustice of colonization, namely, (1) the forcible loss of sovereign title to territory, (2) the slave trade, (3) the depopulation of Africa, and (4) epistemicide.[45]

The Contemporary Global Historical Condition

Today, timocracy has replaced democracy without bloodshed. Paradoxically, it sustains the socioeconomic structure and the system that continues to condone the preventable deaths of the many for the pleasure of the few.[46] This situation reaffirms Marcuse's thesis that the "free election of masters does not abolish the masters or the slaves."[47] On the other hand, the "three great religions of the world" pride themselves with the legitimacy of monotheism. Odd that they seem satisfied with "three" signifying a multiplicity of gods—Yahweh, the God of Jesus Christ, and Allah—rather than one god only. Each of the three gods is so deeply rooted in their respective ground that in practice wars have erupted whenever there was an attempt to uproot one of them. Furthermore, practice shows that none of the three gods is successful in avoiding the veneration of the human-made god called "the market," money being the god in whom all contradictions coincide into an uneasy harmony.[48] The harmony is such that two of the "three great religions of the world" condemn what they deem to be the fundamentalism of the other while they condone their deadly economic fundamentalism.[49]

A well-known adage from Western antiquity teaches that the health of the people is the highest law. Yet, there is compelling evidence revealing that the "Third World health [is] hostage to [the] First World wealth."[50] Holding the health of the conquered of the Earth to ransom in this way is a violation of the human right to life. The right to good health is inseparable from the right to life. Contemporary human rights discourse recognizes the right to food. Yet, practice reveals that for the conquered of the Earth, the enjoyment of this right is subordinated to an economic structure feeding on a political ideology that allows the throwing away of food to ensure the survival of this deadly economic structure.

From the point of view of the conquered of the Earth, the human rights discourse is the inspiration of hope for a better life, while the protagonists of this promise remain resolutely determined to retain and perpetuate the deadly economic structure that prevails globally. The conquered of the Earth are neither blind to this reality nor unaware of the flattery of the beneficiaries from the preventable deaths of the many on a daily basis. Living on a daily survival mode is not the destiny of the conquered of the Earth ordained by nature. It is not an ethical inevitability to which they are condemned.

The condemnation of the conquered of the Earth to live on a daily survival mode is propelled by the global epidemic called "pecunimania": an apparently irrational, incurable, and irresistible love of money. Pecunimania heats up the mind, melting it into a molten organism of production releasing unlimited energy to make profit at any cost. Pecunimania thrives well in and through the bank even though "the world's basic banking principle, [is that] 'The more you have, the more you get'. And conversely that, 'If you don't have it, you don't get it.'"[51] The bank lives on credit, that is to say, trust, yet it is the most untrusting even though credit ought to be "a human right."[52] If indeed the money reflected on my bank account is really mine, why then may I not withdraw the whole credit amount at once and whenever I like from my account? After all, it is my individual money in the bank that I would like to withdraw. Yet, the bank has a decisive as well as determinative say on what my account should look like. If it really is "my own money" because I have worked for it and therefore own it, why is my wish and discretion on how to use it in chains?

The bank uses number to feed the delusion of ownership of money and wealth. It uses its image of power based on money as a means to control and curtail the freedom and discretion of the client to use her or his money. The use of the power of money in this way is not limited to the bank. It happens also in the course of human relations. This happened in antiquity when the problem of the power of money led to moral decay, and it is also happening now because of the attitude that money is "rather a nearly almighty instrument of power capable of guaranteeing everything else. It is in that sense that money is a form of practical totalization, and thus of violence toward others."[53] For this reason, the delusion of number sustained and deployed by the bank must be challenged. It is morally important to seek the truth about the meaning of the bank in our time as part of our quest for justice and peace in the world. In his critical historico-philosophical exposition of the experience and the concept of "money" Toon Vandevelde answers the three questions posed in this paragraph as follows:

> Those who accept money immediately give credit (from the Latin *credere*, to believe, from the Indo-European root "*kred*," trust). There is not a single "real" guarantee for the value of money. The gold reserves in the National Bank's vaults only cover a fraction of the money in circulation, and if everyone decided to reclaim their own little piece of "real" wealth, the economy would collapse. Money rests on suggestion, delusion and magic, on the naïve identification of sign with reality, on the suggestion of solidness and stability.... Those who want to understand the quality of money had better apply themselves to the study of mass psychological mechanisms than to the study of the laws of economics.[54]

The grand delusion of money is anchored on "the naïve identification of sign with reality." The crucial point is to deal with the reality and not indulge in self-deception based on the seduction of the sign.

There is little doubt that in our time money has supplanted the ancient adage that "man is the measure of all things." Today it is 'money is the measure of all things.'[55] We suggest that the latter led to the assassination of President Patrice Lumumba of the Congo: duly and freely elected by the people yet had his life terminated not without interest by foreign powers.[56] Foreign power involvement in state destabilization neither began nor stopped with Lumumba in Africa or other parts of the world. Guatemala, a country of troubled emigration today, is yet another example of clandestine foreign power destabilization of another country.[57] The fanning of wars by the merchants of "corporate warriors" continues to be a worrisome development in international relations.[58] It is a threat to sovereign statehood and democracy. The point here is that scholarship may not gloss over the very important point of the worldwide culture of secret intelligence services and their operations, even if these may not be readily known precisely because of their secrecy. A study of *ujamaa* in Tanzania and *harambee* in Kenya from this perspective can scarcely sustain the orthodox view that both political philosophies failed because they were theoretically inadequate and could not be implemented in practice.

There are two world wars behind us. Their causes are varied and even contested. However, what appears to be constant is wealth and money. As the poet Wilfred Owen observed, many youths were summoned to war to "die as cattle" inspired by the call that "it is sweet and fitting to die for one's fatherland." He writes in his poem *Dulce et decorum est* that

> If you could hear, at every jolt, the blood
> Come gargling from the froth-corrupted lungs
> Bitter as cud
> Of vile, incurable sores on innocent tongues,—
> My friend, you would not tell with such high zest
> To children ardent for some desperate glory,
> The old lie: *Dulce et decorum est*
> *Pro patria mori.*[59]

And so it is that for the poet the youth are being told a lie, an old lie in Latin that few understand, to go to slaughter in war. The reason for waging war is not always truthful, as the invasion of Iraq testifies. Commenting on the invasion of Iraq in 2003 Mohamed El Baradei submits that

> the Iraq War was a war of ideology, motivated by the fantasy of establishing Iraq as an oasis of democracy that would, in turn, transform the geopolitical landscape of the Middle East. Both Blair and Bush have indicated that regime change was at the heart of the motivation to go to war, regardless of the justification cited. Together with a number of their key associates, they significantly inflated the imminence of the threat posed by Saddam Hussein's weapons of mass destruction, weapons which in fact did not exist.... Both were deliberately selective in their use of available facts. And both presided over a war in which, time after time, bombing campaigns and armored assaults made little attempt to protect the civilian population against the indiscriminate use of force, referring euphemistically to civilian deaths as "collateral damage."[60]

Citing El Baradei and adding new information to the above citation, John M. Schuessler corroborates the argument of El Baradei.[61]

The invasion of Iraq happened as if Hiroshima and Nagasaki were not enough to teach us that even the just war doctrine may no longer be invoked to wage any war. "Atoms for Peace," to use former President Eisenhower's phrase, are much better than atoms for war. D. J. Enright the poet cautions us with sarcastic cynicism that the "old lie" of dying for the fatherland is not worth the memorial monuments erected for peace in honor of the dead.

The Monuments of Hiroshima
The roughly estimated ones, who do not sort well with our common
 phrases,
Who are by no means eating roots of dandelion, or pushing up the
 daisies.
The more or less anonymous, to whom no human idiom can apply,
Who neither passed away, or on,
 Nor went before, nor vanished on a sigh.
Little of peace for them to rest in, less of them to rest in peace:
Dust to dust a swift transition, ashes to ash with awful ease.
Their only monument will of others' casting—
A Tower of Peace, a Hall of Peace, a Bridge of Peace
—who might have wished for something lasting,
Like a wooden box.[62]

Our depiction of the contemporary global historical condition suggests that pecunimania is the enduring widespread disease in human relations. We are confronted with a deadly totalizing disease that recognizes only itself as the source and telos of all finitude. The resoluteness of this posture is deeply rooted in an irrational militarism ready to annihilate both itself and all that lives. The basis for this irrationality is said to be the defense of freedom mortgaged to a deity called the capitalist market.

Shall we enter the third millennium under the yoke of this epistemic absolutism? The core of this epistemic absolutism is the negation of justice through the will to sustain the prevailing order of international politics dominated by economic fundamentalism. The critical point, however, is that "socio-political justice and peace in their present forms must never become a definitive regime and this against our western political thinking, with its pretension to universality, and lack of patience for the struggle to improve, exhibiting instead the contrary tendency toward installing itself as an absolute and unchanging system located outside of time."[63] This tendency toward absolutism is the affirmation of dogmatism. This is an antiphilosophical tyrannical posture negating the openness of science. Resistance is the only appropriate response to it. We turn to yet another challenge arising from the contemporary global historical condition before we invite the dialogue between *ubuntu* and *buren* as a response to the challenges.

"WE CHOOSE TO GO TO THE MOON"

We have chosen former president Kennedy's title for this section for the following reasons. First, the direct thrust of the speech was the quest for peace in the world. Second, the speech had the potential to pose the challenge of truthfulness and truth to humanity. The deception and the self-deception induced by pecunimania could be cured if they were to be replaced by truthfulness and truth in practice. This consideration also applies to the challenge posed by the fixation on sovereign statehood. The United Nations is organized on the basis of this concept. Many regional entities such as the Organization of American States, the African Union, the European Union, and the Association of Southeast Asian Nations, for example, are also organized on the basis of sovereign statehood. The apparent absolutization of this theory and practice of the state presents the façade of immutability. Yet, there is evidence that this has been challenged precisely in the sphere of international politics.

The first republican constitution of Ghana made provision for the partial or whole surrender of state sovereignty in pursuit of African unity. This provision saw the light of day in Article 2 of the republican constitution of Ghana of 1960. It is more than noteworthy that no other single African country followed this example of Africanness. This is the first example in international politics of a sovereign state remaining open to partial or whole surrender of itself for the betterment of human relations in Africa and across the entire Mother Earth for all human beings. It is significant also that this predates former president Kennedy's 1961 "We choose to go to the Moon" speech as well as the 1979 Moon Treaty. From our point of view, Ghana gave a shining example of Pan-Africanness to the extent that it is a demonstration that the principle of the sacrosanctity of exclusive territorial sovereignty is contrary to the ontologico-ethical imperative that Mother Earth is the pluriversal communal panarium of all human beings.

Without explicit recognition of Africanness, the agreement governing the activities of states on the Moon and other celestial bodies, the 1979 Moon Treaty, is a reaffirmation of the ontologico-ethical imperative that Mother Earth is the pluriversal communal panarium of all human beings. It also underlines the fact that the principle of the sacrosanctity of state sovereignty is a lie, a grand delusion that humanity ought to divest itself of from here on our livable planet Earth. It is self-deception to surrender state sovereignty only to the Moon and other celestial bodies known to be unfriendly to human life while refusing to do the same with regard to the only planet thus far known to be hospitable to human life, including the lives of all that lives in Mother Earth. Thus the 1960 republican constitution of Ghana and the Moon Treaty are living examples showing that state sovereignty is a lie; it is not the ultimate immutable truth about the organization of human relations despite widespread fixation on it. It is a grand delusion, a deadly obstacle to the betterment of human relations.

Planetary reasoning must be consistent with the findings of contemporary science, especially astrophysics. Among the findings in this field is that the universe has no center. Also, it is found that the universe is "unfolding."[64] Furthermore, it is found that our universe is not the only one.[65] Talk of pluriversality is thus consistent with contemporary science. With each new advance in science, "We seem to be on the verge of discovering not only wholly new laws of nature, but ways of thinking about nature that depart radically from traditional science."[66] In view of this, the idea that the human being is the center of the universe is rather archaic. What is required, given the findings of contemporary science, is planetary reasoning taking decenteredness as its point of departure. The decentered or impersonal perspective calls into question "isms" such as capital-ism and universal-ism. It is an argument for the cultivation of "a cosmic consciousness" that "will revolutionize the pattern of thinking."[67] It is not merely an argument for a "linguistic turn." On the contrary, it is an argument for a linguistic revolution with an unambiguous preferential option for the suffix -ness and the abandonment of -ism. We argue on this basis that the decentered, impersonal, or planetary reasoning exemplified by the Moon Treaty may rightly be called "lunatic" reasoning, but it is not dementia. On the contrary, it is a living ethical challenge to humanity to rethink its apparent escape from truth and truthfulness by honoring the imperative of justice and peace in human relations with regard to the Moon while refusing to abide by the same imperative in the conduct of human relations here on livable planet Earth.

In this section we have described the challenge of truthfulness and truth in the pursuit of justice and peace on Mother Earth. We have shown that the first republican constitution of Ghana, together with the Moon Treaty, exposes the lie inherent to the fixation on the idea that sovereign statehood is immutable and eternal. The basic method revealing this challenge is the conceptual contestation between the suffixes -ism and -ness in philosophical reasoning. We turn to an elaboration of this in the next section by a seriatim explanation of *ubu-ntu* and *buren*.

THE PHILOSOPHY OF *UBU-NTU* AND *UBUNTU* AS A PHILOSOPHY

Ubu-ntu is the root of African philosophy among the Bantu-speaking peoples. The be-ing of an African in the pluriverse is inseparably anchored upon the philosophy and practice of *ubu-ntu*. Similarly, the African tree of knowledge stems from *ubu-ntu,* with which it is connected indivisibly. *Ubu-ntu* then is the wellspring flowing with African ontology, epistemology, and ethics. If these latter are the bases of philosophy, then African philosophy has long been established in and through *ubu-ntu*. Apart from a linguistic analysis of *ubu-ntu,* a persuasive philosophical argument can be made that there is a "family atmosphere," that is, a kind of philosophical affinity and kinship among and between the indigenous peoples of Africa. No doubt there will be variations within this broad philosophical family atmosphere. But the blood circulating through the family members is the same in its basics.[68] In this sense *ubu-ntu* is the basis of African philosophy.

Just as the environing soil, the root, stem, branches, and leaves together as a one-ness give meaning to our understanding of a tree, so is it with *ubu-ntu*. The foundation, the soil within which it is anchored, as well as the building must be seen as one continuous whole-ness rather than independent fragments of reality. Accordingly, African ontology and epistemology must be understood as two aspects of the same reality. We shall adopt a philosophical approach in our clarification of *ubu-ntu* philosophy.

In terms of geographic demarcation, we agree partially with the delimitation of Francesco Elias de Tejada. Thus the *ubu-ntu* philosophy we are about to discuss "goes from the Nubian desert to the Cape of Good Hope and from Senegal to Zanzibar."[69] However, this delimitation is questionable since the Sahara desert is not the indelible birthmark of Africa. For this reason the meaning and import of human interaction before the birth of the Sahara desert must be taken into account. We shall not, however, pursue this line of inquiry here.[70]

PHILOSOPHY IN *UBU-NTU*

It is best, philosophically, to approach this term as a hyphenated word, namely *ubu-ntu*. *Ubu-ntu* is actually two words in one. It consists of the prefix *ubu-* and the stem *-ntu*. *Ubu-* evokes the idea of be-ing in general. It is enfolded be-ing before it manifests itself in the concrete form or mode of existence of a particular entity. *Ubu-* as enfolded be-ing is always oriented toward unfoldment, that is, incessant continual concrete manifestation through particular forms and modes of being. In this sense *ubu-* is always oriented toward *-ntu*. At the ontological level, there is no strict and literal separation and division between *ubu-* and *-ntu*. *Ubu-* and *-ntu* are not two radically separate and irreconcilably opposed realities. On the contrary, they are mutually founding in the sense that they are two aspects of be-ing as a one-ness and an indivisible whole-ness. Accordingly, *ubu-ntu* is the fundamental ontological and epistemological category in the African thought of the Bantu-speaking peoples. It is the indivisible one-ness and whole-ness of ontology and epistemology. *Ubu-* as the generalized understanding of be-ing may be said to be distinctly ontological, whereas *-ntu* as the nodal point at which be-ing assumes concrete form or a mode of being in the process of continual unfoldment may be said to be distinctly epistemological.

The word "*umu-*" shares an identical ontological feature with the word "*ubu-*," whereas the range of *ubu-* is the widest generality, *umu-*, which is also linguistically open to generality, does by virtue of the logic of the language tend toward the more specific. Joined together with *-ntu*, then *umu-* becomes *umuntu*. *Umuntu* means the emergence of *homo loquens*, who is simultaneously a *homo sapiens*. In common parlance it means the human being: the maker of politics, religion, and law. *Umuntu* then is the specific concrete manifestation of *umu-*: it is a movement away from the generalized to the concrete specific.

Umuntu is the specific entity that continues to conduct an inquiry into be-ing, experience, knowledge, and truth. This is an activity rather than an act. It is an ongoing process impossible to stop unless motion itself is stopped. On this reasoning, *ubu-* may be regarded as be-ing becoming and this evidently implies the idea of motion. We propose to regard such incessant motion as verbal rather than the verb *-ntu,* combined with either *ubu-* or *umu-*, may be construed as the temporarily having become. In this sense, *-ntu* is a noun. The indivisible one-ness and whole-ness of *ubu-ntu* means, therefore, that *ubuntu* is a verbal noun.

Because motion is the principle of be-ing for *ubu-ntu,* do-ing takes precedence over the do-er without at the same time imputing either radical separation or irreconcilable opposition between the two. "Two" here speaks only to two aspects of one and the same reality. *Ubu-ntu* then is a gerund. But it is also a gerundive at the same time since at the epistemological level it may crystallize into a particular form of social organization, religion, or law. *Ubuntu* is always a -ness and not an -ism. We submit that this logic of *ubu-ntu* also applies to *hu-* and *-nhu* in the Shona language of Zimbabwe. Therefore it may not be rendered as *hunhuism,* as Samkange and Samkange have done.[71] The suffix -ism gives the erroneous impression that we are dealing with verbs and nouns as fixed and separate entities existing independently. They thus function as fixations to ideas and practices that are somewhat dogmatic and hence unchangeable. Such dogmatism and immutability constitute the false necessity based upon fragmentative thinking. This latter is the thinking—based on the subject-verb-object understanding of the structure of language—that posits a fundamental irreconcilable opposition in be-ing becoming. On the basis of this imputed opposition, be-ing becoming is fragmented into pieces of reality with an independent existence of their own.

Without the speech of *umuntu, ubu-* is condemned to unbroken silence. The speech of *umuntu* is thus anchored in, revolves around, and is ineluctably oriented toward *ubu-*. The language of *umuntu* "relevates," that is, it directs and focuses the entire epistemological domain toward the ontology of *ubu-*. This it does by the contemporaneous and indissoluble coupling of *ubu-* and *umuntu* through the maxim *umuntu ngumuntu nga bantu (motho ke motho ka batho).* Although the English language does not exhaust the meaning of this maxim or aphorism, it may nonetheless be construed to mean that to be a human be-ing is to affirm one's humanity by recognizing the humanity of others and, on that basis, to establish humane relations with them. *Ubu-ntu* understood as be-ing human (human-ness) ontologically, translates into ethics demanding a humane, respectful, and polite attitude toward others. *Ubu-ntu* then not only describes a condition of be-ing, insofar as it is indissolubly linked to *umuntu,* but it is also the recognition of be-ing becoming and not, we wish to emphasize, be-ing and becoming.

In this sense it is simultaneously a gerund and a gerundive since the latter is implied in the imperative, *nga bantu.* In other words, be-ing human in the physical biological sense is not enough. One is enjoined, yes, ethically commanded as it were, to actually become a human being. What is decisive then is to prove oneself to be the embodiment of *ubu-ntu (bo-tho)* because the fundamental ethical, social, and legal judgment of human worth and human conduct is based upon *ubu-ntu*. The judgment, pronounced with approval or disapproval respectively, is invariably expressed in these terms: *ke motho* or *gase motho*. In the original language, in this case the se-Sotho cluster in the Bantu-speaking grouping, these expressions may not be interpreted literally, since in literal terms they mean he / she is a human be-ing or she / he is not a human be-ing. A literal interpretation boils down to an affirmation or negation of the obvious if we restrict ourselves to the biological definition of a human being. Even worse, the negation would ultimately be meaningless since its assertion neither abolishes nor alters the biological definition or nature of a human being. Thus the affirmation or negation of *ubu-ntu (bo-tho)* is a metaphor for ethical, social, and legal judgment of human worth and human conduct. In the sphere of politics, the veritable arena for the making of law, *ubu-ntu* is reaffirmed as the basis of judgment in the three mentioned domains of human life by the maxim *kgosi ke kgosi ka batho,* meaning "the source and justification of royal power is the people."[72] Even here *ubu-ntu* recurs with stubborn consistency because *ba-tho (ba-ntu)* is simply the plural form of *mo-tho (umu-ntu)*. Accordingly, the sphere of politics and law is not only suffused with *ubu-ntu* but is also based upon it. Cumulatively, these considerations constitute the basis for our submission that *ubuntu* is the philosophical foundation of African philosophy among the Bantu-speaking peoples.

Three points emerge from the above explanation of *ubu-ntu*. One is that *ubu-ntu* is predicated on the philosophical perspective that motion is the principle of be-ing. Another is that *ubu-ntu* acknowledges the existence of the plurality and variety of entities that are the manifestation of be-ing. Accordingly, *ubu-ntu* conceives of be-ing as a one-ness, a whole-ness of interconnectedness among beings. The third point arising from this perspective is that *ubu-ntu* is philosophically the open-ness to be-ing as well as beings because of the suffix -ness, which is the special characteristic of *ubu-* or *umu-*. *Ubu-ntu* is thus against the fragmentation of be-ing without denying the existence of the plurality and the variety of beings. We now turn to explain the content of this last paragraph.

THE *RHEOMODE:* THE PHILOSOPHICAL LANGUAGE OF *UBUNTU*

The word "rheomode" is derived from the Greek verb *rheo*, meaning to flow. It is "a new mode of language.... trying to find out whether it is possible to create a new structure that is not so prone toward fragmentation as is the present one."[73]

It is a critique of a thought and language structure that assumes and imposes a strict divide and a necessary sequence in terms of subject-verb-object. It is an appeal for the understanding of entities as the dimensions, forms, and modes of the incessant flow of simultaneously multidirectional motion. This understanding speaks to "be-ing" rather than "be"! It sustains and at the same time preserves the whole-ness and not the whole of be-ing. Whole cannot appropriately describe be-ing since it already implies the fixation of be-ing and its replacement by be-ing. The suffix -ness is indispensable since it underlines the importance of this logical impossibility and puts into sharp relief the ancient opposition between motion and rest as principles of being.[74]

In contrast to the subject-verb-object linguistic structure, the rheomode language takes the verb as its point of departure. In this way the incessant flow of motion as be-ing is preserved because the verb pertains to "do-ing" rather than "do"! Together the suffixes -ing and -ness preserve the idea of be-ing as a whole-ness.[75] Since there is always the doer in the do-ing the rheomode language understands the verb as the verbal noun, that is to say, the gerund.

In our view the verb not only presupposes but is also the embodiment of the doer. The activity or action of the verb is, minus the effect of certain illnesses, inseparable from the doer. The doer do-ing; present continuous tense is in itself at any given moment the embodiment of the potentiality for an infinite variety of an unceasing activity of merging and converging. The present tense, being itself only a specific mode of incessant motion, is always continuous. Accordingly, we hold that the gerund rather than the verb is the ontological basis of the rheomode language.

The logic of *ubu-ntu* is distinctly rheomodic in character. It is the logic of and for the preservation of be-ing as a whole-ness. Accordingly, it is against the fragmentation of be-ing through language. The rheomodic character of *ubu-ntu* underlies the widely held view that the African philosophic view of the "universe" is "holistic." Here it must be emphasized that the correctness of this view would be enhanced by discarding hol-ism as either the definition or description of the African philosophic view of the universe. Instead, the term "holon-ness" should be used. It is appropriate as it speaks directly against the fragmentation of be-ing, especially through language, and defines the African philosophic understanding of be-ing as a whole-ness. Epistemologically, be-ing is conceived as a perpetual and multidirectional movement of sharing and exchange of the forces of life. The African philosophic conception of the universe is, to borrow from the Greek, "pantareic." On this view, "order" cannot be once established and fixed for all time.[76]

The African philosophic conception of the universe is not only pantareic but it is musical as well. It is thus rooted in "its musical conception of the universe."[77] This makes it dynamic. We certainly agree with de Tejada's suggestion that the musical conception of the universe can result in two interpretations of the musical rhythm, namely, the rational and the emotional. However, we definitely disagree with his ascription of the emotional as a distinctive feature of Bantu law and by extension, African philosophy. First, the ascription is an uncritical repetition of the tradition of philosophic racism in Western philosophy.[78] His not infrequent use and appropriation of phrases such as *"unserer Logik"* and *"unserer rationalen Logik,"* coupled with his express ascription of Bantu thought to the "magical" and the emotional speak, to an exclusivism that is psychologically more revealing.[79] Historically, it is an inadvertent transmission of a fundamentally questionable tradition. Second, the ascription does to a large extent undermine his own powerful criticism of researchers and scholars of Bantu philosophy who were bent on finding European thought patterns and institutions in Africa rather than recognize what Bantu philosophy was in its own right.[80]

Third, de Tejada's ascription is inconsistent with our understanding of being as a whole-ness. It undermines its own foundation because the African worldview upon which *ubu-ntu* philosophy is based is fundamentally holonistic. As such it is a criticism of fragmentative thinking, precisely what de Tejada has fallen prey to by maintaining a radical opposition between the rational and the emotional. African philosophy would not subscribe to the radical opposition between reason and emotion. Discourse on the psychosomatic is meaningful even to the Western mind. Understanding thought as a system means recognizing it as a whole-ness that includes not only the indivisibility but also the mutual dependence of the rational and the emotional.[81]

THE *RHEOMODE* AND ITS IMPLICATIONS FOR OUR OVERALL WORLDVIEW

One of the implications of the rheomode language for the dominant worldview based upon fragmentative thinking is that our ideas of fact and truth must change.[82] It is no longer unproblematical to hold that a "fact" is an objective state of affairs susceptible to verification and, by implication, falsification. To make such an assertion without reference to the relationship—and a complex one at that—between the supposedly objective state of affairs and the declarant is to ignore unduly a crucial dimension in the construction of facts.[83]

Our idea of truth must be reviewed from the standpoint of rheomodic thought. According to rheomodic thought, truth may be defined as the contemporaneous convergence of perception and action.[84] Human beings are not made by the truth. They are the makers of the truth.

Even perception is not wholly neutral. In this sense it is more appropriate for humans to live the truth rather than living in and by the truth. The former captures the basic tenet of African philosophy, whereas the latter speaks to the prevailing feature of Western philosophy. To put it in another way, the expression "African time" in its negative connotation, for example, misses the basic point pertaining to the philosophic difference between African and Western philosophy. For African philosophy human beings make time and they are not made by time. Therefore, it is both natural and logical to live time. But for Western philosophy, primacy is accorded to living in time. Quite often time is already there as an empty space to be filled. Hence the proliferation of diaries to note appointments and all that needs to be done to fill up the space of time until death. (It is salutary to note that consonant with contemporary scientific research into space-time, Western philosophy may in the long run persuade the Westerner to live time rather than live in it.)[85] Seen from this perspective, truth is simultaneously participatory and interactive. It is active, continual, and discerning perception leading to action.[86] As such it is distinctly relative rather than absolute.

Furthermore, reasoning from the perspective of -ness, that is, the rheomode, can involve bounded reasoning. For us bounded reasoning, that is, reasoning and acting on the basis of already drawn and yet-to-be-drawn boundaries, attests to the experience that everything is in a flux: a condition of incessant change and changeability because motion, and not rest, is the principle of be-ing.[87] To be is to be in the condition of -ness rather than -ism. This is the ontological basis for the ensuing tension between -ness and -ism. The tension arises as soon as we attempt to construct social reality on the proposition that there is a radical division and irreconcilable opposition between -ness and -ism. On this reasoning, the flux of being necessitates the search for stability. This culminates in the attainment of an -ism. The -ism is then construed to be the reality not only in contrast but also in opposition to be-ing as -ness. Dogmatic absolutism feeds upon this philosophic outlook to reality. Bounded reasoning, insofar as it does not involve the drawing of ontological boundaries beforehand, is neither alien nor necessarily repugnant to *ubu-ntu* philosophy. The -ness perspective of *ubu-ntu* philosophy is posited here as a challenge to dogmatism. We will show this when *ubu-ntu*, in dialogue with *buren*, responds to the contemporary historical condition that we have presented above. We now turn to an exposition of *buren*.

THE MEANING OF *BUREN* 不忍

Our discussion of this subject will be singularly brief. This is because of our total ignorance of Chinese. If we had known the Chinese language, we could have had firsthand access to the relevant sources and be in a position to deliver a solid discussion of the subject. Because of our linguistic deficiency, we will make a brief presentation based on secondary sources.

According to Mencius, one of the transmitters and transformers of the teachings of Confucius, "All men have a mind which cannot bear (to see the sufferings of) others. The early kings, having this 'unbearing' (*buren*) mind, thereby likewise had an 'unbearing' government."[88] Instead of allowing human suffering or being just a passive spectator of it, the "unbearing" mind would seek ways to prevent, remove, or alleviate the suffering. In *ubu-ntu* philosophy, *buren* is conveyed as *goba le pelo,* meaning "to have a humane heart." A human being with a humane heart is struck by the suffering of other human beings as well as other living beings. To this, *motho wa pelo* (the human being with a humane heart) responds positively by doing what is necessary to promote life and avoid killing. Our understanding of killing is that it can be a physical act terminating the life of another human being or other living entities. It can also be a psychological act, in the form of torture, for example, or the spiritual destruction of another human being.

Buren is an ethical imperative in the realm of interpersonal relations and also in the wider domain of politics. It is not only a mere declaration. It is, most importantly, the will to actually die as a matter of necessity in order to give life to others. To give life to others is to die ultimately in the defense of truthfulness in the concrete historical struggle for justice. In both the interpersonal and the political spheres truthfulness and truth are indispensable for the realization of justice and the achievement of peace. A government with an "unbearing" mind is the appropriate vehicle for the administration of distributive justice.

It is significant that *buren* is rendered as "unbearing." The person with this kind of sentiment is a sage and deserves to be the ruler. The understanding of the various aspects of *buren* and its relation to human morality is rendered in *ubu-ntu* ethics as *kgosi ke kgosi ka batho:* that is, the king attains the status of kingship through and with the ruled for the purpose of pursuing justice and peace in the kingdom. The king who acts against this aim is not deemed to be a sage and deserves to be removed from office.

The understanding of the various aspects of *buren* as constitutive of "human nature" is rendered in *ubu-ntu* ethics as *motho ke motho ka batho* in the sphere of interpersonal relations and *kgosi ke kgosi ka batho* in the domain of politics: the king attains the status of kingship through and with the ruled for the purpose of pursuing justice and peace in the kingdom. The king who acts against this aim is not deemed to be a sage and deserves to be removed from office. From both perspectives of African and Chinese philosophies, the sage is the one who must pursue the "Kingly Way" of government.

THE DIALOGUE BETWEEN *UBU-NTU* AND *BUREN*: ON *WANGDAO* 王道 OR THE KINGLY WAY OF GOVERNMENT

In ancient China, the *jingtian* 井田 or "well-field" system benefited the noble class.[89] Mencius converted this into "an economic institution with socialist implications" beneficial to the peasants and the serfs.[90] This conversion reveals a striking coincidence with Tanzanian president Julius Nyerere's *ujamaa.*[91] Whereas

Fung Yu-lan describes this as "socialist" it would, from an African philosophy point of view, be described as communalist. In this context, the institution of *letsema* is the African Kingly Way for the administration of distributive justice. The African philosophical basis of *letsema* is the thesis that life is mutual aid: *obra ye nnoboa*.

Land was indeed allocated to individuals for their own use intended to ensure survival. The cultivation of land was not the exclusive concern of the family. On the contrary, other families participated in the cultivation of land on the understanding that their land would also be cultivated by other members of the community. In addition, communal land for cultivation was also the common concern of the community. The yield from the land was for the people after they had kept some for themselves and delivered the rest to the king to keep in reserve in the *seshego* (silo). The king on the advice of his councillors dispensed of the yield to the community on the basis of need. Underlying this institution was and, still is, co-operation for the sake of the well-being of all. It was indeed competition in its original meaning of seeking together. No one was an employee of another. Under those circumstances, the peoples of ancient China and parts of contemporary Africa were able to live so that they could "nourish their living and bury their dead without dissatisfaction."[92]

This situation was characterized by the primacy placed upon the well-being of everyone and all. This affirmed yet another of the maxims of *ubu-ntu* ethics, namely, *feta kgomo o tshware motho*. It means that whenever one is to make a choice between preserving the life of another human being and accumulating wealth, then the option ought to be for the preservation of human life. Thus, money, if there was any at all, played an insignificant role in the respect, protection, and promotion of the life and well-being of everyone. Unlike today, pecunimania then was the remotest possibility.

The constitution of the community was predicated on the understanding that the family was prior in fact to the gathering together of human beings to form the community, the commonwealth, or the state. These kinds of artificial gatherings of human beings were subject to the achievement of the aim of establishing optimal conditions to ensure individual and collective well-being. Failure to achieve this aim was a warrant to repudiate such associations (see *Rerum Novarum,* issued by Pope Leo XIII on 15 May 1891, paragraph 10). Today the Moon Treaty is a living example of the peaceful repudiation of the state.

Conclusion

We have provided a critique of the Western paradigm of economics, posing the question whether or not it is conducive to the protection of life and the avoidance of killing. We have argued that the question should be answered in the negative.

If capitalism is indeed the best socioeconomic system, why is it that it was forcibly imposed on the colonies? What we have at this historical juncture is the living threat to destroy all forms of human and other lives, including the annihilation of the belligerents. The will to carry out this threat is sustained by the dogma that the only ethical truth is that the prevailing global socioeconomic system, though "unjust at its root," is immutable and eternal. For the protagonists of this dogma, any threat to it ultimately justifies the irrational option of human-made doomsday by resort to strategic nuclear war. The outbreak of the war means that Immanuel Kant shall not be there to witness his *sapere aude!* (dare to reason!) turned into an eternal superstition. No one shall be there to affirm the wisdom of Bertrand Russell that "reason is a very feeble force in human affairs . . . [and] no dogma is so certain as to afford an excuse for widespread cruelty."[93] Before this tragedy befalls humankind, it best to turn to the practice of *buren,* the ethics of *ubu-ntu* and *wangdao* combined, in both the domestic and the international spheres.

Notes

1. H. Kung, *Truthfulness* (London: Sheed and Ward, 1968), p. 100; B. Williams, *Truth and Truthfulness* (Princeton, NJ: Princeton University Press, 2002), p. 1.

2. G. Verbeke, "Unity of Truth and Pluralism in Society," in *Roots of Dogmatism,* ed. M. Wahba (Cairo: Anglo-Egyptian Bookshop, 1984), p. 13.

3. P. Hogan and R. Smith, "The Activity of Philosophy and the Practice of Education," in *The Blackwell Guide to Philosophy of Education,* ed. N. Blake, P. Smeyers, R. Smith, and P. Standish (Oxford: Blackwell, 2003), pp. 174–175; D. H. Wrong, *Power: Its Forms, Bases and Uses* (Oxford: Basil Blackwell, 1979), pp. 32–33.

4. L. Boff, *Church, Charism and Power: Liberation Theology and the Institutional Church,* trans. J. W. Diercksmeier (London: SCM Press, 1985), p. 52.

5. R. Burggraeve, *The Wisdom of Love in the Service of Love,* trans. J. Bloechl (Milwaukee, WI: Marquette University Press, 2007), p. 148.

6. J. Sobrino, *The True Church and the Poor,* trans. M. J. O'Connell (London: SCM Press, 1985), p. 81.

7. Kung, *Truthfulness,* p. 116.

8. F. H. Russell, *The Just War in the Middle Ages* (Cambridge: Cambridge University Press, 1975); J. Y. Calvez, "Just War / Just Defence Today," pp. 48–51; J. Etienne, "Just Way, Just Defence?," pp. 64–73; A. Malone, "The Just War Theory," pp. 91–97; and C. Mellon, "Just War: How Should It Be Viewed Today?," pp. 107–119, in *Studying War—No More? From Just War to Just Peace,* ed. B. Wicker (Kampen, Netherlands: Kok Pharos, 1993); P. A. Messina and J. N. Craig de Paulo, "The Influence of Augustine on the Development of Just War Theory," pp. 23–56; J. N. Craig de Paulo, "The First Symposium on 'Just War Theory and the Wars in Afghanistan and Iraq,'" pp. 57–77; J. N. Craig de Paulo and P. A. Messina, "The Second Symposium on 'Just War Theory, the 2003 War in Iraq and the Significance of the Papacy,'" pp. 78–121; and D. P. Tompkins, "The Question of Just War Theory and the Augustinian

Caveat Praeemptor," pp. 132–153, in *Augustinian Just War Theory and the Wars in Afghanistan and Iraq: Confessions, Contentions, and the Lust for Power,* ed. C. J. N. de Paulo, P. A. Messina, and D. P. Tompkins (New York: Peter Lang, 2011).

    9. R. J. Miller, "The Future of International Law in Indigenous Affairs: The Doctrine of Discovery, the United Nations, and the Organization of American States," *Lewis & Clark Law Review* 15, no. 4 (2011): 847–922.

    10. H. W. Palmer, *Our Empire Overseas* (London: Blackie and Son, 1924), p. 139.

    11. G. Gutierrez, *Las Casas,* trans. R. R. Barr (New York: Orbis, 1993), p. 3.

    12. S. Terreblanche, *A History of Inequality in South Africa 1652–2002* (Pietermaritzburg: University of Natal Press, 2002).

    13. F. Troup, *South Africa* (Harmondsworth, UK: Penguin, 1972), p. 53.

    14. Terreblanche, *History of Inequality,* p. xvi.

    15. Terreblanche, *History of Inequality,* p. 8.

    16. T. Piketty, *Capital in the Twenty-First Century,* trans. T. Goldhammer (Cambridge, MA: Belknap Press of Harvard University Press, 2014), p. vii.

    17. Piketty, *Capital in the Twenty-First Century,* p. vii.

    18. H. Boushey, J. B. Delong, and M. Steinbaum, eds., *After Piketty: The Agenda for Economics and Inequality* (Cambridge, MA: Harvard University Press, 2017).

    19. Piketty, *Capital in the Twenty-First Century,* p. 28.

    20. Piketty, *Capital in the Twenty-First Century,* p. 3 (emphasis added).

    21. Piketty, *Capital in the Twenty-First Century,* p. 20.

    22. Piketty, *Capital in the Twenty-First Century,* p. 41.

    23. H. M. Lange, "European Union: False Hopes and Realities," *Foreign Affairs* 28, no. 3 (April 1950): 442.

    24. E. C. Djamson, *The Dynamics of Euro-African Co-operation: Being an Analysis and Exposition of Institutional, Legal and Socio-Economic Aspects of Association / Co-operation with the European Economic Community* (The Hague: Martinus Nijhoff, 1976), pp. 6–8.

    25. D. K. Fieldhouse, *Black Africa 1945–1980: Economic Decolonization and Arrested Development* (London: Routledge, 2011), p. 4.

    26. Fieldhouse, *Black Africa 1945–1980,* p. 24.

    27. Piketty, *Capital in the Twenty-First Century,* p. 36.

    28. E. S. Riemer and J. C. Fout, eds., *European Women: A Documentary History 1789–1945* (Brighton, UK: Harvester Press, 1983), p. 63.

    29. Riemer and Fout, *European Women,* p. 63.

    30. H. Bokor-Szego, "The Classification of Certain Types of Rights and the Development of Constitutions," in *Questions of International Law,* ed. H. Bokor-Szego (Budapest: Akademiai Kiado, 1991), pp. 21–22.

    31. Piketty, *Capital in the Twenty-First Century,* p. 20.

    32. Piketty, *Capital in the Twenty-First Century,* p. 240.

    33. R. Burggraeve, *Each Other's Keeper? Essays on Ethics and the Biblical Wisdom of Love* (Thrissur, India: Marymatha Publications, 2009), pp. 41–47.

    34. S. Terreblanche, *Western Empires, Christianity, and the Inequalities between the West and the Rest 1500–2010* (Johannesburg: Penguin Books South Africa, 2014), p. xiii.

    35. Piketty, *Capital in the Twenty-First Century,* pp. 31–32.

36. Piketty, *Capital in the Twenty-First Century*, p. 481.

37. S. Brittan, *Capitalism with a Human Face* (Cambridge, MA: Harvard University Press, 1996); S. Dullien, H. Herr, and C. Kellermann, *Decent Capitalism: A Blueprint for Reforming Our Economies* (London: Pluto Press, 2011); J. Richer, *The Ethical Capitalist: How to Make Business Work Better for Society* (London: Random House Business Books, 2018).

38. J. Pilger, *The New Rulers of the World* (London: Verso, 2002).

39. C. Arnsperger, "Competition, Consumerism and the 'Other': A Philosophical Investigation into the Ethics of Competition" (Discussion Paper 9614, Institut de Recherches Economiques, Louvain-la-Neuve, Belgium, 1996), pp. 12–13.

40. Jane Kelsey, *Economic Fundamentalism* (London: Pluto Press, 1995), pp. 348–371.

41. J. Holloway, *Crack Capitalism* (London: Pluto Press, 2010).

42. B. de Sousa Santos, *Epistemologies of the South: Justice against Epistemicide* (Boulder, CO: Paradigm Publishers, 2014).

43. B. de Sousa Santos, *The End of the Cognitive Empire: The Coming of Age of Epistemologies of the South* (Durham, NC: Duke University Press, 2018).

44. Y. Makonnen, *International Law and the New States of Africa* (Addis Ababa: UNESCO, 1983).

45. A. A. Mazrui, "Global Africa: From Abolitionists to Reparationists" (unpublished paper presented at the Seventh Pan African Congress, Kampala, Uganda, April 3–8, 1994), pp. 1–24; B. Bujo, *The Ethical Dimension of Community: The African Model and Dialogue between North and South,* trans. C. Nganda (Nairobi: Paulines Publications Africa, 1998), pp. 176–177.

46. N. Herz, *The Silent Takeover: Global Capitalism and the Death of Democracy* (London: Arrow Books, 2001).

47. H. Marcuse, *One Dimensional Man* (London: Sphere Books, 1972), p. 21.

48. H. Cox, *The Market as God* (Cambridge, MA: Harvard University Press, 2016); G. Simmel, *The Philosophy of Money,* ed. and trans. A. Frisby (London: Routledge and Kegan Paul, 1990), p. 236.

49. J. Kelsey, *Economic Fundamentalism* (London: Pluto Press, 1995).

50. T. H. MacDonald, *Third World Health Hostage to First World Wealth* (Oxford: Radcliffe Publishing, 2005).

51. M. Yunus, *Banker to the Poor* (New Delhi: Penguin Books India, 2007), p. 81.

52. Yunus, *Banker to the Poor*, p. 235.

53. M. Seaford, *Money and the Early Greek Mind* (Cambridge: Cambridge University Press, 2004), p. 159; Burggraeve, "Wisdom of Love," p. 58.

54. T. Vandevelde, "Appropriation and the Sovereignty of Money," in *Law, Life and the Images of Man: Modes of Thought in Modern Legal Theory, Festschrift for Jan M. Broekman,* ed. F. Fleerackers, E. van Leeuwen, and B. van Roermund (Berlin: Duncker & Humblot, 1996), p. 482.

55. M. Ajei and M. B. Ramose, "From 'Man Is the Measure of All Things' to Money Is the Measure of All Things: A Dialogue between Protagoras and African Philosophy," *Phronimon* 9, no. 1 (2008): 22–40.

56. U Thant, *View from the UN* (London: David & Charles, 1978), p. 126.

57. N. Cullather, *Secret History: The CIA Classified Account of its Operations in Guatemala, 1952–1954* (Stanford, CA: Stanford University Press, 1999).

58. P. W. Singer, *Corporate Warriors: The Rise of the Privatized Military Industry* (Ithaca, NY: Cornell University Press, 2003).

59. https://www.poetryfoundation.org/poems/46560/dulce-et-decorum-est.

60. M. El Baradei, *The Age of Deception: Nuclear Diplomacy in Treacherous Times* (London: Bloomsbury, 2012), pp. 86–87.

61. J. M. Schuessler, *Deceit on the Road to War: Presidents, Politics and American Democracy* (Ithaca, NY: Cornell University Press, 2015), p. 109.

62. D. J. Enright, *Collected Poems* (Oxford: Oxford University Press, 1987).

63. Burggraeve, "Wisdom of Love," p. 149.

64. A. Findlay, *The Unfolding Universe* (London: Psychic Press, 1949), pp. 423–456.

65. S. Hawking and L. Mlodinow, *The Grand Design* (London: Bantam Press, 2011), p. 183.

66. P. Davies, *The Cosmic Blueprint* (London: William Heinemann, 1987), p. 142.

67. M. Wahba, "The Cave and the Dogma," in *Roots of Dogmatism,* ed. M. Wahba (Cairo: Anglo-Egyptian Bookshop, 1984), p. 236.

68. J. Ki-Zerbo, quoted by F. E. de Tejada, "The Future of Bantu Law," *Archiv für Rechts- und Sozialphilosophie* (*ARSP*), Beiheft Neue Folge, no. 11 (1979): 304.

69. de Tejada, "Future of Bantu Law," p. 304.

70. B. Davidson, *Africa in History* (London: Granada Publications, 1974), p. 28.

71. S. Samkange and T. M. Samkange, *Hunhuism or Ubuntuism: A Zimbabwe Indigenous Political Philosophy* (Salisbury, Rhodesia: Graham Publishing, 1980).

72. For an extended discussion of this topic, see M. B. Ramose, "African Democratic Tradition: Oneness, Consensus and Openness: A Reply to Wamba-dia-Wamba," *Quest* 6, no. 2 (December 1992): 62–83.

73. D. Bohm, *Wholeness and the Implicate Order* (London: Routledge and Kegan Paul, 1980), pp. 30–31.

74. Charles Sanders Peirce states: "I start from and in and with and as Motion. For me, in the 'spiritual' as well as the physical world, there is of course no Rest as the ultimate goal or as the antithesis of Motion. The changeless is less than the dead, it is the nonexistent.... I often say that I am determined to be free and free to be determined. Why? Because of the unnamed Third yet lying in the womb of Motion, to which both the determinate and the indeterminate have reference.... To me the idea of the new, the young, the fresh, the possible, are deeper than any time-import, and are indeterminate only in a special sense.... The best I can do is say, 'I wish of the Future, we could begin to talk of the Unreached as the Yet distant.'" Quoted in R. Kevelson, *Law as a System of Signs* (New York: Plenum, 1988), p. v.

75. Bohm, *Wholeness and the Implicate Order,* p. 30.

76. M. Griaule, *Conversations with Ogotemmeli* (Oxford: Oxford University Press, 1965). p. 137.

77. de Tejada, "Future of Bantu Law," pp. 306–307.

78. L. T. Outlaw, *On Race and Philosophy* (New York: Routledge, 1996).

79. F. E. de Tejada, "Bemerkungen uber der Grundlagen des Banturechts," *ARSP* 46 (1960): 522–523; L. Adam, "Modern Ethnological Jurisprudence in Theory and Practice," *Journal of Comparative Legislation and International Law,* 3rd ser., vol. 16, no. 4 (1934): 221.

80. de Tejada, "Bemerkungen," pp. 510–514.

81. D. Bohm, *Thought as a System* (London: Routledge and Kegan Paul, 1994), p. 18.

82. The title of this subsection is borrowed verbatim from Bohm's chapter 2 on the rheomode.

83. We have already stated our intention not to discuss the correspondence theory. However, we believe that Bohm's critique of this theory, evidently from the perspective of rheomodic thought, is worth noting. See D. Bohm, *The Undivided Universe* (London: Routledge and Kegan Paul, 1993), pp. 16–17.

84. Bohm, *Thought as a System,* p. 181.

85. H. Kimmerle, "The Concept of Time as a Key-Notion for New Ideas about Development," in *Time and Development in the Thought of Sub-Saharan Africa,* ed. S. B. Diange and H. Kimmerle (Leiden: Brill / Rodopi, 1997), p. 21.

86. Bohm, *Thought as a System,* p. 183.

87. In ancient Western philosophy, Heraclitus may be identified as one of the major exponents of the view that motion, and not rest, is the principle of be-ing. The debate between the adherents and the opponents to this view has hardly been definitively concluded. Both Peirce and Bohm are the modern / contemporary adherents to the view—which we endorse—that motion is the principle of be-ing. That this in many ways is an echo of Hobbes's position in *De Motu* needs no special pleading.

88. Fung Yu-lan, *A History of Chinese Philosophy,* vol. 1, trans. D. Bodde (Princeton, NJ: Princeton University Press, 1983), p. 119.

89. Fung, *History of Chinese Philosophy,* vol. 1, pp. 10–11.

90. Fung, *History of Chinese Philosophy,* vol. 1, p. 118.

91. J. Nyerere, "Ujamaa—The Basis of African Socialism," in *Readings in African Political Thought,* ed. G. C. Mutiso and S. W. Rohio (London: Heinemann, 1975), pp. 512–515.

92. Fung Yu-lan, *History of Chinese Philosophy,* vol. 1, p. 119.

93. Bertrand Russell, *Common Sense and Nuclear Warfare* (Oxford: Routledge, 2009), pp. 53, 57.

CHAPTER 4

Ideology, Quixotism, or Enabling Utopia?

The Notion of *Tianxia* as a Model for a New Form of Global Governance and Coexistence, Seen in the Light of the Japanese Experience

Christian UHL

LET ME START by pausing briefly at the guiding question that the essay at hand seeks to answer: Can Confucian values and the notion of *tianxia* as a model for a new, alternative world order respond constructively to the orogenic shifts and changes of the geopolitical landscape that have been caused by the rise of Asia and of China in particular, and impact a corresponding reassessment also of the prevailing cultural order, "long dominated by a powerful liberalism"?[1] There is, indeed, a lot to unpack here with regard to our understanding of the world as it is and of how it became what it is, of its complexity and the drivers and processes of its transformation, of the significance that we attribute to "values" in these processes, and last but not least, the notion of a *new* world order, the power of which arguably depends also on the degree of scrutiny and the aptitude of our conceptualization of what we conceive of as not new, and old. So, how in the first place do we understand and conceptualize the established world order that would become old in the wake of its replacement by another one, and against which we could perceive this other one as new?

Chimerica

The old global order—or at the least its most recent historical gestalt, that arguably has come to an end, or is in the process of expiring—emerged as well from a massive tectonic shift, caused or enabled by the coincidence of two historically simultaneous events. On the one hand, there was the collapse of Keynesian models of economic and social policy and the corresponding triumph of neoliberalism, first in the two leading Anglophone countries, marked by the election of Margaret Thatcher as prime minister of the United Kingdom in 1979, and the inauguration of Ronald Reagan as president of the United States in 1981. And on the other hand, the third plenary session of the eleventh Central Committee of the Communist Party of China (CPC) in December 1978, and Deng Xiaoping's rise to the position of the paramount leader of China, marked China's turn away from all notions of a direct realization of communism based on predominantly agrarian production, and a big leap instead into capitalism under the rule and guidance of the CPC, resulting in some kind of socialist market economy, Sino-Marxist capitalism, or however the resulting hybrid has been called.[2] The privatization of most of the collectively owned and state-owned enterprises, and the dissolution of the people's communes, created an enormous "industrial reserve army" of tens of millions of migrant workers for the so-called special economic zones that provided ideal hothouse conditions for the transubstantiation of capital, hence giving the liberalization of global trade and finance a direction and purpose and allowing China to outpace other developing economies in the competition for foreign investments.[3] More and more capital flowed into China to be turned by cheap labor into commodities for the export markets, thereby turning China into the "workshop of the world" and the main attractor of foreign capital, first and foremost from the United States, which became in turn the complementary global "borrower and consumer of the last resort."[4] Enabled by the peg of the yuan to the US dollar, the unlimited ability of the United States and the American consumer to go into debt, and the readiness of China to maintain its debtor's buying power by investing its current account surplus in the world's leading reserve currency, the economies of the United States and China established a close symbiotic interdependency. "Globalization, that's Reaganomics + Deng Xiaoping-ideas," wrote a Spanish journalist, inspired by Niall Ferguson and Moritz Schularick's discussion of an economy that had become a virtual "Chimerica."[5]

In this symbiotic relationship of "big saver and big spender" that has become the central hub of the global economy, China for the longest time was in the disadvantageous position at the low end of the supply and value chains.[6] The immense surpluses that were produced by Chinese labor were skimmed off and realized elsewhere. Yet, while precisely for this reason investors did not get tired of investing in Chinese production and human resources, the United States— and to various degrees the other leading economies—deindustrialized themselves and experienced with the progressing degeneration of their own productive capabilities "a second form of the dialectics of master and slave," as W. F. Haug has put it: "Slowly, the power to shape history passed over to the 'slaves.'"[7] The admission of China in December 2001 to the World Trade Organization (WTO)—since its establishment in 1995 the main institutional pillar of the neoliberal "rules-based" world order under US hegemony—was an attempt also at controlling the expansion of China's economy. Yet, China's accession to the WTO rather prompted, among other things, an enormous increase in the country's foreign trade, an increase in real wages, and a significant increase of the inflow of foreign direct investment (FDI).[8] Not even the global financial crisis in the wake of the Lehman Brothers shock in 2007 could hamper the ascent of China to global predominance. The People's Republic of China (PRC) responded to the collapse of its export markets by reducing the reliance of the Chinese economy on exports and by strengthening instead domestic consumption by means of massive stimulus programs, investments in infrastructure, and the promotion of an entrepreneurial culture. Already in 2010, China surpassed Japan as the world's second largest economy in terms of nominal gross domestic product (GDP). As a matter of fact, the PRC even mounted the throne of "the world's king of concrete."[9] In the three short years from 2011 to 2013 China poured more concrete than the entire United States in the continuous twentieth century.[10] Let that sink in for a second.

By its enormous demand for raw materials and other goods, however, China—rather than being an agent for any alternative world order—first of all rescued the existing one from collapsing.[11] This story, arguably, is repeating itself to some degree after China's swift control of the COVID-19 pandemic and the recovery of its economy as the first and only one to expand already in 2020. No doubt, today, the inner tensions and dysfunctionalities in the odd couple's relationship have come to the fore. Tariffs and sanctions have been imposed, flanked by a rhetoric of "decoupling," the "end of globalization," of a "new cold war," and so on. Indeed, China has meanwhile been declared the European Union's (EU), the Group of Seven's (G7), and the North Atlantic Treaty Organization's principal challenge, competitor, and "systemic rival." Obviously, the Chimerican honeymoon is over. Yet, China still depends on the US dollar as much as the United States depends on Chinese production. While China continues to be the "workshop of the world," the country's ever-growing middle class of now approximately 450 million people is also constituting the world's biggest sales market. It is the largest trading partner of now 128 nations, and as of 2021 has replaced the United States as the largest trading partner of the EU.[12] Increasingly, blueprints and specifications too are coming from a spacefaring, quantum-computing, atom-fusing, and growingly competitive and confident China, challenging the innovation lead, and thus the last line of defense of the "old economies" of the Global North. Just recently, the PRC dethroned Germany as the world's mechanical engineering champion.[13] In an ironical twist of the change-through-trade paradigm, a remarkable role reversal has taken place, indeed. Compare, for example, the spirit of Xi Jinping's speech at the World Leadership Summit in Davos in 2017, with that of the US Innovation and Competition Act that was just passed by the US Senate in early June 2021. China, speaking with the voice of liberal, pragmatic reason, appears in the role of the defender of multilateralism and free global trade, whereas an increasingly ideological, defensive, and protectionist West is becoming more and more "like China" by mirroring Chinese economic policies (Made in China 2025, industrial policy, Belt and Road Initiative, focus on Africa, "vaccine diplomacy," etc.). Yet, the theater in which the drama of divorce that we are witnessing since the beginning of Trump's presidency is enacted, is still the "global interior of capital," as Peter Sloterdijk has called it.[14] Moving the armchair from one side of the room to another may challenge established customs, routines, and hierarchies that, seen from an actor's point of view, or from the viewpoint of the think tankers and policy advisors in the stalls, may be all that matters. However, seen from the noble height of the philosophers' box, such reshufflings and rearrangements of the stage set—as entertaining and consequential as they may be—do not really make a new stage, or theater.

Amerinipponica

So much for the degree of novelty and familiarity of the "new geopolitical order," ushered in "by the rise of Asia, and of China in particular." Indeed, we are rather concerned here with "the prevailing *cultural* order, 'long dominated by a powerful liberalism'" (emphasis added). Needless to say, we would not have this concern if Asia and China had not risen so spectacularly in the first place. But why is that liberal order still prevailing, regardless of the recent dramatic geopolitical developments? Is it persisting because it is just a superstructural ramification of what is *not* new about the "new geopolitical order," that is, of its fundamental *economic* logic? Our guiding question seems to point into another direction by implying a certain degree of autonomy of the sphere of culture and values vis-à-vis the spheres of economy and politics, an implication, indeed, that itself may well be understood as a manifestation of liberalism's persisting dominance: "What impact will Confucianism—a philosophy that begins from the primacy of vital relationality—have on the evolving world culture and how will its values play into the ongoing transformation of the geopolitical order?"[15] No question, a world order that fully and unreservedly deserved to be called "new" would also need new values—and who would not be receptive to the beauty of Confucian ethics? Yet, it is not at all self-evident that Confucian values are per se opposed or antithetical to the vital relationships created by globally entangled supply and value chains and to a culture forged by the force of the "coercive laws of competition," as Karl Marx has it.[16] The case of an earlier challenger of US hegemony—postwar Japan—may illustrate this fact. After the defeat in World War II, the Japanese economy experienced a meteoric recovery and growth, marked by the recognition of Japan by the International Monetary Fund (IMF) as one of the eight leading economic powers in 1964. There ensued Japan's accession to the Organisation for Economic Cooperation and Development (OECD) and the hosting of the Summer Olympic Games in Tokyo in the same year, the displacement of Germany as the world's second biggest economy in the course of 1968, and Japan's admission to the circle of the newly founded G7 in 1976, to name just a few milestones of Japan's economic and geopolitical rise. Already in the late 1950s Robert Bellah, in search of an explanation for Japan's postwar "economic miracle" and inspired by Max Weber, discovered Confucian ethics as the true spirit of Japanese capitalism.[17] Two decades later, in the neoliberal 1980s (e.g., privatization of the telephone service, 1984; of tobacco and salt, 1985; of Japan Rail, 1987), such Weberian Confucianism theses experienced a rampant boom in Japan. "In its most general form," as Sebastian Conrad comments, the "Confucianism thesis suggests that Japan's economic success rests upon its special industrial relations—a familial structure within the firm (*kazokushugi*) and a fundamental harmony (*wa*) between employers and employees—which are understood as the legacy of Confucianism. This has been the prevailing view since the 1980s and is highly popular in both Japan and beyond."[18]

Increasingly popular, however, especially in the West, also became visions of Japan replacing the United States as the dominating power, as well as a corresponding anti-Japanese commentary, stretching from accusations of intellectual property theft, a copycat culture, unfair trade practices, and so forth, to the country not being a real democracy, but just an illiberal, tacitly feudal one-party state (from 1955 Japan was ruled uninterruptedly by the conservative Liberal Democratic Party).[19] In 1985, Japan and the United States, France, the United Kingdom, and West Germany (the former Group of Five) agreed on policies to reevaluate the yen and to drop its exchange rate from ¥240 to ¥120 per US dollar in the course of one year (the Plaza Accord). The main purpose of this agreement was to ease the trade deficit of the other countries, and especially of the United States, vis-à-vis Japan. Yet, as an immediate consequence of the accord the world also witnessed the onset (1986) and expansion of Japan's "bubble economy." The cheap dollar incentivized Japanese companies to pick up everything available in the United States from New York (Rockefeller Center) to Los Angeles (Columbia Pictures), a buying spree that prompted a US commentator to go so far as to speak of an "economic Pearl Harbor."[20] The value of Japanese equities quadrupled between 1985 and 1989, representing at the peak 44 percent of the world's equity market capitalization, while the value of the Japanese property market came to exceed that of the entire United States by four times.[21] Nothing else, however, symbolizes the essence of Japan's speculative bubble as appropriately as the feng shui money frog of Ms. Onoue Nui, a restaurant owner, fortune-teller, and fraudster, who used the magic of fabricated deposit certificates to charm major Japanese banks into lending her astronomical amounts of money, turning her for a while into Japan's largest investor and one of the wealthiest people on earth.[22] "Known as the 'Dark Lady of Osaka,' Onoue was supposedly highly accurate in her stock market predictions and held occult midnight ceremonies in her restaurant, beneath the watchful glare of a ceramic toad..., that would be attended by high-powered bankers seeking to divine where they should invest next."[23] There they are, your reputable business leaders!

The bubble climaxed on the December 29, 1989, with the Nikkei stock index climbing to an all-time high of 38,957.44 intraday, and the price for a single square meter of choice property in the Ginza district of Tokyo peaking at US$218,978.[24] When in the following year the bubble began to deflate, ideas of a coming replacement of the Pax Americana by a US-Japanese con-dominion—a "Pax Amerinippon,"[25] as it was called provisionally—or a full-fledged Pax Nipponica eventually deflated as well.[26] What came instead was the first of Japan's "lost decades." Today, the Japanese case occasionally serves some political and economic clairvoyants to describe the rise of China as a mere déjà vu. Yet, history, including that of Japan, teaches us other, more interesting lessons. Apparently, Confucianism, and Asian values in general, can be all kinds of things. They can, as we have seen above, be a discursive device to appropriate and indigenize success in global capitalist modernity. Yet, they can also be ridiculed and trampled upon, or turned into straw puppets and burned in the marketplace as the ghosts of the past who obstruct social and economic modernization. Or they can, as we will see below, be mobilized by intellectuals in wartime Japan to "overcome modernity." However, as different and mutually exclusive as all these uses of the same cultural heritage may be, they have in common that they reinvented this heritage in correspondence to the changing circumstances of the social and economic integration into the emerging world order of globalizing capitalism. Intrinsically essentialist Weberian assumptions that modern social formations and their economic life are based upon a foundation of ancient cultural values and philosophical or religious traditions—such as secular capitalist modernity on Puritan writings of the sixteenth and seventeenth century—are therefore questionable. Of course, "Protestantism," as Marx has already pointed out, "by changing almost all the traditional holidays into working days, plays an important part in the genesis of capital."[27] Yet, we have to adopt a proper materialist perspective to understand *why* Protestantism played this important part, or *why* liberalism, for that matter, assumes a dominant power today.[28]

It is clear, as Marx writes elsewhere, that "the Middle Ages could not live on Catholicism, nor the ancient world on politics. On the contrary, it is the mode in which they gained a livelihood that explains why here politics, and there Catholicism, played the chief part."[29] As a matter of fact, not even the Catholic Church herself can live on Catholicism, as we learned in 2008. Responding to the Lehman Brothers shock and its aftermath, Pope Benedict XVI declared that one must not set up one's life upon the quicksand of material wealth but on the word of God alone, because "we see now in the collapse of the great banks that money disappears, it's nothing."[30] Just one week earlier it was reported that the Vatican Bank had shown a good deal of materialist realism and resolve by unloading stocks and bonds and investing instead in more solid stuff, such as raw materials and precious metals—including "one ton of gold"— in order to hedge its capital assets of about €1.4 billion (as of 2007).[31] The pope, arguably, was right to mobilize old values for another, postcapitalist way of life—and we, arguably, are right calling the pope a hypocrite. Yet, maybe he was just as innocent as Marx's Don Quixote, who "long ago paid the penalty for wrongly imagining that knight errantry was compatible with all economic forms of society."[32] With this in mind, I would like to suggest a slight adjustment of our guiding question. Under what kind of social and economic conditions, I would ask, could the ethics of a social formation that has collapsed long ago, and that rests upon "a philosophy that begins from the primacy of vital relationality," have real impact and realize its utopian potentials, instead of turning into just another Quixotism, or worse, into a mere ideology that rather veils and reinforces what it claims to overcome? Before I come back to this question, I will demonstrate that the latter indeed happened to the Japanese philosopher Nishida Kitarō and his vision of an alternative world order, a vision that, as Shimizu Kōsuke has pointed out, invoked repeatedly "the *tianxia* system as one of the ideal models of the world order of the future generation."[33]

The World as the Dialectical Universal

As the above notions of a "second Pearl Harbor" insinuate, the 1980s was not the first time that Japan challenged an established global order, and the United States in particular. The annexation of Manchuria in 1932, the withdrawal from the League of Nations in 1933, and the repudiation of the Washington Treaties in 1934 were the first acts of this challenge. The year 1937, with the "Incident at the Marco Polo Bridge" in July, and the looting, systematic rape, and mass murder committed by Japanese troops in Nanjing in December, marked the beginning of the second Sino-Japanese War. In 1938 the Chinese communist forces launched the "Anti-Japanese Resistance War," while Japan enacted the National

General Mobilization Act, transforming itself into a militarist "national defense state." In 1940 Japan joined the military alliance of the Axis powers, Germany and Italy, and recalibrated the country's ever-expanding war effort, advertising it as an anti-imperialist "East Asian War" for the establishment of a new order in East Asia and then, after the attack on the US Pearl Harbor naval force and the beginning of the Pacific War in December 1941, as a "Greater East Asian War" for the creation of a "Greater East Asian Commonwealth" under the leadership of Japan as the core of a "new world order." At the ideological front, the state externalized the internal conflicts and contradictions of the Japanese society by presenting the Japanese state itself as a revolutionary on the global stage, which joined the young, "proletarian" nations in their revolt against the unjust, outdated, and "bourgeois" world order of the saturated Anglo-American capitalist democracies. Many fell for this, including many intellectuals, among them some of Nishida Kitarō's disciples, who embraced the war also as a healthy refreshment for the decadent modern Japanese society. Tacitly echoing G. W. F. Hegel's polemics against Immanuel Kant's idea of an "eternal peace," Nishitani Keiji, for example, declared that the war "[taught] the individuals asceticism" and the subordination of their private, selfish interests to the public weal, reunified the disintegrating areas "of the military, art, economy, politics, and thinking," and turned the modern *homo oeconomicus* (*keizaijin*) back into an "original human being" (*honrai no ningen*).[34] "In war is construction—in construction is war," explained Kōsaka Masa'aki.[35] Suzuki Shigetaka agreed: "One cannot contest what Mr. Kōsaka says: War is truth; war unveils the truth of history."[36] And Mr. Kōsaka declared again, more concretely: "The East has been the prehistory of world-history, but it has been the latter's foundation as well. Precisely for this reason, and only for this reason, it did not appear at the surface of world-history. But now the world shall no longer be the West alone, but simultaneously the East as well.... So the East—as if it had stood still for long, but then broke through a dike—becomes the tidal stream of history. And the task of Japan is to become the principal cause of such a world-historical order."[37]

Because of statements like the above, the legacy of Nishida and his entourage—the so-called Kyoto school of philosophy—is controversial.[38] Nishida and his school, so the accusation reads, have provided "Japanese fascism" with a philosophical foundation and helped to legitimize Japan's aggression. Others have rejected such accusations in order to rescue the essence of Nishida's philosophy from its entanglement in wartime politics. As a matter of fact, his political philosophy is an appendix to a much larger philosophical project. This project has a penchant for the late nineteenth and twentieth century's romantic and idealist—and especially German—current in philosophy (e.g., philosophy of life, phenomenology, Martin Heidegger) that, generally speaking, attempted to pre-empt the subject–object dualism on a level prior to that of intellect and reason, and asserted the priority of intuition and of the aesthetic or religious attitude toward the world and the self over against reflection and science. However, Nishida strove "to assimilate Western philosophy and methodology" also in order to "breathe new life into it by means of the Eastern, and, above all, the Buddhist tradition of thinking," as the common encyclopedic wisdom emphasizes.[39] Occasionally, Nishida himself corroborated this assessment, as when he illustrates his point of view by means of the Buddhist notion of emptiness (*kū*) or points out that in Buddhism we can find "the seeds of something like a logic of the self, a logic of the mind (*kokoro no ronri*)," in contrast to the "Western logic" that is, "generally speaking, a logic of things (*mono no ronri*)."[40] Elsewhere, he praises his "logic of the place" (*basho no ronri*) and his core concept of "absolute nothingness" as genuine contributions of the "East" to the "Western tradition" of philosophy, which, as he declares, conceived of the world from the standpoint of "Being" instead.[41] A "world" that is not conceived of from the standpoint of "Being," but that is grounded in "nothingness," forces us to shift our concern away from the individual things that constitute this world and to rather focus on the mutual relationships between these things, and between these things (the many) and the world as a whole (the one). Nishida's world too, indeed, is one "that begins from the primacy of vital relationality."

Yet, should the extension of such a "negative ontology" into the realm of politics not rather take on the form of some sort of "soft empire," unified by a "Leibnizian logic" rather than in any totalitarian fashion, as Karatani Kojin has pointed out?[42] Karatani is hinting here at a formidable shortcut through Nishida's oeuvre. As a matter of fact, Nishida since the 1920s developed a growing interest in Gottfried Wilhelm Leibniz, so much so that he defined his philosophy occasionally as a "dialectical monadology."[43] This label, however, not only expresses Nishida's intellectual indebtedness to Leibniz but emphasizes at the same time what distinguishes his point of view. Nishida's world—the "dialectical universal," as he also calls it—in which everything real is a coincidence of the two contradictory principles of the "self-determination of the individual" (the many) and the "self-determination of the universal" (the one), doesn't comply with Leibniz's concept of truth, according to which "we assess everything as false, which contains a contradiction, and as true everything, which is opposed to falsehood, that is, to that, which is contradictory," as one of Leibniz's renderings of Aristotle's law of noncontradiction goes.[44] The law of noncontradiction—one of the pillars of classical rationalism—is a derivative of the law of identity, which again is the essence of Leibniz's monadology. The law of identity in the sense of the strict tautology, $A = A$, is the reason why Leibniz's individual—the monad—is an indivisible and "windowless" substance. This conception of the individual, however, poses the question of how and why the monads—windowless and self-contained as they are—can come together to constitute—like the parts of a puzzle or the stones of a mosaic—the world as a whole. Leibniz's answer to this question is the concept of a "pre-established harmony," which in his *Theodizee* he defends an chosen by God as the best of all possible worlds.[45] Leibniz, indeed, conceives of the world from a standpoint of Being, and this is the point where Leibniz and Nishida part. Nishida's "dialectical universal" is supposed to exist without such an intervention from above; it is "not a world of pre-established harmony, but a world that creates itself."[46] Leibniz's monads, however, cannot do the job, as they "have no effects. But something which has no effect is not a real individual."[47] Therefore, Nishida flirts with Hegel: "Leibniz's world of pre-established harmony must be Hegel's world of the dynamic idea."[48] Yet, Nishida, who on the one hand criticizes Leibniz's monadological incapability to grasp the world "dialectically," on the other hand also criticizes Hegel's dialectics, arguing "monadologically" that in light of Hegel's logic "the true individual is inconceivable."[49] Hegel's notion of the "identity of the identical and the nonidentical" overcomes the dualism of A and non-A. Yet, Hegel presumes *knowledge* as the absolute (the "absolute idea" of Hegel's *Logic*), the unfolding of which is governed by a strict teleology that does not allow for grasping the relation of the many and the one in any other way than that of a logical subsumption of the former into the latter. Hegel, as Theodor Adorno complains, "presupposes from the start positivity as all-comprehensibility," and in the end "he rakes in the prey of the primacy of logics over the meta-logical."[50] Such a standpoint of positivity, of Being, as Nishida points out, "does not represent the logic of the real historical world" either.[51] In contrast to Hegel's system, Nishida's "historical world" is designed as an open "place" (*basho*) that is infinite, agenetic and not teleological, and is supposed to allow the individual beings, just as they are, to relate to each other by contradicting each other.

"A and B exist independently *from each other*," as Nishida points out (emphasis added), and he continues: "Therefore, correctly speaking, neither does A exist due to A itself, nor B due to B itself. A and B do not exist without being related to each other. A exists due to the fact that it is in opposition to B, and B exists due to the fact that it is in opposition to A."[52] We thus have to specify the above law of identity: $A = A$ *if and only if* $B = B$, and vice versa. This reformulation, however, is obviously not strictly dialectical, but rather a description of a sort of *coincidentia oppositorum* that rather confirms and emphasizes the difference of identity and difference that Hegel tried to overcome, as well as the implications of the abovementioned law of contradiction, namely, the ontological dualism of subject and predicate, self and other, one and many, and so forth. Nishida sides with Leibniz, to prevent his dialectics from taking off and forsaking the independence and self-identity of the individual; and he sides with Hegel to overcome the Leibnizian model in which the only possible relation between the individuals and the individuals and the whole is that of a prefabricated harmony, pre-fixed by the intervention of some rationalist deus ex machina. It is questionable, however, if Nishida is doing justice to Leibniz either, whose God often seems to merely stand in for yet another pillar of rationalist logic—the law of the sufficient reason—but has in the dawn of secular modernity already devolved to an abstract mechanism due to which only the most apt of everything possible becomes real: "From here, one can perfectly understand in which way a divine mathematics or a metaphysical mechanism is at work.... In this way, a world emerges, which gives rise to the most ample production of what is possible."[53] Karl-Heinz Schupp calls this "a kind of ontological Darwinism" (*Seinsdarwinismus*), thereby providing us with a convenient bridge to eventually move on to Nishida's political philosophy.[54]

The most infamous of the more narrowly political writings of Nishida, arguably, is a text of approximately ten pages of Japanese with the title "The Principle of the New World Order." It unfolds an interpretation of the political situation of the time and of Japan's war effort that can indeed be read as an attempt of Nishida at inscribing his "dialectical monadology" into the realm of politics and international relations. The war, as he argues, was an inevitable necessity, because the advances of science, technology, and economies have put the nations and nation-states into a single tight and narrow global space. The institution that was supposed to maintain international peace, however—President Woodrow Wilson's League of Nations—was incapable of fulfilling its task because it was built upon the ideological foundation of mere national autonomy, that is, the idea that all nations are equal and recognize each other's (monadic) independency. This outdated mind-set, as Nishida insists, did "not transcend the narrow horizon of the abstract world ideal of the eighteenth century"—an implicit critique of Kant, who is cited in the League's preamble—"that doesn't meet the requirements of the present day."[55] What according to Nishida would be required instead is that each nation and nation-state, "while remaining in strict conformity with itself" and "constituting a particular world" in accordance with its "local traditions" and specific "historical life," simultaneously "transcend itself" by "awakening to its distinct historical mission" and "contribute to the formation of one global world" (*sekaiteki sekai*, literally "a world of worlds"). "This is the ultimate ideal of the historical development of humankind," as Nishida insists, "and this ideal has to be the principle as well of the new world order the current war is calling upon us. Our country's ideal, as it has manifested itself in the words 'the whole world under a single roof,' must have a similar meaning."[56] The locus classicus of the phrase "the whole world under a single roof" (*hakkō ichiu*), as an encyclopedic dictionary explains, is the third chapter of the *Nihon shoki* (completed in 720 CE), dedicated to the mythical first emperor, Jinmu Tennō. It appears there in the form of the Chinese phrase *yan ba hong er wei yu* (cover the eight cardinal directions and turn them into your realm).⁵⁷ The phrase was rendered into the modern slogan in 1903 by Tanaka Chigaku, a Buddhist scholar and ultranationalist preacher of the Nichiren sect, and signifies the principle of an aspiring Japanese unification of the world (*tenka,* i.e., *tianxia*). Ever since the cabinet of Prime Minister Konoe Fumimarō on the July 26, 1940, mentioned in its *Basic Outline of the National Policy* "the great spirit at the foundation of Japan to bring the world under a single roof" (*hakkō wo ichiu to suru chōkoku no daiseishin*), the slogan was used as a device to legitimize the war effort to establish a "Greater East Asian coprosperity sphere" (or commonwealth), as the Japanese empire was euphemistically called.⁵⁸ Here is what in this context Nishida had to say about the special historical mission of Japan:

> Today we Peoples of East Asia rely on our oriental culture and join forces in world-historical prospect. However, before a particular world can be built and become the center, someone has to take on this mission. In East Asia it is Japan which plays this part today. In the same way the victory of Greece over Persia has determined the direction and development of Europe's history until today, the present Great East Asian War too will determine the history of the world. . . . Our national essence is not simply totalitarian. As being the absolute presence, which encompasses all past and future, our imperial house is the alpha and omega of our world. The merit of our national essence, that is, of our imperial line, being unbroken since countless generations, is manifest in the fact that we built a historical world centered in the imperial house as its hub. However, our imperial house is not just the hub of a single People's state. The imperial way of our country also contains the principle "the whole world under a single roof," that is, the principle of the formation of the world. . . . Not only Great Britain and the USA, but also the Axis Powers should follow it.⁵⁹

The Global Interior of Capital, and the Heaven Beyond

In 1946, one year after Japan's defeat and the death of Nishida, Maruyama Masao presented one of the first, and arguably most influential, analyses of wartime Japan's thought and ideology. According to Maruyama, this ideology was not just a product of the war. On the contrary, all the wars in the history of modern Japan since the Sino-Japanese War of 1894–1895 were results of what he calls the "pathology" of the mental structure of the Tennō system.⁶⁰ In the center of this system, Maruyama saw the institution of the emperor as the incorporation of the highest values of state and society.⁶¹ The relative distance to this deified emperor became the motor that moved the whole hierarchical apparatus of the modern Japanese state. Divinity, however, was not conferred to the emperor as an individual but through the tradition of the imperial house, rooted in the depth of an endless past.[62] According to Maruyama, the particular principle of rule in modern Japan was based on the guarantee of the "eternal emanation of values from out of the center by means of the endlessness of the longitudinal axis," constituted by what Nishida just called the "unbroken imperial line."[63] The entire social order was geared toward the Tennō and structured concentrically by the relative distance of the elites and subordinates to the Tennō as the source of the highest values. In accordance with this inner structure of Japan's social order was Japan's foreign policy, which was determined by a "pan-Asianist" ideology, that is, the idea of a special mission of Japan to liberate the peoples of East Asia from Western imperialism and unify them under Japanese leadership and, moreover, to transfer the inner logics of the modern Japanese state to the whole world and to fit all nations into a concentric hierarchical order centered in the Japanese state, with the Tennō as its innermost core.[64]

The conformity of this analysis and Nishida's "principle" is striking, also because Maruyama does not mention Nishida at all. It has been argued, indeed, that Nishida adopted the language of Japan's wartime regime not in an affirmative way, but in an attempt at usurping it for his own agenda. Between sheer exoneration and the condemnation of Nishida as a fascist is a middle ground for more cautious positions: the well-intentioned philosopher failed in his attempt to rewrite Japan's militarist agenda and to replace it with a morally justifiable purpose, an attempt that undoubtedly ended in a mere justification of Japanese imperialism. Yet the core of Nishida's philosophy and its true intentions are not affected by this circumstantial failure. This, in a nutshell, is also the moral of the "cautionary tale of the Kyōto school" as it is told by Shimizu Kōsuke in his own search for a non-Western theory of international relations. In Nishida's philosophy, he writes, "The place of nothingness appears in the form of concentric circles. The world therefore consists of a number of concentric circles, and the world itself, in this mapping, appears as a larger concentric circle still, that embraces all the others."[65] As these concentric circles do not have clear boundaries, he continues, Nishida's vision of another world order "contrasts sharply with the Westphalian system based on the principle of mutual exclusion."[66] This, however, is consoling only as long as these are really not the same concentric circles that we just saw above through the lens of Maruyama Masao. Terms such as "self-negation," "transcendence of the self," and "affirmation of the other" may have a peaceful Buddhist ring and seem to imply something politically "soft." Yet, what has been said above about Asian values and the fate of Confucianism in postwar Japan applies to Buddhism as well: it can be all kinds of things.[67] In Nishida, "self-negation" rather means to end one's monadic "windowless" existence, to crack one's shell, to go out and become a true "historical, corporeal self" by engaging and grappling with the real world, which is a dialectical battlefield on which "species and species don't connect immediately. Between them there is always only struggle (*tōsō*)," as he explains.⁶⁸

"The historical world as contradictory self-identity is a world of struggle (*tōsō no sekai*), in which species and species wrestle with each other forever," says Nishida.⁶⁹ Or elsewhere: "Heraclitus says that opposite things unite, that from difference, the most beautiful harmony arises, and that war is the father of all things.... In the self-identity of completely diverging, oppositional things, in disharmonious harmony: *there* is life, and the appearance of this disharmonious harmony, of this contradictory self-identity, is the species. In the mutual opposition and conflict of individual versus individual, the formation of the species takes place."⁷⁰ Nishida's vocabulary—"struggle," "life," "species"—is indeed telling. Kobayashi Toshiaki has already underscored the Darwinist spin of Nishida's Heraclitean world, and he has also pointed out that this world's "most beautiful harmony" is perfectly compatible with Leibniz's "pre-stabilized harmony" and his quasi–"Darwinist ontology of being," as Schupp has called it above.⁷¹ Indeed, struggle does not necessarily mean war; it could simply mean competition in the capitalist marketplace. As a matter of fact, social Darwinism and its reified conception of social conflict as transhistorical phenomena of nature are already the result of a retransfer of a liberal theory of society that had previously been assigned to biology: Charles Darwin's evolutionary theory owes its initial inspiration to Adam Smith's "invisible hand."⁷² Yet, if Nishida was just another liberal bourgeois—enthused by the poison of romanticism, indeed, and intoxicated by the gas of war—then we have to weigh the possibility as well that in Nishida's political philosophy the notion of "nothingness" may eventually reveal itself, not as the abyss of fascism, but as just another iteration of this same invisible hand, and his contradictory world of eternal struggle as a mere continuation of the evolving anarchy of capitalism by other means. Nishida's "new world order" of "vital relationality" would not be all that new then. Rather, it would be a veiling ideology as much as a true expression of the conditions and circumstances of one of the many crisis periods in the history of globalizing capitalism.

The question remains, indeed, if the efforts of the Chinese school of international relations are more promising. There are obvious differences between, let us say, Zhao Tingyang and Nishida. Philosophically, Zhao displays rather Kantian leanings, as June Teufel Dryer points out, referring to an essay in which Zhao squares an ancient notion of a universal harmony with Kant's concept of perpetual peace and his own central concept of "world-ness" and the "prioritization of the well-being of all people."⁷³ Elsewhere Zhao argues, "Theoretically speaking, the EU has not gone as far as Kant's idea. A well-organized region such as the EU is essentially something of an enlarged nation / state meant to compete with other world regions or powers, rather than an ideal for the world in its lack of its world-view or world-ness."[74] In contrast to Zhao's concept of "world-ness," the notion of a "world-like world" embraced by Nishida and his school has an obvious Hegelian spin and is explicitly set to rotate in the opposite direction to that of Kant's ideal and the "formalism" of Kantian ethics: "Kant's morals are bourgeois morals," as Nishida comments. "The morals of historical creation, on the other hand, have to be a solemn oath" (*higan,* the oath of Buddha to redeem all humankind) and so forth.[75] The anti-Kantianism of Nishida and his disciples has been mentioned above. Yet, when Qin Yaqing promotes an Asian form of international politics centered in a notion of *guanxi* or "relationality" and rooted in the experience of a genuinely Chinese social structure of interconnected "concentric circles of ripples in a lake," then any connoisseur of Nishida and the Kyoto school must feel compelled to attune to Shimizu's warning of a Sinocentric, Nishida-like preoccupation with the dichotomy of East and West, the nation-state, and the question of who will occupy instead of the United States the center of such an only allegedly new concentric order.[76] The existing "global interior of capital" can be described, and has already been described, as an order of concentric hierarchies in terms of core, semiperiphery, and periphery.[77]

"The current myth of the tributary system ignores historical reality and misleads us about China's true position in East Asia and the world," writes Peter Purdue in the abstract to his essay "The Tenacious Tributary System."[78] We have analyzed this true position in the neoliberal world economy above as the result of the genesis and inner dynamics in the axial "Chimerican" symbiosis of overproducer and overconsumer: "Slowly, the power to shape history passed over to the 'slaves,'" as Haug commented earlier in this chapter, alluding to Hegel's *Phenomenology.*[79] There, the initial asymmetrical unity of master and slave eventually bifurcates as the master has devolved into mere consumption while the slave, reflecting himself in the labor that he has to do in order to satisfy the master's desires, eventually achieves a state of self-conscious independency and demands recognition.[80] This, arguably, is the allegorical equivalent of the point where we are today in East Asia and the world. According to Hegel's scheme, the two sides would now have to come to a new economic arrangement that would sublate their contradiction—and if it is true that the rise of China will inevitably entail the demise of the capitalist world economy, as among many others, Li Minqi argues, then humankind does, indeed, urgently need such a new arrangement, one that is no longer based on the endless increase of exploitative production and accumulation of capital in the hands of a small economic elite, and that promotes a social ethics that emphasizes moderation, fairness, justice, and the common weal.[81] The more disquieting it is, however, that the existing hegemony of global capital has already been conceptualized—ironically enough—as an "American tributary system" or even "American *tianxia.*"[82] So let me conclude by suggesting that the utopian potential of China may not in the first place lay with its Asian values and Confucian heritage, but rather with the fact that it still maintains at the least a formal commitment to the idea of socialism. If this commitment is more than just a euphemism for some market economy with Chinese characteristics, and if China follows "a path of peaceful development to build a community with a shared future for mankind," as Chairman Xi Jinping has promised in his speech at the nineteenth CPC congress in 2017, then maybe we will once find ourselves in a world that is not shaped anymore by the "coercive law of competition," and in which even the idea to live again in accordance with Confucian values is no longer a mere Quixotism, but a real possibility.[83]

Notes

1. "*Tianxia* in Comparative Perspective: Alternative Models of Geopolitical Order," conference outline, April 24, 2021, https://www.berggruen.org/events/tianxia-in-comparative-perspective-alternative-models-of-geopolitical-order/.

2. Here and in the next two paragraphs, I am following Wolfgang Fritz Haug, *Hightech-Kapitalismus in der Großen Krise* (Hamburg: Argument Verlag, 2012), pp. 239–240. Haug has provided in his tenth chapter (pp. 229–271) in my view the theoretically most lucid analysis of the issue at hand.

3. Karl Marx, *Das Kapital: Kritik der Politischen der Ökonomie* (Capital: Critique of the political economy), vol. 1 (Marx Engels Werke [Marx Engels works], vol. 23; editor-in-chief: Institut für Marxismus-Leninismus beim ZK der SED) (Berlin: Karl Dietz Verlag, 1962), pp. 657, 661.

4. Li Minqi, *The Rise of China and the Demise of the Capitalist World Economy* (London: Pluto Press, 2008), p. 73.

5. Lluís Bassets, "La gatomaquia del sieglo XXI" (The Gatomaquia of the twenty-first century), *El País*, December 18, 2008, p. 2; cf. Haug, *Hightech-Kapitalismus*, pp. 229, 241. "Gatomaquia" ("War of the Cats," 1634) is the title of a burlesque poem by Lope de Vega. Niall Ferguson and Moritz Schularick, "'Chimerica' and the Global Asset Boom," *International Finance* 10, no. 3 (2007): 215–239. Cf. Haug, *Hightech-Kapitalismus*, p. 241.

6. Niall Ferguson, "Niall Ferguson Says U.S.-China Cooperation Is Critical to Global Health," *Washington Post*, November 17, 2008, https://www.washingtonpost.com/wp-dyn/content/article/2008/11/16/AR2008111601736.html; cf. Haug, *Hightech-Kapitalismus*, p. 271.

7. Haug, *Hightech-Kapitalismus*, pp. 243–244.

8. Graham Boden, "China's Accession to the WTO: Economic Benefits," *The Park Place Economist* 20, no. 1 (2012), https://digitalcommons.iwu.edu/cgi/viewcontent.cgi?article=1364&context=parkplace.

9. Cf. Niall McCarthy, "China Used More Concrete in 3 Years than the U.S. Used in the Entire 20th Century," *Forbes*, December 5, 2014, https://www.forbes.com/sites/niall

mccarthy/2014/12/05/china-used-more-concrete-in-3-years-than-the-u-s-used-in-the-entire-20th-century-infographic/#256618ae4131.

10. Bill Gates, "Have You Hugged a Concrete Pillar Today?," GatesNotes, June 12, 2014, https://www.gatesnotes.com/Books/Making-the-Modern-World.

11. David Harvey, "Anti-Capitalist Chronicles: The Significance of China in the Global Economy," February 28, 2019, https://www.youtube.com/watch?v=zQk5zd4Y1A0.

12. See "The European Union and Its Trading Partners," Fact Sheets on the European Union, accessed July 18, 2021, https://www.europarl.europa.eu/factsheets/de/sheet/160/die-europaische-union-und-ihre-handelspartner.

13. DPA, "Deutschland nicht länger Exportweltmeister im Maschinenbau" (Germany no longer export champion in machine engineering), *Frankfurter Allgemeine Zeitung*, July 7, 2021, https://www.faz.net/agenturmeldungen/dpa/deutschland-nicht-mehr-exportweltmeister-im-maschinenbau-17426050.html.

14. Peter Sloterdijk, *Im Weltinnenraum des Kapitals* (In the global interior of capital) (Frankfurt am Main: Suhrkamp, 2006). The title is the most valuable part of this book.

15. "*Tianxia* in Comparative Perspective," conference outline.

16. Marx, *Das Kapital,* vol. 1, p. 335 ("Zwangsgesetze der Konkurrenz").

17. Robert Bellah, *Tokugawa Religion: The Cultural Roots of Modern Japan* (New York: Free Press, 1985). The book was first published in 1957.

18. Sebastian Conrad, "Work, Max Weber, Confucianism: The Confucian Ethic and the Spirit of Japanese Capitalism," in *Work in a Modern Society: The German Historical Experience in Comparative Perspective,* ed. Jürgen Kocka (New York: Berghahn Books, 2010), p. 156.

19. Ezra F. Vogel, *Japan as Number One: Lessons for America* (Cambridge MA: Harvard University Press, 1979). For anti-Japanese commentary, see, for example, Karel Van Wolferen, *The Enigma of Japanese Power: People and Politics in a Stateless Nation* (New York: Vintage Books, 1990). For more examples, see Narelle Morris, *Japan Bashing: Anti-Japanism since the 1980s* (Abingdon, UK: Routledge, 2011).

20. Paul Harvey, "Japan Buys US with Our Money," *Kentucky New Era* (Hopkinsville, KY), September 6, 1988, 16. Karel Van Wolferen too used the formulation in a *New York Times* op-ed ("An Economic Pearl Harbor?," December 2, 1991), in which he reminded "believers in the wonders of natural free market forces" of the "unnaturalness" of Japan's governmental-industrial complex. Some geopolitical forecasters even argued in a best-selling book that Japan's "economic encroachment" would lead to a second US-Japanese shooting war: George Friedman and Meredith Le Bard, *The Coming War with Japan* (New York: St. Martin's Press, 1991).

21. Douglas Stone and William T. Ziemba, "Land and Stock Prices in Japan," *Journal of Economic Perspectives* 7, no. 3 (Summer 1993): 249.

22. Cf Wikipedia, "Nui Onoue," accessed July 17, 2021, https://en.wikipedia.org/wiki/Nui_Onoue.

23. Douglas Parkes, "Japan in the 1980s: When Tokyo's Imperial Palace Was Worth More than California and Golf Club Membership Could Cost US$3 million—5 Crazy Facts about the Bubble Economy," *South China Morning Post,* July 1, 2020, https://www.scmp.com/magazines/style/news-trends/article/3091222/japan-1980s-when-tokyos-imperial-palace-was-worth-more.

24. Wikipedia, "Japanese Asset Price Bubble," accessed July 8, 2021, https://en.wikipedia.org/wiki/Japanese_asset_price_bubble.

25. Quoted from Jacques Hersh, "Japan's Ascent to the Status of Economic Superpower in a World System Perspective," *Copenhagen Papers in East and Southeast Asian Studies*, no. 4 (1989): 123.

26. For a contemporary analysis see Richard Leaver, "Restructuring in the Global Economy: From Pax Americana to Pax Nipponica?," *Alternatives* 14, no. 4 (1989): 429–462.

27. Marx, *Das Kapital*, vol. 1, p. 292n124.

28. Cf. Istvan Meszaros, *Social Structure and Forms of Consciousness*, vol. 2: *The Dialectic of Structure and History* (New York: Monthly Review Press, 2011), p. 103.

29. Marx, *Das Kapital*, vol. 1, p. 96n33.

30. Reuters, "Pope Says Financial Crisis Shows Money an Illusion," October 6, 2008, https://www.reuters.com/article/uk-pope-money-idUKTRE49526020081006.

31. "Der Vatikan investiert verstärkt in Gold" (The Vatican invests more in gold), *Frankfurter Allgemeine Zeitung*, September 29, 2008, p. 14; cf. Haug, *Hightech-Kapitalismus*, p. 47.

32. Marx, *Das Kapital*, vol. 1, p. 96n33.

33. Shimizu Kōsuke, "Reading Kyōto School Philosophy as a Non-Western Discourse: Contingency, Nothingness, and the Public," in *Working Paper Series Studies on Multicultural Societies*, no. 31 (Kyoto: Afrasian Research Center, Ryukoku University, 2014), p. 7.

34. Nishitani Keiji, "'Kindai no chōkoku' shihon" (My understanding of the "Overcoming of Modernity"), in *Kindai no chōkoku* (The overcoming of modernity), ed. Kawakami Tetsutarō and Takeuchi Yoshimi (Tokyo: Fuzanbō, 1979), p. 26; "Sōryokusen no tetsugaku" (The philosophy of yotal war), round table discussion in *Chūō kōron* (January 1943): 73.

35. "Sōryokusen no tetsugaku," p. 65.

36. "Sōryokusen no tetsugaku," p. 65.

37. Kōsaka Masaaki, "Rekishiteki sekai" (The historical world), quoted from Hiromatsu Wataru, *"Kindai no chōkoku" ron—shōwa shisōshi e no isshikaku* (On "The Overcoming of Modernity"—An aspect of the intellectual history of the Shōwa period) (Tokyo: Kōdansha, 1989) p. 49.

38. In this section I summarize arguments that I have made elsewhere in a more elaborate form: cf. Christian Uhl, "Nishida Kitarō and the Antinomies of Bourgeois Philosophy," in *Confronting Capital and Empire: Rethinking Kyoto School Philosophy*, ed. Viren Murthy et al. (Leiden: Brill, 2017), pp. 105–140.

39. "Nishida Kitarō," in *Japan: An Illustrated Encyclopedia*, vol. 2 (Tokyo: Kōdansha, 1993), p. 1098; Ueda Shizuteru, "Nishida Kitarō," in *Iwanami tetsugaku shisō jiten* (Iwanami dictionary of philosophy), ed. Hiromatsu Wataru et al. (Tokyo: Iwanami shoten, 2000), p. 1207.

40. Nishida Kitarō, "Shūkyō no tachiba" (The standpoint of religion), in *Nishida Kitarō zenshū* (The complete works of Nishida Kitarō, hereafter *NKZ*), Midorigawa Susumu, editor-in-chief (Tokyo: Iwanami shoten, 1978–1980), vol. 14, p. 307; Nishida Kitarō, *Nihon bunka no mondai* (The question of the Japanese culture), in *NKZ*, vol. 11, p. 289.

41. Nishida Kitarō, "Keijijōgakuteki tachiba kara mita Tōsei kodai no bunka keitai" (The forms of the antique cultures in the East and the West in metaphysical perspective), in *NKZ*, vol. 7, pp. 429–430.

42. Karatani Kōjin, *"Senzen" no shikō* (Thinking of the "prewar") (Tokyo: Bungei bungakusha, 1994), p. 22. The remaining paragraphs of this section of the chapter at hand are based on my more elaborate analysis of Nishida's engagement with Leibniz: see Christian Uhl, "Preliminary Reconsideration on Nishida Kitarō's 'Dialectical Monadology' and Its Political Implications," in "In Search of Non-Western International Relations Theory: The Kyoto School Revisited," in *Research Series in Multicultural Societies,* no. 4, ed. Kosuke Shimizu et al. (Kyoto: Afrasian Research Centre, Ryukoku University, 2014), pp. 3–20.

43. Nishida Kitarō, "Kōiteki chokkan no tachiba" (The standpoint of active intuition), in *NKZ,* vol. 8, p. 96.

44. Nishida Kitarō, "Zushikiteki setsumei 1" (Graphical explanation, no. 1), in *NKZ,* vol. 8, p. 221; Gottfried Wilhelm Leibniz, *Monadologie* (Monadology), in *Vernunftprinzipien der Natur und der Gnade. Monadologie: Französisch–deutsch* (Principles of nature and grace, based on reason. Monadology. French–German) (Hamburg: Meiner Verlag, 1982), p. 41.

45. Cf. Leibniz, *Monadology,* pp. 51–53.

46. Nishida Kitarō, "Rekishiteki sekai ni oite no kobutsu no tachiba" (The standpoint of the individual in the historical world), in *NKZ,* vol. 9, p. 96.

47. Nishida, "Rekishiteki sekai," p. 101.

48. Nishida, "Rekishiteki sekai," p. 94.

49. Nishida Kitarō, "Chishiki no kyakkansei ni tsuite aratanaru chishikiron no chiban" (On the objectivity of knowledge: A foundation for a new theory of knowledge), in *NKZ,* vol. 10, p. 447.

50. Theodor W. Adorno, *Negative Dialektik* (Negative dialectics) (Frankfurt am Main: Suhrkamp, 1997), p. 162.

51. Nishida, "Chishiki no kyakkansei," p. 447.

52. Nishida Kitarō, "Sekai no jiko dōitsu to renzoku" (Self-identity and continuity of the world), in *NKZ,* vol. 8, p. 88.

53. Gottfried Wilhelm Leibniz, *Fünf Schriften zur Logik und Metaphysik* (Five writings on logic and metaphysics), trans. Herbert Herring (Stuttgart: Reclam Verlag, 1966), pp. 42–43.

54. Franz Schupp, *Geschichte der Philosophie im Überblick* (Review of the history of philosophy), Band 3: *Neuzeit* (vol. 3: The modern era) (Hamburg: Meiner Verlag, 2003), p. 259.

55. Nishida Kitarō, "Sekai shin chitsujo no genri" (The principle of the new world order), in *NKZ,* vol. 12, p. 428.

56. Nishida, "Sekai," p. 429.

57. Kisaka Junichirō, "Hakkō ichiu" (The whole world under a single roof), in *Shimpen Nihonshi jiten* (New dictionary of Japanese history) (Tokyo: Sōgensha, 1990), p. 823.

58. Kisaka, "Hakkō ichiu."

59. Nishida, "Sekai shinchitsujo no genri," pp. 430, 432.

60. Maruyama Masao, "Chōkokkashugi no ronri to shinri" (Logic and psychology of ultranationalism), in *Maruyama Masao shū* (Collected works of Maruyama Masao, hereafter *MMS*), ed. Yasue Ryōsuke et al., vol. 3. (Tokyo: Iwanami shoten, 1995–1997), pp. 29, 36.

61. Maruyama, "Chōkokkashugi," p. 20.
62. Maruyama, "Chōkokkashugi," pp. 27, 34.
63. Maruyama, "Chōkokkashugi," p. 35.
64. Maruyama Masao, "Nihon fashizumu no shomondai" (The problems of Japanese fascism), in *MMS,* vol. 3, p. 289; Maruyama, "Chōkokkashugi," pp. 32, 35.
65. Shimizu Kōsuke, "Reading Kyōto School Philosophy," p. 7. See also Shimizu's more elaborate essay, "Do Time and Language Matter in IR? Nishida Kitarō's Non-Western Discourse of Philosophy and Politics," *Korean Journal of International Studies* 16, no. 1 (2018): 99–119.
66. Shimizu, "Reading Kyōto School Philosophy," p. 7.
67. See, for example, Brian Victoria, *Zen at War* (New York: Weatherhill, 1997).
68. Nishida Kitarō, "Shu no sensei hatten no mondai" (The problem of the emergence and development of the species), in *NKZ,* vol. 8, p. 519.
69. Nishida Kitarō, *Nihon bunka no mondai* (The question of Japanese culture), *NKZ,* vol. 12, p. 320.
70. Nishida, "Rekishiteki sekai," pp. 100–101 (emphasis added).
71. Kobayashi Toshiaki, *Denken des Fremden: Am Beispiel Kitaro Nishida* (Thinking the Other: The example of Kitaro Nishida) (Frankfurt am Main: Stroemfeld Nexus, 2002), pp. 115, 137–138.
72. Stephen J. Gould, *The Structure of Evolutionary Theory* (Cambridge, MA: Harvard University Press, 2002), pp. 58–59, 93–94.
73. June Teufel Dryer, "The 'Tianxia-Trope': Will China Change the International System?," *Journal of Contemporary China* 24, no. 96 (April 2015): 1023. Cf. Zhao Tingyang, "A Political World Philosophy in Terms of All-under-Heaven (Tian-xia)," *Diogenes,* no. 221 (2009): 5–18.
74. Zhao Tingyang, "Rethinking Empire from a Chinese Concept 'All-under-Heaven' (Tian-xia, 天下)," *Social Identities* 12, no. 1 (January 2006): 38.
75. Nishida, "Bashoteki ronri to shūkyōteki sekaikan" (Logic of place and religious worldview), in *NKZ,* vol. 11, p. 445.
76. Qin Yaqing, "Guanxi benwei yu guocheng jiangou: Jiang Zhongguo linian zhiru guoji guanxi lilun" (Relationality and processual construction: Bringing Chinese ideas into international relations theory), *Zhongguo Shehui Kexue* (Social sciences in China) 3 (2009): 5–20, 7–8; quoted from Shimizu Kōsuke, "Reading Kyōto School Philosophy," pp. 4, 7.
77. For example: "The axial division of labour in a capitalist world-economy divides production into core-like products and peripheral products. Core-periphery is a relational concept. What we mean by core-periphery is the degree of profitability of the production process. . . . Some states have a near even mix of core-like and peripheral products. We may call them semiperipheral states." Immanuel Wallerstein, *World Systems Analysis: An Introduction* (Durham, NC: Duke University Press, 2004), p. 28.
78. Peter C. Purdue, "The Tenacious Tributary System," *Journal of Contemporary China* 21, no. 96 (2015): 1002.
79. Haug, *Hightech-Kapitalismus,* p. 244.
80. See Georg Wilhelm Friedrich Hegel, *Werke* (Works), vol. 3, *Die Phänomenologie des Geistes* (The phenomenology of the spirit) (Frankfurt am Main: Suhrkamp, 1989), pp. 150–155.

81. Li Minqi (*Rise of China,* 174) quotes Wallerstein: "There comes a point when the contradictions become so acute that they lead to larger and larger fluctuations.... After the bifurcation, after say 2050 or 2075, we can thus be sure of only a few things. We shall no longer be living in a capitalist world-economy. We shall be living instead in some new order or orders, some new historical system or systems. And therefore we shall probably know once again relative peace, stability, and legitimacy. But will it be a better peace, stability, and legitimacy than we have hitherto known, or a worse one? That is both unknown and up to us." *The Essential Wallerstein* (New York: New Press, 2000), pp. 435–453.

82. Yuan Foong Khong, "The American Tributary System," *Chinese Journal of International Politics* 6 (2013): 1–47; Salvatore Babones, *American Tianxia: Chinese Money, American Power, and the End of History* (Bristol, UK: Policy Press, 2017).

83. "Full Text of Xi Jinping's Report at 19th CPC National Congress," Xinhua, November 3, 2017, http://www.xinhuanet.com/english/special/2017-11/03/c_136725942.htm.

CHAPTER 5

Toward a New World Order

Reading *Tianxia* with Marx and Hegel

Viren MURTHY

IN THE PAST few decades, scholars have criticized the concept of universality for being Eurocentric and committing violence to the particular. On this reading, Western nations universalize their particular conceptions in the process of imperialist endeavors. And yet, without the concept of universality, there would be little possibility of transregional dialogue and the fostering of larger communities. This is especially important now because we live in a world where domestic problems are always already mediated by the global, but there exist relatively few transnational mechanisms to address issues that go beyond national boundaries. The recent global COVID-19 pandemic makes the importance of global governance evident in a painful way. The pandemic affects everyone in the world and requires global collective action and yet, everywhere we see merely uncoordinated local and national responses, which have had varying degrees of success. In this context, recent theories of *tianxia* are meaningful because they contend that traditional Chinese theory was always about the world. *Tianxia* 天下 literally means "All-under-Heaven" and ostensibly implied a transregional order in early China. Contemporary Chinese scholars draw on this trope to imagine a new world order. Given the contemporary role of China in the global capitalist world, such theories force us to ask whether they can be successful in creating an alternative to our world of capitalist universality or whether they merely replace one imperialist power with another.

Contemporary China presents a unique situation where a communist party constantly draws on Confucius and other traditional Chinese philosophies as it is increasingly incorporated into the global capitalist world. In this context, China appears to be a space where one could bring traditional Chinese philosophy into dialogue with Marxism. However, perhaps because of the traditional animosity between the two schools of thought—Marxists are seen as progressive and traditional Chinese philosophies (Confucianism and Daoism being the most famous) are labeled as conservative—there has been little systematic attempt to reconcile the two ideologies. On the contrary, Chinese Marxists are usually hostile to *tianxia* theory and to Confucianism more generally. *Tianxia* scholars for the most part ignore a serious encounter with Karl Marx and focus on traditional textual analysis.[1] However, given the recent incarnation of traditional Chinese philosophy in *tianxia* theory, there are immediate areas of overlap with Marxism. In particular, both look toward a new world order, which some *tianxia* theorists think of as a world-state. In the past decades, Marxist theorists have also turned to transnational political structures. For example, Jacques Bidet has written of an incipient world-state (*état-monde*), which could potentially go against the capitalist world order.[2]

But *tianxia* theory seems to proceed from the opposite direction of Marxism—in short, it proceeds from philosophy to politics. While there are many *tianxia* theorists who make this move, below I focus on Zhao Tingyang because, although he does not engage extensively with Marx, his theory lends itself to a Marxist interpretation. Through Zhao's work, I stage a confrontation between *tianxia* philosophy and Marxism to show that *tianxia* theory must confront the problem of a postcapitalist world order. My discussion proceeds in the following five sections. The first section places *tianxia* theory in historical context and suggests that the recent global turn must be understood in relation to the expansion of Chinese capital. The second section examines the philosophical foundations of Zhao's *tianxia* theory, especially his reference to the one-many problem. Zhao invokes Laozi to explicate his version of the one-many problem and so to grasp the specificity of this theory, I place Laozi in the backdrop on G. W. F. Hegel's treatment of the one-many problem in the *Science of Logic*. Through this we shall see that Zhao conceives of the one as an amorphous unity that is capable of enveloping infinite multiplicity, without negating particularity. This is the philosophical ground for his international ideal. The next section turns to how Zhao sees this ideal realize itself in Chinese history. I bring out Zhao's points through a comparison with similar ideas in Japanese history, especially during the interwar period. *Tianxia* becomes an ideal that is to go beyond the competitive world order we live in today. We know that in the Japanese case, claims to create a new order eventually legitimized Japanese imperial expansion, and consequently this is an important vantage point from which to assess *tianxia*. The next two sections treat *tianxia* in relation to the problem of the nation-state and capitalism respectively. In both of these sections, the notion of competition is crucial. Zhao has recently been criticized for being too nationalist and also for proposing a world-state. I suggest that Zhao could rework his theory to counter such objections by drawing on early debates concerning Third World anti-imperialist nationalism. In the final section, I bring Zhao in dialogue with Lin Chun, who has recently criticized *tianxia* theory from a Marxist perspective. Lin makes two criticisms, namely that *tianxia* theory cannot deal with global capitalism and that its proponents have no Confucian program to deal with domestic policy, which should be the first step of a new global politics. My response begins with a Marxist reading of some Confucian texts, and then I turn to Marxists such as Jacques Bidet and Moishe Postone to re-embed Zhao's ideals within a framework that takes capitalism seriously. From this perspective, I respond to Christian Uhl's and Sor-hoon Tan's respective contributions to this volume, both of which in different ways invoke the problems of capitalism to confront *tianxia* theory, and Zhao's philosophy in particular.

By synthesizing Zhao's theory with Marxism, we can both begin to address some of the criticisms and move beyond the unhealthy impasse between traditional Chinese philosophers who shun Marxist political economy and leftists who focus exclusively on the Chinese revolutionary experience and take as their primary standpoint of critique a contrast between the Mao Zedong period and the present. A dialogue between *tianxia* theory and Marxism could help us rethink a postcapitalist politics for the future.

The Transformations of Chinese Nationalism

Zhao Tingyang's recent writings about *tianxia* would be incomprehensible without contemplating how Chinese nationalism and internationalism have changed in the late twentieth and early twenty-first centuries. Mao Zedong proposed a specific type of internationalism, namely Third World internationalism, which fused Marxism with anti-imperialist nationalism. During this time, China supported revolution and development in various Third World regions. However, after Mao's death there were numerous movements against Mao's vision, which changed Chinese perceptions of the world and laid the conditions for a new type of nationalism. From the 1980s until the early 1990s, most Chinese nationalism returned to an evolutionary vision expounded by May Fourth intellectuals such as Hu Shi. On this view, nations were like trains catching up with Western modernity and capitalism. This was a retreat from socialist internationalism, while reinventing the rhetoric of socialism to support nationalist development along capitalist lines.

The Chinese government appeared increasingly legitimate after the collapse of the Soviet Union in 1989 and especially after 1993, when Russian premier

Boris Yeltsin ordered a military attack on a legally elected Duma.³ By this time, elite and popular intellectuals argued that the Chinese tradition was incompatible with Western democracy, but this was connected to a particular path for China rather than a philosophy for a new world order. From this perspective, the recent turn to *tianxia* as a new global order represents a change in the Chinese discourse of the role of China in the world. Previously, Chinese intellectuals were not so concerned with expanding China's sphere of influence.

For example, in the popular nationalist book *China Can Say No* (1996), the authors famously wrote: "The US cannot lead anybody, it can only lead itself. Japan cannot lead anybody, sometimes not even itself. China does not want to lead, it only wants to lead itself."⁴ This book was famously written several years after the Japanese version, *The Japan That Can Say No* (1989), which appeared toward the end of Japan's bubble economy.⁵ The Chinese response is similar in stressing China's own autonomy, without wanting to interfere in the world more broadly. It posits a world where all nations lead themselves. Moreover, we see that the locution is ambivalent with respect to the ability of China. The United States cannot lead anybody, but China does not want to lead anybody. There is an important distinction here between ability and volition, such that it says nothing about whether China has the capacity to change the world. China can say no to the world, which already suggests that it could reject the existing system and create a new one.

Christopher Hughes shows that the desire to expand becomes clear about ten years after the publication of *China Can Say No* with the appearance of *Unhappy China* (2009), which argued for an outward-looking foreign policy. By this time, Chinese capital was rapidly expanding and China had also survived the Asian financial crises of 1997, which seriously affected the Taiwanese and Southeast Asian economies. From 1993 to 1997, the economy grew at an enormous rate, which led to a crisis that could not be solved through mere neoliberal policies.⁶ After the 1997 crises, people had a greater sense of the importance of the state in both the domestic and international economy. This was also the period when China had recently joined the World Trade Organization (WTO) and with the increasing transition to a market economy, people saw problems associated with the polarization of wealth and the deterioration of the environment, among a host of other issues.⁷ All of this suggested that the process of globalization was internal to China and that consequently, China needed to respond.⁸ In addition to the financial crises, which further confirmed the presence of globalization, the bombing of the Chinese embassy in Belgrade during the 1998–1999 Kosovo War suggested that the Chinese should be ready to act in the world.

From the late 1990s to early 2000s, China began what Hughes calls a "geopolitik turn," which meant that China would not just be concerned about its own domestic issues; rather, it to slowly expand its "lebensraum." In *Unhappy China,* which was considered a sequel to *China Can Say No,* the authors wrote: "Once again, we need to let the citizens know the truth that we are totally alone in the world, that Westerners are jackals from the same lair, dispel illusions about any Western country, not to dream that there is any good person among them who will be better disposed toward China, and that in a situation of isolation and adversity the Chinese must ceaselessly strive for self-strengthening (*ziqiang bu xi*) and gain even more expansive lebensraum [*shengcun kongjian*]."[9] The authors of *Unhappy China* are concerned about China being isolated and attacked, especially after events such as the bombing of the Chinese embassy. Note that there is a general indictment of the West and an idea that the Chinese must constantly strengthen themselves. The term "self-strengthening" might cause us to recall intellectuals' and officials' calls for "self-strengthening" after China's loss in the Opium War. However, China has changed greatly from the mid-nineteenth century; it has now entered the world stage as a major player. Three years before the publication of *Unhappy China,* the Chinese international relations scholar Zhang Wenmu argued that for China, as for the United States, self-strengthening and self-preservation implied expansion beyond one's borders. He notes that the national objectives of economic growth place a certain logic in motion. But these national objectives have also locked China into a development path from which there is no turning back. China must continue to move forward, for if it does not, the economy could turn into a destructive one leading to chaos and even violent civil unrest. Maintaining China's economic juggernaut not only requires continuous participation in the global market but also depends on access to energy and other resources.[10]

Zhang's language, including, his invoking of the Marx-like metaphor of the juggernaut, suggests that China is propelled by a capitalist logic that it cannot control. Marx noted that "all the means for the development of production undergo a dialectical inversion so that they become means of domination and exploitation of the producers.... They transform his life-time into working-time, and drag his wife and child beneath the juggernaut capital."[11] Zhang identifies China with the juggernaut of capital, which now must complete its trajectory. Notice that it is the national objectives that have locked China into a directional dynamic that one cannot alter. This suggests that, although the Chinese national state might have begun by propelling this logic into motion by market reforms, joining the WTO and making a host of other decisions, once this logic began it took a life of its own. Now China has to follow this logic and deal with its spatial implications.

However, the gap between capital and the nation-state allows for the possibility that a nation could be part of a project to transform and even sublate the juggernaut of capital so that it becomes something else; this would be the beginning of a new world-system. Although Zhang is not such a visionary, Zhao gestures in this direction. He harnesses various aspects of traditional Chinese philosophy against the present world-system and aims to turn this world-system from one where national juggernauts compete for limited resources, to a world-system where there are transnational institutions to facilitate cooperation and deliberation about the sustainable use of resources. All of this begins with philosophy, which has implications for global politics. So now we will ascend from political realities to the heights of Chinese cosmology and return to politics in a different light.

Tianxia Ontology: The One-Many Problem

Zhao's work presents a representative and highly influential theory of global world order, and I interpret his ideas to bring out their contemporary relevance. Zhao shows how politics and ontology are correlative by invoking a version of the one-many problem. Through the problem of the one and the many, Zhao articulates a relational worldview, which points toward an alternative politics. This includes the relationship between states and the world and also relationships between people and a particular domestic state. I will suggest that these different ontologies relate to competing perceptions of international order. In his *Science of Logic,* G. W. F. Hegel provides a brilliant derivation of the many from the one, and this ontology relates to the idea of a world of nation-states. Hegel's is a relational model where the one generates and is inextricably connected to the many; however, the main mechanism of this generation is that the one first excludes or shuts out the other.[12] Zhao draws on Laozi to construct a different conception of the one and the many, where boundaries are porous and the one is not exclusive, but incorporates others.

Zhao explains his interest in the one-many problem as follows: "History has taught us that it has always been hard to resolve the issue of 'the one and the many' in politics. It is almost impossible to have a perfect system that sets up a common order acceptable to all political parties."[13] Zhao looks to classical Chinese models to resolve the one-many problem and in this context brings ontology / cosmology and politics together. For Zhao, the one-many problem is immediately political because it concerns a communal order that entails acceptance by all members—it cannot be forced on its inhabitants. In his well-known book *Tianxia System* (*Tianxia tixi* 天下體系), he makes the following point directly connecting his idea of the one and the many to Laozi's cosmology:

> Multiplicity must have the control of some type of frame and only then becomes multiplicity. Otherwise, a multiplicity without any control is

merely chaos. Laozi said: "The *dao* begets one, one begets two and three gives rise to the myriad things." Then when there are many new things in the "myriad things," one must of course rethink the "one" to make it possible to incorporate the changes in the myriad things. At this point, there is a mutual relationship between the "many" and the "one." When the many changes, the "one" must also respond. "One" must be more generous and increase its capacity. "Change" is to pursue the "large" up to a standpoint of no-outside.[14]

Zhao begins with cosmology / ontology and then moves to the political idea of tolerance. This idea of tolerance is somewhat different from a similar concept in liberalism, since in the case described above, tolerating the other transforms the self or the unity exhibiting tolerance. To describe this transformation, Zhao combines two conceptions of the one. The first is the classic one-many problem, where Laozi describes how we move from the *dao* to the one to the many. The second concerns the one that envelops the many and is perhaps more directly political.

Hegel and Laozi share this combination of metaphysical and political conceptions of the one-many problem, and contrasting their respective positions highlights how Zhao's position differs from political theories that posit a tolerant state. Hegel and Laozi share an emphasis on correlativity, process, and becoming. Moreover, in both cases, the one mediates between the infinite and finite and shows how they are inseparable. However, Laozi's version of emanation is cosmological rather than logical and this will be an important difference in understanding the idea of one as a harmonious unity in multiplicity. As we shall see, in Hegel's view, the one produces the many because it contains contradictions associated with exclusion and determinacy. This difference is related to their respective political projects. Hegel famously believed that a world-state would be impossible, while classical Chinese thinkers took the government of the whole empire with amorphous boundaries as their starting point.

If we think of Laozi's *dao* as infinite, then we can understand Hegel's transition from the infinite to the one to the many as a significant model to think about Laozi's point. Unlike most philosophical systems, for Hegel, true infinity overcomes the strict separation between the finite and the infinite. This fluid interplay between the infinite and the finite provides a different framework for comparison than the one we see in Takahiro Nakajima's contribution to this volume, which draws on Emmanuel Levinas's *Totality and Infinity* to make comparisons with Taijun Takeda and Atsushi Mori. Levinas makes something of an absolute separation between totality-the finite and infinity, which makes it such that the infinite constantly ruptures totality. However, for both Hegel and Laozi, an infinite that is cut off from the finite is not a true infinite.[15] True infinity is constantly transforming into the finite.

This unity of the infinite and the finite propels Hegel's version of the dialectic of the one and the many. Hegel does not presuppose the one and the many but shows how the concept of being eventually generates determinate being and finitude, which generates infinity, which produces the one, which becomes many ones and begins the transition from quality to quantity.[16] The section in which the infinite turns into the one and then into the many occurs at the end of the first section of Hegel's *Logic,* namely the section on quality or the transition from quality to quantity. This process is completely immanent, which is another similarity with Laozi and most Chinese traditional philosophy.

Let us begin our story where Hegel has already derived infinity from finitude and has shown that infinity is a mode of becoming, which involves passing over into its other. This involves a shift from reality to idealism, namely from seeing things as independent entities to viewing finite things as moments in larger processes. The finite itself becomes infinite in relating to itself through the other. While this might sound obscure, it merely refers to the idea that each finite being ends and becomes something else and through this such a being continues. For example, burning wood becomes ashes and so on.

From a different perspective, we can understand this same process as the infinite returning to itself through the finite. The finite is now seen as a moment in the process in which the infinite returns to itself. Hegel names this infinite "turning back into itself" being-for-self, and the one is precisely a mode of "being for self" or self-relating infinity.[17] The one is a mode of this self-relating infinity, which holds finitude within it. We should already be alert to a paradox here, namely that the one is both determinate (finite) and infinite. This should not surprise us because for Hegel true infinity cannot be something separate from the finite. Earlier in the *Logic,* Hegel showed that being implies being determinate, which entails negation. Being determinate implies being this and not that. We need not go into the full derivation of the many from the one but should note that the one is self-relating infinity, a mode of being-for-self, which explicitly negates everything else.[18] The one is at once infinite and determinate, which means that it contains negation in it. However, since it is only one, there is nothing inside or outside it—such existents would compromise its status as one. Therefore, the one is purely empty, it contains only the void. Hegel therefore calls the one "posited nothing."[19]

The one must abstract from everything else, but at the same time remain determinate as one. One implies distinction because it is finite but should not imply anything that it distinguishes itself from, since that would then already become two. Consequently, the one ends up being completely empty and contains only the void within it, which is connected to its own self-determination through negation. However, in order to be one, it has to shut out even its self-determining, the void within it.[20] Thus, "nothing stands as a void outside the one as existent."[21] But Hegel points out that this "void" is also precisely "posited nothing" and consequently it becomes another one. This process continues ad infinitum to imply many ones, which implies transition from quality to quantity. In Hegel's words, "The one is consequently a becoming of many ones."[22] This is a brief summary of Hegel's version of the transition from the one to the many and shows us that the movement is completely immanent and emphasizes becoming.

From the description above, we see that Hegel's ontology, while emphasizing process and becoming, is also propelled by a logic of exclusion. The one is exclusive and then this leads it to produce another one and so on. If we recall that this is a transition from quality to quantity, we might also think about the beginning of Marx's *Capital,* which is also organized around these categories: use-value is qualitative and exchange value is quantitative. Quantity is a realm of self-externality and is for the most part indifferent to quality. In other words, one can change the quantity of a thing without affecting its quality. To some extent this relation between quality and quantity is there in the contemporary system of nation-states, where each nation qua nation is qualitatively equal to another. They are each relatively stable exclusionary "ones." Zhao and Laozi describe another type of one or unity, which from the beginning is not exclusionary. By focusing on the process of the one becoming many in Laozi's text, we can see how it is a particular cosmology rather than a logic that mediates the generation of the many from the one.

Let us return to the phrase that Zhao quotes from chapter 42 of the *Dao De Jing,* namely that "the *dao* 道 engenders one, one engenders two, two engenders three and three engenders the myriad things." If we interpret the *dao* as the infinite, we see that Laozi tells a story similar to Hegel; the *dao* returns to itself through the finite. In chapter 40, Laozi exclaims that "return is the movement of the *dao.*"[23] Infinity is directly connected to things returning to themselves while becoming other. This movement is described through the *dao* becoming one and then many. The category of "one" is crucial and as in Hegel, it is closest to the infinite. Lü Jifu comments on the above passage: "With the *dao* in the universe there is nothing equal to it. Since there is nothing equal to it, it is simply 'one.' Therefore, it is said that the *dao* becomes one."[24]

In chapter 14 of the *Dao De Jing,* we gain a further perspective on how the Dao becomes one. The passage reads: "We look for it but not perceive it and call it 'unpertruding'; we listen to it but do not hear it and call it rare; we grope about for it, but do not grasp hold of it and call it 'subtle.' These three characteristics do not lend themselves to closer scrutiny. Therefore, they blend together and become one."[25] The *dao* is infinite and indeterminate, which is why it cannot be grasped by the senses; it is not a determinate finite thing. Yet, this lack of distinction makes it "blend" into one. Laozi uses the term *hun* 混, which is translated as "blend" and suggests a movement of becoming mediated by vagueness. It encourages associations with other characters such as *hundun* 混沌, which sometimes refers to originary harmonious chaos. This is different from Hegel's idea of the one, which clearly shuts otherness out and is later associated with repulsion. For Laozi, this haziness is connected to the emergence of determinate things. We see this in sentences such as the following: "In the Dao's constituting an entity, it is hazy and nebulous. Though nebulous and hazy, in the midst there are forms. Though hazy and nebulous in the midst there are things."[26]

This haziness is connected to the above concept of blending, but here he also introduces concepts of determinacy. The Hanshan commentary states that being hazy and nebulous means that the *dao* both is and is not, which shows how the *dao* contains negation within it.[27] In chapter 2 of the *Dao De Jing*, Laozi speaks of being and non-being arising together.[28] Perhaps more clearly, in chapter 40, he writes that "being in turn is engendered from non-being."[29] This is fundamentally different from many philosophers in the Western tradition who take their cue from Parmenides and contend that being and non-being are completely separate.

The key difference between Hegel and Laozi brings us back to the problems of haziness and vagueness, along with the issue of cosmology versus logic. When Hegel argues that determinate being (*Dasein*) emerges from becoming, he performs a logical derivation, which is also an ontological development. Becoming itself as ceaseless unrest logically "collapses into a quiescent result," which is determinate being.[30] In Hegel's view, those philosophers who merely affirm endless becoming overlook the logical consequences of this category. For Laozi non-being is not merely a logical category but part of a cosmological process.

If one is not careful, one will overlook this cosmological dimension. Returning to chapter 42 of the *Dao De Jing*, Laozi explains that one becomes two and two becomes three and three becomes ten thousand things. These numbers are significant, since it appears that three creates the myriad things. This is not a case where one creates another one through a logical derivation; rather, the numbers refer to cosmological principles, which are themselves productive. Ch'en Ku-ying suggests that the number two represents the *yin* and *yang* vapors and that three refers to a state of harmony connected to the coalescing of the *yin* and *yang* vapors.[31] We can support this reading using the following lines: "The ten thousand things are sustained by *yin* (the negative principle) and are encompassed by *yang* (the positive principle)."[32] The chapter ends again with the metaphor of blending (*chong* 冲): "Through the coalescing (*chong*) of these vapors (*qi* 气), a state of harmony is attained."[33] This new state of harmony refers to the reuniting of the one that Zhao mentions above. Zhao contends that it is this new one of vagueness that encompasses the other that he sees in Chinese history and behind the Chinese political ideal.

From Philosophy to History: *Tianxia* and the Problem of Worlding the World

The above philosophical musings about the one and the many have serious political implications with respect to the problem of *tianxia*. The opposition between the Hegelian ontology and Laozi's cosmology above is related to a difference between a system of many unified nation-states and a more porous imperial system. Hegel himself eventually draws out the political consequences of his metaphysics, but for that we would have to take a long detour into how his logic plays out in the *Philosophy of Right,* where for example the idea of unity of the subject makes necessary a certain form of the state. Zhao posits an older vision of the one-many issue against the present resolution in the system of nation-states.

At the level of nation-states, philosophers such as Jean-Jacques Rousseau and Hegel were critical of capitalism and pointed out the limits of abstract individual freedom. For example, Rousseau famously expounded a theory of the general will, which entailed conceiving freedom as communal. Although these theories synthesize the one and the many at the level of the state or in smaller communities, they do not follow through on this promise globally. Rousseau and Hegel both contend that real democratic interaction between the one and the many is only possible in small communities as we witness in ancient Greece and therefore is not possible in either the modern world or in the international sphere. From this perspective, looking to the direct democracy in ancient Athens as an ideal in the modern world would be considered naïve.[34] However, from a perspective inspired by more radical scholars such as Karl Marx and John Dewey, the story of Athens represents a narrative of decline, a story where people once participated in creating a unity in multiplicity and vice versa and now are reduced to mere atomized parts of an inchoate public.[35] Even these more radical critics of capitalism did not deal adequately with the problem of global order.

Although Zhao is not an advocate of direct democracy, he does envision a system in which there is a dialectical relationship between the one and the many or the center and the various peripheries. Like Dewey, Zhao attempts to bring back an earlier form of politics, but now at the level of the world. His *tianxia* theory invokes a Chinese perspective to pose the one-many question where answers seem most difficult, namely with respect to world order, and suggests that the problem of international relations would appear differently if we changed our standpoint from Greece to China. The view from Greece focuses on governing the polis, which becomes the unit of analysis, and consequently the world is conceived as a mere conglomeration of individual states or poleis. From this perspective, there can be no self-conscious unity of the globe and there is bound to be conflict between the various individual states. Zhao argues that as long as we are limited to adjudicating between various warring states, the world is not yet a world. It is precisely this futural dimension of *tianxia* that endows it with critical force.

But the question of how the *tianxia* model would be possible today requires Zhao to put cosmology into history and consequently, he presents a narrative of decline and continuity. There is another way in which we can see this as a response to Hegel. Recall that Hegel's philosophy of history began with China, where one person was free, then went to Greece and Rome, where some human beings were free, and then ended in the modern world, where all were free. In Zhao's view, the historical narrative is reversed and sustainability requires us to go back to the Chinese model, but now this ideal confronts the global system of nation-states. Following Zhao, we must rethink the freedom of the ancient Chinese one as at once many and constituting the amorphous international unity of *tianxia*. Zhao points out that Chinese theory began with something like international relations.

According to Zhao, the Zhou dynasty represents a version of the one-many relation at the level of global politics. He contends that due to specific historical circumstances, the Zhou dynasty had to create a world-system that transcended individual states. In the Chinese context, the individual state always already presupposed a world-system, which was in turn grounded in certain cosmological principles about the Earth, human beings, and Heaven. We might think of Earth, Heaven, and human beings as corresponding to the number three in Laozi, namely *yin, yang,* and the combination of both. Given this worldview, where human beings, Heaven, and Earth are united, distinctions between ontology and politics are not absolute. In other words, the interdependence that we have seen at the cosmological level informs the structure of politics. This is why Zhao contends that the Chinese worldview is a political theology, but we have to understand this in a specifically Chinese setting, where there is no transcendent God.[36] Rather the infinite way is inseparable from the finite, with which it blends and transforms.

According to Zhao, this divine infinite element is expressed in Heaven, while the Earth is that which selflessly gives. He asserts that "Heaven is the largest one, which contains the many." However, given our above analysis, rather than containing, we should emphasize becoming and blending into one. Heaven constantly becomes the many through an infinite process. But this becoming is not merely abstract; rather it produces specific things, perhaps most importantly life. *Tianxia* then creates the conditions for mutual coexistence of all species.[37]

Creating the conditions for sustainable life forms the telos of Heaven, Earth, and *tianxia;* this goal becomes a regulative ideal against which we can measure the present. Zhao asserts that *tianxia* "will remain a theoretical concept until the political world converges with the natural world."[38] The political world here implies the actual system of institutions associated with *tianxia,* which emerged during the Zhou dynasty. The point of course is that they could emerge again. In the above sentence of Zhao, the natural world could appear to be apolitical, as something outside the political world. However, we have seen above that the concept of *tianxia* is inseparable from the movement of nature itself. *Tianxia* expresses a Laozian idea of the one at the level of politics. Until this goal of a universal order that is sustainable for all living things is attained, *tianxia* will remain a regulative ideal, a theoretical construct needing to be realized.

The Zhou dynasty was something like an originary moment, where theory and practice coincided to some extent. There has been much discussion about the historical accuracy of *tianxia,* but I believe that for Zhao and the whole project of *tianxia,* the normative content of *tianxia* does not rest solely on historical accuracy. While *tianxia* presents itself as a return to a past, we must think of this as a return back to the future. *Tianxia* as an ideal in a global capitalist world will have to find a different institutional form than it had in the Zhou dynasty, but it is nonetheless infused with this history.

Given that this normative ideal emerged in the Zhou dynasty, we need to ask with Zhao, what happened to this history, and indeed this trajectory looks extremely different in the 2020s than it did during the late Qing dynasty. By the early twenty-first century, scholars became critical of a world based on competition in a way very different than it was in the late nineteenth century. For example, in his *Outline of a Theory of Civilization* (1875), Fukuzawa Yukichi praises the pre-Qin period for reasons diametrically opposed to Zhao. Rather than focusing on the one that unites the many, he believes that it is precisely the dispersion into different groups that is laudable. This allows for competition just like in feudalism, which led to capitalism. Moreover, according to Fukuzawa, because the ruler of *tianxia* only has symbolic power over the various lords, there is a separation between theocratic and military domains. In this narrative, the Chinese pre-Qin period is interesting precisely because it embodies a distinction between religion and the state, which was later picked up by the West. Indeed, for Fukuzawa, this explains why there were so many different schools of thought vying for hegemony. However, China was not able to maintain such a decentralized system once the Qin unified. About a thousand years after this point, medieval shogunal Japan actually embodied the spirit of early China. Fukuzawa explains that this later difference characterizes Japanese and Chinese civilizational difference more generally: "I say that China has endured as a theocratic autocracy over the centuries, while Japan has balanced the element of military power against the element of theocracy. China has had but one element, Japan two. If you discuss civilization in these terms, China has never once changed and thus is not equal to Japan in her development. It is easier for Japan to adopt Western civilization than for China."[39]

In the above passage, Fukuzawa finds liberalism in the Japanese shogunal system.[40] But this was only one side of Fukuzawa's argument for the superiority of Japan. He also mentioned the emperor system, which he believed showed the continuity of the Japanese bloodline. In his *Outline of a Theory of Civilization,* Fukuzawa spoke of a difference between political legitimacy (*seitō* 正統) and the bloodline (*kettō* 血統).[41] He argued that because Japan continuously had an unbroken line of an emperor system, it retained a continuity that Korea and China did not have. In particular, he contends that China did not have such a continuity because it had lost its sovereignty to the Mongols and then to the Manchus. About sixty years after Fukuzawa made this argument, in 1935, Nishida Kitarō returned to the problem of the emperor to show Japan had resolved the one-many problem in a unique manner. He writes:

> If we look back at the thousands of years at the traces of our country that developed with the imperial house at the center, is it not the contradictory unity of the one as totality and the many singulars, which moves from something that is made to something that makes? . . . The one as totality that is a historical subject has undergone many changes. . . . But I believe that the imperial house goes beyond these subjects and is a place in the world that limits itself by bringing the one as totality and the singular many into a contradictory unity in itself.[42]

Nishida contends that the Japanese emperor represents an active synthesis between the one and the many. Notice that according to Nishida, the emperor follows a process beyond himself, namely the logic of the world limiting itself. In this way, the cosmological problem lines up with the problem of political order. Giving the timing of this essay around the start of World War II, some might argue that Nishida mobilized the ideology of the one and the many to promote Japanese imperialism and fascism. This will be a specter that haunts the Chinese case, so let us now turn to how Chinese history might be different.

In Chinese intellectual history, thinkers did not underscore the connection between *tianxia* and one individual. On the contrary, in the late Ming and early Qing dynasties, Huang Zongxi (1610–1695) complained that emperors had changed from seeing *tianxia* as a common good to appropriating *tianxia* for their own personal gain.[43] The problem here is precisely that emperors monopolized the one at the expense of the many. The difference between the Japanese and Chinese cosmologies is crucial here. In the Japanese case, the emperor can never lose the mandate of Heaven, since he is a descendent of the sun goddess Amaterasu. In China, on the other hand, emperors can always lose the mandate of Heaven and so the cosmology of the one refers to *tianxia* rather than to an individual. Consequently, unlike the case with the Japanese emperor, in China *tianxia* can be a critical vantage point against the present.[44] For example, during the late Qing, Liang Qichao (1873–1929), having read Fukuzawa, made a comment echoing Huang about the Chinese emperor monopolizing the public.

Although Huang has been appropriated as a liberal since he chastises the Chinese emperor for using the empire for his personal gain and also legitimates the pursuit of private interests among the masses, his writings also have a communal dimension. One of the key ideas of *tianxia* is that it belongs to no one. Zhao cites Confucius stating that an all-inclusive world pursues "*tianxia* as the common good." He then quotes Lu Buwei, anticipating Huang and asserting that "*tianxia* is not one person's *tianxia,* but all people's *tianxia.*"[45]

However, Huang's and Fukuzawa's respective approaches present an interesting contrast to the historical narrative that Zhao gives us in the first decade of the 2000s. By this time, it is China rather than Japan that appears as the giant of East Asia. Moreover, now rather than being able to catch up to the West, China might provide an alternative to the present Euro-American world order. Zhao looks to ancient China to develop his own theory of the world. He takes such comments about public ownership of the world to their logical conclusion, namely a type of world-socialism, which is governed for the common good. In the traditional Confucian narrative, the unification of China in 221 BCE represented a decline, and Zhao rethinks this transformation to emphasize continuity. Zhao describes the transition to the Qin in the following manner: "In 221 BCE, the Qin dynasty unified the country through wars, discontinued the *tianxia* system, and created a grand unity system of centralized governance. The rise and fall of the Zhou dynasty teaches us an important lesson: a highly benevolent political system may not be the most robust one. This means that for any idealism to be sustainable, it must simultaneously be realistic. By the same token, any realism must be idealistic in order to be meaningful."[46]

From this perspective, unlike Huang, Zhao writes an evolutionary type of perspective in which there is a necessity to the transition from the Zhou to the Qin because the Zhou did not develop the conditions to reproduce a *tianxia* system. At this point, the *tianxia* ideal enters into a complex dialectic with history, where it constantly searches for an institutional form that is true to the goals of peaceful coexistence and sustainability. The Qin represents a dialectical continuation of the *tianxia* perspective.

The *Tianxia* system of the Zhou dynasty was the first systemic revolution in China. In 221 BCE, the Qin dynasty launched a second revolution, effectively terminating the *Tianxia* system by building a China of grand unity instead. This marked a change in direction from the world construction to state construction. The grand unity model that began during the Qin dynasty was consolidated during the Han dynasty, putting an end to the period of China's world history and ushering in an era of state history. However, grand unity China still retains the heritage of the *Tianxia* concept, transforming the *Tianxia* spirit into a state spirit, changing a world structure into a state structure and consequently turning China into a "world-structured" country.[47]

Unlike Huang and Liang, Zhao does not merely describe a narrative of decline after the Qin emperor's unification. Rather, the earlier ideal is sublated and gets a new institutional form, while preserving the *tianxia* structure within it. We move from a *tianxia* system to *tianxia* as a world-structured country. The *tianxia* concept turns into a country. To follow the spirit of Zhao's thought, we must understand *guo* as both state and empire. The manner in which *tianxia* mutates after the Qin is not so much that it becomes a country among others; rather it becomes an empire that by the Han period is able to incorporate difference within it. It is in this sense that Lucien Pye famously said when speaking of a later period that China is a civilization pretending to be a nation-state.[48]

This idea of civilization implies *tianxia*'s ability to incorporate difference within itself and presents a model of continuity. Like Fukuzwa, Zhao stresses historical continuity. However, Zhao turns the tables on this framework by attempting to think of China beyond the opposition of inside and outside. Indeed, Fukuzawa was writing in 1875 when Japan and much of Asia was facing Western imperialism, and consequently he hoped that Japan could create an independent nation-state.

Against this, in a perhaps unconscious gesture toward Mizoguchi Yūzō, Zhao argues that China is a methodology.[49] In 1989, Mizoguchi famously argued for "China as method," which implied decentering Europe and emphasizing the cultural particularity of various nations.[50] Mizoguchi's goal was to construct a new universality out of the various singular cultures. Zhao makes the stronger claim that Chinese culture from the beginning went beyond the opposition between particularity and universality in its concept of *tianxia*. China in the early twenty-first century aims at creating a universal global order that brings with it some of the characteristics of older empires without being imperialist. Zhao brings Fukuzawa and Mizoguchi together by underscoring Chinese continuity: "Chinese civilization has not been interrupted since its known inception, indicating its strong sustainability; Chinese civilization has always comprised multiethnicities and multicultures ... ; and Chinese civilization has never produced a universal monotheism or transcendental religion, a phenomenon that has been interpreted as indicating the Chinese civilization to be highly non-religious."[51]

While Fukuzawa locates continuity in the persistence of the emperor, Zhao underscores the prolongation of Chinese culture. Within this framework, what Fukuzawa construes as evidence of the loss of China, namely conquest by the Mongols and the Manchus, Zhao interprets as the malleability and compatibility of Chinese civilization. Zhao connects this ability to the absence of monotheistic religions of transcendence, which he associates with an exclusive idea of the one. In his *Tianxia tixi,* he asserts that the Western idea of absolute transcendence implies that there is something outside that cannot be incorporated.[52] Against this, he emphasizes the blending unity of which Laozi spoke. Chinese civilization does not depend on race and incorporates difference at its core. In this way, it entails a new type of universality that incorporates difference. Focusing on the Manchu and Mongol conquests, Zhao explains: "Even when the northern ethnic groups (particularly Mongolian and Manchu) ruled the Central Plains [*zhongguo*], the culture of the Central Plains was still the chief cultural resource. The fundamental reason for this is, as we discussed before, that the embedded Chinese historical line is where the northern ethnic groups find their maximum interests.... Whether the Yuan dynasty or the Qing dynasty, their political legitimacy can always find justifications in Chinese thought, at least in the tradition of *tianxia.*"[53]

Zhao thus turns the Manchu and Mongol conquests from something negative to something positive. The dialectic between the conquered and the conqueror made it such that the Manchu and Mongols were themselves transformed by *tianxia* as they tried to take over the Central Plains. Note that the political legitimacy of *tianxia* does not lie in the state or in a bloodline; rather, it lies in the continuity of certain cultural practices and rituals, which the Mongols and Manchus eventually accepted and developed. The late-Qing reformer Kang Youwei (1858–1927) developed this form of thought. Against Chinese revolutionaries who, like Fukuzawa, saw sovereignty in terms of race, Kang emphasized that Chinese civilization was based on a vision of culture that implies this amorphous one at the center. On this view, the one and the many do not exclude one another; rather, the one incorporates the many. Here we see *tianxia* construct a new vision of the one and the many, in which the one is not only inseparable from the many, it is constituted out of the many.

Kang's idea of the great community and Zhao's *tianxia* exemplify this correlative understanding of the one and the many. In short, Kang recognized that during the nineteenth century, the world was not unified and that China had to take on the characteristics of the nation-state. This is a world where there are numerous nation-states, which do not form a whole. He was indeed one of the first who proposed learning from the Meiji Restoration. However, he did not see this as the final goal and believed that the world of warring nation-states would eventually have to be sublated and reunited under *tianxia,* which would preserve the singularities of the many. This sublated community is precisely Kang's great community.

Zhao follows Kang's logic and argues for *tianxia* in the contemporary world. He notes that after the imperial system collapsed in 1911, China tried to model itself after European nation-states but retained a "grand unity" structure from the imperial system. "No matter how complex modern China is, its *tianxia* spirit remains constant, highlighting that the concept of *tianxia* is a stable gene in the country."[54] The *tianxia* gene actually has a telos. Zhao writes, "Since grand unity China encompasses a world structure, its political intention is to unify all states under its governance, include all peoples in one family and put *tianxia* ideals into practice in one country, therefore defining a political form in which a country limited in its territory, expresses the all-inclusiveness concept of *tianxia.*"[55]

The above passage deals with China from the Qin to the Qing, namely China as empire, but we can add that this logic and impulse continue beyond the nation-state. This could be the theoretical basis for the world as *tianxia* and would continue Kang's thought. In other words, although the above passage discusses unifying states under China's governance, the impulse is to create a well-governed world. The ideal of *tianxia* within the Chinese state points beyond it toward an internationalism. Given the dialectical ontology of the Chinese tradition that stresses process and that we have seen when discussing the one and the many, we should not think of *tianxia* as a finished product. Rather the significance of *tianxia* continues to evolve as the world unfolds historically.

From the above description of Zhao's ideal of *tianxia,* we see that it fundamentally addresses the problem of unity in difference that is especially relevant not only for China but around the world, where the politics of identity and partition haunts the various nation-states of the world. Even without a unified world, it seems difficult to resolve the one-many problem within any individual nation-state. Pye's point about China being a civilization is relevant here, since we could also say that China is a world in itself—a microcosm that provides us a glimpse of what would happen if its model were generalized to encompass the globe. For example, we can wait and see how China deals with the tensions in Hong Kong, Xinjiang, and Tibet and this might provide us with a vision of how *tianxia* would work more broadly. From this perspective, we can understand *tianxia* as a challenge to the current government and an ideal to which it could be held accountable.[56]

However, even if we concede that China is a miniature world in itself, it has to find a way to realize a *tianxia* in a world of global capitalist competition.

Consequently, Zhao and others interested in realizing *tianxia* must describe how *tianxia* articulates with capitalism and nationalism. *Tianxia* must begin as both a national and transnational movement that overcomes capitalism. Moreover, the issue of capitalism mediates the various tensions in Tibet, Xinjiang, and Hong Kong, since the problems in each of these regions are connected to inequality and political disempowerment.

Competition, Nationalism, and Cosmopolitanism

In the modern period, we must understand the ideal of *tianxia* in the context of a global capitalist arena where nation-states compete for resources and military dominance. Consequently, we will follow Zhao's discussion of *tianxia* as an alternative to competition and relate this to the problem of nationalism. I provide a dialectical reading of anti-imperialist nationalism as a way of realizing the *tianxia* ideal. Let us begin with Zhao's vision of *tianxia* as an alternative game. As Zhao's describes the dialectics of *tianxia* further, he brings us into the realm of contemporary political economy. Zhao points out that as a concept that unfolds historically, *tianxia* has the structure of a certain type of game. He writes, "When a historical order or a game of competition becomes the common interest of all peoples, it becomes a historic and political focal point. This is a game concept from Thomas C. Schelling, where the focal point refers to a selection made by all without prior consultation."[57]

The idea of a selection that is made without prior consultation suggests something akin to John Rawls's original position in which people decide on principles of justice before actually entering the world. This ahistorical starting point is not quite adequate to the Chinese concept of *tianxia,* since as Zhao points out, the assumptions of people following material interests and individual liberty cannot explain the ancient adherence to *tianxia*. Zhao notes that although politics usually pursues wealth, that was not what made China as the central kingdom attractive. The various nomadic tribes were more technologically advanced, so they found something else in *tianxia* beyond mere material wealth.

At some level this point is trivial, since the appeal of *tianxia* is precisely that it is a global structure for mutual flourishing, which serves as an alternative to competition based on self-interest, be it national or individual. Speaking of the spiritual dimension of *tianxia,* Zhao makes the following comment: "It can be found that the temptations stronger than material ones can only come from the spiritual world, which has a magical power. In contrast to the consumable material world, the spiritual world increases in value and its gains are infinite."[58]

With this opposition between the infinite / spiritual and the finite / material, we seem dangerously close to a bad infinite, which would go against the assumptions associated with Laozi and many other Chinese thinkers. I would suggest interpreting this infinite of the spiritual as inextricably connected to the material, including institutions and practices, while pointing beyond it toward a future. The infinite is a process that points beyond itself. In other words, although one cannot reduce the spiritual dimension of Chinese culture to any specific matter, one cannot also not separate it from matter; in short it requires institutional embodiment and this project is not finished. In this way, the term "Chinese" transcends itself and refers to something global.

While Zhao mentions aspects of Chinese culture, such as the writing system, he returns to a political theology, which implies institutional structures, which go beyond the local. It was precisely these aspects that overcame the Manchus and Mongols as they conquered China. They became wedded to larger ideals beyond ethnic identity. Through invading China, they continued the project of *tianxia* in a manner very different from the British who colonized India. Put simply, the British did not become Indian in the way the Manchus became Chinese. The Chineseness mentioned here is that of the Chinese empire / state before modern nationalism. But Zhao advocates *tianxia* in a world where the nation-state is the most dominant form of community. Consequently, we must ask what is *tianxia*'s relation to the nation-state and nationalism. This is especially the case since many would contend that *tianxia* is merely a mask for Chinese nationalist expansion.

Tianxia and the Problem of Nationalism

Given that *tianxia* transcends the nation, one might immediately judge that it is incompatible with the nation. However, the *tianxia* perspective is one that is not static and consequently allows or even necessitates different institutional forms at different periods in history. Contemporary political philosophers Daniel Bell and Sor-hoon Tan each argue against Zhao's idea that *tianxia* is best embodied in a world-system. Bell underscores the compatibility between *tianxia* and the nation, while Tan attempts to outline nonnational opportunities for realizing *tianxia*. Tan follows Sin-yee Chan in claiming that Bell overlooks that the Confucian idea of gradated love implies human relationship rather than the group consciousness implied by nationalism. Tan is of course correct to point out that terms such as *guo* 國 and *jia* 家 in the texts of Confucius and Mencius cannot map onto our contemporary ideas of nation-state and family.[59] But Tan's normative point goes beyond this: "The *tianxia* ideal might work better if, instead of a single state becoming the 'world government,' a truly global organization with participation and legitimacy worldwide provides the leadership in solving problems beyond the abilities of national governments, or when a government commits acts against its own citizenry that results in deaths and suffering *en masse*. It might be something similar to humanitarian intervention under the control of the United Nations."[60]

Somewhat like Karatani Kojin, Tan relates a future postnational order to existing structures such as the United Nations.[61] She further mentions different relationships that could be built through various group memberships and transnational organizations with peaceful objectives. The key in all of this is that the *tianxia* ideal would give no special consideration to the nation.[62] All of this echoes Jacques Bidet's work on the world-state (*état-monde*), where he notes that the United Nations is not a state: "It is the matrix, denied, the symptom of a world-state. It possesses the silent and powerful existence of the repressed."[63] From this perspective, there is clearly some truth to the idea that the United Nations could be a symbol of the struggle for global justice. However, this overlooks the extent to which the United States has dominated the United Nations and consequently, has often supported American dominance in Korea and other parts of the world.[64] Moreover, as I will touch on below, imperialism can continue in different forms. It is in this sense that we have to think of the United Nations as merely a symptom of a deeper repression, which certain types of nationalism might resist.

A key issue here concerns the relationship between our present moment and the idea of a period of anti-imperialist nationalism. Zhao himself mentions Mao and Third World nationalism favorably in relation to the theories of Thomas Piketty and Michael Hardt and Antonio Negri. He writes, "Even though there are some new ideas in their theories, none of these thinkers are able to adequately respond to Mao's Three Worlds theory, which directly addressed the problem of global inequality."[65] By comparing Mao to Hardt and Negri, Zhao invites us to juxtapose Third World nationalism with more recent visions of global struggle, including Hardt and Negri's concept of the multitude, which has no nation. Zhao does not discuss Third World nationalism in detail, but he makes the following incisive point: "We have already analyzed the problems of imitation in tactical deployments and counter-strategizing. Both of these problems deal with forms of resistance open to weaker parties within structures of domination, and in such dynamics we find that the weaker party's counterstrategies can always have a certain destructive effect on imperialist orders."[66]

Zhao describes a strategy of imitation, where the dominated groups or nations imitate their oppressor and through this process resist and destabilize the system. Although he contends that such a process cannot completely change the system, this was precisely the goal of Third World nationalists, who did not really think of what they were doing as a simple mimesis. The conflict between these positions hinges on how one conceives of nationalism. The position that overemphasizes imitation assumes that both imperialist and anti-imperialist nationalism are basically the same because they both rely on the nation-form. However, the Third World nationalists claimed that anti-imperialist nationalism aimed to create a world beyond imperialism and that this made both the form and the content of their nationalism different.

This debate is not new, and we can learn from the Japanese Marxist historian Ishimoda Shō's defense of the Third World nationalist position in the early 1960s. Discussing the cases of China and other weaker nations in postwar Japan in an essay published in 1961 entitled "Kotoku Shusui to chūgoku [Kotoku Shusui and China]," Ishimoda vehemently argued against the anarchist Kotoku Shusui, who in the early twentieth century opposed any form of nationalism. Ishimoda's response is especially relevant to cosmopolitan readings of *tianxia*. Ishimoda's argument overlaps with Wang Ban's chapter in this volume, where he discusses the nationalism of Kotoku's Chinese contemporary, Liang Qichao, as something that goes beyond itself.

The basic premise of Ishimoda's position concerned a difference between the oppressed and imperialist nations. By the time Ishimoda was writing, the globe was witnessing numerous anticolonial and Third World movements, many of which linked themselves to the Chinese Revolution. The main point was similar to one made by Zhang Taiyan, a contemporary of Kotoku, namely that although, in an ideal world, nation-states would no longer exist, in a world of imperialism and capitalism, movements based on the nation-state were an essential moment in the struggle for a new order. Ishimoda's point, however, is not merely that the nation-state is necessary for resistance against imperialism. This would make it blind and indeterminate. Rather, he contends that the nationalism of oppressed nations could point to a different future, one beyond both imperialism and capitalism. If we interpret *tianxia* as a world-socialist ideal, then such anti-imperialist nationalism intended something similar to *tianxia*.

Some might question the relevance of the paradigm of imperialism for understanding the world and *tianxia,* especially because Zhao does not explicitly connect *tianxia* to an anti-imperialist movement. Zhao's conception of the game of competition and the pursuit of wealth, which he opposes to *tianxia,* is precisely behind the imperialism we see today. The context of this discussion is a world where global capitalism unwieldily undermines national self-determination, and this appears to make the concept of imperialism nugatory. However, global capitalism does not imply an even playing field, and this new system of global inequalities is related to imperialism. From this perspective, we can endorse Sam Gindin and Leo Panitch's thesis that postwar imperialism consists in the United States making the world safe for global capitalism.[67] In Gindin and Panitch's view, the real nature of American empire emerges during the Cold War and the idea of the containment of communism, which provided an ideology for the US government to change regimes around the world. This is a world in which countries are brought into a high degree of interdependence by either force or ideology, but the logic behind these connections is blind. Zhao's intervention should be read as a call to bring the current world under global control. His intervention also emerges at a time when China appears to be transitioning from the periphery to the center of the global capitalist system, and therefore the question of whether China could change the game becomes crucial. Zhao explicitly points us in this direction when he says, "This world-ideal is obviously not aimed at systematizing a new authoritarian power operating with the trinitarian logic of global capitalism, technology, and comprehensive services."[68] However, Zhao does not discuss capitalism extensively, and for this reason Marxists have recently criticized his theory.

Realizing *Tianxia* and Overcoming Capitalism: Marxist Criticisms

The Chinese Marxist Lin Chun has recently made an important critique of recent *tianxia* discourse by highlighting the importance of the Communist Revolution in China and the struggle against capitalism. According to her, the Communist Revolution was the moment of real internationalism, which has now receded into the background. She writes, "This internationalism confronted a global capitalist system, in which the independent survival of any socialist regime would depend on the sustenance it could draw from wider resistance to that system. Despite its own acute difficulties, China thus aided anti-colonial movements and postcolonial developments beyond its borders, often in the complicated circumstances of an international united front replete with internal tensions."[69]

Lin contrasts revolutionary China and the contemporary international turn represented by Zhao and others. She repeatedly chastises Confucianism for being reactionary, obsolete, and premodern. In her words, Confucianism represented a "repressive hierarchy" and is "toothless when facing a global order sustained by a powerful capitalist industrial-financial and military complex."[70] Some of these criticisms might be offset by presenting more nuanced readings of Confucianism throughout its various historical transformations, but the more important point concerns the structuring power of global capitalism and how *tianxia* discourse could articulate with earlier revolutionary movements. Up to now, *tianxia* discourse has more or less avoided both the problem of China's revolutionary legacy and the issue of capitalism and therefore has brought on the rebuke of leftist critics such as Lin. For this reason, Lin calls the *tianxia* ideal a "fantasy."[71]

In his *Philosophy of Right,* Hegel makes a similar criticism of ideals becoming mere fantasy and writes, "But however lofty, however divine, the right of thought may be, it is perverted into wrong if it is only this [opining]."[72] Zhao and *tianxia* theory clearly have to address this point. However, with respect to the issue of translating theory into practice, Marxists are in a similar situation, since it is not clear how one would realize Marxist ideals today. Consequently, we might compare Lin and *tianxia* scholars further in terms of their ideals.

Lin and the *tianxia* scholars have a common goal, namely to overthrow the present order and create a new global order that harmonizes national self-determination and global equality, justice and human flourishing. Zhao creates a philosophical plan for the future that refers primarily to premodern Chinese philosophy without much reference to the revolutionary period, while Lin connects internationalism to continuing China's revolutionary period. Mao took concrete steps to realize a world beyond global capitalism, and *tianxia* discourse could remold itself as a mode of continuing both the Chinese Revolution and Third World nationalism. Mao's revolution is a promise that has remained unfulfilled and on Lin's account has made way for a pernicious new type of globalism. Zhao's *tianxia* discourse could be reconstructed to complete the Maoist project in new conditions without being nostalgic. The debate between Confucians and Marxists could quickly dwindle into a tale of two fantasies.

To counter the charge of irrelevance, Zhao's project needs a more dynamic vision of Gan Yang's "unity of the three" (*tong san tong*) that goes beyond any of the three (Confucius, Mao, and Deng Xiaoping).[73] It has to affirm the dialectical relationship between the Confucian / premodern China, the Mao period, and the post-Mao opening to the global capitalist world. To return to the ideals of Confucius or even Mao is not to wish the return of either of these regimes, but a challenge to think the past so as to help create a new future. Gan Chunsong hints at this when he claims that *tianxia* echoes Kang Youwei's attempt to use the past for reform in an era of globalization.[74] In other words, the principles of *tianxia* and new postcapitalist global order have yet to be realized.

Zhao himself points in the direction of how to proceed to understand the conditions of realizing *tianxia* today when he approvingly speaks of Marx. He notes, "Today to belong to China is to belong to the world. This is a fact. The weight of the economy determines the weight of politics, culture and thought. Economic problems drive political, cultural and ideological problems (Marx's theory of the 'economic base' is still effective)."[75] This is an important passage that Zhao does not develop. Capital is at once political, economic, and cultural and so the question of base is perhaps gratuitous. *Tianxia* theorists must rethink both Mao and Confucianism in relation to a more expansive conception of capitalism. Capitalism provides the key to answering the Hegelian question of how one *tianxia* or a new postcapitalist world order is not merely fantasy but a process that begins in the present. Focusing on the temporal implications of his critique, Hegel warns that a work of philosophy "cannot consist in teaching the state what it ought to be."[76] At first site, such statements would appear to condemn philosophy to conservatism, but the point of such statements is to force one to think the relationship between the ideal future and the present. In our case we need to ask both why previous attempts to go beyond capitalism failed and how capitalism, in our own present, points beyond itself. Moreover, we must ask what Confucianism might contribute to such a project.

Tianxia, Communism, and the Cunning of Reason

In addition to criticizing Confucianism for being toothless against global capitalism, Lin suggests China should begin with domestic policies to show the world that it has a better model. If we were to develop Zhao's perspective, we could say that the power or teeth of Confucianism arise precisely from its conceptual framework, which advocates connection between the domestic and international order. Leading by example is one of the key principles of Confucianism, and so we can begin by responding to Lin's second criticism with a Marxist reading of the first chapter of the *Mencius*. The opening of the *Mencius* echoes Tan's chapter in this volume and deals with how domestic order should serve as a model for other states and his addresses the issue of inequality. When King Hui asks Mencius about profiting the state, Mencius responds, "What is the point of mentioning the word profit. All that matters is that there should be humanity and correct disposition." He further explains that if the ruler asks about how to profit the state and people ask about profiting their person, then "those above and those below will be trying to profit at the expense of one another and the state will be imperiled." He suggests that the logic of profit leads to an endless series, in which the poorer country will always be struggling to overcome the richer. However, the logic of humanity and correct disposition change the logic of the game and go beyond profit toward collaboration: "No man of humanity ever abandons his parents and no dutiful man ever puts his prince last."[77] Mencius here speaks of a transformation from a bad infinity where one is obsessed with competing and overcoming the other to another type of infinity, where one sees oneself in the other. From this perspective, completing oneself involves completing the other.

Once one breaks the logic of profit, a new type of politics can take place. The politics of leading by example emerges in the next paragraph when King Hui asks why his state is not more populated than others. Mencius points out that the king is again following the logic of competition and advises a paradigm shift, which involves governing effectively and thereby drawing the respect of the people and neighboring nations. Interestingly, well-governing concerns human flourishing and overcoming structural inequality. He writes:

> Now when food meant for human beings is so plentiful as to be thrown to dogs and pigs, you fail to realize that it is time for garnering, and when

men drop from starvation by the wayside, you fail to realize that it is time for distribution. When people die you simply say, "It is not my doing. It is the fault of the harvest." In what way is that different from killing a man by running him through, while saying all the time, "It is none of my doing. It is the fault of the weapon."[78]

This passage shows that poverty and inequality are not natural phenomena; they must be thought of politically, and part of this requires overcoming the logic of competition and creating the condition for mutual flourishing. Lin would counter that the Chinese Revolution did this and so any new Confucian theory is superfluous. Zhao and other *tianxia* scholars must respond to such claims and do so in a way that resituates the possibility of an alternative future, a new configuration of the one and the many at a global level, in the present.

Zhao could point out against Lin that the whole communist experience must be understood in terms of a process that it turned into something else, somewhat along the lines of what Hegel called "the cunning of reason." This is not unrelated to the concepts that Mencius and Zhao use, namely the opposition between competition and a world of humanity. In the context of capitalism, competition eventually makes possible something else. If we place the Chinese Revolution in this larger history of global capitalism, it expresses a new meaning at the beginning of the twenty-first century. Hegel explains the concept of the cunning of reason in the following manner: "But that the purpose posits itself in a mediate connection with the object, and between itself and this object inserts another object, may be regarded as the cunning of reason."[79] Seen from the twenty-first century, Mao's China plays the role of this inserted object, which aided in the realization of capitalism in China. Antonio Gramsci famously said that Lenin created a revolution against capital by creating socialism in Russia. Throughout the twentieth century, capital appeared to be having its revenge and making earlier revolutions appear like means.[80]

In wake of this transformation, we must face the larger question of how an anti-imperialist movement or any movements confronting a capitalist and imperialist world can also go beyond the global capitalist system that promotes inequality and a game of self-interested competition. How do we make the possibility of a path beyond capital concrete? How can anticapitalist movements avoid becoming engulfed in the cunning of capital? Zhao and other *tianxia* people give us a goal, but they do little to help us make the path concrete. On the other hand, Lin and others who cogently show how Mao's China was trying to build a socialist system and true internationalism have little to say about how China could continue such a path today. For that, we must return to recent interpretations of Marx that uncover the conditions of the possibility of socialism as coming out of the contradictions of capitalism. Antonio Negri, Moishe

Postone, and more recently Nick Nesbitt have each highlighted Marx's *Grundrisse* and the "Fragment on Machines" as being keys to understanding the contradictions of capitalism, along with the possibility of socialism. By focusing on this fragment, Postone and Nesbitt show how Marx's theory goes beyond mere issues of distributive justice and points to the heart of how communal life should be organized and how people can have control over the conditions that govern their lives. Marx believed that there were contradictions inherent in capitalism that pointed beyond it. These contradictions are especially relevant to Zhao's vision of *tianxia,* because he also comments on technology. He claims that a "revolution in technologies is likely to totally transform the human experience in all aspects."[81]

Drawing on a passage from Marx's *Grundrisse,* we can develop a modified version of Postone's vision of capital as the subject of history. In other words, unlike Postone, we should make a space for the potential of anti-imperialist struggles as going beyond capitalism. This requires recognizing the potential of organization both in the form of the state and in terms of social movements. Consequently, we must synthesize Postone's emphasis on the crises associated with increasing technological mediation, which we will discuss below, and Jacques Bidet's understanding of capitalism as being doubly mediated by market and organization.[82] In both theories, we confront the problem of how capitalism itself could make possible another world.

First let us turn to the problem of how competition for profit, or surplus value in Marxist terms, could lead to a qualitatively different system conducive to realizing global human flourishing, which Zhao and other *tianxia* theorists take as their goal. For this reason, the problem of capital should be a key element of what Gan Chunsong calls drawing on the past to reform the system in an era of globalization. We must underscore that the manner in which the past relates to the present and future in a world of capitalist globalization is different than in previous periods. In particular, extending Mencius to the present, we must understand profit in terms of global capitalist competition and the crises and opportunities that this entails. Marx describes these possibilities in the following controversial passage:

> Capital itself is the moving contradiction [in] that it presses to reduce labour time to a minimum, while it posits labour time, on the other side, as sole measure and source of wealth. Hence it diminishes labour time in the necessary form so as to increase it in the superfluous form; hence it posits the superfluous in growing measure as a condition—question of life and death—for the necessary. On the one side, then, it calls to life all the powers of science and of nature, as of social combination and of social intercourse in order to make the creation of wealth. On the other side, it

wants to use labour time as the sole measuring rod for the giant social forces thereby created, and to confine them within the limits required to maintain the already created value as value.[83]

The above citation might appear to be distant from the Confucian world of rituals and music or Laozi's world of the *dao*. However, if we interpret Mencius beyond his historical context, we could say that the above passage is precisely about the opposition between a world governed by profit and the creation of a new type of society of harmony and humanity. It is about moving from a world governed by quantitative unities embodied in money to a world where the one and the many dialectically respond to one another.

Before we tackle the significance of the above text, we must address briefly a basic criticism of using this passage to explicate Marx. Clearly, the *Grundrisse* is similar to a first draft and commentators such as Jacques Bidet astutely point out that there are mistakes in the language: for example, value does not measure wealth.[84] Moreover, labor-time was never really a measure of wealth but rather a measure of value. The difference between Marx and the political economists is that the latter proposed a labor theory of wealth, while Marx developed a labor theory of value. However, I believe that the passage contains a rational kernel beyond the terminological infelicities and that this kernel is continued in Marx's later works. The point is that as the composition of capital increases and labor or variable capital becomes increasingly superfluous, capitalism becomes increasingly crisis prone. Capital develops in two contradictory directions: it makes labor obsolete and yet retains labor as necessary for the creation of surplus value / profit. So the key distinction is between production of wealth and production of surplus value, which concerns wealth in the abstract, eventually represented by quantities of money. Consequently, although labor-time has never measured wealth, it does measure abstract wealth and surplus value. The "Fragment on Machines" cited above suggests that the gap between wealth and abstract wealth—as distinction between quality and quantity—becomes increasingly pronounced. This process has implications for the one-many problem that have yet to be fully explored. For example, domination of quantity over quality gives rise to a separation between the abstract one and the qualitatively different many. Zhao discusses this from the standpoint of political organization and Marx tackles this question in his "On the Jewish Question." However, in the *Grundrisse*, the abstract unity of the one works in relation to time, whose singular units are indifferent to qualitative difference. Value is measured in terms of this abstract, socially necessary labor-time and so, as this average increases with technological innovation, one needs to produce more wealth and qualitatively different things to produce the same amount of value. Before the working day was limited to eight hours, capitalists could increase surplus value by extending the amount of time that workers labored. In *Capital*, Marx argues that once the working day is fixed, capital must increase productivity and technology to create surplus value. This leads to a constant increase in fixed capital (machines and technology) in relation to variable capital (labor). In this process, labor becomes increasingly superfluous from the standpoint of producing wealth or use-values, but as long as society remains capitalist, proletarian labor remains essential for the production of surplus value, which is fundamental to capitalist society. As a result of this dynamic, the situation of workers becomes increasingly precarious as capitalism develops and unemployment or underemployment will tend to rise.

However, the above passage suggests that capitalist development opens the possibility of creating a world order beyond the capitalist globe in which social relations are not mediated by proletarian labor. It might appear that the abolition of proletarian labor and the creation of a postcapitalist society are far removed from Zhao's goal of creating a new world order, but what Marx understood was that proletarian labor sustains a capitalist system, which in turn entails precisely the game that Zhao seeks to overcome. Proletarian labor is connected to a dynamic in which capitalists pursue profit and production for their own sake, which implies a world of competition and self-interest rather than one of harmony and mutual flourishing. But the above scenario described in the *Grundrisse* shows how global competition itself might produce a way to realize a world beyond it. From this perspective, *tianxia* is not just opposed to a world of competition; rather competition, and capitalist competition in particular, creates the conditions for the realization of *tianxia*. This is of course only a possibility and one that must be realized through political action.

Conclusion

The idea that capitalist competition makes possible a new global order allows us to ground Zhao's idea of *tianxia* in our current historical moment. As we have seen, since the early 2000s, China's politics have turned toward the international realm as we see in the Belt and Road Initiative. As I mentioned in the introduction, the goal of *tianxia* overlaps with Marxism to the extent that they both seek an alternative to the contemporary global order. One could eventually continue this argument by explaining how global capitalism creates the condition for a new world order. Here Bidet's concept of world-state (*état-monde*) could be useful for *tianxia* theory because he shows how capital itself creates such a transitional state through various organs including the Global Agreement on Tariffs and Trade and the WTO. Although such transnational entities are the conditions for the possibility of the market, they represent an organizational power that is not reducible to the market. The question for the future concerns how one could capture this organizational power for other purposes. On Bidet's view, what

Marxists have up to now not understood adequately is that global socialism requires bringing both the market and organization under democratic control, and in the current crises, we might see increasing pleas for such control. This would require a struggle, which is perhaps a missing term in *tianxia* discourse. The problem is that this struggle must take place at the national, international, and popular levels. Bidet puts the question in the following way: "What type of global citizen can human beings make recognized at a global level when political decisions are only recognized by nation-states?"[85] This turns the question of *tianxia* or a new global order to one of a new type of citizen in the making, and we can add that such a citizen would be made in the process of the struggle to transform capitalism. This opens an avenue for further research, namely, how we must rethink agency and citizenship not only in *tianxia* but in the process of realizing *tianxia*. I have tried to show how *tianxia* could remake itself as continuing China's revolutionary agency, and this was always both individual and communal. Mao suggested such a revolutionary path has twists and turns, and perhaps *tianxia* theory could be part of such a trajectory of liberation.

Notes

A version of this chapter appeared in Viren Murthy, *The Politics of Time in China and Japan: Back to the Future* (London: Routledge, 2022).

1. I am speaking primarily of contemporary works. There was of course a period where Marxists dealt with Confucius from the perspective of historical materialism, and in the 1980s, scholars such as Li Zehou attempted to bring the two together. However, by the late 1990s and early 2000s, I believe we can speak of a global Confucian culture, where Marxism slipped to the background. Part of the reason for this is that while Confucians kept up with much modern political theory, they rarely engaged with recent Marxist scholarship.

2. Jacques Bidet, *État-monde: Libéralisme, socialisme et communisme à l'échelle globale* (Paris: PUF, 2011).

3. Wang Hui, *End of the Revolution: China and the Limits of Modernity* (London: Verso, 2009), pp. 50–51.

4. He Beilin, foreword to Song Qiang, Zhang Zangzang, Qiao Bian Tang Zhengyu, and Gu Qingsheng, *Zhongguo keyi shuo bu: Lengzhan hou shidai de zhengzhi yu qingganjue ze* (China can say no: Political and emotional choices in the post–Cold War era) (Beijing: Zhonghua gongshang lianhe chubanshe, 1996), p. 3. Cited in Christopher Hughes, "Reclassifying Chinese Nationalism: The Geopolitik Turn," *Journal of Contemporary China*, 20, no. 71 (September 2011): 603.

5. Shintaro Ishihara, *The Japan That Can Say No*, translated by Frank Baldwin (New York: Simon and Schuster, 1991).

6. Wang Hui, *End of the Revolution*, p. 56.

7. Wang Hui, *End of the Revolution*, p. 57.

8. Wang Hui, *End of the Revolution*, p. 57.

9. Wang Xiaodong, "Sakeji jian Dalai: Liao wu xin yi de youxi" (Sarkozy sees the Dalai: Understanding a game with no novelty), in Song Qiang, Huang Jisu, Song Xiaojun, Wang Xiaodong, and Liu Yang, *Zhongguo bu gaoxing: Dashidai da mubiao yiji women de neiyouwaihuan* (Unhappy China: A great period, great goals and our internal worries and external threats) (Jiangsu: Jiangsu renmin chubanshe, 2009), p. 164. Cited in Hughes, "Reclassifying Chinese Nationalism," p. 604.

10. Zhang Wenmu, "Sea Power and China's Strategic Choices," *China Security* (Summer 2006): 17.

11. Karl Marx, *Capital*, vol. 1, trans. Ben Fowkes (London: Penguin, 1993), p. 799.

12. We should understand that Hegel's transition from quality to quantity eventually involves concepts such as repulsion and attraction, which shows that the one simultaneously attracts and repels the other. We do not need to delve into such complexities here because it would take us into Hegel's eventual discussion of quantity and the natural sciences.

13. Zhao Tingyang, *Redefining a Philosophy for World-Governance,* trans. Liqing Tao (Singapore: Palgrave Macmillan, 2019), p. xiv.

14. Zhao Tingyang, *Tianxia tixi: Shijie zhidu zhexue daodu* (*Tianxia* system: An introduction to a philosophy of global order) (Nanjing: Nanjing jiaoyu chubanshe, 2004), pp. 13–14; my translation.

15. I would venture to say that many thinkers in classical China shared this vision of the infinite as becoming.

16. There are many interpretations of Hegel's *Logic,* but on the above topic, I have found helpful Stephen Houlgate, *The Opening of Hegel's Logic: From Being to Infinity* (West Lafayette, IN: Purdue University Press, 2005). See also Stephen Houlgate, "Hegel on the Category of Quantity," *Hegel Bulletin* 35, no. 1 (2014): 16–32.

17. G. W. F. Hegel, *The Science of Logic,* trans. George Di Giovanni (Cambridge: Cambridge University Press, 2010), p. 127 (hereafter *Logic*).

18. Hegel has another step before this: namely, because the infinite implies a process with moments, there must here also be structure of being-for-one, which simply means being a moment of something. But when dealing with the infinite, there cannot be a simple thing of which being for one could be a moment, and so being for one must be a moment of being for self. Through this process being for self turns into a moment and becomes identical to being for one. The infinite at this point is in the relation and between the two moments, each a being for one passing into the other. Hegel departs from Kant, where being-for-one remains as an in-itself, while being-for-self is understood as self-consciousness. Hegel shows how being-for-one becomes identical with being-for-itself and this becomes the one, which is a mode of being-for-itself, but as an abstract limit and a self-relating negation.

19. Hegel, *Logic,* p. 133.

20. Hegel, *Logic,* p. 133.

21. Hegel, *Logic,* p. 134.

22. Hegel, *Logic,* p. 136. We should note that at this point the various ones are "presupposed, posited as non-posited; their being-posited is sublated, they are existents with respect to each other such as refer only to themselves" (Hegel, *Logic,* p. 136). So the various ones will appear independent even though they are fundamentally connected.

23. Ch'en Ku-ying, *Lao Tzu: Text, Notes and Comments,* trans. Roger T. Ames and Rhett Y. W. Young (Beijing: Chinese Materials Center, 1981), p. 201.

24. Ch'en, *Lao Tzu,* p. 207.

25. Ch'en, *Lao Tzu,* p. 100. Ames and Young translate *yi* as "one entity," but literally *yi* only means "one."

26. Ch'en, *Lao Tzu,* p. 130.

27. Ch'en, *Lao Tzu,* p. 131.

28. Ch'en, *Lao Tzu,* p. 58.

29. Ch'en, *Lao Tzu,* p. 201.

30. Hegel, *Logic,* p. 81.

31. Ch'en, *Lao Tzu,* p. 207n2.

32. Ch'en, *Lao Tzu,* p. 207.

33. Ch'en, *Lao Tzu,* p. 207, translation amended by the author.

34. See G. W. F. Hegel, *The Philosophy of History* (New York: Dover, 1956), p. 255. Hegel writes, "It must also be remarked, thirdly, that such democratic constitutions are possible only in small states—states which do not much exceed the compass of cities.... The living together in one city, the fact that the inhabitants see each other daily, render a common culture and a living democracy possible. In Democracy, the main point is that the character of the citizen be plastic, all of a piece." He further diagnoses a problem that Dewey would see much later in *The Public and Its Problems.* Hegel continues: "In a large empire a general inquiry might be made, votes might be gathered in several communities, and the results reckoned up—as was done by the French Constitution. But a political existence of this kind is destitute of life, and the World is ipso facto broken into fragments and dissipated into a mere Paper-world" (Hegel, *Philosophy of History,* pp. 255–256).

35. John Dewey, *The Public and Its Problems* (Athens: Ohio University Press, 1954).

36. Zhao, *Redefining a Philosophy for World-Governance,* p. 9.

37. Zhao, *Redefining Philosophy for World-Governance,* p. 10.

38. Zhao, *Redefining Philosophy for World-Governance,* p. 6.

39. Fukuzawa Yukichi, *An Outline of a Theory of Civilization,* trans. David A. Dilworth (New York: Columbia University Press, 2008, 29); Fukuzawa Yukichi, *Bunmeiron no gairyaku* (Outline of a theory of civilization) (Tokyo: Iwanami bunko, 2004), p. 40.

40. The Japanese political theorist Maruyama Masao follows this line of argument to claim that there was a space of openness in both ancient China and the shogunal system, but adds that during the Meiji, Japan also gave up this separation, by uniting the state under the emperor. Maruyama Masao, *Bunmeiron no gairyaku wo yomu* (Reading *An Outline of the Theory of Civilization*), vol. 1 (Tokyo: Iwanami bunko, 2007), p. 158. Indeed, Maruyama points out that during World War II, it is precisely the future that Fukuzawa feared that happened. Fukuzawa wrote, "But if today, as some imperial way scholars would have it, the people were to be set under a ruler who united in himself both political and religious functions, the future of Japan would be very different. We Japanese are fortunate that things have turned out the way that they have." Fukuzawa, *Outline,* p. 29; Maruyama, *Bunmeiron,* p. 40.

41. Fukuzawa, *Outline,* pp. 32–33; Maruyama, *Bunmeiron,* pp. 44–45.

42. Nishida Kitarō, "Nihon bunka no mondai" (The problem of Japanese culture), in *Nishida Kitaro Zenshu* (The complete works of Nishida Kitarō) (Tokyo: Iwanami shoten,

1980), vol. 12, p. 335; Hiromatsu Wataru, *Kindai no chokoku ron: Showa shisoshi yeno yichi shikaku* (On overcoming modernity: A perspective of Showa intellectual history) (Tokyo: Kodansha gakujutsu bunko, 1989), p. 207.

43. See Tsung-hsi Huang (Huang Zongxi), *Waiting for the Dawn: A Plan for the Prince*, trans. Theodore de Bary (New York: Columbia University Press, 1993).

44. Indeed, this is one of the reasons that in Meiji Japan, the government and officials did not want to translate many Confucian texts such as the *Mencius,* since they claimed that they could incite revolution.

45. Cited from Zhao, *Redefining a Philosophy for World-Governance,* p. 13.

46. Zhao, *Redefining Philosophy for World-Governance,* p. 17.

47. Zhao, *Redefining Philosophy for World-Governance,* p. 22.

48. Lucian W. Pye, "International Relations in Asia: Culture, Nation and State" (Sigur Center for Asian Studies, George Washington University, Washington, DC, June 1998), p. 9.

49. Zhao, *Redefining a Philosophy for World-Governance,* p. 32.

50. Mizoguchi Yūzō, *Hōhō to shite no chūgoku* (China as method) (Tokyo: Tokyo daigaku shuppansha, 1989).

51. Zhao, *Redefining a Philosophy for World-Governance,* pp. 22–23.

52. Zhao, *Tianxia tixi,* p. 14.

53. Zhao, *Redefining a Philosophy for World-Governance,* pp. 35–36.

54. Zhao, *Redefining a Philosophy for World-Governance,* p. 24.

55. Zhao, *Redefining a Philosophy for World-Governance,* p. 24.

56. For a discussion see Judd Kinzley, *Natural Resources and the New Frontier: Constructing China's Borderlands* (Chicago: University of Chicago Press, 2020), esp. chapter 8.

57. Zhao, *Redefining a Philosophy for World-Governance,* p. 26.

58. Zhao, *Redefining a Philosophy for World-Governance,* p. 29.

59. Sor-hoon Tan, "Nationalistic Guo, Cosmopolitan Tianxia? Possibility of World Order Based on Confucian Relational Ethics," in *Reimagining Nation and Nationalism in Multicultural East Asia,* ed. Kim Sungmoon and Hsin-Wen Lee (New York: Routledge, 2017), pp. 64–65.

60. Tan, "Nationalistic Guo, Cosmopolitan Tianxia?," p. 71.

61. Karatani Kojin, *The Structure of World History: From Modes of Production to Modes of Exchange* (Durham, NC: Duke University Press, 2014).

62. Tan, "Nationalistic Guo, Cosmopolitan Tianxia?," p. 73.

63. Bidet, *État-Monde,* p. 258.

64. For a discussion of how various nations defended imperialism at the United Nations, see Jessica Lynn Pearson, "Defending Empire at the United Nations: The Politics of International Oversight in the Era of Decolonization," *Journal of Imperial and Commonwealth History* 45, no. 3 (2017): 525–549.

65. Zhao Tingyang, *All under Heaven: The Tianxia System for a Possible World Order,* trans. Joseph E. Harroff (Berkeley: University of California Press, 2021), p. 189.

66. Zhao, *All under Heaven,* p. 190.

67. Sam Gindin and Leo Panitch, *The Making of Global Capitalism: The Political Economy of American Empire* (London: Verso, 2012).

68. Zhao, *All under Heaven,* p. 233.

69. Lin Chun, "China's New Globalism," *Socialist Register* 55 (2019): 152.
70. Lin, "China's New Globalism," pp. 162, 163.
71. Lin, "China's New Globalism," p. 162.
72. G. W. F. Hegel, *Philosophy of Right,* trans. with notes by T. M. Knox (Oxford: Oxford University Press, 1952), p. 4.
73. Gan Yang, *Tong san tong* (Uniting the three) (Beijing: Sanlian chubanshe, 2014).
74. Gan Chunsong, *Zhidu ruxue* (Institutional Confucianism) (Beijing: Zhongyang bianyiju, 2017), p. 96.
75. Zhao, *Tianxia tixi,* p. 2.
76. Hegel, *Philosophy of Right,* p. 11.
77. Mencius, *Mencius,* trans, D. C. Lau (London: Penguin, 1988), p. 49; Mengzi, *Mengzi yizhu* (Mencius with notes), ed. Yang Bojun (Beijing: Zhonghua shuju, 1996), p. 1.
78. Mencius, *Mencius,* p. 52; Mengzi, *Mengzi Yizhu,* p. 5.
79. Hegel, *Logic,* p. 663.
80. I first heard this idea of the "revenge of capital" from Moishe Postone in 2011 in Beijing at the conference entitled "Rethinking Twentieth Century China," University of Chicago–Beijing Center.
81. Zhao, *All under Heaven,* p. 224.
82. Such a synthesis of course goes beyond the scope of this chapter and I hope to devote another paper to this topic.
83. Karl Marx, *Grundrisse,* trans. Martin Nicolaus (London: Penguin, 1993), p. 706.
84. Jacques Bidet invited Moishe Postone to Paris and, after his talk, wrote him a detailed letter (dated 2008) on precisely this point. I thank Jacques Bidet for showing this letter to me.
85. Bidet, *État-monde,* p. 263.

PART II

From Nation-States to a Relational Ecology

CHAPTER 6

Why Does *Tianxia* Need a Nation-State?
Nation and *Tianxia* in Modern China

Ban WANG

THINKERS WITH *TIANXIA* outlooks often view the Western nation-state as a major roadblock to world peace. In his *Datong shu* 大同書 (Book of great community), Kang Youwei identified the state as the culprit for war, chaos, and misery in the past and the present. Bent on the expansion of power and conquest of territory, both ancient warring states or belligerent modern nation-states are aggressive and self-serving. In order to achieve world peace and unity, Kang wrote, the warring nations should make treaties for disarmament, erase their borders, and ultimately abolish the nation-state.[1] Liang Qichao, however, disagreed with the view of his mentor and deemed it unrealistic and impossible to abolish nation-states, especially in a time when China was besieged by Western powers. Liang confronted and engaged the Western-style nation-state and sought to bring elements of *tianxia* 天下 into a broader definition of nation-state.

Hence the idea of a cosmopolitan state. While he traveled in Europe in 1919 and observed modern ways of life, Liang had an opportunity to observe the Paris Peace Conference. What intrigued him most was the cosmopolitan idea that motivated the League of Nations. Having done homework about the leading figures (US president Woodrow Wilson, French prime minister Georges Clemenceau, and UK prime minister David Lloyd George) and inspired by the league's peace-making initiatives, Liang contemplated the prospect of the "cosmopolitan state" (*shijiezhuyi de guojia* 世界主義的國家). In a section in his essay "My Travel Impressions in Europe" (*Ouyou xinying lu* 歐游心影錄), Liang notes that the league's peace-making efforts resonate with the ancient Chinese *tianxia* vision. Sober minded about the disruptive tendency of major Western nations, Liang felt that as long as geopolitical rivalry drives interstate relations, the nation-state stands as the major barrier to world peace. China was barred from being a player in the decision-making procedures of the world organization. For all its cosmopolitan wisdom of *tianxia,* the country had no voice in interstate negotiations. All major powers were eyeing China's vast territory, markets, and natural resources. To count on the powerful nations to recognize China and look after its interest was a dangerous illusion.[2]

But silver linings were on the horizon. To Liang, the initiatives of the League of Nations heralded the stirring of an aspiration that might "reconcile cosmopolitanism and nation-state" (*shijiezhuyi he guojiazhuyi de tiaohe* 世界主義和國家主義的調和). Premised on the reciprocity and cooperation of nation-states, cosmopolitanism was discussed and explored at the peace conference. The peace-making procedures presumed that the state's sovereignty is not absolute and must be curbed and regulated by forces beyond nation-states through networking and negotiation. The vision of the cosmopolitan state could launch nation-states on the way to a cosmopolitan world. At present the nation-state is the major cause of interstate rivalry and colonial wars. In such a conflicted world, individuals and communities are left to fend for themselves and have to find shelter in the bosom of a nation. It is thus natural, legitimate, and even imperative to promote nationalism and to foster patriotic feelings. But one cannot love one's nation, Liang cautions, in a "style of thought that is obstinate, narrow-minded, and old fashioned." We cannot just favor our own country without considering individuals; nor can we merely appreciate our nation without understanding the world. "Under the protection of one's nation, we will each fulfill our innate potential and make great contributions to the world and human civilization."[3]

Nation-building is indeed necessary for China, and the nation-state paves the way toward the cosmopolitan state. Liang's trajectory entails a notion of nation-state that is not self-interested, narrow-minded, and parochial but envisages a planetary ethic. The journey progresses in a spiral from the individual to the family to the nation-state, culminating in a cooperative and unified world. Drawing on the Confucian doctrine of "cultivate the self, order family ties, govern the country, and bring peace to All-under-Heaven" (*xiushen qijia zhiguo ping tianxia* 修身齊家治國平天下), Liang describes a self that is not self-serving but sociable, and a nation-state that is not aggressive but a team player:

> The ultimate aim of an individual's life is to make contribution to humanity as a whole. Why? The reason is that humanity as a whole is the upper limit of the self. If you want to develop yourself, you need to move in that direction. Why must the state exist? The reason is that with a state, it is easier to rally the cultural power of a national group, to perpetuate and

grow it so that a country will be able to contribute to humanity as a whole and help the world grow as well. Building a state is thus a means of advancing humanity, just as the coordination of a municipal government with self-governing local regions is a means of building a state. In this light, individuals should not rest content with making their own country wealthy and powerful but should instead make their nation an addition to humanity. Otherwise the nation-state is built to no purpose.[4]

Liang's cosmopolitan state was a recurrent theme among modern Chinese thinkers, who sought to engage and overcome the nation-state while looking forward to a world community à la *tianxia*. From Kang Youwei and Liang Qichao to Li Dazhao and Mao Zedong, thinkers engaged and worked through the nation-state by enfolding it within their world visions.

In 1944, Luo Mengce, a high-ranking official of the Guomindang, published a book titled *On China* (*Zhongguo lun* 中國論) from his lecture notes. Luo proposed a self-understanding of China in terms of a *tianxia* state. China's impending victory in the War of Anti-Japanese Invasion and its diplomatic gains in the abolition of extraterritoriality of the Western powers caused fears of the country as being a rising imperialist power or an old-fashioned oriental empire. Refuting these views, Luo insisted that China is not a regular nation-state. Neither is it an imperialist, colonialist power, or an oriental empire. China's political identity is derived from the *tianxia* system, and it should be defined as a *tianxia* state. As a *tianxia* state, China should not remain complacent with its age-old, premodern empire; rather, Chinese leaders and people must reform and transform the country into a modern nation-state. The new Chinese nation should stress "national consciousness and state thinking" and push for national sovereignty, industrialization, and modernization in order to become a *tianxia* state. Such a state would be ready and willing to make contributions to the world at large.[5] Luo's combined *tianxia* and nation-state echoed Sun Zhongshan's claim that China should establish itself as a sovereign nation-state before it extended a helping hand to other colonized countries in pursuit of cosmopolitan ideals.[6]

In a much-quoted passage in *Reflections on the French Revolution*, Edmund Burke argued that "to be attached to the subdivision, to love the little platoon we belong to in society, is the first principle (the germ as it were) of public affections. It is the first link in the series by which we proceed towards a love to our country, and to mankind."[7] While the nation-state seems to rise from the little platoon of local communities and next of kin, it is a stage in a moral trajectory toward human unity. In his *Tianxia System* (*Tianxia tixi* 天下體系), Zhao Tingyang made a similar observation that Western political priorities are arranged in the order of "the individual—community—nation-state," with the nation-state as the ultimate threshold of politics and legality. In reverse, the Chinese vision runs the series of "*tianxia*—state—family," with *tianxia* as the top priority of political thinking.⁸

Writers of *tianxia* and cosmopolitanism, in refuting the flawed concept of nation-state, tend to ignore or bypass its republican politics and popular constitution. Liang, often seen as a staunch nationalist thinker, bestowed much thought on the Western-style nation-state. With the long tradition of *tianxia* behind him, Liang sought to find a way to work through the nation-state and transcend it. To him the nation-state was both a scourge and an opportunity. On the one hand, it was a scourge because it was the prime source of world conflict and anarchy. At the turn of the twentieth century, the major colonial nation-states were aggressively carving up China, bent on controlling its markets, pillaging its resources, and taking its lands. This imperialist and colonial tendency seemed endemic to the expansionist behavior of the nation-state's economic system, which Liang called "nationalist imperialism of great powers" (*lieqiang de minzu diguozhuyi* 列強的民族帝國主義). Imperial China was caught up in this maelstrom of imperialist-nationalist expansion and its survival was in grave danger. On the other hand, Liang recognized the inner political strength and popular power fundamental to the Western nation-state. The beauty of the Western national institution was its self-rule, popular sovereignty, and solidarity, which China must emulate. "Unless we pool together the strength of our nation and foster our own nationalism, China has no way to resist Western nationalist expansion," declared Liang. The nation-state presented a great opportunity and a role model. An open-minded national republic, based on self-rule, popular sovereignty, and an enlightened citizenry, offered an indispensable means for China to survive in the forest of nations.⁹

The vision of *tianxia* entails a cosmopolitan ethic, whereas the nation-state pledges a parochial allegiance to one's own particular community. The question is how to reconcile *tianxia* with the nation-state. The idea of the *tianxia* state concerns whether one's membership in a national community can align with the particular obligations and belonging of family and kin. What are the merit and virtue of the nation-state to a *tianxia* realm based on culture, reciprocity, and cooperation? I will show how Liang Qichao, Sun Zhongshan, and Mao Zedong squared the nation-state with *tianxia* in creating the national-international nexus for modern China.

Reconciling Private Morality with Public Morality

As the Western powers encroached on China in the late nineteenth century, Chinese intellectuals perceived the nation-state as a menace and danger. Kang Youwei's explicit judgments gave valence to Liang's indictment of narrow-minded, self-serving nationalism. Kang listed the nation-state's moral flaws, its crimes against humanity, and its menace to world peace. The belligerent nation-states bring about calamities of war, grind people down, and cause huge waste and bloodshed. Poisoned by narrow-minded patriotism, "Everyone looks to the advantage of his own state and aggresses against other states." Large states fight wars to swallow up a small one, causing no end of calamity and bloodshed. Nation-states constantly fight over land and cities, and "people are trained to be soldiers." The death toll of one single battle amounts to thousands and tens of thousands. "When selfishness and strife bring people to such a pass, how can one but admit that it is due to the fact of existing, sovereign states." Narrow-minded, brutal patriotism has its own perverse morality and honor. The nationalist elites "cannot help but be partial each to his own state." Patriots are "fixated upon and limited to their own state"; "they consider fighting for territory and killing other people to be an important duty and great accomplishment."[10]

The term "narrow-minded patriotism" occurs frequently in Kang and Liang, referring to the expansionist, self-interested, and self-aggrandizing Western nation-states in their colonial encroachment into China. Later, in the War of Anti-Japanese Invasion, Mao used "narrow-minded patriotism" (*xia'ai aiguo zhuyi* 狹隘愛國主義) to describe both the loyalty of Japanese soldiers to the imperialist mandate and the chauvinism of the Guomindang that privileged the ruling elites at the cost of Chinese territories and populations. Powerful, lethal, greedy, and out to colonize lands and populations, the nation-state appeared to Liang as an alien political entity antithetical to the *tianxia* vision. The modern aggressive nation-states recalled the brutal conflict of belligerent kingdoms in the Spring and Autumn and Warring States eras. In those proto-nation-state conditions, geographical barriers and local inhabitants separated groups and kingdoms, and ambitious states rivaled and fought with each other in grabbing land, amassing populations, and plundering resources. This situation was a fertile ground for the kings and their advisors to preoccupy themselves with statecraft and state building. As a result, "state thinking" (*guojia sixiang* 國家思想) prevailed. State builders and advisors were recruited and eagerly sought after.[11] But state thinking was contested by Confucian political thought. The *Spring and Autumn Annals* proposed the *tianxia* order as a solution to interstate rivalry. *Tianxia* aimed to break down the boundaries of states, rallying all states under one ruler and, through normative values and universal civilization, realizing peace in the world (*yiwen zhi taiping* 以文至太平).

> Since the birth of Chinese civilization, Chinese have always refused to recognize the nation-state to be the highest form of human community. Chinese political philosophy frequently takes the whole of humanity as its end. Its goal is to pacify all multitudes and to preserve peace, safety, and

stability for all under heaven. The state, incidentally, like family and kinship, is only a stage toward the formation of *tianxia*. China's political culture has tended to preoccupy itself not merely with a particular region or a specific group in the world of humans. Chinese political thought deems this type of [nation-state] politics unnecessary, because the state just seeks unity and solidarity within one community and expresses antagonism toward the outsiders.[12]

The modern nation-state, however, could not be ignored. Liang weighed the pros and cons of the nation-state as a political entity. European nation-states stem from the political community of the city-state. National ideology promotes inner unity and core values within the communities, but national strength thrives on antagonism toward outsiders. It appeals to human distrust and hatred, and draws boundaries between us and them.[13] Liang's analysis echoes a concept of nationalism rooted in a primordial belonging and particular allegiance. Comparing *tianxia* with the nation-state, Liang suggests that *tianxia* is a politically weak concept, whereas the nation-state provides a strong institution. The latter, endowed with autonomy, ethnic coherence, solidarity, and the capacity for self-defense, was what China sorely lacked and badly needed. For centuries, the state thinking of the Warring States era had given way to a complacent *tianxia* mentality under the imperial mode of governance. Absent state thinking, *tianxia* cannot foster the cohesion of a race and has no potential to build a tightly knit political community. Liang's famous lament, that for millennia Chinese knew only *tianxia* and have no sense of nation-state, calls into question *tianxia* as something outdated and as a sign of China's vulnerabilities and crises.[14] A *tianxia* regime is unfit for the modern interstate world, unable to pull the population together for self-defense, and is at risk of being wiped out from the world map. It stands as the barrier to regaining China's strength in interstate competition.

Under the threat of colonialism and imperialism, China badly needed a form of nation-state. "To resist the imperialism of the major nation-states and to prevent calamity and save lives, we must implement policies of the nation-state," Liang writes.[15] The nation-state is a desirable trend embraced by all peoples in the world and is an important modern institution. Teetering on the brink of collapse, China's millennial political culture must draw strength and inspiration from the nation-state. The world has become a world of nation-states, and to enter and join the world you need to stand up with and match other nations with strength and sovereignty: nation-building is the ticket to the arena of nations.

In *Discourse on the New People* (*Xinmin shuo* 新民說), Liang defines the nation as "a people who share the same ethnicity, language, religion, and custom and regard each other as blood kin. They strive to achieve independence and self-rule and establish a comprehensive government in order to serve public goods and to ward off foreign rules."[16] The first part of this definition reveals an understanding of nationalism in terms of primordial roots and embeddedness in family and kinship relations, echoing Burke's "little platoon" as well as the apolitical, nonnational nature of *tianxia*. Under *tianxia*, Chinese only have obligations to their family and allegiance to their kin, village, and region. This circle of identification and belonging, ironically, resembles the primordial definition of nationalism and fits the bill of cultural, ethnic, prepolitical nationalism. It confirms the "narrow-mindedness" that Kang and Liang associated with the selfishness, inwardness, blood ties, and antagonism of the Western nation-states. Linking selfishness to private morality and self-seeking communities, Liang suggests that just as private morality undermines public space, the self-serving nation-states tear the world apart. In their refusal to take the world as a larger whole, the Western nation-states treat it as an empty space up for grabs—open to free completion, occupation, and annexation. The world is fragmented and torn apart: it is but an arena of struggle and competition among selfish colonialist and imperialist powers.

The second part of Liang's definition contains a political dimension: the creativity and empowerment of the nation-state. As a republic, the nation-state does not have to be a natural outgrowth from primordial and prenational roots. Although it may inherit ancient roots, a national formation must take the primordial kinship and blood relations to a higher political plane. Building a nation-state entails a transformation of its cultural tradition and an updating of primordial, prepolitical allegiance, elevating these historical givens onto the imagined community and solidarity. This insight hints at the creative and genuinely political aspect of nation-building. The prior historical, cultural, and ethnic relations can be carried over and updated into modern relationships among members of modern society, nationals and citizens. The people, though hailing from disparate villages, ethnicities, and families, must strive to build a government of their own and pursue common goods. National citizens must go beyond their primordial relations, forge new associations and alliances, and make a contribution to the commonweal. The nationals are political actors, and instead of being passive recipients of past heritages and traditions, they participate in building a new political community with independent spirit.

According to Liang, the Chinese should foster the public ethos and citizenship of a nation-state, but rather than rejecting *tianxia*, the new nation is to fulfill *tianxia*'s potentials at both national and international levels. The *tianxia* ethic seems alien to the ethos of a national republic, because it is confined to private, personal, and kinship attachments captured by the term *si* 私. Under *si*, one's love and obligation are toward the nearest kin and personal relations governed by traditional hierarchies. This morality has made Chinese politically apathetic and unaware of themselves as constituents of a political community. The empire has survived for ages without a tight unity, solidarity, and territorial integrity. The loosely governed *tianxia* order contrasts sharply with the cohesiveness of a national body politic. Far from a world of unity and autonomy, *tianxia* looks like a natural landscape, an extensive empire with mixed ethnicities, a decentered condition for the economic and social reproduction of life, and a society where ordinary men and women are born, live, and die within families, villages, and communities. Everyone is an individual with particularistic ties to their next of kin. *Tianxia,* in short, refers to a world of particular, unconnected communities marked by disparate and diverse pursuits of livelihood and interests. In the face of assaults by colonial nation-states, the system's vulnerability and fragility became self-evident. The absence of national cohesiveness and solidarity is what prompted Sun Zhongshan to deplore Chinese as "a slate of loose sands." On the other hand, state thinking became desirable and imperative.

The most essential element of national consciousness is an ethic that Liang calls *gongde* 公德 (public morality). Public morality is opposed to *side* 私德 (private morality). A legacy of *tianxia,* private morality is concerned with the individual's moral integrity and is attainable through a program of self-cultivation. The self of private morality is disengaged from public affairs and is unconcerned with the common good. The most pernicious form of private morality is manifest in the single-minded pursuit of private interest and profit, eroding and destroying public space. By contrast, public morality insists on commitment, service, and devotion to the common good, upholding a reciprocal relationship between the individual and the collective.

Private morality undermines common goods and leads to political decay. In imperial administration, private morality fosters corrupt behavior rooted in a relationship of patronage and favors, leading to what Francis Fukuyama calls the "tyranny of cousins." Private pursuits regulate "a reciprocal exchange of favors between two individuals of different status and power, usually involving favors given by a patron to the client in exchange for the client's loyalty and political support."[17] In the governance of empire, the emperor and his ministers are supposed to relate to each other under a broad mandate of civil service and public administration. But this "public" arena frequently degenerates into a private exchange of personal favors and benefits as if among families and kin. Yet an empire, Liang asserts, is by "no means an exclusive property at the disposal of the emperor and his subjects" (*fei junchen suo neng zhuanyou* 非君臣所能專有). If the political order runs on private morality through the swapping of benefits and advantages, politics is reduced to a trade-off between two private persons and has nothing to do with the totality of common goods.[18] Political institutions decay into an exchange between two self-serving individuals at the expense of public resources and well-being. If *tianxia* governance is about caring and providing for all people, private dealings are nothing short of stealing from the commonweal.

Self-interest at the expense of public affairs has corrupted morality and poisoned human relations. The phrase *jia tianxia* 家天下 (privatizing the whole world under Heaven) denotes the way emperors and nobles treated all the lands and population as their own family estates. When private morality prevails, the Chinese are unconcerned about common interests beyond their local attachments. The contrast between private and public morality prompts Liang to lament that Chinese, accustomed to *tianxia,* know nothing about *guojia* 國家 (nation-state), and though attached to family, kin, and local community, they have no sense of themselves as a political community.[19]

Here is a paradox. By associating private morality with *tianxia,* Liang is suggesting that *tianxia* has no way of fostering a public ethos and is far from a universal order. This claim calls into question the familiar consensus about *tianxia*'s universality and inclusivity. Most accounts of *tianxia* view it as a governing principle based on a broad public morality in terms of *gong* 公, which is the source of legitimate sociopolitical order for all multitudes under Heaven. The moral foundation of *tianxia* makes sense only under the rubric of *gong*. *Gong* has two meanings. The first is that all people under Heaven are the most important resources and the care of their well-being and needs is the criterion for good government. The second meaning is that whoever presides over and maintains the order is not supposed to take possession of the land and territories for his private enjoyment but to carry the mandate of Heaven by winning the hearts and minds of all people. *Tianxia,* in its ideal form, attracts people to the benevolent king, unites them under one order, and rallies them under one system of values. This sweeping capacity and goodness is the essence of the word *de* 德 (morality or virtue), which could be translated as "political morality." According to Xun Zi, whoever loses the state loses people, but whoever gains people's support will achieve a good political order. "When you have *de,* you have the support of people, you would have lands, wealth, and have many uses." In this light, the *tianxia* order describes the unity of all people (*wanmin* 萬民) across the realm, far and near, under *dezheng* 德政—-the moral-political order.[20]

Gong denotes a form of publicness. Frederic Wakeman translated *tianxia weigong* 天下為公 into "render public all under heaven" and "commonweal."[21] The crucial question is, how does Liang insert *gong* into the public space of a modern nation-state? *Gong* is the most prominent concept in the canonical statement of *tianxia* in *Records of Rites* (禮記), a work of Confucianism compiled during the Han dynasty (206 BCE–220 CE):

> When the Great Way was practiced, the world was shared by all alike (大道之行，天下為公). The worthy and the able were promoted to office and men practiced good faith and lived in harmony. Therefore they did not regard as parents only their own parents, or as sons only their own sons. The aged were cared for till the end of their lives, the able-bodied pursued proper employment, while the young were nurtured in growing up. Provisions were made to care for widows, the orphaned, and the sick. Men had their tasks while women had their hearths. They hated to see goods lying about in waste, yet they did not hoard them for themselves; they disliked the thought that their energies were not fully used, yet they used them not for private ends. Therefore all evil plotting was prevented and thieves and rebels did not arise, so that people could leave their outer gates unbolted. This was the age of Great Harmony.[22]

Gong has been taken to mean All-under-Heaven, commonweal, common good, world community, and a broad public space of equity. The term projects a broad commitment and fealty beyond personal, family, and kinship ties. In its emotional outreach, mutual care, and universal benevolence, *gong* looks very much like civic virtue and mutual empathy in a modern citizenry. It envisages a society in which all have their interests cared for and are as ready to empathize with others as they do with family and kin.

This moral capacity resonates with Jean-Jacques Rousseau's ideas of civic virtue and citizenship. Civic virtue describes, as Terry Eagleton reminds us, a citizen's "passionate affection for his fellow citizens and for the shared conditions of their common life." It is about the pity we feel for each other or for animals in trouble. Citizens are able to project "a kind of empathetic imagination" that "enables us to transport ourselves outside ourselves, identify with suffering humans and animals."[23] In the *Records of Rites* passage, loving one's parents is a less desirable form of private morality, but the capacity to extend love to others' parents is part of *gong*, public morality. It is in this extension of private attachment to a broad sympathy that prompts Liang to say that "private morality is by nature not incompatible with public morality (私德公德，本並行不悖也)."[24] Filial piety, gratitude, and duty are the essence of private morality, but these virtues can be cultivated and expanded into a citizen's obligation to the national community. Just as we owe our parents our life, so we owe our political community our well-being, identity, and protection. Private morality and public morality are intertwined as two sites of one coin. Initially embedded in primordial kinship ties, private morality is broadened into a citizen's virtue (*minde* 民德) and the public ethos of a nation. We remember that *minde* is the first element in Liang's account of the trinity of national strength: *minde, minzhi* (民智 "people's intelligence"), and *minli* (民力 "people's sovereignty").

Hence an updated *tianxia* reconciled with public morality is essential to a national community. The *tianixa* state begins with the intimate ties of family and kin but reaches beyond them to a broad moral and social horizon. In carrying over from private to public morality, it treats all people as members of one family and gives equal care to all. The patrimonial exchange and pursuits of private interests are frowned on. The "modernity" of *tianxia* lies in a broad extension of private bonds to public morality and to civic virtue, which is extendable to a cosmopolitan ethos.

For all its desired harmony, empathy, reciprocity, and care for the commonweal, the ancient *tianxia* order lacked a politically integrative power, popular constitution, representative mechanism, national economy, military, and legal system—the essential features of the nation-state. It is true that *tianxia* was concerned with all people under Heaven and showered benevolence from the top down, and wise emperors such as Yao and Shun were wise and capable leaders. They worked hard to serve the people with benevolence and treated the whole empire as a commons shared by all.[25] The sage king was manifest in the policy of *yangmin* (養民), which means fostering people's morality and caring for their well-being and needs. Under the Kingly Way (*wangdao* 王道) as opposed to "the overbearing way" (*badao* 霸道), *tianxia* describes the way in which the wise king inculcates people with moral ideas and correct behavior. But this paternalist order runs counter to the popular sovereignty of a modern nation: it leaves people with little room for initiative, agency, and participation. Pointing to this glaring lack, Liang comments that the ancient mode of governance was "for the people and of the people," but not "by the people."[26] To update and modernize *tianxia* requires enabling the people to build their own society and to govern themselves. Individuals, through their self-directed moral reform, will educate themselves and become equipped with public morality. Instead of the Kingly Way showering benevolence, governance by the "public" means delegating self-education to the people themselves so that they become citizens of a modern nation. In this argument, the notion of popular sovereignty replaces and supersedes *tianxia*'s paternalistic and universal care of multitudes.

If a national people can build a nation-state with a broad public ethos, the Chinese nation would be on the way to the *tianxia* state. Particularistic obligation and allegiance can grow and become open-minded: moral sentiments would spiral out from one's family to other families, from one's village to the nation, and from the nation to other nations. Although this moral outreach starts from private entities, the journey traverses them as a stage toward the broadest goal of *tianxia*. *Tianxia* politics does not only work on behalf of a nation's interest and security. It goes on to serve the interests and peace of the whole world. Young people in the open-minded republic would be able to value Chinese traditions as well as learn from and respect all other traditions. China must learn from the West and synthesize all precious cultural elements to create a world culture. This is how China as a national republic would make contributions to a world community.²⁷

Sun Zhongshan: Nationalism Is the Basis for World Unity

Liang's concept of the *tianxia* state anticipates Sun's broad-minded nationalism. Japanese scholar Mizoguchi Yūzō suggested that Sun's vision of the Chinese nation-state, indebted to the *tianxia* tradition of morality and peace, radically departs from Japan's model.²⁸ One special feature of Sun's vision involves the care of *shengmin* 生民, meaning lives and livelihood of ordinary men and women, their rights to economic well-being and equality as well as political independence.

With the mission of toppling the Manchu rule and resisting colonialism, Sun took Liang's "state thinking" more seriously. Recognizing the key concept of national self-determination advocated by Woodrow Wilson, he saw an opportunity in that principle for the colonized to emancipate themselves from colonial powers and achieve independence. Of his three key principles for saving China, nationalism goes first. The principle of national self-determination, though manipulated by the League of Nations, would enable China to resist the great powers that dominated the international order. Although Wilson advocated national self-determination for remaking the world order, the Paris Peace Conference turned out to be a betrayal of that principle. The major powers simply redistributed their war spoils, redrew boundaries, and remapped spheres of influence.

To resist colonialism, Sun called for recovering national sentiments, which deepens Liang's "state thinking." To achieve national strength and unity, the Chinese could resort to historical kinship, clan, and family relations and treat them as stepping-stones to a higher end. Particular groups, blood ties, native place and belonging, and emotional linkages could be broadened to rally diverse populations for national unification. Instead of being impediments to national cohesion, these primordial relations provide an enabling condition for fragmented communities and diverse ethnicities to rally themselves into a nation. "Family relations (*zongzu* 宗族) can be extended to become the relation of nationality."²⁹ Beginning with family loyalty, one moves to clan loyalty and finally extends to national loyalty, knitting together small groups into a large national group. In the past, one's loyalty was due to kings, but a modern nation-state cannot dispense with a deep sense of loyalty. Instead of monarchs, modern loyalty should be attached to the country, and more importantly to the people.³⁰

Sun's reading of *gong* in the *Records of Rites* text echoes Liang's invocation of people's power by putting popular sovereignty into the mouths of Confucius and Mencius, who somehow understood people's rights and power. "The statement 'When the Great Way was practiced, the world was shared by all' was a plea for a great community of *datong* ruled by the people's power," proclaimed Sun.³¹ *Tianxia* politics is "the affairs of multitudes and governing means the people running governmental affairs."³² To Sun, strife among monarchies for hegemony was the main source of war and chaos. But a peaceful *tianxia* world would arise from a modern democracy. "After the founding of a republic, who is to be the emperor? The people would be emperors. Four million would be emperors."³³

Sun's notion of nation-state also entails a cosmopolitan outlook. He regards nationalism as a way station toward the cosmopolitan world. The October Revolution of Soviet Russia had achieved national self-determination and succeeded in building a modern nation-state. Vladimir Lenin's notion of self-determination fueled a movement to combat the domination of the imperialist and colonialist powers over the colonized. It called for mobilizing and assisting the 1.2 billion people to fight one million oppressors and promoted the independence of the movement of Asian peoples. National self-determination of all colonized and weak nations is the basis for a broad internationalist alliance and movement. This cosmopolitanism dovetails with the *tianxia* tenet of "assisting the weak and helping the fallen" (濟弱扶傾)—a "true cosmopolitan spirit."³⁴

But the dream of cosmopolitanism is unrealistic and impossible without nationalism and without the buildup of a nation-state. The cosmopolitanism touted by the major imperial powers is a mirage and a trick to maintain the unjust international order and is hostile to national self-determination by colonized and oppressed people. China is a colony under foreign rule, and it is premature for Chinese educated elites to talk about cosmopolitanism. The urgent task is to promote nationalism and achieve national independence. Sun devoted a whole lecture to the topic titled "Nationalism Is the Basis for World Unity" (*Minzu zhuyi shi shijie datong de jichu* 民族主義是世界大同的基礎) in the collection *Three Peoples' Principle* (*Sanmin zhuyi* 三民主義). National independence means achieving the status of equality and freedom with other nations. To achieve it, China must first become a nation:

> Today we should revive China's lost nationalism, rallying a people of four hundred million strong to fight for peoples of the world in the name of justice.... Out of fear of this thinking, the imperialist powers come up with a dubious doctrine and they seek to trick us with cosmopolitanism. They say the world must progress, that humanity's vision should be far and wide, and that nationalism is too narrow.... It is under such a misleading

influence that some Chinese new youth advocate a new culture and oppose nationalism. But the doctrine of cosmopolitanism should not be accepted by a subordinated nation. We are a subordinated nation, and we must restore our nation to the status of equality and freedom with other nations before we discuss cosmopolitanism. If we are to promote cosmopolitanism, we must first strengthen nationalism.[35]

Assisting the weak and helping the fallen is "what a strong nation is supposed to do," and constitutes a project of "ordering the nation and preserving the world peace (治國平天下).[36]

The appeal to *tianxia* and *datong*—a world order of international coexistence and mutual respect—deepens the connections between nation-building and an international outlook. The Chinese nationals should appeal to *gongli* 公理, the universal principle, by supporting the weak and helping the fallen. Sun's thinking, as Mizoguchi noted, brings the nation-state into the *tianxia* framework.[37]

The People Can Be Nationalist and Internationalist

Liang envisaged a national republic that is not antagonistic and aggressive but stands on an equal footing with other nations. The nation takes on a cooperative attitude and is open to a cosmopolitan world. Sun valorized the nation-state as a new republic replacing the Manchu rule and a bulwark of resistance against colonialism and imperialism. Once established, the Chinese republic was ready to assist the colonized and oppressed before attaining the *datong* dream. In their accounts, the nation-state is not inward but outward, not narrow minded but broad minded: it is the threshold to the *tianxia* vision.

Socialist thinkers, for all their internationalist aspirations, did not dispense with the national question. That national independence is the first step toward socialist internationalism informs thinkers such as Li Dazhao and Mao Zedong. They saw China as an actor in unison with other nations in shaking up the colonial and imperialist world. An admirer of Kang and Liang, the young Mao was more internationalist than nationalistic. He proposed the union of popular masses and the founding of a national party as the means to achieving it. He divided the world into two parts: a small ruling class of aristocrats and capitalists, and workers and laboring people of the whole world. The ruling class exploited laboring people economically, oppressed them politically, and dominated the masses through military and police. Perceiving the injustice and inequality in the global expansion of capitalism and colonialism, Mao viewed the violent rebellion of worker movements in Europe as an attempt to resist oppression: "Do unto others as they do unto you." Evoking Russian anarchist Pyotr

Kropotkin, Mao articulates the union of the popular masses by blending anarchist ideas into *tianxia* language. The anarchist movement promoted the morality of mutual aid in economic production and envisaged a world where working classes work for themselves voluntarily. The ruling aristocrats and capitalists are made to work and help working people rather than harming them. Going beyond the working-class interests, however, the ideas of anarchism "are broader and more far reaching." Anarchists "want to unite the whole globe into a single country, unite the human race in a single family, and attain together in peace, happiness, and friendship—an age of prosperity."[38] The global union of the popular masses, however, would grow from numerous small unions. Segments in region, class, and profession would be integrated into larger groups until the groups were united into a working-class nation. The Soviet Russians had set an example, and Hungary had risen up, where a "new toilers' and peasants' government [has] also appeared in Budapest. The Germans, Austrians, and Czechs have done the same."[39] In China, social movements by small groups would be led by a revolutionary party that would finally be a party with national sovereignty.

Two analytical categories mark Mao's analysis of the nation-*tianxia* nexus: class and nation. The class analysis points to shared victimhood, an internationalist alliance, and mutual aid among working classes in the colonies. The national category, on the other hand, points to the nation-state as an effective emancipatory movement aimed at decolonization, independence, and territorial integrity.

In the war against Japanese imperialism, the nationalist concern was high on the agenda in the United Front between Communists and Nationalists. Observing that the Chinese must be nationalists before they joined the international movements, Mao extended Sun's notion of national self-determination in the war of self-defense and resistance. All Chinese at this critical moment should be nationalist actors in the struggle to resist colonialism and imperialist invaders. This wartime nationalism sought to invoke cultural heritage and roots: it required a cultural revolution in consciousness and morality to carry on traditional culture and emotional structures to a higher level. In 1938, Mao stated that the modern Chinese nation had grown out of the China of the past and that we "must not lop off our history. We should sum up our history from Confucius to Sun Yatsen and take over this valuable legacy." An internationalist outlook is intertwined with nation-building: "Communists are internationalists, but we can put Marxism into practice only when it is integrated with the specific characteristics of our country and acquires a definite national form."[40]

The promotion of national culture and tradition was not nostalgic or a glorification of national pasts: it was intended to build up confidence and rally the Chinese for much-needed unity, as articulated in Liang's "state thinking." Mao qualified revolutionary nationalism with the claim that revolutionaries are not just nationalists but also communists. Communists are not only patriots committed to national defense but also internationalists. Communists are broad-minded patriots, and their patriotism makes good sense only in the context of the international struggle against fascism and imperialism. Good patriotism is congenial to internationalism because oppressed nations and peoples share a common fate of victimhood and should work in concert to change the world order dominated by colonialist nations.[41]

In an interview with Mao in Yan'an, the American journalist Agnes Smedley raised the question of the connection between nationalism and internationalism. To her question "if the policy of a united front implied that the Chinese communists had abandoned the class struggle and turned into simply nationalists," Mao replied: "The Communists absolutely do not tie their viewpoint to the interests of a single class at a single time but are most passionately concerned with the fate of the Chinese nation . . . the Chinese communists are internationalists. They are in favor of the world communist movement. But at the same time, they are patriots who defend their native land . . . this patriotism and internationalism are by no means in conflict, for only China's independence and liberation will make it possible to participate in the world communist movement."[42]

Like Sun Zhongshan, Mao cited Kang's word *datong* to refer to internationalism.[43] Joseph Levenson linked *tianxia* with what he called "communist cosmopolitanism."[44] To achieve this goal, Chinese communists must mobilize the toiling masses in the national liberation movement to achieve socialism. It was the same principle of emancipation that prompted Karl Marx to "distinguish between the nationalism of the developed bourgeoisie states and the nationalism of oppressed, colonized people."[45] Self-determination of a nation and emancipation of worldwide working classes fit into a national-international nexus. As Pheng Cheah puts it, "Proletarian emancipation necessarily involves the emancipation of the oppressed peoples elsewhere because the exploitation of other peoples through colonization is intimately connected to the exploitation of workers within the 'domestic' space of a colonial power."[46] The key to this link of nation to the world is the emphasis on the people first as decolonizing nationalists and then as liberators of themselves as working classes. These two aspects make Chinese revolutionaries both nationalist and internationalist.

The new national people are both "nationalist and internationalist at the same time."[47] Peoples of different nations are capable of understanding each other, not because they are individuals with cosmopolitan empathy, but because they belong to the same international class. As Joseph R. Levenson wrote, "Cultural cosmopolitanism, *on a class basis* (italics in the original), seemed to pair with nationalism, not to impair it. For the *jenmin* [*renmin*] of all nations were supposed to have a common cause, while the *jenmin* of each nation was supposed virtually to constitute the nation. If the local bourgeois failed to make the common cause with 'the people' (*jen-min*), they were denationalized, as imperialists or running dogs of imperialists, disqualified for the *min-tzu* [*minzu*] variant of 'people.'[48]

The nationalism of the Guomindang affirmed the narrow-minded patriotism and self-serving patriotism that work against the public space and the common good. When the Guomindang, under the banner of nationalism, failed to represent the will of the Chinese people, it lost legitimacy as a national government and became a comprador entity subordinated to the imperialists. However, a nation constituted by its people is able to identify with other national people as well as other laboring classes, opening the door to international affinity and class solidarity. This people-to-people, class-to-class relation is the basis for mutual support and sympathy on an international scale and underlies socialist internationalism.

The nexus between nationalism and internationalism marks the *tianxia* state. It breaks away from the logic of ethnic and cultural identity rooted in the parochial line of blood ties and family relations. Internationalism manifests itself in the alliance of peoples with the shared fate of victimhood and oppression, an awareness of the common fate of working classes across national boundaries, and the need for mutual understanding and sympathy. The people must first stand up as a sovereign nation-state and then extend a helping hand to peoples in the world in order to forge internationalist affinity and solidarity. Internationalism, a form of political cosmopolitanism, is "to pair with nationalism, not to impair it."[49] Peoples of diverse nationalities are peer groups whose separate pursuits of independence make a common cause.

Notes

1. Kang Youwei, *Datong shu* 大同書 (Book of great community) (Shanghai: Shanghai guji, 2005), pp. 68–69, 85–86.

2. Liang Qichao, *Liang Qichao quanji* 梁啓超全集 (Complete works of Liang Qichao) (Beijing: Beijing chubanshe, 1999), p. 2978.

3. Liang, *Liang Qichao quanji*, p. 2978.

4. Liang, *Liang Qichao quanji*, p. 2985.

5. Luo Mengce, *Zhongguo lun* 中國論 (On China) (Shanghai: Shangwu yinshuguan, 1944), pp. 11–12.

6. Sun Zhongshan, *Sun Zhongshan quanji* 孫中山全集 (Complete works of Sun Zhongshan), vol. 9 (Beijing: Zhonghua shuju, 1986), p. 226.

7. Edmund Burke, *Reflections on the Revolution in France* (London: Cambridge University Press, 1912), p. 46.

8. Zhao Tingyang, *Tianxia tixi* 天下體系 (World system) (Nanjing: Jiangsu jiaoyu, 2005), p. 17.

9. Liang, *Liang Qichao quanji*, p. 657.

10. Kang, *Datong shu*, pp. 68–69.
11. Liang, *Liang Qichao quanji*, p. 666.
12. Liang, *Liang Qichao quanji*, p. 3604.
13. Liang, *Liang Qichao quanji*, p. 3604.
14. Liang, *Liang Qichao quanji*, p. 665.
15. Liang, *Liang Qichao quanji*, p. 657.
16. Liang, *Liang Qichao quanji*, p. 656.
17. Francis Fukuyama, *Political Order and Political Decay* (New York: Farrar, Strauss, and Giroux, 2014), p. 86. Fukuyama considers China in the Qin and Han dynasties as the first modern state, with its impersonal bureaucracy and meritocracy. But the patrimonial pull of private, kinship, and family ties constantly eroded the broad, impersonal administrative system, which was in fact the *tianxia* system. Liang is deploring the same patrimonial relationship.
18. Liang, *Liang Qichao quanji*, p. 661.
19. Liang, *Liang Qichao quanji*, pp. 413–414.
20. Quoted in Zhao Tingyang, "Cong shijie wenti kaishi de tianxia zhengzhi" 從世界問題開始的天下政治 (*Tianxia* politics from a global perspective), in *Dongya zhixu: Guannian, zhidu yu zhanlue* 東亞秩序：觀念、制度與戰略 (Asian order: Ideas, system, and strategy), ed. Zhou Fangyin and Gao Cheng (Beijing: Shehui kexue wenxian, 2012), p. 50.
21. Frederick Wakeman, *History and Will: Philosophical Perspectives of Mao Tse-tung's Thought* (Berkeley: University of California Press, 1973), pp. 30, 100.
22. The English translation is from Theodore de Bary and Irene Bloom, eds., *Sources of Chinese Tradition,* 2nd ed. (New York: Columbia University Press, 1999), p. 343.
23. Terry Eagleton, *The Ideology of the Aesthetic* (Oxford: Blackwell, 1990), p. 24.
24. Liang, *Liang Qichao quanji*, p. 661.
25. Sun, *Sun Zhongshan quanji*, p. 327.
26. Liang, *Liang Qichao quanji*, p. 3605.
27. Liang, *Liang Qichao quanji*, p. 2987.
28. Mizoguchi Yūzō, *Zuowei fangfa de Zhongguo* 作為方法的中國 (China as method) (Taipei: National Institute for Compilation and Translation, 1999), pp. 97–98.
29. Sun, *Sun Zhongshan quanji*, pp. 238, 240.
30. Sun, *Sun Zhongshan quanji*, p. 244.
31. Sun, *Sun Zhongshan quanji*, p. 262.
32. Sun, *Sun Zhongshan quanji*, p. 255.
33. Sun, *Sun Zhongshan quanji*, p. 270.
34. Sun, *Sun Zhongshan quanji*, pp. 225–226, 231.
35. Sun, *Sun Zhongshan quanji*, p. 226.
36. Sun, *Shun Zhong quanji*, p. 253.
37. Mizoguchi, *Zuowei fangfa de Zhongguo*, pp. 97–98.
38. Stuart Schram, ed., *Mao's Road to Power: Revolutionary Writings 1912–1949*, vol. 1 (Armonk, NY: M. E. Sharpe, 1992), p. 380.
39. Schram, *Mao's Road to Power*, p. 386.
40. Mao Tse-tung, *Selected Works of Mao Tse-tung*, vol. 2 (Beijing: Foreign Language Press, 1965), p. 209.

41. Mao, *Selected Works*, p. 196.
42. Stuart Schram, *Mao Tse-Tung* (Baltimore: Penguin, 1966), p. 201.
43. Schram, *Mao Tse-Tung*, p. 201.
44. Karl Marx and Friedrich Engels, *The German Ideology* (New York: International Publishers, 1970), p. 7.
45. Pheng Cheah, *Spectral Nationality* (New York: Columbia University Press, 2003), p. 188.
46. Cheah, *Spectral Nationality*, p. 189.
47. Joseph R. Levenson, *Revolution and Cosmopolitanism* (Berkeley: University of California Press, 1971), p. 6.
48. Levenson, *Revolution and Cosmopolitanism*, p. 8.
49. Levenson, *Revolution and Cosmopolitanism*, p. 8.

CHAPTER 7

Comparing the Ancient Chinese *Tianxia* Order and the Postwar UN-Centric International Order

Qingxin K. WANG

IT HAS NOW become almost a truism to say that there are major differences between the ancient Chinese *tianxia* (天下) order and the modern international order due to different cultural and historical backgrounds. At least two important differences can be identified.

First, the ancient Chinese *tianxia* order as the entire known world for the Chinese was a highly centralized empire, while the modern international system that originated in the Treaty of Westphalia of 1648 is characterized as a multi-state system that upholds state sovereignty. Whereas modern states have enjoyed a large degree of sovereignty, states under the *tianxia* order in ancient China during the Spring and Autumn period (*Chunqiu shidai,* 春秋時代), which was a prototype *tianxia* order, enjoyed no sovereignty, with the Zhou king possessing authority to enforce states' obligations.[1] Second, whereas the modern international order consists of diverse cultures and ethnicities and upholds the principle of national equality, the Chinese *tianxia* order was constructed on the basis of one single culture, that is, the Confucian culture, which is sometimes referred to as the Sino-centric world order.[2]

This chapter compares the ancient Chinese *tianxia* order during the Spring and Autumn period with the postwar United Nations (UN)-centric international order. It argues that there are some important similarities despite the apparent differences. These similarities may have important implications in light of China's rapid rise. Specifically, this chapter argues that there are three major similarities between the two international orders: First, both international orders are hierarchical with a nominal power center at the top of the hierarchy. At the top of the hierarchy of the postwar international order is the UN Security Council. At the top of the hierarchy of the ancient Chinese *tianxia* order during the Spring and Autumn period was the Zhou king. Second, both international orders have relied on a body of ethical norms that form the foundation of the international rules and laws for the maintenance of the two international orders. In the case of the postwar UN-centric international order, there is a body of international law that draws on the combination of the natural law tradition and legal positivism (namely, the customary and case laws and precedence of state practices). In the ancient Chinese case, it is the body of *Zhouli* (Zhou rites or rules of propriety 周禮制度) that formed the foundation of ethical rules and laws for the maintenance of the Zhou empire. Third, due to the weak nature of the nominal power center at the top of the hierarchies, both international orders have relied on dominant states to assemble a multistate military coalition in the maintenance of both international orders on behalf of the power center at the top of the hierarchies. These similarities between the two international orders suggest that the differences between the UN-centric postwar international order and the future Chinese international order that draws on the ancient Chinese *tianxia* order may not be as great as are commonly assumed and that the two international orders can complement each other, rather than contradicting each other or being in perpetual conflicts.

The first section of this chapter examines the origin of the modern international order and changes in the underlying sources of international law that formed the backbone of the international order. Attention is given to how the UN-centric postwar international order was created and what role the United States has played in the maintenance of this order. The second section of this chapter surveys the origin and the evolution of the Zhou empire in the Spring and Autumn period in ancient China. It examines the body of the Zhou rites, which is similar to the body of international laws that draws on the natural law tradition and legal positivism, and what role it played in the maintenance of the Zhou *tianxia* order.

The third section discusses four cases of actual practice of maintaining the ancient Chinese *tianxia* order as documented in the historical narrative of the *Zuozhuan* (*Zuo's Commentary* 左傳). They focus on how ethical norms of Zhou rites were used to regulate the interstate relations among the states of the *tianxia* order and the role that the dominant state(s) played in maintaining the Chinese *tianxia* order on behalf of the Zhou king. The fourth section draws some implications of these similarities for the future Chinese role in the UN-centric postwar international order in light of China's rapid rise.

The Evolution of Modern International Order

The modern international order originated in the signing of the Treaty of Westphalia in 1648 when France, Spain, and German states agreed to recognize the Dutch independence from Spain and their right to maintain its own Protestant religion, thus ending the Thirty Years' War. As a result, there emerged many states and principalities that could rightfully conduct their own foreign policies.

The Treaty of Westphalia stipulates three major tenets and laid the important foundation for the rise of the modern sovereign state system. These tenets are as follows. First, each prince or monarch has the right to determine the religion within their own state. Second, religious freedom is guaranteed, that is, Christians (e.g., Protestants) who live in a place where their denomination is not the established religion have the right to practice their faith in public. Third, the treaty guarantees that each state or principality has exclusive sovereignty over the territories it controls and the people residing in the territories. The corollary principles are the principle of national self-determination and the principle of nonintervention.[3] The rise of nationalism subsequently reinforced the sense of sovereignty.

The law of nature served as the foundation of international law that regulated interstate relations during the early part of the post-Westphalia period. French philosopher of the Renaissance period Jean Bodin (1530–1596) coined the term "sovereignty" and suggested that monarchs have sovereign power, which means that monarchs have absolute political power and there is no higher authority than monarchs on earth. Namely, monarchs are not accountable to the Catholic Church in Rome and to the authority of the Holy Roman Empire. But Bodin adds that the only higher authority that monarchs are held accountable to is God or the law of nature. In other words, although every nation-state is sovereign in the absence of world government, it does not mean that states can do whatever they want and that there are absolutely no external constraints on states. Such constraints are international norms and laws derived from the natural law tradition and Biblical precepts. Bodin also proposed that states are equal regardless of their size, which is the precursor of the principle of sovereign equality. Furthermore, Bodin used the example of the theory of just war, which draws on the natural law tradition, to suggest that monarchs are subject to God or the law of nature.[4] The theory of just war was heavily influenced by the writings of St. Augustine (354–430) and Thomas Aquinas (1225–1274) on the issue of just war, with the Bible providing an important source of the theory of just war.

As St. Augustine suggests, just wars are those that "avenge wrongs."[5] Thomas Aquinas famously suggests three principles for just war. First, the war must be waged by a legitimate authority. Second, there requires a just cause in that the war should be directed against those who commit an offense and deserve punishment or should return what has been taken away unjustly. Third, there should be a right intention on the part of those who are making the war: that is, a just war should aim at achieving some good such as peace or avoiding some evil such as genocide. A just war should meet all these three conditions.[6]

Dutch philosopher Hugo Grotius (1583–1645) focused on international treaties and stressed that it is a law of nature for states to fulfill their treaty obligations. He also emphasized other important moral precepts constraining states' international behaviors such as the humane treatment of prisoners of war.

The Enlightenment gave rise to positivist law, which provided an important new basis for international law. Influenced by renowned Italian legal scholar Alberico Gentili (1552–1608), the international legal scholars of the Enlightenment era believed that states possess the inherent right to wage war as a foreign policy instrument. As Gentili argues, men cannot know the divine truth as to on which side justice lies in international disputes on the basis of just war tradition. We humans "for the most part are unacquainted with that truth. Therefore we aim at justice as it appears from man's standpoint." As long as sovereign princes need to make a final decision to guarantee international peace—just or unjust— we must abide by the final outcome of a regularly conducted trial of strength between sovereign equals because we have no better way of determining where justice lies in international disputes. In other words, war is a viable, albeit nonideal, means to render a judgment in international disputes between sovereign equals.[7]

In the post-Enlightenment era, the actual practice of states in the conduct of international relations such as precedents, customs, and usages replaced the law of nature or the just war tradition as the major sources of international law. Swiss international lawyer Emer de Vattel (1714–1767) made important contributions to the codification of international law based on case law and customary law. In the words of well-known contemporary scholar of international ethics Terry Nardin, "The main works of the late eighteenth century concerning international law make it clear that European practice was almost completely replacing natural law as the most important source of legal rights and duties."[8]

Jeremy Bentham's (1748–1832) utilitarianism also became a moral basis for the theory of international law prevalent in that era. According to Bentham, international law is the positive law based on the prevailing acceptable practices of states, having nothing to do with natural law. For Bentham, whether or not an international law is morally justifiable is based on whether the international law maximizes the well-being or utility of relevant states.[9]

Another factor contributing to the decline of natural law as the main source of international law was the expansion of European international relations to include non-Christian states; chief among them was the Ottoman Empire, with which Europe had increasing interaction. The Christian tradition of natural law was no longer applicable to the increasing cultural diversity of the international society of states. To maintain the unity of the new emerging international society of states with cultural diversity, the body of international law gradually came to rely on legal positivism as a guiding principle, and the actual practices of states in international relations such as customary law and case law became the major basis of international law.

A corpus of international laws was codified in the two Hague Peace Conferences at the turn of the twentieth century. The first Hague Peace Conference, held in 1899, dealt with international law regulating the conduct of war. It also created the Permanent Court of Arbitration to resolve interstate disputes arising out of international agreements. The second Hague Peace Conference, held in 1907, focused on the peaceful settlements of international disputes.

The lessons of the disastrous World War I forced international jurists to reevaluate the importance of natural law and called for the supplement of the natural law tradition for the positivist international law. The natural law tradition has regained its influence. They also began to consider the enforcement of international law through the creation of a hierarchical power structure or world federation. German philosopher Immanuel Kant's proposal for eternal peace from the eighteenth century received a lot of recognition. Kant postulates the creation of a federation of republics to establish international peace on the basis of three principles: the creation of constitutions within republics, the signing of a peace treaty among republics, and the encouragement of cosmopolitanism through international commerce.

The growing influence of natural law was evident in the creation of the League of Nations. It was also evident in the subsequent renunciation of war as an instrument of foreign policy in the 1928 Kellogg-Briand Treaty sponsored by Germany, France, and the United States, and signed by sixty-two states. The pact clearly embodied a strong sense of moralism.

The creation of the UN after World War II, which embodied humanity's new aspiration for international peace, once again witnessed the stronger influence of natural law. While the UN Charter has continued to enshrine the principle of sovereign equality and its corollary principles such as nonintervention and territorial integrity, new moral idealism drawing on the natural law tradition has also been injected into the UN Charter. As is stipulated in the UN Charter, the notion of sovereignty is to be qualified in the light of the lessons of two disastrous world wars. For the first time, states no longer have absolute sovereign rights and states can no longer do whatever they want to other states. States' sovereign rights are to be qualified. Instead, states not only have sovereign rights, but they have obligations as well. This gives rise to the notion of "limited sovereignty," which can be seen in following three aspects.

First, states are obligated to maintain friendly relations with other states and to resolve their international disputes through peaceful means. For example, the UN Charter's Article 2(4) stipulates that states no longer have the absolute sovereign right to war. In other words, war is now prohibited as an instrument of foreign policy. The UN Charter says that states only have the right to self-defense only (Article 51).

Article 2(4) of the UN Charter says:

> All Members shall refrain in their international relations from the *threat or use of force* against the territorial integrity or political independence of any state, or in any other manner inconsistent with the Purposes of the United Nations.

Article 51 of the UN Charter provides a qualification of Article 2(4) with the following clause:

> Nothing in the present Charter shall impair the inherent right of individual or collective self-defense if an armed attack occurs against a Member of the United Nations, until the Security Council has taken measures necessary to maintain international peace and security.

Second, the UN Charter links the protection of individual human rights with international peace, namely, in Article 1(3). There was the belief that the abuse of human rights may disturb domestic peace, and this may spread across borders. Thus, the UN Charter treats the improvement of human rights as one of the UN's major goals. Subsequently, the UN has played an important role in the further codification of international laws regarding the protection of individual human rights. This can be seen in the signing of the UN Universal Declaration on Human Rights in 1948 and the signing of the two UN covenants on human rights subsequently.

The 1966 UN Covenant on Civil and Political Rights provides for a long list of various social and political rights that national governments are obligated to protect. (As of July 2022, there are 173 signatory states.) Article 6 stipulates the protection of the individual's right to life and forbids arbitrary killings by security forces. While Article 6 did not forbid the death penalty, it restricts the application of the death penalty to the most serious crimes and forbids its use on children and pregnant women. Articles 7 and 8 guarantee individual freedom from torture, cruel punishment, and slavery. Articles 9, 11, 14, and 15 guarantee freedom from arbitrary arrest and detention, and the right to a fair and impartial trial. Articles 12 and 13 provide for the individual's right to free movement. Article 18 mandates the freedom of religion and beliefs. Article 25 guarantees the individual's right to political participation including the right to vote for their governments. Articles 26 and 27 guarantee the individual's right to nondiscrimination and equality before the law.

Third, the UN Charter also stipulates the establishment of collective security as a supranational enforcement mechanism to ensure the major principles of the UN Charter are to be carried out. There has been clearly a gradual drive toward the creation of a supranational enforcement mechanism in the postwar period. The cosmopolitanists or idealists believed the reason why the League of Nations failed to deter World War II was because of its lack of military power. They advocated the creation of the UN, which would address the deficiency of the League of Nations. The UN was created with the belief that some kind of supranational military enforcement should be created to provide teeth to the UN's collective security operation. The UN Charter's articles 43 and 47 stipulate that a standing army is to be created and that such standing army is to be directed by the UN Military Staff Committee, which would be held accountable to the UN Security Council. If this materialized, the UN would become a quasi–world government with its own standing army.

Unfortunately, due to the deepening Cold War conflicts between the United States and the former Soviet Union, the two superpowers could not agree on the actual mechanism of collective security, and the idealists' aspiration for a supranational military enforcement mechanism did not materialize. While the UN did not realize its hope of creating a standing army, it eventually settled for something less, that is, the establishment of a collective security operation with the contribution of contingent military forces from member states in the absence of a UN standing army.

The UN Security Council has twice invoked the UN collective security operation since its inception in ways that came close to the ideal model of the UN collective security mechanism. The first UN collective security operation was a multistate military coalition led by the United States to repel North Korean aggression during the Korean War in the 1950s. The Soviet representative boycotted a UN Security Council vote on the UN collective security operation in Korea. The UN operation in Korea was dominated by the United States, which contributed most of the naval and air forces. A UN military command was created to lead the multistate coalition, but it was totally dominated by General Douglas McArthur.

The second UN collective security operation was a multistate military coalition led by the United States to repel the Iraqi forces from Kuwait in 1991. While the end of the Cold War allowed the UN Security Council to achieve unanimity for the UN collective security operation in the 1991 Gulf War, the entire military operation was once again dominated by the United States, which contributed the majority of the armed forces to the operation. There was not even the establishment of a UN command this time. The multistate coalition was entirely under direct control by the US commander, General Norman Schwarzkopf. There have also been numerous UN-sponsored humanitarian peacekeeping operations after the Cold War that aimed to protect human rights such as the UN operations in Somalia, Bosnia, and Kosovo, for instance.

The drive to create a quasi–world government after the Cold War has also made some concrete progress in the nonmilitary aspects. The idealists have concentrated the endeavor on the creation of a supranational judiciary with compulsory jurisdiction. The 1998 Treaty of Rome provides for the establishment of the International Criminal Court (ICC). The treaty stipulates that the ICC has supranational compulsory jurisdiction over crimes against humanity and genocide. Traditionally, compulsory jurisdiction on states is difficult. Conventional international law stipulates that international jurisdiction on individuals follows the principle of territoriality or the principle of nationality. The principle of territoriality says that the state on whose territory a crime takes place has jurisdiction to try the criminal. The principle of nationality says that the state whose nationals commit the crime has jurisdiction to try criminals. There is also the concept of universal jurisdiction, which says that every state has jurisdiction to try the crimes of piracy and the slave trade.

The Treaty of Rome stipulates that the ICC has compulsory jurisdiction to try crimes only if either state where the crimes take place is party to the ICC or state whose nationals commit crimes is party to the ICC (a compromise between traditional and universal jurisdiction). Yet this is an important step toward creating a quasi–world court that has compulsory jurisdiction and it is a clear indication of the erosion of national sovereignty. For example, US peacekeeping forces may be prosecuted in Bosnia or Iraq for abusing civilians if Bosnia and Iraq are ICC parties even if the United States is not a party to ICC because the crimes are committed in ICC signatory states. This is compulsory jurisdiction on the United States. This is a controversial issue that has consistently incurred the US government's strong objection. The US government's objection has been that the ICC should not have compulsory jurisdiction on states that are not party to the ICC. This is because compulsory jurisdiction may lead to the trial of US troops without US consent.

The concept of compulsory jurisdiction has also been introduced in the Dispute Settlement Board (DSB) of the World Trade Organization (WTO) in the 1994 Treaty of Marrakesh that laid the legal foundation for the creation of the WTO. This treaty states that the WTO's DSB has compulsory jurisdiction to hear member states' complaints about unfair international trade practices against other member states. The WTO agreement stipulates that the DSB has the automatic jurisdiction to form a panel of specialists to hear trade complaints against member states unless the DSB decides unanimously against forming the panel. This is a revolutionary change from the jurisdiction arrangement of the General Agreement on Tariffs and Trade (GATT), which stipulates that a panel can only be formed when the dispute settlement body votes unanimously to form such a panel. While this is a modest step toward the creation of a quasi–world court, it is a clear erosion of traditional notions of sovereignty.

Many cosmopolitan scholars want to see the further strengthening of the UN as a quasi–world government. For example, renowned German philosopher Jürgen Habermas calls for the creation of a global parliament modeled after the European Union Parliament. British political scientist David Held advocates for the establishment of a global assembly of nongovernmental agencies to give private interest groups a stronger voice in global affairs.

The Nature of the Zhou Empire

The Zhou dynasty (1122 BC–222 BC) lasted some nine hundred years. The early Zhou dynasty was noted by its political consolidation, continued expansion, and the gradual weakening of the Zhou royal authority. In the face of the onslaught of barbarian tribes along its fringes around 771 BC, the capital of the Zhou empire was moved eastward from Gaojing (稿京) to Luoyang (洛陽). As a result, the Zhou empire was significantly weakened. This marked the beginning of the Spring and Autumn period, which was the early part of the so-called Eastern Zhou empire. The later Zhou dynasty consisted of two periods. The Spring and Autumn period (771 BC–464 BC) was characterized by the continued weakening of the Zhou royal authority and the rise and fall of different leading vassal states in replacing the Zhou royal authority to play the stabilizing role for the Zhou empire. The second period (463 BC–222 BC) was known as the Warring States period, which was marked by the intense military contest among seven major states for reunifying the disintegrated Zhou empire.[10]

The Zhou empire encompassed the entire known world for the Chinese, and the Zhou king was the universal king for All-under-Heaven, or what the Chinese called *tianxia*. The territories of the Zhou empire could be drawn within a few concentric squares. At the very center was the royal domain, which was about one thousand *li* (half mile) in diameter. The geographical distance between the royal domain and the vassal states indicated the political closeness between the royal rulers and the vassal rulers. Broadly speaking, there were four kinds of vassal states: most of the key vassal states that were controlled by the princes or blood relatives of Zhou rulers, some key vassal states that were controlled by the military generals who helped the Zhou rulers to overthrow the Shang rulers (e.g., the state of Qi 齊國), the vassal states that were controlled by the surviving relatives of the overthrown Shang rulers (e.g., the state of Song 宋國), and the barbarian states that bordered the Zhou empire (e.g., the state of Chu 楚國).

The authority of rulers in the vassal states was delegated by the Zhou king, and their vassalage was conditional on their allegiance to the Zhou king and their compliance with the institution of *Zhouli* (Zhou rites or rules of propriety), a body of ethical rules and norms that governed the relations between the Zhou king and vassal states, the relations between vassal states, and the relations between the people and their rulers. When vassal rulers violated the terms of delegation or failed to maintain allegiance to the Zhou king, their authority and land tenure could be withdrawn and the vassalage could be ended. By and large these vassal rulers enjoyed a large degree of political independence and autonomy as long as they abided by the terms of delegation.

That the Zhou empire was maintained for more than eight hundred years was a remarkable feat despite the intense military contests during the Warring States period. The stability of the Zhou empire rested on two essential pillars: First, there was an elaborate system of ethical rules and laws that governed the relations between the Zhou king and all the vassal states and the relations between vassal states, as well as rules and norms that regulated the domestic affairs of vassal states. Second, there was a powerful military possessed by the Zhou king, with the support of vassal states, that helped the Zhou court to enforce this system of ethical rules and laws. The Zhou rulers enforced the system of rules and norms by relying on the royal court's military as the last resort. The Zhou kings had fourteen armies, which were stationed in garrisons and could be dispatched anywhere within the imperial territories at the Zhou king's disposal. The imperial armies were used to repel barbarian invasions outside the Zhou empire, to suppress internal rebellion, and to punish the vassal states that violated imperial rules and regulations.[11] Moreover, the rulers of vassal states were supposed to pay proper visits to the Zhou court each year. If the ruler of a vassal state failed three times to make his proper visit to the royal court in accordance with the rules, the Zhou rulers could send the imperial armies to remove him.[12]

As the empire declined in the Spring and Autumn period, there was a lot of internal strife and conflicts, coupled with the continued presence of external threats. Many Zhou rites were no longer observed. Incidents of regicide took place frequently and some dozens of vassal states also went out of existence. As Confucius would later on lament, this period witnessed the collapse of *li* (rites) and the abandonment of *yue* (musical education) (禮崩樂壞).

Nonetheless, parts of *Zhouli* survived and remained influential during this period. The institution of *Zhouli*, which was comparable to the Western tradition of natural law, merits attention here. *Li* was the most important concept in the institution of *Zhouli* and had an important religious basis. The ancient Chinese believed that Heaven, which is the equivalent of the Judeo-Christian God, was the creator of the myriad of all things. While there were many gods, Heaven was the king of all gods in the hierarchy of gods. For the ancient Chinese, Heaven (*tian* 天) created the laws of physics to govern the natural world and even the movements of celestial objects in order to maintain natural harmony. Heaven also legislated ethical rules and norms to regulate sociopolitical and family relations so that there would be harmony in family and society. This body of physical laws and ethical rules and norms came to be known as *li*. Just as Western medieval theologians like Thomas Aquinas believed that natural law reflected the moral will of God, the ancient Chinese believed that the body of *li* was created by Heaven as a reflection of Heaven's moral will. And the sage kings did not make the body of *li;* rather they discovered the *li* through self-reflection.[13] Just like natural law, *li* is self-enacting mostly. But in some cases, *li* needs to be enforced by political authority through coercion.

Nonetheless, *li* is very different from the legalist conception of law, which is based on the careful calculation of material interests. Whereas the legalist conception of law is made in accordance with the situation and is malleable, *li* is supposed to be a reflection of Heaven's moral will and is objective and unchangeable. The legalist law needs to be strictly enforced by political authority. Those who comply with the law will be rewarded with interests and honors, and those who flaunt the law will be meted with severe punishment. But for Confucians, *li* is mostly self-enacting.

The *Zuozhuan,* a Confucian classical text, postulates an ideal ethical society as based on observing *li* properly, such as having a just king (君義), a practical minister (臣行), a father who is generous (父慈), an elder brother who knows how to love others (兄愛), and a younger brother who knows how to respect others (弟敬). If everyone observes these *li,* there will be social harmony. A famous passage in the *Zuozhuan* says, "It has been a long time for the *li* to regulate the state and the society since the beginning of time. When the king issues the order and the minister obeys, when the father is benevolent and the son is filial, when the older brother loves the younger brother and the younger brother respects the older brother, when the husband takes good care of the family and the wife submits to him, when the aunt loves and the woman listens, these are rites at work."[14] Likewise, as Confucius suggests, "If a man is able to govern a state by observing the rites and showing deference, what difficulties will he have in governing a state? If he is unable to govern a state by observing the rites and showing deference, what good are the rites to him?"[15]

The concept of *li* extends to include the rules and norms that govern interstate order, with *li* specifying the rights and obligations of states under the *tianxia* order. The so-called Code of Nine Principles for Royal Expedition (*Jiufazhifa* 九伐之法) exemplifies this body of international rules and norms. This code is recorded in the *Book of Zhou Rites (Zhouli: Book Four)*《周禮. 夏官司馬第四》. This code elaborates on the rights and obligations of the vassal rulers and the conditions under which the imperial army will be sent to punish vassal rulers for wrongdoing. The Code of Nine Principles reads as follows:

—Those who bully the weak and the small will be punished with the reduction of territories.
—Those who harm the wise people and abuse the ordinary people will be punished by military force.
—Those who oppress their own people and bully neighboring states will be removed from power and sent into exile.
—Those who allow the people's fields to be empty and let the people flee to foreign states for food will be punished by reduction of territories.
—Those who embark on aggressive or surreptitious attacks on foreign states will be punished by military force.
—Those who harm or murder their parents will be punished with capital punishment.
—Those who send their lords into exile or murder their lords will be punished with capital punishment.
—Those who do not show allegiance to the Zhou king and do not observe the Zhou rites will be forbidden from conducting diplomacy with other states.
—Those who act like animals and commit incest will be punished with capital punishment.

As we can see from the above, the Code of Nine Principles is composed of three parts. The first part focuses on the obligations that vassal states had in maintaining friendly relations with other vassal states and not launching aggressive war against other vassal states. This suggests that vassal states enjoyed a large degree of political independence and territorial autonomy. These principles were somewhat similar to the principles of noninterference and territorial integrity in the modern sovereign state system. It is tempting to say the rights enjoyed by vassal states were similar to the notion of sovereign rights of modern states. But it is important to note that there are two significant differences between the rights of vassal states and the sovereign rights of modern states. The most important difference is that vassal states did not enjoy the absolute territorial rights because there was a higher authority—that is, the Zhou king— which in theory could withdraw the delegation of power or land tenure if they violated the Code of Nine Principles. Modern states enjoy absolute territorial rights or have permanent entitlement to their territories and no higher authority or world government can take them away. Moreover, the code mainly emphasizes the obligations that vassal states should comply with, rather than their sovereign rights or entitlements in the modern sense of the term. Even though sovereign rights of modern states are qualified by their legal and moral obligations that are stipulated in the UN Charter and UN-sponsored international covenants on human rights, the concept of sovereign rights in the modern sense connotes the much larger degree of rights that states are entitled to claim such as the principles of self-determination, noninterference, and territorial integrity in comparison with the rights of vassal states in the Zhou empire.

The second part of the code focuses on the obligations that vassal rulers owed to their people or individual subjects. As it stipulates, the main responsibilities of vassal rulers were to provide a basic livelihood for the people, to protect the people's physical security, and to ensure a degree of social justice. This included nourishing the children, providing a decent life for the parents and elders, helping the poor, relieving the people in need, and exonerating the people of heavy tax burdens. Failure to comply with these obligations would be punished severely by the Zhou king.

It is no coincidence that later on Mencius frequently lectured to the kings in the Warring States period that the states have obligations to provide a basic livelihood for the people. Mencius even endorsed foreign intervention in a state that oppressed its own people. Specifically, he supported the state of Qi's intervention in its neighboring state of Yan (燕) to rescue the people from being oppressed by its ruler. The ruler of the state of Yan usurped his power, which caused civil war and led to the miserable suffering of the people. When asked by the ruler of Qi if Qi has the right to intervene in the state of Yan, Mencius replied that the state of Qi has the right to intervene on behalf of the people of Yan and that if the state of Qi intervened militarily, the people of Yan would treat the military of Qi as their saviors and would welcome the military of Qi with open arms and great food.[16] In other words, Mencius's endorsement of foreign intervention on behalf of the oppressed people is consistent with the modern conception of human rights and resembles modern humanitarian intervention.

While the second part of the code is mainly concerned with the obligations that vassal rulers owed to their individual human subjects in protecting their lives and dignity, to say vassal rulers are obligated to protect the lives and dignity of their subjects and to provide a basic subsistence is an equivalent of saying that the individual subjects have innate entitlements to claim certain benefits from the rulers. This presupposes that the people have an innate dignity and human worth that deserve to be respected, which resembles to a certain degree the modern concept of human rights protection that is enshrined in the

Universal Declaration of Human Rights and the two UN covenants on human rights. Even though there are important differences in the scope of protecting human rights between the system of Zhou rites and the UN-sponsored International Covenant on Civil and Political Rights, they share the fundamental principles of protecting human life and dignity.

The third part recognizes the higher authority of the Zhou king over all vassal states and emphasizes the importance of maintaining the allegiance of the vassal rulers to the Zhou king. This reminds us of the obligations of UN member states to comply with UN Security Council resolutions as stipulated in the UN Charter.

In short, the three parts of the code nicely correspond to the three important aspects of postwar international order centered around the UN discussed above: First, states are obligated to maintain friendly relations with each other and to refrain from the use of force or the threat of force to settle their disputes. Second, states are obligated to protect the basic human rights and dignity of their subjects. Third, states are obligated to comply with the decisions made by the UN Security Council, the supranational authority.

When in the Spring and Autumn period the authority of the Zhou king was in decline and he was no longer able to send his own army to punish territorial aggression and other violations of other Zhou rites, some vassal states simply ignored the leadership of the Zhou king and engaged themselves in fierce competition and struggle for power expansion and territorial aggrandizement. Yet despite the decline of the Zhou king, some portions of Zhou rites survived. The leading states or hegemonic states of the Zhou empire took up the responsibility of maintaining the Zhou empire (or the *tianxia* order) on behalf of the Zhou king. More often than not, the hegemonic states usually formed a multistate military coalition with other allies to enforce the institutions of Zhou rites to repel foreign aggression.

In the light of the decline of the Zhou kings, the limited entitlement of vassal states to their territories gradually became permanent. To put it differently, these vassal states might enjoy the right to limited sovereignty to a certain extent, which was comparable to the modern sense of the term. Thus, the decline of the Zhou kings has made it possible to compare the interstate relations of these vassal states with the international relations of modern states. The following section provides some examples of how hegemonic states took up the responsibility of maintaining the *tianxia* order on behalf of the Zhou king.

The Maintenance of the *Tianxia* Order

This section discusses four cases drawn from the historical narratives of the *Zuozhuan*. They reveal the important role the Zhou rites played in regulating interstate relations and the important role the dominant states assumed in enforcing the Zhou rites and in the maintenance of the *tianxia* order during the Spring and Autumn period. The *Zuozhuan* is a Confucian classic that documents the political history of ancient China spanning some 250 years during the Spring and Autumn period. It also evaluates the personal conduct of political rulers in the empire on the basis of the ethical standards of the Zhou rites.

To a certain extent, the major ethical principles that governed the interstate relations among the states of the Zhou empire resemble some international rules and norms established by the UN Charter. These ethical rules and norms include the principles regarding states' rights, just war (or just war theory), self-defense, and territorial integrity. There are also rules and norms in the body of the Zhou rites concerning how war should be conducted and how prisoners of war should be treated. The following section provides four cases to illustrate the respective influence of the principle of peaceful settlement of conflicts, the principle of just war, the principle of self-defense, and the principle of territorial integrity in the conduct of interstate relations during the Spring and Autumn period as recorded in the *Zuozhuan*.

THE CONCEPTION OF JUST WAR

The state of Qi's hegemonic leadership in the *tianxia* order received the formal blessing of the Zhou king in the famous Covenant of Kui Qiu (葵丘之會) in which Duke Huan assembled a large multistate military coalition. As the Zhou empire was in decline during the Spring and Autumn period, the Zhou king had become dependent on a multistate coalition led by Qi for some forty years.

In 655 BC, there was an internal conflict over the succession of the Zhou king between his two sons. Qi and its many allies supported the eldest son as the legitimate heir to King Hui's throne in accordance with the system of Zhou rites. Yet King Hui of Zhou (周惠王) somehow favored his youngest son as heir and persuaded the state of Zheng to provide political support for the youngest son as the legitimate heir. The eldest son eventually succeeded to the throne due to the support of Qi and its many allied states.

In order to uphold the integrity of the institution of Zhou rites, Duke Huan of Qi put military pressure on Zheng to support King Hui's eldest son as the legitimate heir by assembling a multistate military coalition along its border with Zheng. The ruler of Zheng sent his eldest son, the designated successor to his father's lordship, to negotiate with Qi. The Zheng prince made a secret offer to support Qi's position on King Hui's eldest son as the legitimate heir under the condition that Qi attacked his political enemies inside Zheng and removed the political obstacles to his succession as the new Duke of Zheng. Duke Huan of Qi thought it was a good idea as he had tried several times to subdue Zheng without success. But his chief minister, Guan Zhong, disagreed and thought the prince's offer was morally wrong. Guan Zhong said that Qi's military alliance with other states was to uphold Zhou rites on the behalf of the Zhou king and that any use of force must be to defend Zhou rites and uphold the common interests of *tianxia*. Only when moral persuasion has failed can military force be used for the purpose of upholding Zhou rites. If Qi resorts to the use of force to attack Zheng for the self-interests of Qi and for the personal gain of the Zheng prince, it would be defeating its public purpose of upholding Zhou rites. Consequently, Qi's alliance with Zheng would not be formed on the basis of the common good and could not last long.

Duke Huan was persuaded by Guan Zhong and declined the prince's offer. A few months later, the ruler of Zheng decided to join the multistate coalition voluntarily and supported the legitimately designated new political principles of the state. The prince of Zheng was executed when he returned to Zheng.[17]

To sum up, it is clear that the reason Qi decided not to take up the prince's offer and launch a military attack against Zheng for Qi's self-interest was because of Guan Zhong's deep moral conviction that war should only be fought for promoting the common interests of the *tianxia* order and for upholding Zhou rites, rather than for the promotion of the private interests of a particular state or a person. This is very consistent with Aquinas's just war theory that war should be fought only for a public purpose.

THE CONCEPTION OF SELF-DEFENSE

After Duke Huan of Qi died, the state of Qi experienced a long period of internal turmoil, which gradually weakened Qi's long-standing hegemonic leadership. The state of Jin (晋), under its ruler Duke Wen of Jin (晋文公), emerged as the new dominant state in the *tianxia* order to exercise hegemonic leadership on the behalf of the Zhou king.

Shortly after Duke Wen of Jin was inaugurated, the King of Chu launched a new bid to challenge Jin's hegemonic leadership in the Zhou empire. Chu had brutally conquered its neighboring state of Cao and also formed a close alliance with another neighboring state, Wei, through matrimony. Both states were core members of the Zhou empire. Thus, Chu's military aggression continued to pose a major threat to the *tianxia* order.

In 633 BC, Chu sent a military force to surround the state of Song, another core state of the Zhou empire. Chu's goal was to break Song's alliance with Jin and force Song to defect to the side of Chu. Song's ruler had provided a tremendous amount of material support for Duke Wen of Jin while he was in exile in Song before he became the ruler. The ruler of Song believed then that Chong Er (重耳, Duke Wen's name before he became the ruler) was the most suitable candidate to assume the leadership of Jin and intended to establish a close relationship with the state of Jin after Chong Er became its ruler.

Because of the previous support he had received from Song, Duke Wen felt obligated to come to the defense of Song, which was under attack by Chu. His advisers proposed a strategy to help Song: that is, to attack Chu's allies Cao and Wei. Chu would have to divert its troops from Song to defend Cao and Wei, and Chu's military pressure on Song would be relieved. It also implied that Jin could avoid direct military confrontation with Chu.

Duke Wen of Jin fought hard battles to conquer Cao and Wei on the advice of his ministers. Chu's military commander, Ziyu, proposed that if Jin withdrew its military from Cao and Wei and restored the status of the lordship in these two states, Chu would pull back its troops around Song. Duke Wen then agreed to withdraw troops from Cao and Wei, but he also demanded the leaders of Cao and Wei openly denounce their alliance relationship with Chu. Ziyu was furious about Duke Wen's demand. He immediately moved troops out of Song and pursued the troops of Jin in the hope of crushing them.

Before Duke Wen took over his lordship, he had stayed in Chu for quite some time and received a lot of support and help from King Cheng of Chu (楚成王). When he was leaving Chu, King Cheng asked him how he would pay back his debts to Chu. Duke Wen had replied that if he would be lucky enough to return to his state as ruler, and the military of King Cheng's state and the military of Duke Wen's state ever encountered each other, Duke Wen's troops would retreat in three stages, so that the troops would not fight each other directly. So when Chu's military leader, Ziyu, ordered his troops to pursue Jin's troops, Duke Wen ordered his troops to retreat in three stages (one stage was about fifteen kilometers) in order to show his appreciation for the previous help he had received from Chu. Duke Wen did this because he firmly believed that a benevolent ruler should not betray the people who once helped him. Failure to comply with this ethical principle might incur the wrath of Heaven. Duke Wen's action provoked strong opposition within his own military, as some of his military commanders felt his retreat was a sign of weakness and cowardice in the face of the barbarian enemy, which was humiliating for a leading state of the Zhou empire. But Duke Wen simply ignored these commanders' opinion. His strategy of retreating in three stages has since become a legendary story in Chinese history.

Nonetheless, Ziyu, the maverick Chu military commander, was determined to crush Jin's troops and ordered his troops to pursue Jin's military despite Duke Wen's retreat. Ziyu's military action even went against the warning of the ruler of Chu. At this point, Duke Wen decided that direct military confrontation was unavoidable, and he ordered his troops to get prepared for the battle. The battle was then joined and ended in Chu's humiliating defeat and Jin's triumph. This war, which came to be known as the War of Chengpu (城濮之戰) marked the emergence of Jin as the new hegemonic leader of the Zhou empire.[18]

To sum up, Duke Wen believed it is morally wrong to launch offensive war and that his attack against Cao and Wei was a reaction to Chu's military aggression against the *tianxia* order. Clearly, Duke Wen's military strategy is very much consistent with the conception of self-defense and use of force as a last resort under Article 2(4) and Article 51 of the UN Charter. Nonetheless, even when Duke Wen was morally justified to attack Chu after Chu committed aggression first, Duke Wen still felt hesitant to confront Chu militarily because of another moral consideration. That is, he believed it is also morally wrong to engage in military conflict with the people who once helped you. It suggests that the ancient Chinese conception of military restraint went further than the conception of self-defense in the UN Charter. It also includes the moral precept of not engaging in war with the people who once helped you.

PRINCIPLES OF INTERNATIONAL COOPERATION AND MUTUAL ASSISTANCE

The hegemonic role played by the state of Qi was greatly weakened after the death of Duke Huan. Three states were competing to replace Qi for the new hegemonic leadership. The state of Jin (晉國) was situated in the northern part of the Zhou international system, the state of Qin (秦國) in the west, and the state of Chu in the south. The state of Qin, situated on the western flank of the Zhou empire, was growing rapidly in strength and its leader, Duke Mu of Qin, was ambitious to take up the hegemonic role left over by the declining Qi.

The leader of the state of Jin at the time was Duke Hui, the second son of Duke Xian, who succeeded to his father's position after a court plot led to the death of his eldest brother (the designated heir) and two other brothers. Duke Hui escaped from the country for some time and returned to Jin to take up his father's lordship with the political support of the state of Qin. Duke Hui of Jin offered to cede five cities in the western part of Jin bordering Qin to Qin in exchange for the political support of Duke Mu of Qin for Duke Hui's takeover of the lordship. Duke Mu of Qin was looking for an opportunity to expand his state eastward and agreed to the deal. But after Duke Hui took power, he reneged and did not give the five cities to Qin as he promised. There were officials inside Qin who advised Duke Mu to use military force to get the cities as Qin was promised. But Duke Mu of Qin did not go along.

In 647 BC, the state of Jin under Duke Hui suffered from severe famine and requested economic assistance from the state of Qin. Duke Mu of Qin sought advice from his advisers as to whether Qin should provide economic assistance to Jin. One adviser said, "Let us help Jin one more time. If the people of Jin return the favor as they promised, your highness will get what you wanted. If they do not return the favor, Duke Hui of Jin will lose his credibility and will lose the political support of his own people. Then if we use force to take away the cities, it will be much easier." Another adviser said that "natural disaster happens in every country, it is in accordance with the way of Heaven that people help each other and that neighboring states provide assistance to each other in times of natural disasters. If we follow the way of Heaven, we will be blessed." Duke Mu of Qin then concurred, saying, "although I despise the leader of that country, the people of Jin are innocent and deserve our help." Shortly after, Duke Mu ordered the provision of large quantities of food and crops to be shipped to Jin.[19]

Confucianism believes men are innately good, as evident in Mencius's conception of four potentially good human qualities: benevolence, justice, rules of propriety, and wisdom. Being compassionate to people is evidence of such benevolence as preordained by Heaven. When people practice filial piety to their parents at home, such compassion can be made to develop to its fullest extent and can even transcend politics and temper political animosity. As the above case suggests, such compassion was extended even to the people of an enemy state when the people in that state were suffering from natural disaster. Facing the moral dilemma between launching a punitive expedition against Duke Hui of Jin for reneging on his promise to cede territories and meeting the urgent humanitarian needs of the suffering people of Jin in time of natural disaster, Duke Mu of Qin clearly opted for the latter. The moral principle of compassion toward humanity mitigated the impulse of territorial ambition and prevented Duke Mu of Qi from using force to seize the territories that Duke Hui of Jin had promised to give him. In the end such an ethical principle also induced Duke Mu of Qin to provide massive economic assistance to the suffering people of Jin despite his animosity toward Duke Hui.

This story suggests that there are some similarities between Confucian ethics and Christian ethics. In the New Testament, Jesus preached that one should love one's neighbor as oneself, which includes one's enemy, in the parable of the Good Samaritan.[20] Similarly, Confucians also touted the principle that humans have a moral obligation bestowed by Heaven to love fellow human beings outside their family or outside their own community.

To a certain extent, this Confucian conception of mutual assistance among nations resembles the UN Charter's Article 2(3), which states that the UN's goal is "to achieve international co-operation in solving international problems of an economic, social, cultural, or humanitarian character, and in promoting and encouraging respect for human rights and for fundamental freedoms for all without distinction as to race, sex, language, or religion." Moreover, this Confucian principle of mutual assistance is identical to the principle of mutual assistance in times of drought and famine in John Rawls's proposal for the law of peoples to govern the interaction among the peoples of the world. Rawls's law of peoples includes some major principles of the UN Charter such as the principles of nonaggression, nonintervention, and self-defense.[21]

TERRITORIAL INTEGRITY AND PROPORTIONALITY OF PUNITIVE FORCE

The state of Chen (陳國), like the state of Zheng, was situated between the two competing dominant powers, Jin and Chu. In 599 BC, there was internal political turmoil within the state of Chen. The minister of war, named Xia, killed Duke Ling of Chen because Duke Ling was having a love affair with the beautiful mother of the minister of war. Xia installed himself as ruler.

King Zhuang of Chu (楚莊王), the grandson of King Cheng of Chu, felt it was his moral responsibility to punish this outrageous act of regicide. King Zhuang of Chu sent a military force to the state of Chen and arrested the new ruler and had him executed. But King Zhuang of Chu did not withdraw his military from the state of Chen. He had his troops stationed there and formally annexed the state of Chen as a county of the state of Chu.

When King Zhuang's close adviser Shen returned to Chu from a foreign mission, he criticized the king's conquest of the state of Chen. As the adviser explained, there was no question that the new ruler of Chen deserved punishment because he committed regicide. It is a morally right thing for a king to punish such an egregious crime. But it is morally wrong to annex the state of Chen and make it a part of Chu. The adviser used an analogy to explain to the king why he and many other high-ranking officials disapproved of the king's military action.

The analogy is like this: When someone allows his ox to trample on the crops in your field, you confiscate his ox. It is of course wrong to allow the ox to trample on the crops. But when you confiscate the ox, the punishment is certainly way out of proportion. Many of us supported your highness's sending troops into the state of Chen only because they wanted to punish the man who committed regicide. But when you took the possession of the state of Chen by annexing it, it was motivated by greed and it was morally wrong. You started the campaign as a moral crusade, but ended it as an act of greed. King Zhuang of Chu was taken aback by these criticisms but was delighted by Minister Shen's candid advice. He then decided to end the annexation and restore the territorial integrity of the state of Chen.[22]

Clearly, the ancient Chinese during the Spring and Autumn period conceived the territory of a state as some kind of possession bestowed on the rulers of states by the Zhou king. Based on the Code of Nine Principles for Royal Expedition, the rulers of states did not have absolute control over their territories. Their territories could be taken away as punishment if rulers violated ethical principles as stipulated in the Code of Nine Principles.

Nonetheless, with the authority of the Zhou king having weakened, it seems the mutual recognition of territorial rights among states within the *tianxia* order had become an important source of territorial rights. It appears that it had become a norm that the territory of a state, like the private possession of property, could not be taken away without the consensual approval of other states in the *tianxia* order. This is somewhat similar to the modern conception of territorial integrity, which suggests that the control of states over their territories is conferred through the mutual recognition among states.

Conclusion

The hierarchical nature of the *tianxia* order in ancient China has been often contrasted starkly with the sovereign nation-state system of the modern era. Nonetheless, despite the important differences between the two systems, it is worth noting the similarities between the ancient Chinese *tianxia* order and the postwar UN-centric international order as the above analysis shows. These similarities are most pronounced during the Spring and Autumn period as the power of the Zhou king declined considerably and his need to rely on the power of hegemonic states to maintain the empire became more acute.

This chapter has identified three major similarities between the ancient Chinese *tianxia* order and the postwar UN-centric international order, notwithstanding the important differences between the two international orders. First, both international orders are hierarchical with a strong sense of cosmopolitanism. In both orders, there has been a nominal power center sitting at the top of the hierarchy, or something that resembled a world government. In the postwar international order, the UN Security Council is the power center at the top of the hierarchy when it comes to the operation of UN collective security. In the ancient Chinese world order, the Zhou king is the power center at the top of the hierarchy. Arguably, the composition of the power centers at the top of the two international orders is very different. The power center of the UN Security Council is represented by its five permanent members, whereas the power center at the top of the Chinese *tianxia* order was the Zhou king.

The two international orders are both hierarchical, for two reasons. First, the UN is not just simply an international organization; rather it resembles a world legislature to a certain extent. The UN Charter's Article 2(4) outlaws the use of aggressive war as a foreign policy instrument and only legalizes defensive war (Article 51). The UN legislates international law through the codification of international law in the UN Assembly, such as the adoption of the Law of the Seas. The UN also legislates and adjudicates international trade law through the GATT and the WTO. Furthermore, the UN does not simply just legislate international law; it also enforces international law through the UN Security Council in the case of a collective security operation against aggression. The power center at the top of the UN-centric hierarchy sometimes is nominal, but at times it exercises real and substantial influence. While the UN Charter upholds national equality, the power structure of the Security Council operates in violation of the principle of national equality in that the five permanent members of the Security Council enjoy the exclusive privilege of veto power. This extraordinary privilege is the most important evidence to attest to the fact that the UN-centric postwar international order is a hierarchical order dominated by the five permanent members of the Security Council, and at times by the United States single-handedly.

Second, both international orders have relied on a system of international ethical rules and norms in the maintenance of the international order. The UN Charter and the UN-sponsored codification of international law have served as the major ethical basis in the maintenance of the postwar international order. In ancient China, it was the body of *Zhouli* that formed the major ethical foundation in the maintenance of the *tianxia* order.

Third, although both international orders have a nominal power center at the top of the hierarchy, in reality both of these power centers do not exercise real power. It is the most powerful state, or the hegemonic states, that exercises the de facto leadership on behalf of the power center in the maintenance of both international orders. The hegemonic states usually form a multistate military coalition to enforce the international order. In the postwar international order, while the UN Charter has envisioned an ideal collective security mechanism whereby the five permanent members of the UN Security Council would exercise collective responsibility in the UN's collective security operations, it is in fact the United States that has dominated the UN's collective security operations. In the ancient Chinese case, it was one of the dominant states, be it Qi, Jin, or later on Chu, that exercised the hegemonic leadership on behalf of the Zhou king.

There has been a lot of concern in the Western world that in light of China's rapid rise, China may adopt an alternative vision of world order based on the ancient Chinese *tianxia* order, which may lead to major conflicts between the United States and China.[23] Nonetheless, if this study is correct, it might have important implications for future Chinese-American relations. As this analysis has shown, despite important differences, there are some areas in the ancient Chinese vision of international order that may complement, rather than contradict or challenge, the UN-centric postwar international order. This includes, for example, the notion of limited sovereignty, the conception of just war, the obligation of states to exercise self-restraint in the use of force, the obligation of states to protect human dignity and worth, the legitimacy of humanitarian intervention, and the role and responsibility of the dominant states in the maintenance of international peace. The future Chinese vision of international order inspired by the *tianxia* concept in the Spring and Autumn period might not necessarily be in irreconcilable conflict with the UN-centric postwar international order.

Notes

1. Many Western Sinologists have treated the interstate relations in ancient China during the Spring and Autumn period as a universal empire identical with the tributary system of later China and believed that the ancient *tianxia* order was in sharp contrast with the modern sovereign state system, and this is why it was very difficult for Chinese to adapt to the sovereign state system in the late nineteenth century by abandoning the *tianxia* order. See Cho-Yun Hsu, "Applying Confucian Ethics to International Relations," *Ethics and International Relations* 5 (March 1991): 15–31; and H. G. Creel, *The Origins of Statecraft in China: The Western Chou Empire,* vol. 1 (Chicago: University of Chicago Press, 1970). See also Benjamin Schwartz, "The Chinese Perception of World Order: Past and Present," in *The Chinese World Order: Traditional China's Foreign Relations,* ed. John K. Fairbank (Cambridge, MA: Harvard University Press, 1968), pp. 278–284. It is worth noting that Richard Louis Walker has provided a unique study in which he identifies the interstate system of the Spring and Autumn period closely with the modern sovereign state system. See Walker, *The Multi-state System of Ancient China* (Hamden, CT: Shoe String Press, 1954).

2. John K. Fairbank, "A Preliminary Framework," in *The Chinese World Order: Traditional China's Foreign Relations,* ed. John K. Fairbank (Cambridge, MA: Harvard University Press, 1968), pp. 5–10.

3. Terry Nardin, *Law, Morality and the Relations of States* (Princeton, NJ: Princeton University Press, 1983), pp. 52–53.

4. Murray Forsyth, "The Tradition of International Law," in *Traditions of International Ethics,* ed. Terry Nardin and David R. Mapel (Cambridge: Cambridge University Press, 1992), pp. 32–33.

5. Cited in Terry Nardin, "The Moral Basis of Humanitarian Intervention," *Ethics and International Affairs,* 16, no. 2 (March 2002): 58–59.

6. Paul E. Sigmund, ed., *St. Thomas Aquinas on Politics and Ethics* (New York: W. W. Norton, 1988), pp. 64–65.

7. Forsyth, "Tradition of International Law," pp. 32–33.

8. Nardin, *Law, Morality,* p. 63.

9. Anthony Ellis, "Utilitarianism and International Ethics," in Nardin and Mapel, *Traditions of International Ethics,* pp. 161–164.

10. Hsu, "Applying Confucian Ethics," pp. 15–31.

11. Creel, *Origins of Statecraft in China,* pp. 54–55.

12. Creel, *Origins of Statecraft in China,* p. 306.

13. As Benjamin Schwartz suggests, "The *li* is in essence a kind of 'natural law' in the stoic and medieval sense. Like natural law, it is not self-enacting. Yet it would appear that what the ancient sages did in bringing the order of society into existence was not invent an arbitrary system of *li* but 'discover' it by a process of arduous reflection." Schwartz, *The World of Thought in Ancient China* (Cambridge, MA: Harvard University Press, 1985), pp. 301–302.

14. The original Chinese text reads: "君令臣共，父慈子孝，兄愛弟敬，夫和妻柔，姑慈婦聽，禮也."《左傳. 昭公 26 年》(*Zuozhuan* Duke Zhao year 26).

15. Translation adapted from Confucius, *The Analects,* trans. D. C. Lau (London: Penguin Classics, 1979), book IV:13, p. 74.

16. Mencius, *Mencius,* trans. D. C. Lau (London: Penguin Classics, 2003), p. 25.

17. James Legge, *The Ch'un Ts'ew with the Tso Chuen* (Beijing: Beijing Normal University Press, 2011), book V (Duke He), year V, pp. 142–146; year VII, pp. 147–148.

18. Legge, *Ch'un Ts'ew,* book V (Duke He), year XXVIII, pp. 202–212.

19. Legge, *Ch'un Ts'ew,* book V (Duke He), year X and year XIII, pp. 155–156, 160.

20. Joseph Boyle, "Natural Law and International Ethics," in Nardin and Mapel, *Traditions of International Ethics,* p. 125.

21. John Rawls, "The Law of Peoples," *Critical Inquiry* 20, no. 1 (Autumn 1993): 47.

22. James Legge, *Ch'un Ts'ew,* book VII (Duke Seuen), year XI, pp. 308–309.

23. For example, see William A. Callahan, "Chinese Visions of World Order: Post-Hegemonic or a New Hegemony?," *International Studies Review* 10, no. 4 (December 2008): 749–761.

CHAPTER 8

Tianxia and Islam

Mustapha Kamal PASHA

APPARENT DIVERGENCES OFTEN conceal latent points of contact, dialogue, and convergence. Drawn from alternative cosmological principles, *tianxia* (天下) and Islam display essential differences, not only in their grounding metaphysics but also in the shape of the political orders imagined in the shadows of opposing cosmologies.[1] On a cursory reading, *tianxia* congeals an immanentist cosmological principle devoid of theological pretensions.[2] Islam, in its pristine cosmological purity, rests principally on Transcendence.[3] The registers of *tianxia* and Islam, on this swift appraisal, could not be more divergent. An axiomatic source of difference is the absence of the notion of a singular transcendent entity in Chinese philosophy that grounds *tianxia*. Confucianism, the major source of that philosophy, enjoins its followers to exemplify righteous conduct, not religious piety.[4] Islam is unimaginable without an unshakeable belief in a monotheistic God whose power permeates the universe.[5]

Contrary to a reductive capture of Islamicness, however, the immanent register is no less important in Islam than its transcendent counterpart.[6] Both transcendental and immanentist elements must combine to nurture authentic belonging within the religious fold. Hence, personal piety is an insufficient prerequisite to actualize faith; the spiritual life is intertwined with other immanentist spheres of expanding human sociability: family, community, and humanity. While seeking transcendence, the community of faith in Islam materializes within an immanent political space in anticipation of the Hereafter. Similarly, the salience of Heaven (*tian*) in Chinese cosmology rescinds the notion of its assumed singular attachment to immanence.[7] Heaven may not be a visible presence in human affairs, but it remains a critical force in harnessing the social and political order. Hence, de-essentialized mappings of *tianxia* and Islam show that the register of immanence is not entirely absent from Islam, nor is *tianxia* lacking in intimations of transcendence, albeit in a language that resists monotheistic entrapment. The Heaven that lurks behind *tianxia* may be uninhabitable for the Abrahamic God, but its effects for humankind are no less compelling.

Intimations of a transcendence / immanence dualism find fortification in modernist claims of elective affinity between immanence and secularity, and between transcendence and religiosity. On this reading, the absence of secularity in Islam matches Confucianism's assumed secularity. Cosmological divergence also materializes on the plane of history. The cultural codes linked to Confucianism and Islam realize radically different processes and outcomes. Despite sustained interaction and dialogue between China and the Islamic world and the production of a plethora of hybrid cultural forms—in architecture, poetic expression, and the arts, among others—neither Confucianism nor Islam permits cosmological convergence or synthesis.[8]

What affinities can be discerned between these opposing cosmologies against the stubborn picture of divergence? The first step toward finding affinities is to shun dualistic thinking, allowing instead a detection of deeper sources of confluence. First, in both cosmologies, *moral conduct* is an indispensable prerequisite for human perfection, a transcendent value reaching up to Heaven or the Abrahamic God. Human conduct must conform to a determinate set of inviolable moral principles, not expediency. These principles are binding, both to shape society and to create social harmony. In both cosmologies, social purpose must subordinate individual self-interest.[9]

A second step toward seeking convergence is the recognition that the imagined space of human sociability and belonging is unhinged from modern constrictions of nation and state: "All-under-Heaven" (*tianxia*) in Chinese philosophy or the notion of the human community (*Ummah*) in Islam.[10] The spatial sphere of human belonging resists parochial attachments. Hence, the expansive understanding of the imagined community in both cosmologies breaches notions of mutually exclusive bounded (e.g., national) spaces linked to Western modernity; *tianxia* and the *Ummah* present alternative cartographic horizons.[11]

These alternative mappings of the constitution of human community acquire even greater salience in present times. The quest to find pathways of confluence between non-Western cosmologies emerges not simply as a philosophical exercise but as a practical necessity elicited by the deepening crisis of Western modernity and its attendant ecological crisis.[12] In particular, the sacralization of the modern state attending the Westphalian model of global governance has effectively exposed its limits, hindering cultural tolerance and harmony on a world scale. In turn, by furthering a culture of competition and widening global inequality, Western modernity exposes its intrinsic opposition toward building universal society. The ecological crisis underscores the growing discordance between Western modern political and economic reason on the one hand and the planet's sustainability on the other.

Embedded in the recesses of moral philosophy and historical practice, therefore, different conceptions of imagining political space and identity offer *other* possibilities for structuring social relations and nurturing a more harmonious relation between nature and humankind. A comparative engagement with *tianxia* and Islam offers rich resources for imagining alternative worlds. While the centrality of moral conduct in both Islam and Confucianism bridges the cosmological divide and its divergent origins and principles, transcendence from the Westphalian prison house and its associated exclusivities carries the seeds of a common horizon of a post-Westphalian imagined community. *Tianxia* and the Islamic notion of *Ummah,* especially, escape the exclusivist logic that lies at the heart of the Westphalian system. Affording alternative notions of human connectivity and interdependence, *tianxia* and the *Ummah* can help denaturalize the modern world-system.

This chapter resists the urge to find specious points of similarity, overlap, or convergence between the two cosmological orders or worldviews. While seemingly useful in revealing homologies, simple comparisons suppress recognition of the distinctiveness of the quest for the universal. Rather, the central aim here is probe the presence of deeper affinities occasioned by similar challenges. On the surface, Islam and *tianxia* do not supply common horizons, but in a more profound sense both recognize human finitude as a basic ontological condition. This attitude stands in stark opposition to available rationalities of organizing international space and the fictitious pursuit of individual freedom.[13] Ensnared in Westphalian containers of political being, a fractured human community is catechized to realize freedom through competition or conflict. Westphalian sovereignty naturalizes human divergence, obviating the possibility of a universal community. Conversely, the culture of competition forged by the fiction of a sovereign individual inhibits the pursuit of societal harmony and coexistence with the natural world. Driven by the twin impulses of national sovereignty and sovereign individuality, the post-Westphalian Enlightenment subject takes Otherness merely as a vehicle for self-valorization, against humanity and nature alike. *Tianxia* and Islam envision a different order of being.

On this post-Western premise, even a cursory engagement with past encounters and exchanges between China and the Islamic world helps contravene received narratives of European diffusion and the peripheralization of the non-West.[14] A more sustained re-examination of the normative aspects of *tianxia* and Islam can show the contours of alternative universalisms. No longer appended to the story of European exceptionalism and the rise of the West, alternative pictures of world-making can also become legible. An awareness of civilizational encounters between China and the Islamic world, predating the advent of Western ascendance and hegemony, also helps to contribute toward a refutation of Eurocentric conceptions of world politics.[15] Pivoted around the Old Silk Road, exchange between Islam and China, in particular, uncovers the existence of different pathways in the making of the modern world.[16] As an alternative to the assumed universalism of Westphalian political reason, different conceptions of international relations resurface, conceptions usually lurking behind civilizational exchange.

Recent scholarship provides ample evidence of intercommunication between the Chinese and Islamic civilizational zones, especially during the Qing period.[17] The expansion of these zones, as is usually the case with cultural encounters, is marked by conversion, mutual borrowing, and distribution of people and objects. A knowledge of these interactions is a small step toward revitalizing civilizational energies once ruptured or depleted by Western intrusion and European hegemony.[18] Dispelling the assumed refrain, retrieval of the past is linked neither to imperial nostalgia nor to civilizational wistfulness, but toward refamiliarization with (normative) principles informing alternative designs. Reworked to meet current challenges, these principles can offer the kernel of rethinking the constitution of international society.

Although intimate connections between universalisms produced within the two civilizational spheres are not immediately apparent, closer probing suggests that the universal community promised in *tianxia* avoids parochial attachments to Westphalia, nation, or tribe. Similarly, Islam offers a horizontal nexus to humankind secured by a vertical relation to the One.[19] Both *tianxia* and Islam share the value of ontological parity, although they both foster cosmological hierarchy to instantiate universalism, creating the difficulty of reconciling inclusion with otherness. The ethical principles grounding *tianxia* and Islam, however, contain the potential to overcome this difficulty.

A fruitful site to explore the above possibility lies in the normative foundations of *tianxia* and Islam. In defiance of sovereign individuality, Confucian and Islamic ethics both advance the idea of a nested individual, anchored in obligations. Regard for the family, society, and humanity replaces the idea of exchange as the principle of human connectivity. Similarly, the world is viewed not as a theater of perpetual conflict but as a terrain of sociability and harmony. Resting on these principles, alternative visions emerge that seek transcendence from the competitive nature of the extant world order. Responding to the need for a more humane and equitable world order, these principles serve as a counterpoint to available political reason. *Tianxia* and Islam, therefore, also offer the hope of confronting the man-made ecological crisis that threatens the planet. At a minimum, these principles not only expose the constricting horizon of the status quo but suggest that other worlds are imaginable. On this reading, the hegemonic conceit that erases all alternatives can be denaturalized.

Tianxia

As with any complex cosmological system, *tianxia* invites diverse understandings and interpretations. A growing field of scholarship on *tianxia* underscores the importance attached to its post-Westphalian horizon, which carries the potential to combat the twin political and existential crises produced by competing sovereignties and the climate emergency.[20] While robust defense of the Westphalian order is not lacking, nuanced formulations from scholars on and from China on *tianxia* and its philosophical anchoring underscore the risks of oversimplification.[21]

A useful place to initiate an abridged account of *tianxia* is Wang Mingming's reworking of the philosophical mapping of nineteenth-century thinker Liang Qichao, which captures some key features of the concept.[22] Engaging Liang's work, Wang identifies two central elements of *tianxia* (All-under-Heaven): (1) the world (*shijie* 世界), which comprises all "the realms on earth," distinct from the (territorial) nation; and (2) a different conception of the world (*shijie sixiang* 世界思想). Critical to *tianxia* is a rejection of the constrictive spatio-political horizon embedded in the concept of nation that essentially links territoriality with blood or an imagined community premised on impersonal relationality.[23] The universalism embedded in *tianxia* encompasses hierarchically distributed polities of dissimilar size and significance. According to Wang, "*Tianxia* historically conveyed a certain supra-societal system in the classical and imperial periods; it is thus referred to as a political entity whose topographical scope was far greater than a kingdom (*guo* 國)."[24] Wang's reading of *tianxia* implicitly equates territorial China with the Universe itself. Keeping the image of the Westphalian system in the background can help provide a vivid contrast with *tianxia*. The political order conceived in *tianxia* cultivates *relational*, not substantive, ontology, one of the core features in Confucian cosmology.[25] This feature directs inquiry into the normative edifice of the concept. Being-in-relation challenges the notion of atomistic existence.

For Wang, the second component of Liang's formulation "concerns the interrelationship between cosmology and the perception of the 'real world'":

> [As] a cosmological totality, *tianxia* was given meanings in the varied activities of those who endeavored intellectually and politically to come to terms with an *asymmetrical relationship* between earth and heaven. This asymmetrical relationship, on the one hand, refers to a proportional truth: the earth is smaller than heaven. On the other hand, in relationship to

tianxia as a polity, this asymmetrical relationship specifically referred to the gap between the *realistic geography* of the territorial coverage of *tianxia* as an actual political system and the *imaginary cosmography* in which *tianxia* was situated. The former is limited, whereas the latter is infinite. *Tianxia*, in other words, was a *world-scape*, built into the larger cosmology that covered earth, heaven, and everything in-between.[26]

The notion of a *world-scape* advances a Universalist notion of political space, not the fractured space associated with Westphalian sovereignty. In the latter instance, the world order is built upon the logic of mutual exclusivity. A system of separate nation-states privileges the "inside" over the "outside." The "outside," as international relations scholars propose, is the realm of Hobbesian anarchy. In essence, this is a system of self-help, competition, and potential conflict.[27] Disguised in this system of "equal" political entities, however, is an intrinsic asymmetry between the rich and the powerful, on the one hand, and the poor and the weak, on the other. Although *tianxia* rests on the principle of hierarchy, it spurns an ethos of competition and conflict.[28] For critics, it is the hierarchical nature of *tianxia* that draws fire. In the present political climate, the easy association of *tianxia* with the rise of China further emboldens these critics. Observed through the Realist framework, the revival of *tianxia* and China's growing global ascendance appear incontrovertible.

The Realist framework, however, thwarts the possibility of examining *tianxia*'s philosophical meanings at two principal levels. Trapped within the constricted horizon of international politics, *tianxia*'s *moral* dimension is eclipsed by the narrative of legitimation for Chinese dominance or hegemony. As mentioned, what separates *tianxia* from the Westphalian system is the former's explicit relational ontology. Merging a notion of an ordered world with a conception of relations "between the Self and the Other," *tianxia* is premised not on relations between polities or states but on *human relations*, "relations between persons and things, humans and divinities."[29] Despite its "secular" appearance, *tianxia* conceives of the world as "a territorial-cum-celestial totality." On Wang's summary of Liang's formulation, this totality comprises "three levels: heaven above, earth below, and mountains, rivers, seas, trees, and divinities in the middle."[30]

Tianxia captures a Chinese civilizational ideal and a worldview linked to that ideal. Some proponents of this worldview (All-under-Heaven) no doubt mobilize it to legitimatize China's rising power in the world. *Tianxia*'s current protagonists, however, see it as an alternative to empire or hegemony. In their estimation, *tianxia* provides an alternative language of recognition and aspiration. Borrowed from the ancient past, *tianxia* unites the old and the new China, healing the wound of historical rupture produced by Western colonial / imperial adventure. *Tianxia*'s supporters also stress its cosmopolitan appeal, *tianxia* serving as a vehicle for discarding the shackles Westphalian sovereignty places on the Chinese civilizational-state.

Another source of contention is *tianxia*'s supposed illiberal character, one suffused by a nostalgic yearning for an imperial past. Speaking principally to the disciplinary community of international relations, for instance, Chu Sinan stresses this element in his long list of flaws in "*tianxia* theories," including their reliance on a strict binary distinction between the West and the non-West, a "selective and arbitrary reading of the Chinese philosophy," and rationalization of hierarchy and "advocating a Sinocentric world order."[31] A counterpoint of this critique is the delinking of the notion of "universal civilization" from any distinct culture, but also stressing decentralization and nonhierarchy as structuring principles of *tianxia*.[32]

Tianxia blends a normative and a political order that thrived in imperial Chinese theory and practice. In its revised manifestation, *tianxia* forsakes its reliance on a civilized–barbarian divide that gave the old *tianxia* its raison d'être. Instead, the new *tianxia* seeks to promote a culture of openness to the world, underscoring its recognition of a radically transformed historical context. This pathway seeks to decouple *tianxia* from nationalism, inwardness, and Sino-centrism. On this revised reading, the emergence of the nation-state is seen only as a recent episode in Chinese history, chiefly the product of interactions with Western modernity. Implicit in the new *tianxia*-ism is a repudiation of the idea of historical rupture; Chinese civilization never abandoned its Confucian past and the normative system embedded in that past.[33]

The relational ontology specific to the new *tianxia*-ism also stresses China's historical willingness to learn from others and an attitude of tolerance, not nationalist conflict, with the West. This stance presents China as a cosmopolitan state that advances universal values of harmony, cooperation, and coexistence. Avoiding the culturally coded particularism of the old *tianxia*-ism, its purported successor offers a vision of a post-Westphalian world order. A similar tendency is discernible in cosmopolitan correctives to the religious particularism of certain interpretations of the *Ummah*.[34] A dialogue between the new *tianxia*-ism and Islamic cosmopolitanism in this context becomes highly desirable.

The Islamic Cosmological Order

A proper understanding of the Islamic cosmological order cannot rest on the familiar caricature of a much-advertised Islamic State.[35] This portrait largely circumvents the deeper resonances of a universal order that rejects exclusion as an ordering principle. Islam's cosmological map affords an alternate Universalist topography of human entanglement with the cosmos.[36] The envisioned community (*Ummah*) remains essentially an intermediate zone between Divinity and the earth. Unlike the Westphalian universe of divided, albeit sovereign, political units, the *Ummah* is not simply a fixed association of sameness but a universal community. The universalistic dimension of the *Ummah* has eluded virtually all standard accounts; the *Ummah* is not simply a closed union of the faithful—an ideal that pulls the believers toward an ideal polis—but a community of human oneness nurtured against the anticipation of union with the Divine. The universalistic character of the *Ummah* puts into question notions of a perfect Islamic state imagined by its current advocates. These fervent believers import modern notions of sovereignty into a cosmological field inseparable from the demands of eschatology.[37]

More broadly, a formidable obstacle to direct access to the universalistic message in Islamic cosmology is its reduction to a particularistic doctrine addressed principally to Muslims.[38] Another hurdle is the Orientalist prejudice that denies Islamic cosmology either self-sufficiency or autonomy. This bias takes two principal forms: the notions that much of Islamic cosmology is derivative from Greek metaphysics or that it is merely "a synthesis of Greek heritage and Islamic revelation."[39] The more charitable view reflected in the second version provincializes the importance of the principle of *Tawhid* to the Islamic cosmological order. This Abrahamic principle certainly does not require pantheistic mappings afforded by Greek speculation. While Greek philosophy certainly allows religious ideas an important source for rational interrogation and mathematical validation, it is the concept of unity that is distinctive about Islam.[40] *Tawhid* is not simply the affirmation of God's transcendent singularity but the idea of harmony that permits homologies between all forms of existence. Transferred to a picture of human entanglement, singularity allows universality. The vertical attachment to God creates a basis for horizontal unison among living things.

The distribution of existent things in which the human emerges as a privileged ontological entity is essentially hierarchical. This image comports with a cosmological design in which reflexivity and capacity for moral judgment separate humanity from other beings. The capacity for knowledge and its deployment are crucial to the process of defining the vocation of the human in the cosmos: "Through his knowledge of all the Divine names, or aspects, regarded as the key to the knowledge of Nature, man has gained superiority over all other terrestrial beings and even in a certain way over angels."[41] Yet, the misuse of knowledge is also the cause of much mischief. Humanity's abuse of nature and others deemed less capable of making sense of the cosmos litters history, neither intended by Creation nor permitted in the Qur'an.

The hierarchical structure of the cosmos in the Qur'an allows the one and the many to coexist in a dialectical mode. Through knowledge of God and Creation, Oneness becomes intelligible. God's transcendent nature points to a singular source. On the other hand, existent beings also divulge differences that emerge from their location within a hierarchical order, reaching up to their singular source. At the level of humanity, however, Islamic cosmology brooks no divergence. Neither phenotypical difference nor divergences in aptitude split humanity. Even a divide between those who embrace or reject God's Oneness does not distort the cosmological design. Only in its political instantiation does distinction in religious commitment produce gradations, reflected in the ambivalent nature of the concept of the *Ummah*. The distinction between the cosmological and the political in Islamic history offers poignant warnings of inclusive and exclusive pathways available to the community in different epochs and often within the same epoch.[42] Building on the notion of "unity of humankind" Islam contains within its deeper core a cosmopolitan impulse.

The cosmopolitan impulse, nonetheless, stands in plain opposition to the conventional division of the world in Islamic legal thought between *dar al-Islam* (the territory where Muslim law prevails) and *dar al-harb* (literally "the realm of war," where Muslim law does not prevail). The intermediate zone, *dar al-sulh* (the territory where a peace treaty or armistice between Muslims and non-Muslims prevails), softens the binary between war and peace, but it fails to inject a cosmopolitan impulse in Islam's relations with its others.[43] To meet current challenges, however, that impulse is best recovered by revisiting the originary Qur'anic notion of "unity of humankind." This would also require prioritization of principle above practice but also delinking Islam's normative appeal from political reason. A similar attitude is warranted in rethinking the notion of humankind as *ashraf ul makhluqat* (the noblest of all creatures) in view of the Qur'anic awareness of the sanctity of all life.

Hence, the cosmological order sanctioned in Islam does not give unlimited license to humans to subordinate other existent beings.[44] Nor does Islam privilege the individual over society, an attitude that signifies the modern sovereign individual. Despite the elevation of the human in the chain of existent beings, the moral code demands restraint, caution, and humility in social relations and between society and nature. In turn, this code rests on an awareness of basic human finitude. Hence, the transient character of human existence serves as a constant reminder of the distinction between the eternal and the ephemeral. Human finitude melds the notion of impermanence with the idea of God's timeless existence. Annihilation is not simply a biological fact but a necessary ontological ground to build the Islamic cosmological structure. Viewed on a comparative scale, *tianxia* may not harbor notions of human finitude so explicitly, but the recurrent rise and fall of empires suggests an implicit embrace of the primacy of Heaven over earth.

The generative power of Faith (*iman*) separates Islam from secular and pantheistic cosmologies that struggle to reconcile spiritual oneness with notions of a graded human order, such as classifications between the civilizer and the barbarian, or between the native and the foreigner. The notion of hierarchy advanced in Islamic cosmology repudiates racial or cultural correlates of inclusivity. Membership in the Islamic community is not contingent upon birth, inheritance, or filial relations. Rather, it lies in a recognition of Oneness as the principle that unifies the universe. Acknowledging the sovereignty of the One integrates both the Cosmos and Humanity. The Islamic community can only emerge by accepting this elementary principle. Hierarchy guarantees human coevalness. Once God's undivided sovereignty is embraced—the *vertical* principle—the human community that emerges is liberated from primordial difference—the *horizontal* principle.

Notwithstanding redemptive currents in actually existing Islam, the absence of a conception of original sin characterizes the last of the Abrahamic faiths as a religion of perfectibility. Carrying the seeds of goodness at its essential core, imperfection is merely an obstacle, not destiny.[45] The capacity to gain knowledge and moral judgment gives the believer in Oneness the freedom to write an autonomous script unhinged from natural determination. On this reading, Islam is a religion of freedom with infinite possibilities to marvel and understand the mysteries of the universe. God demands obligation to fulfill the purpose of Creation but spares the human from natural determination. Affirmation of God's unity, and the unity of the created world, gives life purpose. This ontological condition is not a trap to elude but a human entitlement, as a knowing being, as *ashraf ul makhluqat* (the noblest of all creatures).

The mission of perfectibility receives its finest rendition in Sufi conceptions of the union of the Divine with the believer.[46] Usually dismissed in literalist variants of Islam (and their political equivalents) as asceticism, the quest for perfection relies on attaining integration within the Self as a passage toward oneness with the Divine. The confluence between inner unity and unity with the Divine paves the way toward perfection. This spiritual journey stands in stark contrast to the desire for sovereignty within Western modernity.

While the path toward perfection is available to all humans, few traverse its steep hills and mountains. The spiritual journey rests on discipline of the body and soul. As humans are exposed to distraction, material enticement, or avarice, the journey can be easily interrupted or abandoned. The only guarantee to complete the passage to perfection is steadfast commitment to *Tawhid*. Hence submission is a not a one-time step to steer the journey but imperative in all phases of the spiritual voyage. Ritual is no less important, but unlike ritual in literalist Faith, where it merely becomes a simulacrum of Faith itself and emptied out of its spiritual content, ritual always remains subservient to Faith.

On a conventional interpretation, the Sufi path inescapably collides with the political aspects of Islamicity. The image of a totalizing Islam in which there are no autonomous and differentiated spheres illuminates the problem. As Mohammed Arkoun notes, "The tensions between the religious and the political—considered in their anthropological dimensions—are expressed in such well-known opposite pairs as esoteric meaning and obvious meaning (*batin/zahir*), delightful initiatory knowledge and argumentative knowledge (*Irfan/'ilm*), spiritual leadership and temporal leadership with religious responsibility (*imama/khalifa*), the principle-source-foundation and derived legal qualifications (*asl/far'*), the truly real and the conjectural (*haqq/zann*) and so on."[47] Abandoning customary thinking, "the re-evaluation of the mystic way leads to the transgression of conceptual boundaries inherited from dualistic thinking based on the well-known dichotomies between faith and reason, revealed truth and rational truth, religious law and human norms, earthly life and eternal life, good and evil, true and false, and so on."[48] Arkoun reads into the Sufi way a nondualistic metaphysics. The mystic does not deny the ontological reality of the terrestrial realm but prefers closer engagement with the transcendent for a more perfect personhood. As Sufi masters have consistently stressed, cultivation of the rational faculties is a precondition for the spiritual journey. Without knowledge of the exoteric world, its inner secrets are inaccessible, as well as the possibility for transcendence. The dichotomy between Reason and Revelation and its assumed absence in the Islamic civilizational sphere, on a Sufi reading, is plainly untenable.[49] Yet, this dichotomy has persistently performed the function of relegating Islam to the zone of premodernity. A long tradition of orientalist scholarship and its fraternal discourses have cast doubt on the Muslim capacity to drink at the well of rationality and science. The entire trope of the need to modernize Muslims to domesticate their assumed irrationality is a dominant and recurrent theme in scholarship on Islam.[50]

A Moral Community

Comparisons between *tianxia* and Islam inevitably involve the Islamic concept of the *Ummah*, the moral community of Islam. On closer scrutiny, the popular notion of *Ummah* does not fully capture the deeper resonances of Islamic cosmology. In essence, *Ummah* signifies not merely a community of the faithful but a *universal* community. This elementary intuition directs inquiry into the spiritual edifice of Islam, not its political expression.

In its oversimplified connotation, *Ummah* suggests a religious amalgam of like-minded believers in a community, principally Muslim. United by a common belief (*Tawhid*) in the Oneness of Allah and the finality of the Prophet Muhammad (PBUH) in the prophetic order, *Ummah* is a commonwealth without discrimination of caste, creed, race, or tribe. On the vertical axis, it is the Oneness of God, "God's transcendent singularity," that produces common attachment.[51] The horizontal axis represents the materialization of the *Ummah* in space-time. Awareness of these separate axes discloses heterodox mappings of the concept. The community sanctioned by attachment to the idea of Oneness, therefore, is not merely the historical community that has existed in Muslim-majority cultural zones and its apparition in Muslim-minority regions but an idealized community of the Faithful. As an Ideal, the *Ummah* embodies a perfect union. The historical community envisaged in the concept originates with the founding of the first Muslim community during the lifetime of the Prophet and its subsequent expansion as civilizational space, followed by its decline and renewal within Westphalian political space. In the Westphalian context the *Ummah* takes the shape of a political commonwealth of Islamic states with its nominal and material expression in the Organization of Islamic Cooperation.[52] It is, however, the idealized form—more aspiration than fact—that provides Muslims across transnational space a common reference point of belonging.[53]

The vertical axis that rests on *Tawhid* cannot be visualized independently of the Qur'anic sources of the concept. Apparently derived from the Arabic word *umm* (meaning "mother"), *Ummah* is inconceivable without a notion of religious piety. *Ummah* is also interchangeable with the idea of the human community itself; and the plural use of the term refers to the communities that have preceded the Islamic community. Both conceptions are noted in the Qur'an, where *Ummah* in some form or another appears a total of sixty-two times.[54]

The varied connotations of the concept legitimate divergent interpretations with important implications. An understanding of the *Ummah* as the *human community* advances a cosmopolitan impulse.[55] Restricting the term to only permit People of the Book (*ahl al-kitab*) into the community separates Abrahamic from non-Abrahamic believers. In turn, further curtailment in the membership to an exclusive community of Muslims removes the notion from its expansive cosmopolitan meaning. Civilizational decline and the consolidation of global Western hegemony have been accompanied by a striking diminution in Islam's cosmopolitan appeal. This development is one of the more potent correlates of "political" Islam and its sectarian projects. The cosmological principle of *human oneness* and its moral implications offer a more productive site of comparison with *tianxia* than either the imagined transnational *Ummah* inscribed in Westphalian space or a political union of actually existing Islamic states. Building on the vertical axis of *Tawhid* and its expansive horizon, a moral community (All-under-God) that comprises all of humanity presents more determinate concurrences. Within this frame, parallels with Confucian ethics, notably the idea of righteous conduct in Islam, are particularly salient.

The tension between alternative conceptions of the *Ummah* provides both the possibility to return to First principles, eschewing common depictions of the exclusivist character of Islam, and the persistence of internal struggles within a politically fractured Muslim community. In the former instance, the principle of *Tawhid* and its isomorphic rendition in the notion of the unity of humankind return Islam to its originary cosmopolitan promise. However, in the second instance, Islam's relation to the Other, primarily in exclusivist language, severely restricts the scope for common humanity. The Other (in religious, sectarian, heretical, pagan form) cannot enter the zone of coeval existence. Westphalian entrapment only exacerbates the problem. The main effect of Westphalian sovereignty is not restricted to an external sphere, but it is transposed into internal space. As the organizing logic of political habitation, nationalism seeks and effects erasure of internal difference.[56] The nation-state tolerates external others but is unfailingly resistant to internal difference. Westphalian sovereignty accentuates external difference but remains abundantly intolerant of any deviations from the ideals of a homogenized political community.

Islam's resistance to a blanket repudiation of *this-worldly* obligation in favor of eschatological salvation or an acceptance of theodicy moves Islam closer to the immanent register of being. Melding belief in the Final Judgment and righteous moral conduct, Islam rejects the notion of original sin. Equally salient is the recognition of human imperfection that dictates moral vigilance of an autonomous agent. Yet, the believer is not a deracinated creature within a society of separate individuals but a nested subject seeking solace, succor, and belonging within a community. The Islamic community, in this sense, is an extended family, albeit a family defined by neither blood nor tribal filiation. The act of submission (*Islam*) frees the human from societal markers of difference. All-under-God carries the connotation of unity. While the "secular" underpinnings of *tianxia* stress a spatial mapping of relationality, Islam's spatial boundaries resist fixity. The notion of unity of humankind embodies the essence of the *Ummah*. This conception has been increasingly driven to the margins in place of narrower circles of religious or political filiation.

While unity is the end product of submission, obligation remains hierarchical. The affairs of the Divine take precedence over human affairs. Within these two poles lies an extended field for action with corresponding levels of obligation. These levels are concentric circles of moral conduct, distributed across family, friends, community, and strangers. A key element of moral conduct toward others is *regard,* which comes with responsibility for their wellbeing. Unlike the self-possessed sovereign individual of capitalist modernity, it is not aggrandizement or instrumentality that dictates conduct but the fulfilment of primary duties. Obligation rests on an expanded conception of relationality that mirrors the concentric circles of belonging. The *Ummah* is another way of capturing the totality of openness toward the Other, not as other.

To recapitulate, the familiar distinction between a religious and secular worldview rests on the assumed divergence between transcendental and immanentist registers. Arguably, without the presence of transcendence, moral obligation can only materialize in relative terms. The absoluteness religious belief ensures is unavailable within *this-worldly* zones of relationality. Yet, this line of thinking misrepresents the immanent force of human relationality; it also exaggerates the human capacity to implement the Law of God.[57] Imperfection retains its primal presence; the ideal of righteous conduct assumes imperfection. The notion of obligation lies in direct contradiction to the idea of the autonomous, self-serving individual. The humanness of the human lies in relationality—an awareness of finitude. Without others or God, the individual is not fully human; it is moral worth that makes a person human. The essence of morality rests upon a self-conscious rejection of sovereignty, either in individualistic form or in the supposedly naturalized (atomistic) structure of the state system. To recognize finitude is to reimagine sovereignty, but the obstacles to an alternative world remain.

Affinities

The *moral* element in the two cosmologies extends to a common desire in both to seek alternative visions of world order. Drawn from historical memory, future imaginings of a post-Westphalian world are, indeed, discernible. Both *tianxia* and Islam repudiate naturalization of difference. While humanity has never existed as a unified community or even as a community of coexistence, the aspiration for oneness permeates both Islam and *tianxia*. Both cosmological orders seek to repair a fractured human community. Reading into their deeper content, a common recognition of human finitude recasts relations with the Cosmos and Nature.[58] In place of the consolidation of borders and difference, generalized hospitality and harmony in *tianxia* and Islam offer the promise of a universal society. *Tianxia* nurtures a relational ontology that presupposes the possibility of human cooperation and harmony in a divided world. Islam envisions a moral community extended to the entire humanity.

Undeniably, the philosophical visions offered by *tianxia* and Islam remain ideal-typical. In their historical instantiation, however, complex and diverse orientations and commitments appear. Both Islam and *tianxia* are entwined with changeable political practice, the *conditioning* force responsible for materializing the ideal-typical visions. Often the process of materialization has produced radical deviations from the norm. Despite apparent stability, both *tianxia* and Islam need to be seen in dynamic terms, in the specific context in which *tianxia* and Islam have been "thrown" in historical time. Since the advent of European hegemony, the weight of national sovereignty cannot be discounted. Above all, the assumed naturalization of the Westphalian political form for organizing the human community remains the principal barrier against any imagined or real alternatives. While Confucian relational ontology finds parallels in Islam, both appealing to an expansive terrain of human connectivity and advancing the notion of moral righteousness in conduct with others, the container of the nation-state has acquired a mythical status. The consolidation of national difference and the culture of competition hangs above both *tianxia* and Islam. In this context, the biggest task facing alternative projects is to delineate the necessary steps that offer realizable pathways of transcending the political form in which humanity remains trapped.

The principal hurdle in realizing the universal message contained in *tianxia* and Islam is the imagined community supplied by the modern state. Can the revival of the *tianxia* narrative avoid its axiomatic linkage with the notion of a world-state or world empire, or an assumed hegemony?[59] This linkage clearly weakens its Universalist appeal. Similarly, can Islam avoid its political materialization in exclusivist schemes of an Islamic State, denying Islam's cosmopolitan impulse? The latter question derives from the intuition that politicization of faith imperils Islam's Universalist message. Both *tianxia* and the *Ummah,* therefore, must confront the problem of particularism embedded in the available political form.

The above challenges and constraints, however, need not preclude active explorations of alternative visions of human connectivity. A growing awareness of other possibilities is augmented by the twin crises of Western modernity and the climate emergency. These are extraordinary times in the sense that the twin crises arise on a singular temporal scale. On the one hand, the limits of the Westphalian order to effectively address these challenges increasingly acquire visibility. On the other hand, realignment of a world order to nature's demands no longer appears simply as a theoretical possibility but as a political necessity. Despite the hegemonic prevalence of Panglossian ethics attending neoliberal reason, human extinction increasingly approaches the realm of actuality.[60] While the basic templates of Baconian modernity remain stable, the fiction of normalcy is difficult to sustain. To proceed as normal becomes abnormal.

As moral, not political, constructs the new *tianxia* and cosmopolitan Islam present alternate sources of human renewal in the face of existential threats. These constructs entail both a critique of human possibility hemmed within neoliberal attachments to sovereign individuality within fixed containers of nation-states, and an outlook of responsibility toward, and coexistence with, others. Transcending narrower parameters of societal functioning, both Islam and *tianxia* avoid excessive reliance on individual civil or political rights. In Confucian understandings of the Self, which ground the cosmological structure of *tianxia,* "a distributive sense of justice" is paramount.[61] Countenancing social responsibility is not to deny the individual its autonomy but to prioritize collective good. The sovereign individual imagined in neoliberal theorization remains confined to its own shores, which progressively grow shallower and narrower within the expanded global culture of competition. Especially in its denial, the ideal of distributive justice furnishes a persistent reminder of the fateful excesses of neoliberal caprice toward humans and nature alike. A similar awareness of collective good and social responsibility informs Islamic ethics. In recognizing the failings of liberal individualism, both as a regulative ideal for societies experiencing an exhausted phase of Western modernity and as an aspiration for humanity in its ceaseless quest to modernize and develop, *tianxia* and Islam offer correctives. The perils generated and advanced by national sovereignty and neoliberalism continue to confirm their unworkability.

To a large degree, most alternatives appear utopian and impractical in relation to their hegemonic counterparts; the latter imbibe a natural attitude toward the Westphalian and neoliberal order. A deeper source of the problem, however, lies in the limiting notion of the human that persists in alternatives to the status quo. The hegemonic conception of the human that travels across international space remains unruffled. Wedded to the template of post-Enlightenment Western modernity and its institutionalization as *homo economicus* and the liberal political subject, this conception also appears in alternatives. If the new *tianxia* and cosmopolitan Islam are to make any inroads, the celebrated post-Enlightenment human subject must be discarded. The originary terrain of relational ontology and the notion of the unity of humankind need to replace the sovereign subject of liberal modernity and its habitation in the Westphalian political form. Return to cosmological principles alone can only build a halfway house. A different conception of the human also needs to be recovered.

To reiterate, alternative conceptions of the human represented within *tianxia* and Islam rest upon the recognition of human finitude. Largely removed from the script of Western modernity, recognition of finitude reframes relationality with Otherness in its human and natural materializations. Resisting vectors of domination, this recognition provincializes the liberal sovereign subject; it also provincializes humanity. On this different reading of convergence between *tianxia* and Islam, the place to begin is not in the political order produced in the image of cultural plenitude but in different conceptions of the human in the cosmological order.

Admittedly, the conception of the human envisaged in the backwaters of *tianxia* and Islam is not the same. On the one hand, the religiously tempered human in the last of the monotheistic faiths receives legitimation only upon a disavowal of its sovereignty. Despite invocations of an existent Heaven, on the other hand, the nested human in the *tianxia* framework is largely confined within a (secular) zone of immanence. Yet, in both *tianxia* and Islam, this human is not the post-Enlightenment artifice of self-assertion nor a creature of secular reason. The temporal universe conceived in *tianxia* and Islam requires a transcendent frontier that bequeaths humility as a condition for human sustenance. Against the horizon afforded by secular modernity and its seductions, the alternate cosmological promise—either in the transcendent quest for Oneness or in the capacious universe of human singularity—affords a different mapping of the world and the Cosmos.

The obvious demurral in notions of the human as a nested entity within wider circles of attachment is the attendant demotion that claims of centering inevitably encompass. In reality, however, the expanded realm lifts the human out of spaces of self-centeredness into a cosmological world of mutual recognition and wonder. God or Heaven may not offer practical technological fixes, but their presence in the planetary scheme curtails the excesses of the culture of narcissism. Apprehensions of fragility also expose the human to the delicate balance with nature and others currently trapped within containers of exclusion. The nation-state and the presumed sovereign individual both inhabit worlds of self-enclosure. These worlds continue to find sustenance in the belief that autonomous existence is both necessary and desirable. Fictionally separated from relationality to the cosmos, though, the human increasingly becomes a convict of sovereign desire in both the interiority of individual space and the space of the nation. These confined and confining zones of assumed self-fulfillment are ultimately illusionary. The unhinged subject now is fully exposed both to the whims of the nation-state that increasingly structures spaces for realization and the tyranny of abstract valorization that capitalism necessitates.

Civilizational and political dimensions of *tianxia* and Islam, therefore, need to be distinguished. Common to both *tianxia* and Islam is a notion of moral community based on human cultivation. Neither *tianxia* nor Islam advances the idea of a political community without giving primacy to a moral community. In both *tianxia* and Islam, Heaven remains above humanity and the earth. While *tianxia* principally concerns the world under Heaven, Islam's constitutive principle links transcendence with immanence. It is the appeal to a transcendental reality that unites what is beneath. Hence, the "secular" principle of unity proposed in *tianxia* matches Islam's cosmological norm of unity of humankind. In both cases, humanity and earth remain subordinate to Heaven.

Conclusion

Salvaging *tianxia* and Islam from the political and its instantiation as fractured space of difference opens up the possibility to acknowledge the *moral* character of humanity. Missing in both Westphalian and post-Westphalian (world society) theorizing is the need to approach humankind not as politically fractured beings—divided by the narrative of sovereignty, but as fragile agents united by a higher purpose. Attempts to realign *tianxia* or the *Ummah* to the template of Westphalian sovereignty impoverishes the philosophical and theological aspects of imagining global community. Once the stubborn hold of Westphalian framing is embraced, it is unlikely to yield space for alternatives. Clearly, the moral community decreed by official Islam restricts membership only to those with similar or same convictions of faith. This constrained view, however, contravenes the higher principle of the unity of humankind. Similarly, only by delinking *tianxia* from nationalism can permit the consolidation of a cosmopolitan outlook, countering Westphalian nation-state consciousness.

Traditional *tianxia* divides the world into the civilized and the barbarian. Official Islam constructs a divide between *dar al-Islam* (the realm of peace) and *dar al-harb* (the realm of war). Hierarchy is common to both. In the context of a changed and changing world, however, recovery of cosmopolitan impulses within both *tianxia* and Islam generates the basis to envision a post-Westphalian order. Any attempt to subordinate those impulses to Westphalian reason will fail to provide access to the moral aspects of the two cosmologies. Furthermore, within the Westphalian frame, concurrencies between *tianxia* and Islam are more likely to appear as a shared anti-Westernism or as a united front against the modern settlement. Rather, as moral frames of reference, both *tianxia* and Islam offer alternate imaginaries of forging political community whose key features are harmony and *human relations,* not merely transactional encounters.

Each society's idea of the Self is closely linked to the moral burden placed on its constituents. The idea of moral righteousness permeates both Islam and *tianxia*. Affirming the dynamic character of human nature, Confucian virtue stresses becoming.[62] *Tianxia* provides the universal framework for the cultivation of human perfection. Similarly, the Islamic notion of righteous conduct overcomes dark depictions of the fixity or depravity of human nature. Attaining different levels of perfection through knowledge, self-abnegation, and spiritual affirmation of Oneness, the true believer can negate originary templates of selfhood. Both *tianxia* and Islam, therefore, provide resources to exorcise the Hobbesian demons that have governed Westphalian political space, at least since the mid-seventeenth century.

In the case of cosmopolitan Islam, the quest for perfection presupposes God's confidence in moral cultivation. Negating original sin, this quest affirms the purpose of Creation.[63] Doubtless, the world is imperfect and the potential for malevolence permeates human existence. The persistent moral challenge to contest this condition, however, is precisely the source of ontological meaning. Despite the woeful record of human wickedness and deficiency, the quest for moral excellence retains its originary purpose. The hierarchized field of human action made available in the terrestrial realm prepares humanity for the afterlife. Worldly existence is not an illusion since it is the materiality of moral conduct that determines the quality of the world thereafter. The intrinsic nexus between *this-worldly* and *other-worldly* realms merges immanence with transcendence.

Ranging from the most mundane to the most extraordinary, the moral code permeates all zones of conduct. On this reading, the mistaken image of Islam as a totalizing belief system conflates different realms of social action and the essential moral quality of all conduct. The Islamic weltanschauung recognizes both differentiation and hierarchy in human conduct. All action is not the same and righteousness is not a matter of crude choice. Human beings are enjoined to do "what is right, forbidding what is wrong."[64] Unified by *Tawhid*—the first metaphysical principle—concentric circles of human action require particular values to guide proper conduct. Filial piety conditions relations within the family; loyalty is an essential prerequisite for friendship; justice is indispensable for societal harmony; and so on. Without moral obligation toward others—both proximate and distal—humanity remains imperfect and incomplete. The terrestrial world, therefore, is where the purpose of Creation is activated. Extended to the political sphere, the essential component of governance is trust between the ruler and the ruled. Echoing Confucian ethics, "moral responsibility of the ruler toward the ruled" is not only desirable but necessary. Islam supplements the idea of trust with a commitment to justice. Equally salient is the ideal of *maslaha* (public interest) that finds parallels with the Confucian regulative ideal of the Good. These moral principles bring *tianxia* and Islam much closer than either realpolitik or a presumed alliance of convenience against Western modernity.

Notes

1. The term "cosmology" is used throughout this chapter to connote the structuring framework of human cognition of the universe in its metaphysical sense, involving any culture's deep understanding of humanity's place and purpose in the scheme of existence. This usage departs from the purely "scientific" comprehension of the physical laws of origin or evolution the universe. For a useful definition, see Elizabeth Reichel, "Cosmology," in *The Encyclopedia of Religion and Nature,* ed. Bron Taylor and Jeffrey Kaplan (London: Thoemmes Continuum, 2005), pp. 420–425.

2. Liu Junping, "The Evolution of *Tianxia* Cosmology and Its Philosophical Implications," *Frontiers of Chinese Philosophy* 1, no. 4 (2006): 517–538.

3. Fabio Vicini, "Thinking through the Heart: Islam, Reflection and the Search for Transcendence," *Culture and Religion* 18, no. 2 (2017): 110–128.

4. Justin Tiwald, "Confucianism and Neo-Confucianism," in *The Oxford Handbook of Virtue,* ed. Nancy E. Snow (Oxford: Oxford University Press), pp. 171–189.

5. Asma Afsaruddin, "Monotheism in Islam," in *Monotheism and Its Complexities: Christian and Muslim Perspectives,* ed. Lucinda Mosher and David Marshall (Washington, DC: Georgetown University Press, 2018), pp. 33–44.

6. Habibollah Babaei, "Standards of Islamity in Islamic Civilization," *Kom: Journal of Religious Sciences* 5, no. 3 (January 2016): 19–36.

7. Chenyang Li, "Chinese Philosophy," in *The Oxford Handbook of World Philosophy*, ed. William Edelglass and Jay L. Garfield (Oxford: Oxford University Press, 2011), pp. 1–5, doi:10.1093/oxfordhb/9780195328998.003.0002.

8. See Hyunhee Park, *Mapping the Chinese and Islamic Worlds: Cross-Cultural Exchange in Pre-Modern Asia* (Cambridge: Cambridge University Press, 2012); Cai Yanxin, *Chinese Architecture* (Cambridge: Cambridge University Press, 2011); Amin Banani, Richard G. Hovannisian, and Georges Sabagh, eds., *Poetry and Mysticism in Islam: The Heritage of Rūmi* (Cambridge: Cambridge University Press, 1994); and Rachel Harris and Rahilä Dawut, "Mazar Festivals of the Uyghurs: Music, Islam and the Chinese State," *British Journal of Ethnomusicology* 11, no. 1 (2002): 101–118.

9. For a perceptive understanding of the common good, see Jacques Maritain, "The Person and the Common Good," *Review of Politics* 8, no. 4 (October 1946): 419–455.

10. As it becomes more noticeable in a subsequent section, the notion of the *Ummah* deployed in this chapter diverges from its restrictive use as "a community of the faithful" restricted to Muslims. For a brief historical account of the concept, see Rudy Paret, "Ummah," in *The Shorter Encyclopedia of Islam*, ed. H. A. R. Gibb and J. H. Kramers (Leiden: E. J. Brill, 1954).

11. Jeremy Larkins, *From Hierarchy to Anarchy: Territory and Politics before Westphalia* (New York: Palgrave Macmillan, 2010).

12. Simon Lumsden, "The Logic of Modernity and the Ecological Crisis," *Environmental Values* 30, no. 3: 277–296. See also Victor M. Toledo, "Modernity and Ecology: The New Planetary Crisis, *Capitalism Nature Socialism* 4, no. 4 (1993): 31–48.

13. Islam, for instance, ventures a different notion of the self. See Seyyed H. Nasr, "Happiness and the Attainment of Happiness," *Journal of Law and Religion* 29, no. 1 (February 2014): 76–91. See also Fazlur Rahman, "The Status of the Individual in Islam," in *The Status of the Individual East and West*, ed. Charles A. Moore and Aldyth V. Morris (Honolulu: University of Hawaii Press, 1968), pp. 217–225. On a Confucian perspective, see Luo Shirong, "Happiness and the Good Life: A Classical Confucian Perspective," *Dao* 18, no. 1 (March 2019): 41–58.

14. See Osman Bakar and Gek Nai Cheng, *Islam and Confucianism: A Civilizational Dialogue* (Kuala Lumpur: University of Malaya Press, 1997). For a forceful critique of diffusionist thinking, see James M. Blaut, *The Colonizer's Model of the World: Geographical Diffusionism and Eurocentric History* (New York: Guilford Press, 1993).

15. John H. Hobson, *The Eurocentric Conception of World Politics: Western International Theory, 1760–2010* (Cambridge: Cambridge University Press, 2012).

16. Peter Frankopan, *The Silk Roads: A New History of the World* (London: Bloomsbury, 2015).

17. See Zvi Ben-Dor Benite, *The Dao of Muhammad: A Cultural History of Muslims in Late Imperial China* (Cambridge, MA: Published by the Harvard University Asia Center and distributed by Harvard University Press, 2005); Sachiko Murata, William C. Chittick, Tu Weiming, and Jielian Liu, *The Sage Learning of Liu Zhi: Islamic Thought in Confucian Terms* (Cambridge, MA: Published by the Harvard University Asia Center for the Harvard-Yenching Institute and distributed by Harvard University Press, 2009).

18. As Dariush Shayegan notes: "The decline of these Asian civilizations brought their mutual cross-fertilizations to an end. The era of the great translations leading to fruitful

encounters between India and China, Iran and India, China and Japan, came to an end. These great civilizations turned away from each other and towards the West. They withdrew from history, entered a phase of passivity, stopped renewing themselves and lived increasingly on their accumulated fat. They were like rich aristocratic families overtaken by events, ruined by a shift in economic reality, who keep up appearances for a time by selling off their inheritance bit by bit: jewelry, paintings, carpets, silver, everything, until the bitter day comes when there is nothing left." Dariush Shayegan, *Cultural Schizophrenia: Islamic Societies Confronting the West* (Syracuse, NY: Syracuse University Press, 1997), p. 44.

19. On the relation between the one and the many in Islam, see Habibollah Babaei, "One and Many in Islam, the Path and the Ways in the Qur'an," *Kom: Journal of Religious Sciences* 3, no. 1 (January 2014): 97–112.

20. Several chapters in this volume provide nuanced readings of *tianxia*. The present discussion offers a highly simplified sketch of the concept, principally to contrast it with the Islamic notion of the *Ummah*.

21. For a defense of the Westphalian order, see June Teufel Dreyer, "The 'Tianxia Trope': Will China Change the International System," *Journal of Contemporary China* 24, no. 96 (April 2015): 1015–1031. For philosophically anchored accounts, see Roger T. Ames, *Seeking Harmony Not Sameness: Comparative Philosophy and East-West Understanding* (Beijing: Peking University Press, 2002); Junping Liu, "The Evolution of Tianxia Cosmology and Its Philosophical Implications," *Frontiers of Philosophy in China* 1, no. 4 (December 2006): 517–538; Zhao Tingyang, "Rethinking Empire from a Chinese Concept 'All-under-Heaven' (Tianxia)," *Social Identities* 12, no. 1 (2006): 29–44; Zhao Tingyang, "A Political World Philosophy in Terms of All-under-Heaven (Tian-xia)," *Diogenes* 56, no. 1 (February 2009): 5–18; and Zhang Lei and Zhengrong Hu, "Empire, Tianxia and Great Unity: A Historical Examination and Future Vision of China's International Communication," *Global Media and Culture* 2, no. 2 (2017): 197–207.

22. Wang Mingming, "'All under Heaven (Tianxia)': Cosmological Perspectives and Political Ontologies in Pre-Modern China," *HAU: Journal of Ethnographic Theory* 21, no. 1 (2012): 337–383.

23. Benedict Anderson, *Imagined Communities: Reflections on the Origin and Spread of Nationalism*. rev. ed. (New York: Verso, 2016).

24. Wang, "'All under Heaven (Tianxia),'" 338.

25. See Peter Hershock's chapter in this volume.

26. Wang, "'All under Heaven (Tianxia),'" 338.

27. Kenneth N. Waltz, *Man, State, and War: A Theoretical Analysis* (New York: Columbia University Press, 1959).

28. Romeyn Taylor, "Chinese Hierarchy in Comparative Perspective," *Journal of Asian Studies* 48, no. 3 (August 1989): 490–511.

29. Wang, "'All under Heaven (Tianxia),'" 338.

30. Wang, "'All under Heaven (Tianxia),'" 340.

31. Chu Sinan, "Whither Chinese IR: The Sinocentric Subject and the Paradox of Tianxia-ism." *International Theory* 14, no. 1 (2022): 57–87, doi:10.1017/S1752971920000214.

32. Xu Jilin, "Xin tianxia zhuyi: Dui minzu zhuyi yu chuantong tianxia zhuyi de shuangchong chaoyue" (New tianxia-ism: Dual transcendence of nationalism and tradi-

tional tianxia-ism), *Exploration and Free Views* 5 (May 2020). Cited in Chu, "Whither Chinese IR."

33. David L. Hall and Roger T. Ames, *Thinking through Confucius* (Albany: State University of New York Press, 1987).

34. Annulling the universal appeal of the notion of the unity of humankind, the dominance of sectarian and parochial tendencies in "political" Islam has erected insurmountable barriers against either a dialogue of civilizations or the harnessing of material lineaments of a post-Westphalian world order. The challenge for the Islamic civilization is to revitalize its cosmopolitan impulse.

35. Hassan Hassan, *The Sectarianism of the Islamic State: Ideological Roots and Political Context* (Washington, DC: Carnegie Endowment for International Peace, 2016).

36. Seyyed H. Nasr, "The Cosmos and the Natural Order," in *Islamic Spirituality: Foundations*, ed. Seyyed Hossein Nasr (New York: SCM Press, 1985), pp. 345–357.

37. Mustapha Kamal Pasha, "Political Theology and Sovereignty: Sayyid Qutb in Our Times," *Journal of International Relations and Development* 22 (2019): 346–363.

38. Seyyed H. Nasr, *An Introduction to Islamic Cosmological Doctrines* (Cambridge, MA: Belknap Press of Harvard University Press, 1964).

39. Edith Jachimowicz, "Islamic Cosmology," in *Ancient Cosmologies*, ed. Carmen Blacker and Michael Loewe (London: George Allen & Unwin, 1975), pp. 143, 144.

40. Majid Fakhry, *A History of Islamic Philosophy* (New York: Columbia University Press, 1983).

41. Jachimowicz, "Islamic Cosmology," p. 145.

42. For a pioneering account of Islam's place in history, see Marshall G. S. Hodgson, *The Venture of Islam: Conscience and History in a World Civilization*, 3 vols. (Chicago: University of Chicago Press, 1974).

43. The classical statement on the Islamic law of nations is the work of eighth-century jurist Muhammad Shaybani, *Kitab al-Siyar al-Kabir*, which was translated with an extended commentary in 1966 by the noted scholar Majid Khadduri as *The Islamic Law of Nations: Shaybani's Siyar* (Baltimore: Johns Hopkins University Press, 2001). Khadduri's translation and commentary, however, have been the target of sustained criticism for their failure to accord Shaybani the status of one of the pioneering international jurists, eight centuries before Hugo Grotius. See Jean Allain, "Khadduri as Gatekeeper of the Islamic Law of Nations?," in *International Law and Islam: Historical Explorations*, ed. Ignacio de la Rasilla and Ayesha Shahid (Leiden: Brill / Nijhoff 2018), pp. 127–145.

44. Mawil Izzi Dien, "Islam and the Environment: Theory and Practice," *Journal of Beliefs & Values* 18 no. 1 (1997): 47–57.

45. Mohammed Arkoun, "The Unity of Man in Islamic Thought," trans. R. Scott Walker, *Diogenes* 35, no. 140 (1987): 50–69. See also Seyyed H. Nasr, "The Quran as the Foundation of Islamic Spirituality," in Nasr, *Islamic Spirituality*, pp. 3–10.

46. Fabio Vicini, "Thinking through the Heart: Islam, Reflection and the Search for Transcendence," *Culture and Religion* 18, no. 2 (May 2017): 110–128.

47. Arkoun, "Unity of Man," pp. 58–59.

48. Arkoun, "Unity of Man, pp. 59–60.

49. Paul R. Powers, "Interiors, Intentions, and the 'Spirituality' of Islamic Ritual Practice," *Journal of the American Academy of Religion* 72, no. 2 (June 2004): 425–459.

50. For a typical example, see Bernard Lewis, "The Roots of Muslim Rage," *The Atlantic*, September 1990.

51. Stuart E. Brown, "A Note on Islamic Spirituality," *The Ecumenical Review* 38, no. 1 (1986): 72.

52. Turan Kayaoglu. *The Organization of Islamic Cooperation: Politics, Problems, and Potential* (Abingdon, UK: Routledge, 2015).

53. Shahrbanou Tadjbakhsh, "International Relations Theory and the Islamic Worldview," in *Non-Western International Relations Theory*, ed. Amitav Acharya and Barry Buzan (London: Routledge, 2009), pp. 174–196.

54. As the Qur'an says: "Mankind was one single nation, and Allah sent Messengers with great tidings and warnings; and with them He sent the Book in truth, to judge between people in matters wherein they differed; but the People of the Book, after the Clear Signs came to them, did not differ among themselves, except through selfish contumacy. Allah by His Grace guided the believers to the Truth, concerning that wherein they differed. For Allah guides whom He will to a path that is straight." *The Holy Qur'an*, trans. Abdullah Yusuf Ali (Ware, Hertfordshire, UK: Wordsworth Classics of World Literature, 2000), 2:213. And, again from the Qur'an: "If Allah had so willed, He would have made you a single people, but (his plan is) to test you in what He hath given you: so strive as in a race in all virtues," 5:48.

55. Bruce Lawrence, "Afterword: Competing Genealogies of Muslim Cosmopolitanism." In *Rethinking Islamic Studies: From Orientalism to Cosmopolitanism*, ed. Carl W. Ernst and Richard C. Martin (Columbia: University of South Carolina Press, 2010). See also Lenn Goodman, *Islamic Humanism* (Oxford: Oxford University Press, 2003).

56. Ernest Gellner, *Nations and Nationalism* (Ithaca, NY: Cornell University Press, 1983).

57. Rémi Brague, *The Law of God: The Philosophical History of an Idea*, trans. Lydia G. Cochrane (Chicago: University of Chicago Press, 2007).

58. Syafaatun Almirzanah, "God, Humanity, and Nature: Cosmology in Islamic Spirituality," *HTS Teologiese/Theological Studies* 76, no. 1 (2020), https://hts.org.za/index.php/hts/article/view/6130/16250.

59. William A. Callahan, "Chinese Visions of World Order: Post-Hegemonic or a New Hegemony?," *International Studies Review* 4, no. 4 (2008): 749–761.

60. Clive Hamilton, *Defiant Earth: The Fate of Humans in the Anthropocene* (London: Polity Press, 2017).

61. Roger T. Ames, "On How to Construct a Confucian Democracy for Modern Times (or Why Democratic Practices Must Not Lose Sight of the Ideal)," *Philosophy East and West* 65, no. 1 (2017): 65; Tu Wei-ming, *A Confucian Perspective on Human Rights: The Inaugural Wu Teh Yao Memorial Lecture* (Singapore: Singapore University Press, 1996). See also Stephen C. Angle, "Contemporary Confucian and Islamic Approaches to Democracy and Human Rights," *Comparative Philosophy* 4, no. 1 (2013): 7–41.

62. Ames, "On How to Construct," p. 3.

63. Ismail R. Al-Faruqi, "On the Raison d'être of the Ummah," *Islamic Studies* 2, no. 2 (1963): 159–203.

64. The Holy Qur'an, 3:10.

CHAPTER 9

Tianxia

A Process of Relations

QIN Yaqing

IT IS WIDELY accepted that *tianxia* is a holistic concept, meaning "All-under-Heaven." It is understood as the whole world under Heaven, or the entire universe.[1] In other words, it is a world system that takes the whole world as a unit and "a whole political existence" with the most important principle of nonexclusivity.[2] Even though *tianxia* was a concept of ancient China when it was limited to the known sphere of the Zhou dynasty, it, as a conceptual construct, meant the totality of the physical domain where humankind lived, largely within the boundary of human knowledge. In today's international relations (IR), it refers primarily to the whole world or our common global village.

Zhao Tingyang's *tianxia* theory is most original and inspiring. It encourages people to think from the perspective of the world rather than think merely about the world, to establish a worldwide system of institutions to best govern the world's affairs, and to adhere to and implement the principle of nonexclusivity or all-inclusiveness for perpetual peace, which is more reliable than what Immanuel Kant suggested.[3] However, *tianxia*, defined as such, is fundamentally a spatial sphere and its inclusiveness refers to "including all political entities in the world."[4] Thus the *tianxia* theory is more about coexistence of individual entities in a space that is holistic to the extent that our knowledge reaches, more about converting externality to internality (or alien-ness to family-ship), and more about making the fragmented world into a world in its entirety. *Tianxia* is therefore a tangible structure with substantial entities as its units and nonexclusivity as its organizing principle. Even if we lay particular emphasis on all-inclusive institutions, it is still an institutional space where set institutions govern individual entities. It is quite a static structure, physically and institutionally.

Behind this spatial theory of *tianxia* is a firm ontological position. There are two ontological tendencies in our understanding and interpretation of the world. One is the substantialist ontology and the other the processual (or relational) ontology. As Mustafa Emirbayer argues, in sociology the most important issue is not "material versus ideal," "structure versus agency," or "individual versus society," but substantialism versus relationalism.[5] It is even more important because this issue concerns not only the highly specific dyadic pairs Emirbayer has mentioned, such as the material and the ideational, but also how our worldview is shaped or how we perceive the world in general. Taking *tianxia* as a spatial sphere and an all-inclusive structure reflects a firm Newtonian worldview that seeks general laws to govern and control for certainty and stability.

Modernity and modernist sciences depend heavily on the substantialist ontology, consciously or unconsciously. It is a fact that this ontology continues to dominate in general. It assumes that the world is composed of substances or tangible entities, discrete and independent, hanging together by rules and norms. This ontology focuses on substances with their defining features. It orients people to thinking *from* substances, and therefore any difference means difference of substances that have a priori and fixed properties and attributes. It necessarily leads to a taxonomy that groups substances with similar properties together. Modern sciences rely heavily on such taxonomies, and so does modernity itself. It is exactly this dominant worldview that has been internalized to a large extent in Western societies, which took the lead in modernization and made great achievements during the process. Along with its success, the ontology behind it has been spreading all over the world and gaining a status of dominance and a power of preponderance.[6]

Along this line, *tianxia* is first of all a whole system of entities as often suggested, and the dominant entities, themselves a product of modernity, have been nation-states ever since the Westphalian peace treaties. These entities or substances coexist in the world. The *tianxia* theory tries to deal with the inside-outside boundary that is spatially drawn and, arguably, spatially eliminable with a system of world institutions. "If *tianxia* is understood as a dynamic process, then it means the worldization of world," meaning a gradual elimination of the boundary between Ego and Alter, or the self-nation and other-nation.[7] Today's international system is largely organized on the principle of sovereignty monopolized by nation-states, which, as a most important legacy of the Westphalian peace, are the tangible entities, self-organized, independent, and territorially integrated. This international system, together with its principle of sovereignty, is undoubtedly a product of modernity rooted deeply in the substantialist ontology. *Tianxia* intends to change this principle of sovereignty and replace it with the principle of all-inclusiveness. Then the whole world would become a holistic entity with no nation-state as an alien, something very much like the Zhou dynasty in its ideal form. Thus, in the final analysis, such a *tianxia* continues to be based on the substantialist ontology, though it shifts from the individual entity to a larger and more holistic entity. In this respect, it is not very much different from the transformation from the city-state system to the nation-state system. Such a *tianxia* is still a substantialist *tianxia*.

The processual ontology differs. It sees the world as composed in the first place of dynamic and flowing processes. A process differs from an entity mainly in that it is moving all the time, changing and indefinite, and it includes both the spatial and the temporal dimensions. Generally speaking, it is a series of connected events rather than discrete entities and as such the temporality is very much stressed, for "the primary constituents of every event are the threads which come to it from earlier events, and live anew in it."[8] From the perspective of the processual ontology, therefore, social reality is not defined in terms of the performance of independent and substantial entities but depicted in "dynamic, continuous, and processual terms."[9] In this sense, *tianxia,* both an ideational worldview and a social reality, is a process with a strong temporal, as well as a spatial, dimension, for it itself is an event that connects the past and the future and relates events around.

Then what is process? I define process in general as relations among all, things and people alike. Furthermore, it is relations in motion: flowing relations that generate the dynamism of the process. For Alfred North Whitehead in philosophy, Emirbayer in sociology, and Patrick Jackson and Daniel Nexon in international relations, it is clear that process is always the temporal-spatial connections and relations.[10] Emirbayer distinguishes between substantialism and relationalism, focusing on relations and explicitly maintaining that relations are connections between terms or units, linking persons, places, meanings, and events.[11] Jackson and Nexon define their theory as processual/relational. It is the *relations* among All-under-Heaven, rather than all entities under Heaven, that constitute the *tianxia* system and *tianxia* per se indeed. If process is defined in terms of relations, a processual ontology is a relational ontology.

This relational ontology orients us to think *from* relations and rests on the fundamental assumption: *Tianxia* is an ontology of relations. It is true of both the natural and the social worlds. In the natural world, everything is related to everything else; in the social world, everyone is related to everyone else; and across the natural and social worlds humans and things are also related. Interacting together they constitute a whole cosmos, a cosmos of meaning.[12] It is not to deny the self-existence of an entity, but it does stress that the self-existence gains meaning only when simultaneously related through practice to other-existence and coexistence. It looks different from the world perceived and conceived by the substantialist ontology, for at the metaphysical level such a *tianxia* is visualized as composed of continuous events and ongoing relations, temporally and spatially, rather than substantial objects and discrete entities interacting on a billiard board. In this sense, *tianxia* is relations.

We may use a *weiqi* or *go* board as an example; Chinese tend to see more the lines that link the pieces rather than the pieces themselves. In fact, the pieces have no a priori identity and attributes before they are put onto the board. They gain identity and meaning once they are on the board and are connected by the lines to other pieces there. A similar story is told when the traditional Chinese medicine pays greater attention to the invisible channels or the network of passages through which vital energy circulates than the body itself. This relatedness decides that relations are real and important though they are not as tangible and as substantial as physical objects. In other words, without relations nothing would meaningfully happen and be, and the *tianxia* would be null or non-*tianxia*. Thus, from the perspective of the relational ontology *tianxia* is no longer a substantialist *tianxia*. It is a processual *tianxia* or a relational *tianxia*. It is not a static space, but a dynamic, fluid process full of cosmic and human meanings.

This *tianxia* is what David Hall and Roger Ames have described as an immanent cosmos—everything is in everything else and all are related to one another as well as to the context, and "correlativity" is the most significant word to describe it.[13] The substantialist ontology provides a deeply embedded worldview that has biased the modernist Western thinking toward a cosmos composed of discrete objects and self-organized, self-subsistent actors. From a relational perspective, however, the world represents itself always as a complexly relational whole for which actors are always actors-in-relations and in which actors live and co-live, act and interact, inclusively and immanently.

Tianxia is thus a totality of relations in motion, on which traditional Chinese thinkers focused. Since Chinese philosophers from generation to generation paid more attention to relations especially involving humans, they tended to be keener observers of relations between nature and humanity (*tianren guanxi* 天人關係), relations among humans or self–other relations (*jita guanxi* 己他關係), and relations between heart and body (*shenxin guanxi* 身心關係).[14] Altogether, these various types of relations are correlated. It is not a material space where only tangible entities like nation-states count. Neither is it a purely ideational world where only ideas matter. It is where the ideational meets the material via the practice of relationality and where the practice of relationality matters most. Moreover, it is the human that goes through all these types of relationships and makes these universes meaningful. In this sense human agency and human practice constitute the most significant factor and the key link for the *tianxia* system.

Zhongyong Dialectics and Harmony of Relations

A basic assumption about the state of nature is usually provided as the starting point for understanding "All-under-Heaven." We may assume, as Thomas Hobbes has done, that it is a jungle where everyone fighting against everyone else is the normal phenomenon, or we may agree, as Thomas Moore has imagined, that it is a utopia where all actors live happily in peace and forever. Even though these assumptions rest primarily on the agential level—that is, they take the individual actor as the unit based on which the assumptions are made—they in fact describe the state of relations or the nature of relationships. Hobbes's jungle depicts eternal enmity while Moore's Heaven depicts eternal amity. Both enmity and amity describe the nature of relationships among actors. The meaning world is thus constructed through these various relationships.

The relational ontology requires that relations, rather than individual agents, be used as the unit of analysis because it assumes that the universe is composed of relations. As "relation" is taken as the central focus, questions follow: If we conceive *tianxia* as composed of dynamic relations, then how do we understand the multiplex relations that are always in motion? What is the nature of such relationships? Without answering these questions, all complex and fluid relations would appear a complete mess. For any research taking a relational perspective, therefore, it is necessary to assume the nature of relations as the starting point. The state of nature is what I call the original state of relations.

Let me use again examples in my discipline, international relations (IR). As I have just discussed, mainstream IR theories all have explicit or implicit assumptions on the original state of relations, for none of them can avoid this fundamental question. Now the study of international relations is still dominated by the so-called three bigs: realism, liberal institutionalism, and constructivism.[15] They are largely theories developed in the United States and used widely in the United States and other places in the world.[16] Realism, still a most influential IR theory, assumes that the original state of relations among nation-states is enmity due largely to the anarchic nature of the international system, which is the Hobbesian jungle where everyone fights against everyone else and might is right.[17] Liberal institutionalism is somewhat more optimistic, taking the anarchic assumption and recognizing the competitive relations among selfish international actors, but believing that institutions, or rules and regimes, can reduce the (original) anarchic nature of the international system and facilitate cooperative relationships among actors.[18] Constructivism, stressing the social construction of actors, argues that the original state is neither antagonistic nor friendly. It depends on the intersubjectivity of agency. Anarchy, for example, is constructed by nation-states in their interaction and may have different meanings due to the different ways of construction.[19]

With these fundamental questions in mind, we now turn to the Confucian tradition to see how the original state of relations is understood and interpreted. Since we assume that the universe is composed of relations, we need to understand how the original state of relations is perceived or understood, for it shapes our understanding of the fate of All-under-Heaven.

The first step is perhaps to identify what elsewhere I termed "meta-relationship," which is a prototype of relationships of all kinds.[20] As we have just discussed, mainstream IR theories believe that conflict is the nature of relationships, such as realism, neoliberal institutionalism, and radicalism do, or that at best it is neutral, as constructivism proposes. Going back to both Daoism and Confucianism, we can find clearly that the *yin–yang* relationship is assumed as the meta-relationship even though this particular term has not been used.[21] I call it the meta-relationship because all other relationships are derived from it. It is the simplest, but at the same time the most natural and the most representative in the universe, for traditional Chinese philosophy believes that life, as well as the cosmos, starts with this most fundamental relationship.

Once we focus on this meta-relationship, what we need to do next is to see how traditional Chinese philosophical thinking interprets the nature of the *yin–yang* relationship. The *zhongyong* dialectics explains it. Simply put, it is harmony. In other words, the *yin–yang* relationship is a harmonious relationship as represented at its original state. The *zhongyong* dialectics expounds this harmony in three aspects.

First, *yin* and *yang* are immanently inclusive. *Yin* is in *yang* and vice versa.[22] In other words, they are two expressions of the same phenomenon. On the one hand, *Yin* and *yang* are two different halves, something like thesis and antithesis or Ego and Alter. But unlike thesis and antithesis, or Ego and Alter, *yin* and *yang* together form an immanent entirety, depending on each other for life and coexisting as life. Life does not exist without either. Thus, the two halves are not thesis and antithesis, but co-theses, a term I have coined to explain the non-alternativeness and non-contradictiveness of *yin* and *yang*. It is intersubjectivity in a certain sense, but it is not the intersubjectivity between two independent and discrete subjects like Ego and Alter, but the intersubjectivity between two immanent subjects that are inclusive of each other. The *yin–yang* symbol or the Chinese cosmological diagram vividly illustrates such a relationship: *yin* and *yang* are two fish-shaped halves complementing each other and forming together a harmonious and holistic circle. Without either half of the double-fish shape, the circle is nonexistent; without the circle, the two fish cannot form a complete and perfect life. *Yin, yang,* and the circle are in and of one simultaneously.

Second, *yin* and *yang* are mutually complementary. The strength of *yang* makes up for the weakness of *yin* and vice versa. It is not a subject–object relationship and neither takes ontological priority over the other. Furthermore, the *yin–yang* mutuality is a process, which is defined in terms of fluid relations. It is a process of mutual complementation, maintaining a dynamic balance of life energy and facilitating a coevolution of cooperation. As Hellmut Wilhelm has commented, "The explanation of the creative process in terms of the interaction of complementary oppositions is fundamental to the Chinese tradition."[23] Back to the origin, it is this creative process of *yin* and *yang,* the simplest form of all other pairs of polar terms, that starts the movement and dynamic life of all in the universe.

Third, *yin* and *yang* are fundamentally in harmony. The *yin–yang* interactive process is one epitomized by equilibrium, which, however, does not present itself as a symmetrical evenness, structural and static.[24] Rather it is a dynamic balancing and the balance is maintained by cooperative mutuality, processual and continuous. In this sense I define "harmony" in terms of maximum cooperation and "harmonization" in terms of the dynamic process of maximizing cooperation. As the simplest and most natural relationship, *yin* and *yang* generate, create, maintain, and sustain life through immanent cooperation. This process is dynamic and open, nurturing cooperation in continuous inclusivity and complementarity. The core of the *zhongyong* dialectics is harmony and its practice continuous harmonization. It sees polarities in everything, but it argues that change and progress are not ignited by conflict and crisis but rely on the harmonizing process of the *yin–yang* trans-subjective mutuality.

Immanent intersubjectivity and complementary mutuality are both expressions and articulations of the original state of harmony, which in turn facilitates and promotes immanency and complementarity. This is why we say that the original state of the meta-relationship is harmony. We do not deny conflict but rather see conflict as a deviation from the original state that therefore does not have the ontological significance that harmony enjoys.[25] In this sense, conflict is ultimately resolvable.

It is useful to make a brief comparison here between the Hegelian dialectics and the Chinese *zhongyong* dialectics. Both identify the two forces or poles, and both see the interaction of the two forces as the prime mover of progress. But they differ in one crucial aspect: whether the nature of relationship is conflict or harmony. While the former comprehends it largely as conflictual, as the terms "thesis" and "antithesis" suggest, the latter understands it mainly as harmonious, as the term "co-theses" implies. Furthermore, the former tends to see the confrontational interaction between contradictory and conflictual forces result in progressive change, while the latter sees harmony and concord lead to sustainable order. Thus, the logic of the dialectics of conflict is recognizing the essentially contradictory nature of the relationship between two different terms, seeing difference as the root of conflict, identifying the most fundamental contradiction, and pushing it to the extreme for change.[26] The logic of the dialectics of harmony is recognizing the fundamentally harmonious nature of the meta-relationship, seeing differences between the two terms as assets for mutuality and complementarity, and resolving conflict through appropriate centralizing to correct the deviation. Simply put, the former is a dialectics of conflictualization while the latter is one of harmonization.[27]

The immanent inclusivity and complementarity of *yin* and *yang*, the process of their transforming toward each other, and the dynamic centrality that stresses the transforming movement unfolding with due measure and degree, constitute the essential elements of the *zhongyong* dialectics and reflect an important worldview of the Chinese: The *yin–yang* relationship, or the relationship of any polarities in this sense, is fundamentally harmonious and is always in the process of reaching and realizing harmony through constant centralization.[28] The state of nature is harmony, which is also the home of any polarities. Moreover, the *zhongyong* dialectics assumes that the *yin–yang* relationship is a constantly and continuously harmonizing process. It is important for understanding *tianxia* as a process of relations because it assumes the fundamentally nonconflictual and harmonious nature of all relations, supporting the belief that harmony is not only desirable but also realizable, for it is the state where the world is in and of its true self.

Global Governance as an Illustration

In the previous sections, two propositions have been made: *tianxia* is a totality of relations and the original state of the relational *tianxia* is harmony. Nowadays, global governance is both a reality and a failure. In the case of governance, a more spatially and structurally focused *tianxia* would require, on the one hand, an all-canopying institutional arrangement to govern equal units, while a more processually and relationally oriented *tianxia* needs governance of relations among the units rather than the units per se. In other words, governance means governing relations, and global governance is to manage complex relations in an increasingly interdependent and complex international and world society for overcoming the collective-action problem and managing the global commons.

Mainstream IR literature on global governance is based on the worldview that the international system is composed of independent and sovereign nation-states and that therefore global governance is to regulate the behavior of individual states and orient them toward cooperative action for the good of the commons. There are various approaches to such regulation. Exercise of coercive power is one. Hegemonic governance basically places emphasis on the key role of the hegemon's material power in leading and performing global governance. When Charles Kindleberger analyzed the Great Depression, he argued that the economic disaster occurred because there was a vacuum of leadership in the world. He believed that the world needs a leader, and one single leader, to govern for order.[29] Pax Britannica and Pax Americana are telling examples in this respect. Simply put, power rules—it is the power of the hegemon that regulates, coercively when necessary, the behavior of states and maintains the governance in the international system.[30]

The most influential literature on global governance to date (or at least to the Obama administration) is the IR theory of neoliberal institutionalism. Its key idea is "institutions rule." It began to emerge during the 1970s and 1980s when the power of the United States seemed to be declining. The US failure in Vietnam and the decoupling of the US dollar with the value of gold caused great concern in international governance and the "Kindleberger fear" spread rapidly in the world. Neoliberal institutionalism, to some extent drawing on the practice of the European regional integration, argued that international order and governance would continue after hegemony. The most important factor is international institutions that perform the function of ruling and regulating.

Robert Keohane took the lead in developing this powerful theory.[31] He converted the supply theory of institutions provided by the hegemon to a demand theory of institutions needed by members of the international community. It argues that international institutions are not merely supplied by any hegemonic actor; rather they are demanded by members of the international system for the realization of their own interests. International institutions work to reduce transactional costs and increase transparency, thus lessening the problem of free-riding and facilitating the likelihood of cooperation. Though it does not completely solve the collective-action dilemma, it at least reduces the negative effect of the logic of collective action in anarchy. Global governance became a top priority in the study of international relations in the 1990s when the Cold War was over and the legacy of neoliberal institutionalism continued to dominate the agenda.

Neoliberal institutionalism is no doubt today the most relevant literature in the field of governance, and rule-based institutionalism continues to be the most relevant form of global governance. However, it is far from adequate. In 2004, Kofi Annan, the then–secretary general of the United Nations, organized a high-level panel to identify the most serious challenges to the world and put forward suggestions for dealing with them. The panel, membered by prestigious statespersons, diplomats, and experts, worked out a report entitled "Our Shared Responsibility: For a More Secure World," which pinpointed several formidable threats to all humankind, including poverty, environmental deterioration, terrorism, and international and domestic conflict. While recognizing transnational threats as the most formidable to humankind, it redefined collective security in the era of globalization and placed special emphasis on multilateralism and institutionalized cooperation as effective measures to deal with new, transnational threats.[32] Nearly twenty years have passed and the threats in these areas have not been effectively dealt with. Rather, they tend to be more serious in the 2020s, as the COVID-19 pandemic has shown. Looking at the serious phenomenon of governance failure in various fields of the global commons, from terrorism to climate change, people in general believe that there should be reform of the existing institutions.[33]

For me, one of the problems of institutionalism is the substantialist ontology embedded in its worldview. It takes the world as composed of independent and discrete nation-states, which are self-existent and instrumentally rational. When international institutions are designed, the designers' background knowledge works for them to make rules and regimes for governing such individual actors through regulating their behavior.

The relational ontology differs. It takes relations as the most significant unit of analysis and thinks about governance from relations. It is what the term "relational governance" means. This terminology appeared perhaps first in the literature of business management, especially when the focus was on East Asian business firms and their management, for relational governance, though practiced almost everywhere, is most conspicuous in East Asia.[34] These studies, however, largely take the approach of transactional cost economics and see relational governance as a mere measure for reducing costs by instrumentally rational actors.

I understand relational governance from a different perspective. I define it as a process of negotiating sociopolitical arrangements that manage complex relationships in a community. The objective is to enable members of the community to behave in a reciprocal and cooperative way with mutual trust evolving over a shared understanding of social norms and human morality.[35] This definition gives priority to relations. It pinpoints at least three important elements in relational governance: governing of relations, governing by relations, and governing for relations.

Governing of relations shifts the governed from individuals to relations among them. The governed are no longer individual members of a society, as most governance literature assumes. They are relations among them. We need to recognize there are various members who have various interests; we need also to recognize that we cannot and should not turn the variety and diversity into homogeneity. But at the same time, we need to recognize that relations among various actors can be governed and managed, and therefore interests of various kinds are defined or redefined so that cooperation rather than conflict will result. In international relations, politics is defined in terms of power, which determines who gets what and how much. From a relational perspective, however, politics means more the ability to govern relations and manage relationships. Well-balanced and cooperative relationships reflect the true wisdom and art of politics.

Governance by relations means that the exercise of governance relies very much on the relational context. The existing IR literature places emphasis on rules as neoliberal institutionalism does, and governance by rules has become a motto for global governance because of the predominant influence of institutionalism in world politics. It is true that international institutions, rules, and regimes play a crucial role in governance, but rules alone cannot govern all and well. Once friendly and cooperative relations are established and maintained, it is easier to exercise governance. Even if we have a homogenous set of rules and institutions throughout the *tianxia,* the collective-action problem would remain unsolved. Relations select, and good relationships orient people to cooperation.

Governance for relations places particular emphasis on establishing friendly and cooperative relationships among members in a community. It means that maintenance and enhancement of good relations is not only a means for some end but also an end in itself. Governance and order are first of all reflected by relations among members of a community, and good governance and order are expressed by harmonious human relations in society. Specifically, as I have discussed before, harmonious human relations refers to maximum cooperation among social members for both the common good and individual interests. We are able to harmonize the relations among the various members and to reach a maximum level of cooperation in society. To some important extent, politics is defined not in terms of power. Rather, it is the art of managing human relationships.

Accordingly, behavioral rules and norms are extremely important in this harmonizing process, but they are or should be designed more for managing human relations in society than for regulating individual behavior, for individual behavior varies according to the nature of relationships. Relational thinking assumes that the individual has no social identity until she is in relation with other social members, just as a piece in the Chinese game *weiqi* or *go*. The whole *weiqi* board is a relational *tianxia,* and a piece has no identity at all before it is placed on this board. For any particular social actor, others exist just like irrelevant general existences until she is related to them. Then they have identities, play roles, and acquire meanings. In other words, they are not existent until related to one another.[36] Think about the five cardinal relationships Confucius discussed; each of the pairs is defined by the other. To govern relationships, rules and norms are made for the purpose of governance: loyalty for the emperor-minister relationship, filial piety for the father-son relationship, and sincerity for the relationship between friends. Moreover, rules and norms are always morally oriented. External rules and norms are always transformed into internal morality, so that governing relations depends very much on what can be called the "moral noumenon."

The Association of Southeast Asian Nations (ASEAN) is an example in this respect. Frequent visits to meet and see counterparts and friends are common among leaders in ASEAN states to enhance their relations in an informal way. Kishore Mahbubani, a diplomat-scholar from Singapore, tends to say that peace in Southeast Asia has been inseparable from golfing and that many thorny issues were solved "after a happy round of golf that generated friendship and camaraderie." Former foreign minister of Singapore Wong Kan Seng readily agreed, saying that golfing was important because it reduced tension and promoted friendship. ASEAN golf matches were organized at the weekend when ASEAN delegations were attending the annual UN Assembly, which, in Wong's words, "was a show of unity. Ministers' wives would come and shake people's hands—that was not seen in other regional organizations. There were memorable but simple gifts as well. Orchids would be given at the end of the reception. A lot of people would turn up, including the UN secretary-general."[37] It is thus interesting that informal friend making seems quite often more relevant than formal institutions in the practice of ASEAN multilateralism. To some extent, this example illustrates how governance of, by, and for relations is practiced in everyday diplomacy among nations.

Relational governance is not a replacement of or an alternative to rule-based governance. Following the *zhongyong* dialectics, they are complementary. We need to recognize that there is more than one way of global governance and that different initial perspectives or worldviews may lead to different practices. It is more effective and reasonable, for example, to synthesize the wise elements of rule-based and relational models of governance for more effective and humane governance of our global commons.

Conclusion

Taking a relational ontology, I have depicted a processual *tianxia* composed of relations. It is not a *tianxia* that, holistic as it is, is co-lived by discrete, self-organizing entities that have a priori properties, interacting as such with one another. Rather, it is a temporal-spatial process of relations: spatial because All-under-Heaven are related to one another and temporal because the present is related to the past as well as to the future.

This approach gives priority to dynamic and flowing relations. As such, the pivot of the universe is relations rather than individual actors per se. It does not deny the existence of individual entities but places emphasis on the fact that they are meaningful only when getting related. It does not deny self-existence but stresses the simultaneity of self-existence, other-existence, and community-existence, all being related in a generative process. Without dynamic relations, paraphrasing Wang Yangming, all are lonely and silent.[38] Once they get related through practice, all become bright and colorful in a constructed world of meaning.

It is important to recognize that all relationships, represented by the *yin–yang* meta-relations, are fundamentally harmonious, for it tells us that relations are governable and our common global home therefore does have a future. The Chinese *zhongyong* dialectics, one of harmonization, understands that the state of nature or the original state of relations is harmony. Despite all the deviations from this original state, in the form of conflict and discord, harmony is achievable. I in particular define harmony in terms of maximum cooperation and following the *zhongyong* dialectics, I also believe, as Martin Nowack has believed, that humans are super co-operators who have proved most successful because they cooperate.[39]

The relational ontology also means that the most significant unit of analysis in the social sciences is relations rather than individual actors. Using global governance as an example, I shift the unit in the international system from the individual actor per se to social relations among them. Global governance, whose purpose is to manage the global commons for the public good, is thus governing of, by, and for relations. The governed are relations rather than individual international actors including nation-states; the way to governing is more through building friendly relationships, which shape a most favorable context for collaboration; and the objective is to establish, maintain, and develop good and balanced relationships so that maximum cooperation can be obtained for managing the global commons through joint efforts. It is the way of governing *tianxia* if we agree that *tianxia* refers today primarily to our common globe that links all of us as well as our past, present, and future.

Notes

1. Zhao Tingyang, "Rethinking Empire from a Chinese Concept 'All-under-Heaven,'" *Social Identities* 12, no. 1 (2006): 30.

2. Zhao Tingyang, "Rethinking the Concept of Politics via '*Tianxia*': The Problems, Conditions and Methodology," *World Economics and Politics* 6 (2015): 4–22.

3. Zhao, "Rethinking Empire," 37–38.

4. Zhao, "Rethinking the Concept of Politics," p. 3.

5. Mustafa Emirbayer, "Manifesto for a Relational Sociology," *American Journal of Sociology* 104, no. 2 (September 1997): 281.

6. Amitav Acharya and Barry Buzan, *The Making of Global International Relations: Origins and Evolution of IR at Its Centenary* (Cambridge: Cambridge University Press, 2019), pp. 19–24.

7. Zhao, "Rethinking the Concept of Politics," p. 2.

8. Alfred N. Whitehead, *Process and Reality*, corrected edition, ed. David Ray Griffin and Donald W. Sherbourne, 2nd ed. (New York: Free Press, 2010); Victor Lowe, *Understanding Whitehead* (Baltimore: Johns Hopkins University Press, 1966).

9. Emirbayer, "Manifesto for a Relational Sociology," p. 281.

10. Patrick Thaddeus Jackson and Daniel Nexon, "Relations before States: Substance, Process and the Study of World Politics," *European Journal of International Relations* 5, no. 3 (1999): 291–332.

11. Emirbayer, "Manifesto for a Relational Sociology," p. 294.

12. Wang Yangming, *Chuanxilu* (Records of the instructions and reviews), collated by Ye Shengtao (Beijing: Shidai huawen shuju, 2014).

13. David L. Hall and Roger T. Ames, *Thinking through Confucius* (Albany: State University of New York Press, 1987), pp. 12–17.

14. Feng Youlan (Fung Yu-lan), "Why China Has No Science—An Interpretation of the History and Consequences of Chinese Philosophy," in Feng Youlan (Fung Yu-lan), *Selected Philosophical Writings of Fung Yu-lan* (Beijing: Foreign Languages Press, 1991), pp. 571–595.

15. Daniel Maliniak, Susan Peterson, Ryan Powers, and Michael Tierney, *TRIP 2014 Faculty Survey* (Williamsburg, VA: Institute for the Theory and Practice of International Relations, 2014), https://trip.wm.edu/dashboard/faculty-surveys; Wiebke Wemheuer-Vogelaar, Nicholas J. Bell, Mariana Navarrete Morales, and Michael J. Tierney, "The IR of the Beholder: Examining Global IR Using the 2014 TRIP Survey," *International Studies Review* 18, no. 1 (March 2016): 16–32.

16. Robert M. A. Crawford and Darryl S. L. Jarvis, eds., *International Relations Theory: Still an American Social Science?* (Albany: State University of New York Press, 2001).

17. Edward Hallet Carr, *Twenty Years' Crisis, 1919–1939: An Introduction to the Study of International Relations* (New York: Harper and Row, 1964); Hans J. Morgenthau, *Politics among Nations: The Struggle for Power and Peace* (New York: Alfred A. Knopf, 1961); Kenneth Waltz, *Theory of International Politics* (Reading, MA: Addison-Wesley, 1979).

18. Robert O. Keohane, *After Hegemony: Cooperation and Discord in World Political Economy* (Princeton, NJ: Princeton University Press, 1984).

19. Alexander Wendt, "Anarchy Is What States Make of It: The Social Construction of Power Politics," *International Organization* 46, no. 2 (1992): 391–425; Alexander Wendt, *Social Theory of International Politics* (Cambridge: Cambridge University Press, 1999).

20. Yaqing Qin, *A Relational Theory of World Politics* (Cambridge: Cambridge University Press, 2018), pp. 152–194.

21. Pang Pu, "*Zhongyong* pingyi" (An analysis of *zhongyong*), *Zhongguo Shehui Kexue* (Social Sciences in China), no. 1 (1980): 75–100; "Daojia bianzhengfa lungang" (An outline of the Daoist dialectics), part 1, *Xueshu Yuekan* (Academic Monthly), no. 12 (1986): 4–10; "Daojia bianzhengfa lungang" (An outline of the Daoist dialectics), part 2," *Xueshu Yuekan* (Academic Monthly), no. 1 (1987): 29–33.

22. L. H. M. Ling, "World beyond the Westphalia: Daoist Dialectics and the China Threat," *Review of International Studies* 39, no. 3 (2013): 549–568.

23. Quoted in Tian Chenshan, *Chinese Dialectics: From Yijing to Marxism* (Lanham, MD: Lexington Books, 2005), p. 10.

24. This equilibrium is understood as appropriate centrality, as the concept of harmony in traditional Chinese philosophy always implies the "centralizing" process, such as the meaning of 中和 (Tu Wei-ming translated it as "centralizing harmony") indicates. In other words, the process of constant centralizing generates and keeps dynamic harmony. See Tu Wei-ming, *An Insight into Zhongyong,* Chinese and English bilingual edition (Beijing: People's Press, 2008), p. 2.

25. Chung-ying Cheng, "Toward Constructing a Dialectics of Harmonization: Harmony and Conflict in Chinese Philosophy," *Journal of Chinese Philosophy* 33, no. 1 (2006): 36.

26. Robert W. Cox, "Social Forces, States, and World Orders: Beyond International Relations Theory," in *Neorealism and Its Critics,* ed. Robert O. Keohane (New York: Columbia University Press, 1986), pp. 204–254.

27. Chung-ying Cheng, *Lun Zhong Xi Zhexue Jingshen* (On the spirits of Chinese and Western philosophies) (Shanghai: Oriental Press, 1991).

28. Tu, *An Insight into Zhongyong,* p. 16.

29. Charles Kindleberger, *The World in Depression: 1929–1933* (Berkeley: University of California Press, 1973).

30. Stephen Krasner, ed., *International Regimes* (Ithaca, NY: Cornell University Press, 1983).

31. Keohane, *After Hegemony.*

32. United Nations Department of Public Information, *A More Secure World: Our Shared Responsibility: Report of the Secretary-General's High-Level Panel on Threats, Challenges and Change* (New York: United Nations Department of Public Information, 2004).

33. Yaqing Qin, "Global Governance Failure and Ideational Reconstruction for a Sustainable World Order," in *China under Xi Jinping: Its Economic Challenges and Foreign Policy Initiatives,* ed. Shao Binhong (Leiden: Brill, 2015), pp. 98–116.

34. As for relational governance in business management, see the following literature: Jeffrey H. Dyer and Harbir Singh, "The Relational View of Cooperative Strategy as Sources of Japanese Comparative Advantages," *Organization Science* 7, no. 6 (1998): 649–666; Laura Poppo and Todd Zenger, "Do Formal Contracts and Relational Governance Function as Substitutes or Complements?," *Strategic Management Journal* 23, no. 8 (2002): 707–725; John Shuhe Li, "Relation-Based versus Rule-Based Governance: An Explanation of the East Asian Miracle and Asian Crisis," *Review of International Economics* 11, no. 4 (2003): 651–673.

35. Qin, *Relational Theory,* p. 335.

36. It is useful to recall Wang Yangming's argument, "Yi zhi suozai bian shi wu" (Where there is a meaning, there is a thing). See Yang Guorong, *Zouxiang Liangzhi: "Chuanxilu" yu Yangming Xinxue* (To attain innate knowledge: Records of the instructions and reviews and Wang Yangming's mindology), Chinese and English bilingual edition, trans. Gong Haiyan (Shanghai: Shanghai Foreign Languages Educational Press, 2018), p. 19.

37. Kishore Mahbubani and Jeffrey Sng, *The ASEAN Miracle: A Catalyst for Peace* (Singapore: Ridge Books, 2017), pp. 50–51.

38. Wang Yangming, *"Chuanxilu,"* p. 233.

39. Martin Nowak with Roger Highfield, *Super Cooperators: Evolution, Altruism and Human Behaviour or Why We Need Each Other to Succeed* (Edinburgh: Canongate, 2011).

CHAPTER 10

Universalizing *Tianxia* in an East Asian Context

Takahiro NAKAJIMA

WHAT DOES IT imply to talk about *tianxia* 天下 in today's world? Viewed in light of the "conceptual history" suggested by the German philosopher Reinhart Koselleck (1923–2006), we might discuss the history of *tianxia* as a concept: that is, how the concept of *tianxia* has been transformed. In fact, some scholars have attempted to understand *tianxia* using this approach, primarily in mainland China. If we trace the conceptual history of *tianxia,* as a complement to previous studies, particularly in Korea and Japan (which are China's neighbors), we find a distinctive understanding of the concept of *tianxia* and can provide some worthwhile insights to the discourse that concerns it.

However, it is more important to seek the philosophical meaning of the old term *tianxia* by restating it in a broader context, wherein the right of discourse or the decolonization of philosophy has been restored. Hence, what we contemplate must go beyond the constraints or barriers of the "world," a modern and universal concept. Simultaneously, we must remain alert so as not to return to a Japan-centered discourse on "overcoming modernity," as found expression in prewar Japanese philosophy. This discourse was in fact "overcome by modernity" (Harootunian 2000) and, in the end, it came to only replace Eurocentrism with Japan-centrism. If we, in a similar fashion, propose a Sino-centric *tianxia* in place of a Eurocentric understanding of the "world," it would become meaningless.

Instead, it is necessary to think how to restate what has been called the "world" or the "universe" from East Asia through *tianxia*. For this, we would need to revisit and reassess the limits and possibilities of the European discourse on the "world" or the "universe" and search for the possibility of a differentiated *tianxia*. In this regard, I would like to use the following pages to explore the possible ways of defining *tianxia* with reference to the postwar Japanese writers / thinkers / novelists Taijun Takeda and Atsushi Mori, whose thoughts notably differ from the discourse on "overcoming modernity."

Tianxia and the World

In the first place, what kind of concept is *tianxia*? To pose this question differently, we might ask if it is a specific concept or a universal one.

If we consider it as a specific concept, *tianxia* indicates the proper concept of grasping the world in the sphere of Chinese civilization. This is the predominant understanding of *tianxia*. By presupposing a cultural and ethnic hierarchy as a *hua–yi* 華夷 distinction, this understanding suggests that there is a ruler called *tianzi* 天子, the Son of Heaven, who inhabits the center of the civilized world called *zhonghua* 中華, while there is *tian* 天, Heaven, which secures the *tianzi*'s legitimacy. In this structure, we recognize *tianxia* as the governing space. One caveat is that its meaning and contents change constantly, according to where the center (*zhonghua*) is situated, which signifies that it is not necessarily confined to mainland China geographically. For instance, it is well known that China's neighboring countries, such as Korea and Japan, had considered themselves to be another *zhonghua,* or followed an even more orthodox understanding, which led them to create their own *hua–yi* distinction or *tianxia*. Despite these variations, this way of understanding *tianxia,* as a worldview based on Chinese civilization, was prevalent in East Asia.[1]

However, the situation changed drastically in the nineteenth century as modern Europe introduced the "world" as another universal concept to East Asia. As a universal concept, *tianxia* hitherto gave way to the "world," a brand-new concept. Thus, *tianxia* as the specific concept that represents the worldview proper to the sphere of Chinese civilization solely remained. Here, we might ask: Why was the modern European concept of "world" considered more universal when compared with *tianxia*? Among various plausible reasons, I would like to consider this question in relation to the concept of totality. Immanuel Kant, by understanding God, the soul, and the universe as the "unconditioned" in the *Critique of Pure Reason,* raised critical questions: Can a human being, who is by definition finite and conditioned, be able to think of something that transcends human reasoning? How can the conditioned get close to the absolute totality of conditions?

Under this problematic, Kant thought of the "world" as the totality of the objects and events we can experience. Although the "world" can be ideally a totality, it is not the object of our experience. The "world," therefore, is an idea. Stated more precisely, it is a regulative idea postulated by human reason.[2] If that is the case, what East Asia confronted became a totality (or an ideal totality) called the "world," which became understood as more universal, because it was not a mere concept but an idea. On the contrary, *tianxia* remained a specific concept, upholding a distinctive system as incorporated into the totality as the "world." *Tianxia* was not understood as an ideal totality.

The Aspiration for Universality and a Critique of Totality

Here, we need to consider the next step. In recent years, the concept of *tianxia* has been re-examined in China, especially by Tingyang Zhao, Jilin Xu, and others. While there are nuanced differences between their interpretations, they seem to share a common interest in the deconstruction of the historically structured concept of *tianxia* such as the *hua–yi* distinction and Chinese civilization, and in its elaboration as a universal concept once again. Even so, these movements, seeking *tianxiazhuyi* 天下主義 (a theory of All-under-Heaven) or *xin tianxiazhuyi* 新天下主義 (a new theory of All-under-Heaven) are exposed to the criticism that they still reflect Sino-centrism, as the Korean historian Young-Seo Baik has argued. The position of these critics is likely due to a deep-seated doubt concerning the universality of the concept of *tianxia*. In other words, they seem to presuppose that *tianxia* is not adequate as a universal concept, that is, that it is unfailingly entangled with the specific geographical, cultural, and ethnic connotations of China.[3]

However, this does not automatically mean that the concept of the "world" as advocated by modern Europe can boast of its usefulness in the moment. More specifically, the "world," an ideal totality, cannot be held as it is. For instance, the German philosopher Markus Gabriel questions the concept of the "world" as an ideal totality (e.g., a whole) as follows:

> To put it briefly, Kant says, and with him Habermas, that the world is a "regulative idea." This means that we presuppose a world whole, and that everything we experience and know must be understood as a section of the world whole. In this way we guarantee that we can have a coherent and contradiction-free picture of the world, for the world itself is a unity whose sections we are able to represent. Habermas's point is that the world in this sense, of course, is not a thing, nor can it be identical with the universe. In this model the world itself is not found as a section of the world; rather, it is only an idea which we presuppose in order to be able to make the sections intelligible. (Gabriel 2017, p. 47)

We only experience and perceive fragments of experience, and what makes the fragments intelligible is the "world," as a "regulative idea." Gabriel, however, dismisses this stance, which stems from modern European philosophy. "By analogy, so it is with the world as a whole. This exists just as little as a connection which encompasses all connections. There is simply no rule or world formula that describes everything. This is not contingent on the fact that we have not yet found it, but on the fact that it cannot exist at all" (2017, p. 11). And further, "We cannot know everything simply because there is no principle that holds everything together and organizes it all. The world does not exist" (p. 181).

The background of this critique may be understood as the so-called New Realism, which serves to reconstruct a philosophical interrogation of the anthropocentric worldview that emerges in modern Europe. Is anthropocentrism, which relates everything to human beings, likely to support attitudes of contempt toward beings other than humans and the denigration of their actual existence? Was the concept of the "world" in fact a totality that reinforced anthropocentricism? Along with this line of philosophical interrogation, Gabriel's critique contains an ethical response to totalitarianism, the political experience of the twentieth century. Reflection that starts from totality and returns to it, along with the totalitarianism this produces, is not considered ethical. Here, we should bear in mind the significance of Emmanuel Levinas's argument in *Totalité et infini* (Totality and infinity, 1961) concerning the events of the twentieth century. Levinas criticizes European philosophy as a philosophy of totality and presents the dimension of others irreducible to totality as infinity.

On the Type of Plurality

Then how should we envision *tianxia* or the "world" in the present day? The concept of plurality can play a key role here. In recent years, for example, the multiverse theory has emerged in astronomy. However, the plurality discussed in the field of astronomy is still one viewed in light of a transcendent being, such as God. Insofar as each universe can be constructed by following completely different principles, multiple universes are fundamentally distinct. However, the viewpoint that sees them is located outside the universes, as if it were the perspective of God. Moreover, the universes are understood to carefully avoid overlapping one another. For instance, in the notion of "bubble" universes in the multiverse theory, the case of multiple overlapping bubbles is not considered.[4]

In this context, a consideration of Gottfried Wilhelm Leibniz might help to provide a better understanding of the question at hand. When Leibniz encountered another world, China, in which a completely different set of principles were in effect, his worldview, rooted in the Christianity of his day, was challenged. But rather than abandoning God, he started to ponder the notion of simultaneous, parallel worlds, which is well known as the "theory of possible worlds." He contends that while there are an infinite number of "worlds," God has chosen the "actual world" as the best of all "possible worlds." Accordingly, this provides the ground to uphold the plurality of the "world" and at the same time the notion of God as the creator of all "worlds" and, moreover, the one who selects the "actual world" as the best among all possible worlds. In Leibniz's *Monadology*, the assertion of a "windowless monad" serves as a point of reference for plural worlds that represent each other insofar as they are "worlds," but a "world" that is windowless cannot be directly connected with another "world."

All in all, this plurality is derived from the notion that one "world" is regarded as a certain totality. As long as we belong to "this world" as a totality, we cannot be interconnected with "that world" at the same time. This is the case in Leibniz's account, regardless of the possibility that plural "worlds" could represent each other. Nonetheless, what I would like to consider here is nothing less than *tianxia* or a "world" that escapes the totality. In this situation, the condition of plurality should also be unlike God's point of view.

"The Astounding Phenomenon of Worlds Existing in Parallel"

As a way of approaching some of these questions, it is worth devoting attention to the endeavors of the Japanese writer Taijun Takeda (1912–1976). In *Sima Qian: The World of Shiji* (1943), Takeda depicted the "astounding phenomenon of worlds existing in parallel" regarding *Shiji* (The Record of the Grand Historian) of Sima Qian.

> You realize simply by reading the *benji* 本紀 [the imperial biographies that form the first 12 of the *Shiji*'s 130 volumes] that imperial biography does not fully encompass the world of the *Shiji*. When at last the peoples known as the *shijia* 世家 make their appearance, you come to understand at a visceral level the astounding phenomenon of worlds existing in parallel. This kind of response is very different from that to the unified phenomenon of imperial biography.
>
> The center of the world is not only one and moreover it does not halt. If this were the case, this world would inevitably stand in parallel. This world sticks to its propensity for returning to a single thing as well as reaching out in every direction. If it reaches out, there we see plural centers in parallel, and thereupon the content of each center is likely to be undetermined, and even the fragile shape of each center could be easily skewed. Therefore, the different *shijia* ceaselessly combine, are intermingled, pass in and through the inside of other *shijia*, increase or vice versa; they never know a standstill. (Takeda 1943, pp. 99–100)

The center of the world is not a single one. While the *benji* present the unification of the world, the history of peripheralized people called the *shijia* illustrates the "astounding phenomenon of worlds existing in parallel." Incidentally, the *shijia* appear only in the *Shiji,* eliminated from the later authentic history—Sima Qian wrote the *shijia* in thirty volumes in order to show the "astounding phenomenon of worlds existing in parallel."

Despite this, Takeda did not leave the *benji* as a unified world. What makes the *benji* of the *Shiji* bizarre is that they place Xiang Yu in line with Liu Bang, the founder of the Han dynasty, although the two were rivals. Takeda tried to read the *Shiji* as "human astronomy" (Takeda 1943, p. 85), but as a matter of fact there were "two suns" in the world. "The fun of the 'meeting at *Hongmen*' in itself reflects the fun of the '*benji*'; if you enjoy the 'meeting at *Hongmen*,' you can have confidence you fully grasp the '*benji*.' In the 'meeting at *Hongmen*,' two suns encounter one another. This alone is extraordinary in the human universe. The 'centers of the world,' Xiang Yu and Liu Bang, meet face to face" (pp. 84–85).

Admittedly, it is very exceptional to put Xiang Yu in the *benji*. If one intends to honor the *yitong* (one lineage) of the Han dynasty alone, Xiang Yu should be involved in a *liezhuan* (a series of biographies) like *Hanshu* (the *Book of Han*). Sima Qian, however, purposely put Xiang Yu in the *benji,* while stating specifically under the rule of Emperor Wu, the heyday of the Former Han. The *benji,* then, state explicitly that there can be plural centers of the world. This is a very daring description of history, to the extent that we can easily imagine it even endangered the writer's life. Moreover, Takeda also made a bold decision to write about Empress Lu, a wife of Liu Bang, in the *benji*. "*Luhou benji* [*benji* of Empress Lu] is the story of a woman who travels back and forth through the space between that of Heaven and the individual. Sima Qian here articulates that even a woman becomes an absolute being, who is capable of drawing close to Heaven. To put it in another way, the identity and content of the absolute being can both be clearly enunciated by delivering the episode of a woman. It is the *benji* that even a woman can become the center of the world, and can be a part of it" (Takeda 1943, p. 95).

Here, Takeda sees the world described by Sima Qian such that, not only are there plural centers, but also the world is ceaselessly agitated. This is the very secret of the "astounding phenomenon of worlds existing in parallel"; that is, it is not the eyes of God that arbitrate here.

In accordance with this, Yoshimi Takeuchi's (1910–1977) critique of Takeda seems to miss the mark.

> History sometimes appears stagnant. It may seem like paths of circulation are not moving. However, unpredictable and volatile energies may be building up internally. If one looks to these areas, revolution may take a more important place alongside the *longue durée*. If *Sima Qian* was written presuming an apocalyptic world stands against a sustaining world, it

is fair to say that as a piece it would be finished with more dignity. I know that this judgement is based on my insatiable desire. Concerning the time when it was written, resisting the trend of a historical view of the times or a historical view of *bansei ikkei* (the unbroken imperial line, reigning since time immemorial), it might have been the best he could do. (Takeuchi 1981, p. 161)

Both Takeuchi and Takeda studied Chinese literature at Tokyo Imperial University, and together they established an academic society on Chinese literature called the "Association for Chinese Literature." They were friends who criticized the *Shinagaku* (Sinology) of the times. According to Takeuchi, what Takeda resisted by any means was the then "historical view of the times" and the "historical view of *Bansei ikkei* (unbroken imperial line)." These entail narrating the past sequentially in order to affirm the present, weighing the "paths of circulation" much like the putative natural laws that govern it. In this historical view, the world is a single totality (i.e., posited as a whole). Takeda, to the contrary, focused on the "internally" "unpredictable and volatile energies"; that is, he turned his eyes toward another possibility laid out in history: that is, by envisioning plural worlds existing in parallel and the encounter of plural centers.

One caveat is that Takeda's worldview did not extend to the "revolution" or "apocalyptic world" that Takeuchi desired. Presumably, Takeuchi had a God's-eye view or regulative ideal in mind, while for Takeda, by not engaging with a "revolution" or "apocalyptic world," the radicality of his view was far more pronounced than that of Takeuchi. In other words, for Takeda worlds are posited horizontally rather than vertically, which strongly signifies the power of his radical imagination.

Edgar Allan Poe and Blaise Pascal

It is important to bear in mind that Takeda referred to "associating E. A. Poe's 'Eureka'" (Takeda 1943, pp. 104–105) as a thought of the "astounding phenomenon of worlds existing in parallel." Edgar Allan Poe's (1809–1849) *Eureka* (1848) is a poetic cosmology written in his last years, dedicated to Alexander von Humboldt (1769–1859), the author of *Cosmos* (published between 1845 and 1862). Poe nonetheless addresses the difference between Humboldt and his own views as follows: "But even of treatises on the really limited, although always assumed as the *un*limited, Universe of *stars,* I know none in which a survey, even of this limited Universe, is so taken as to warrant deductions from its *individuality*. The nearest approach to such a work is made in the 'Cosmos' of Alexander Von Humboldt. He presents the subject, however, *not* in its individuality but in its generality" (Poe 1965, pp. 186–187; emphasis in original).

Stated differently, while Humboldt observes the universe in its "generality," Poe sees it in its "individuality." What is the difference? It would be the point at which Poe considered "infinity."

> Let us begin, then, at once, with that merest of words, "Infinity." This, like "God," "spirit," and some other expressions of which the equivalents exist in all languages, is by no means the expression of an idea—but of an effort at one. It stands for the possible attempt at an impossible conception. Man needed a term by which to point out the *direction* of this effort—the cloud behind which lay, forever invisible, the *object* of this attempt. A word, in fine, was demanded, by means of which one human being might put himself in relation at once with another human being and with a certain *tendency* of the human intellect. Out of this demand arose the word, "Infinity"; which is thus the representative but of the *thought of a thought*. (Poe 1965, p. 200; emphasis in original)

"Infinity" here is regarded much like Kant's regulative ideal. Viewed in light of what we have discussed so far, Poe sees the universe not via a totality but rather via infinity, but because it is guided by a regulative ideal in the end, his contention on infinity does not extend to the infinity going beyond it.

For Poe, this point implies a subtle difference with Blaise Pascal's (1623–1662) conception of the universe:

> This was the untenable idea of Pascal when making perhaps the most successful attempt ever made, at periphrasing the conception for which we struggle in the word "Universe." "It is a sphere," he says, "of which the centre is everywhere, the circumference, nowhere." But although this intended definition is, in fact, *no* definition of the Universe of *stars*, we may accept it, with some mental reservation, as a definition (rigorous enough for all practical purposes) of the Universe *proper*—that is to say, of the Universe of *space*. This latter, then, let us regard as "*a sphere of which the centre is everywhere, the circumference nowhere.*" In fact, while we find it impossible to fancy an *end* to space, we have no difficulty in picturing to ourselves any one of an infinity of *beginnings*. (Pascal 1972, pp. 204–205)

The passage of Pascal's *Pensées* that Poe quotes reads like this: "C'est une sphère infinie dont le centre est partout, la circonférence nulle part" (It is a sphere whose centre is everywhere, its circumference nowhere) (Pascal 1972, pp. 26–27; emphasis in original). Concerning this passage, Poe gave credit in that he felt it adequately defined the "the Universe proper," but he had already stated, "This was the untenable idea of Pascal." Why is that? It is because they have different conceptions of "infinity." Describing the "sphere of infinity," Poe also mentioned "the '*utmost conceivable expanse*' of space" in the same passage (Poe 1965, p. 204; emphasis in original). By contrast, Pascal sees "infinity" as unknowable and frightening, for example: "Donc il est vrai qu'il y a un infini en nombre, mais nous ne savons ce qu'il est" (Thus, it is true that there is an infinity in number, but we do not know what it is) (Pascal 1972, p. 112), or "Le silence éternel de ces espaces infinis m'effraie" (The eternal silence of these infinite spaces frightens me) (p. 105). Here, it seems that for Pascal, the plurality is astonishing enough to demolish the process of thought.

Needless to say, Poe also touches upon the plurality of the universe:

> My question, however, remains unanswered:—Have we any right to infer—let us say, rather, to imagine—an interminable succession of the "clusters of clusters," or of "Universes" more or less similar?
>
> I reply that the "right," in a case such as this, depends absolutely upon the hardihood of that imagination which ventures to claim the right. Let me declare, only, that, as an individual, I myself feel impelled to the *fancy*—without daring to call it more—that there *does* exist a *limitless* succession of Universes, more or less similar to that of which we have cognizance—to that of which *alone* we shall ever have cognizance—at the very least until the return of our own particular Universe into Unity. *If* such clusters of clusters exist, however—*and they do*—it is abundantly clear that, having had no part in our origin, they have no portion in our laws. They neither attract us, nor we them. Their material—their spirit is not ours—is not that which obtains in any part of our Universe. They could not impress our senses or our souls. Among them and us—considering all, for the moment, collectively—there are no influences in common. Each exists, apart and independently, *in the bosom of its proper and particular God*. (Poe 1965, p. 276; emphasis in original)

If it is the case to see the universe from "individuality," Poe also came to think of the plurality of the universe. As noted in this quotation, he even presupposed an "interminable succession" of multiple universes. What differs here, however, is that these plural universes have no casual relations—each one exists "in the bosom of its proper and particular God"—which recalls the multiverse theory. In Poe, then, we find no insight akin to what Takeda identifies, that is, worlds existing in parallel and the encounter of plural centers. We must go beyond Poe.

Two "Worlds": Atsushi Mori

Born the same year as Taijun Takeda, Atsushi Mori (1912–1989) is a writer well known for mathematics and novels concerned with Buddhist themes. It is alleged that Mori was greatly influenced by Poe.[5] What characterizes Mori's thinking most, however, is that he transcends Poe's thought and proposes a path to connect with other worlds or other universes, by breaking through a closed totality. This was possible in part due to Mori's topological imagination, of which he was fond and for which he had a talent.

The first step is as follows: "Taking an arbitrary point as an origin, draw a circle with an arbitrary radius. If we consider the circumference as a boundary, the world is thus divided into two areas. The boundary must belong to one of these two areas. In this case, the area to which the boundary does not belong is called a neighborhood, while the area to which the boundary does belong may be called an exterior" (Mori 1993, p. 33). Mori first divides the "world" into two areas: an inner side, which he calls a "neighborhood," and an outer side, its "exterior." The role of the "boundary" here is intriguing, for it does not belong to the inner "neighborhood" but rather belongs to the outer "exterior." Insofar as there is no "boundary" in the "neighborhood," this "neighborhood" may also be understood as the "world."[6] Furthermore, since the "boundary" belongs to the "exterior," the "world" consists of the sum of "neighborhood," "boundary," and "exterior" ("neighborhood" + "boundary" + "exterior" = "world"). We now gain two "worlds" by drawing a "boundary" line.

Following this idea, what does it mean that a "neighborhood" is the "world"? Mori suggests the following definition:

> The "neighborhood" is hermetically closed, for it is the area to which the boundary does not belong. In addition, the "neighborhood" is opened, for it is the area to which the boundary does not belong. That is, since it can be said that the "neighborhood," as long as it is hermetically closed and opened, any point in the "neighborhood" can be set as an origin. The boundary does not need to be a circle, for in some cases an arbitrary point in the exterior could also be an origin. The origin also constitutes and combines with the neighborhood. (Mori 1993, p. 34)

The "neighborhood" is hermetically closed, insofar as it is delimited by the "boundary." However, since the "neighborhood" is that to which the "boundary" does not belong, it is opened and constitutes the "world." As long as it is the "world," an "arbitrary point in it can be an origin." Even if it is an "arbitrary point in the exterior," this is so. This clarifies that Mori's proposition exactly corresponds to the aforementioned passage of Pascal: "a sphere whose centre is everywhere, its circumference nowhere."

Mori's thoughts proceed as follows: what is the relationship between the "neighborhood" and the "exterior"? Stated differently, what relationship do these

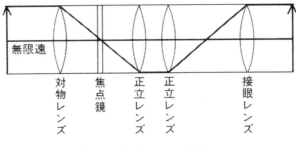

Mori's "telescopic sight." From Mori 1993, p. 23.

two "worlds" have with each other? Here, Mori introduces a device, which is a lens, as if Spinoza had thought of it. Concretely speaking, for him, it is a telescope. "A telescope is the one that realizes the area that constructs an outer side in the area that constructs an inner side and proves the reality that constructs an inner side is solely inside" (Mori 1993, p. 19).

By realizing the outside inside, the outside is connected to the inside. The two worlds overlap. But the overlap is not that simple. What is emphasized here is how Mori shows the mechanism of a telescope (i.e., a telescopic sight). With a simple structure using a mirror and four lenses, an external image that stands vertically is realized inside. Further, Mori gave careful attention here. Since the external image looks smaller with a lens of 1x magnification, he uses a lens of 1.25x magnification, to give the viewer a sense of connectedness. "The boundary has a dreadful meaning in that it converts the inside into the outside and vice versa. And yet if you look at things through a frame, you feel they are somehow smaller and not 'connected.' I endeavor to overcome this" (Mori 1993, p. 26). Mori also noticed that an external image appears connected with a lens of 1x magnification if the mechanism of "optical sight" is adopted. What is critical here is that the boundary itself is the secret of converting inside and outside; it is necessary to have made some other maneuver—for example, an "illusionary trick" (p. 22)—in order to uncover this secret.

What, then, does this imply? It elucidates that what matters most in understanding the "world" based upon "totality" and "plurality" is the conduct of drawing a "boundary" line. The "boundary" is not granted beforehand; the "boundary" is established when someone draws it, and in this way a "world" emerges. Once a "world" emerges, however, the "boundary," which does not belong to it but is unintentionally included in it, has vanished from sight. Therefore, we need an "illusionary trick" or some specific maneuver in order to re-emphasize the "boundary."

In addition, Mori asserts that this "boundary" is "infinity": "Naming the inside or outside, whatever it is; it is only either converged into infinity or converging infinity" (1993, p. 15). In the end, how can we envision the "world" as open to "infinity" rather than to "totality" in our problematic?

The Praxis of "Questioning"

As for the "way" and "time," Mori describes them as follows:

> "If the way changes, the world changes. We should change the way so as to change the world. Namely, not only are the way and the world in a functional relationship, but the way can even attach significance to the world. Likewise, if possibly time signifies the world, would we be able to change time, by changing the world? Very interesting, but it is impossible. Yes. There is only one difference between the way and time."
> "One difference?"
> "Yup. We are always in the neighborhood with an origin as I. The neighborhood is an area where a boundary does not belong. Any way cannot reach its boundary. But . . ."
> "But?"
> "But there is only one way to reach a boundary. That is the way as time, which leads us even to the Great Divide." (Mori 1993, pp. 48–49)

The way and time can even signify the world itself. But while the way cannot reach the boundary, time can reach it. How and why can this "way as time" reach the boundary? It is because time is "questioning" in itself.

> Let us liken that world to the white flesh of an apple at hand; though saying the boundary that should be called the Great Divide belongs to it, it is within the extent in which I peel away red skin, akin to life, with a knife of time, in order to obtain the white flesh, which is imminently and largely pressed without doubt. If I quit peeling, the boundary cannot belong to any part of its areas; it is just a "being left as it is," or nothing-to-be, neither white flesh or red skin, neither inside nor outside. (Mori 1993, p. 73)

The boundary reveals its secret at the moment you put a knife of time to it. Otherwise, whether inside or outside, it is just a "being left as it is," or "nothing-to-be." It cannot be even a "world." Moreover, it cannot also long for the realization of another "world" in this "world." To apply the "knife of time" is exactly "questioning." "But what if you do not give up questioning? The sphere to be realized is always higher than the boundary in its dimension. . . . If so, life, which is only realized in the Great Divide as just a one-dimensional sphere, so far, is not lost, but revives to a higher sphere in its dimension, the Great Divide heightened with more dimensions" (Mori 1993, p. 73).

As for this question, Mori seems to have an image that Christianity and Buddhism should have posed this type of question. Nevertheless, it is not necessarily religious, but related to a wide range of the "transformation of meaning," as the title of his book suggests. That the "meaning is transformed into a religion" and "even history is becoming a philosophy by transforming the meaning" means "its reasoning is congruent" (Mori 1993, p. 63). In a sense, this may be what surpasses Poe and leads back to Pascal. In any case, without "questioning," we can never be engaged in the "world."

Conclusion

In this chapter, I have sought the significance of the concept of *tianxia* in today's world. To summarize, first, *tianxia* is not a specific concept that presupposes the *hua–yi* distinction or Chinese civilization, which was a pervasive influence in premodern East Asia. It then became a subcategory of the "world," which is a modern concept. *Tianxia*, however, should not inherit the "world," especially one in which a totality becomes an ideal. We should not naively presume the totality of the world, which resulted in the vain experiences of the twentieth century. Accordingly, *tianxia* should be a concept that embraces infinity instead of a totality. It is the concept that opens toward radical plurality, reflecting the status of plural "worlds" existing in parallel. Here, though, we need to be cautious by understanding that it is not necessarily a "place" where plural "worlds" exist in parallel. This is because it includes a nested structure for plural other "worlds" to be realized in the midst of this *tianxia*. For this, it is essential to make efforts to bring *tianxia* to a far higher dimension, by repeatedly drawing a boundary line of *tianxia*. This effort will pay off; otherwise, *tianxia* will immediately become a "being left as it is" or "nothing-to-be," which falls into the state of affirming the status quo.

What should we do then? As Atsushi Mori keenly contends, we must continue to put the "knife of time," which is "questioning," on *tianxia*. This ultimately leads *tianxia* to a "transformation of meaning."

The concept of *tianxia* is meaningless unless it is a praxis; and that praxis is "questioning" itself. Will then *tianxia* eventually reach the boundary?

Notes

1. Regarding the concept of *tianxia* or the "world" in Japan, see Sueki 2017, pp. 65–104.

2. Regarding Kant's contention on the "world," see Saito 2002, pp. 642–645.

3. Regarding the recent contention on the concept of *tianxia* in China, see Nakajima 2016.

4. Yasunori Nomura, one of the advocates of the multiverse theory, offers a diagram of "bubble universes" and explains it as follows: "In fact, it is generally expected that all the different universes in string theory are physically realized as bubble universes in this manner. This process of eternally creating bubble universes in exponentially expanding ambient space is called the eternal inflating multiverse. This setup, therefore, is exactly the one needed by Weinberg to solve the problem of small vacuum energy. According to this picture, our universe is only one of the (infinitely) many bubble universes formed through eternal inflation" (Nomura, Poirier, and Terning 2018, p. 188). These "bubble universes" are disjunctive with respect to one other.

5. See the account of Mori in *Tokyo Sports*, January 18, 1974: http://www.mori-atsushi.jp/k-012.html (accessed April 5, 2019).

6. By the way, Atsushi Mori came to avoid the term "totality" afterward. Until then, the object of the "total concept" was replaced with the "world." In other words, he came to describe a "neighborhood" as "I will not call it a total concept here, rather will call it the world as you said sometime before" (Mori 1993, p. 33).

References

Gabriel, Markus. 2017. *Why the World Does Not Exist*. Cambridge: Polity Press.
Harootunian, Harry. 2000. *Overcome by Modernity: History, Culture, and Community in Interwar Japan*. Princeton, NJ: Princeton University Press.
Levinas, Emmanuel. 1961. *Totalité et infini: Essai sur l'extériorité*. La Haye: M. Nijhoff.
Mori, Atsushi. 1993. *Transformation of Meaning*. In *Atsushi Mori Complete Collection*, vol. 2, pp. 3–78. Tokyo: Chikuma shobo.
Nakajima, Takahiro. 2016. "Recovery of *Zhonghua*: A Discourse on Chinese Universality." In *Iwanami Lecture Series: Contemporary Religion and the New Era of a Mind*, edited by Masachi Osawa et al., pp. 67–90. Tokyo: Iwanami shoten.
Nomura, Yasunori, Bill Poirier, and John Terning. 2018. *Quantum Physics, Mini Black Holes, and the Multiverse* Cham, Switzerland: Springer.
Pascal, Blaise. 1972. *Pensées*. Paris: Livre de poche.
Poe, Edgar Allan. 1965. *The Complete Works of Edgar Allan Poe*. Edited by James A. Harrison. New York: AMS Press.
Saito, Yoshimichi. 2002. "The World." In *The Encyclopedia: Tree of Philosophy*, edited by Hitoshi Nagai et al., pp. 642–645. Tokyo: Kodansha.
Sueki, Fumihiko. 2017. *Range of the History of Japanese Thought*. Tokyo: Keibunsha.
Takeda, Taijun. 1943. *Sima Qian—The World of Shiji*. Tokyo: Kodansha.
Takeuchi, Yoshimi. 1981. "Commentary on *Volume Nine of the Complete Works of Takeda Taijun*." In *The Complete Works of Takeuchi Yoshimi*, vol. 12, pp. 148–162. Tokyo: Chikuma shobo.

CHAPTER 11

Virtuosic Relationality and Ethical Diversity

A Buddhist Revisioning of International Relations beyond Anarchy and Hierarchy

Peter D. HERSHOCK

HISTORY IS WRITTEN by the victors. If this well-known adage is true, it must also be true that histories have been rewritten every time a winning streak has broken. Among the motivations for differently theorizing international relations (IR) and global justice is the mounting evidence that Western theories of international relations and justice—at least as they have been applied thus far—have passed the apogee of their practical efficacy. Not only have they proven incapable of motivating and sustaining effective responses to such long-term global structural challenges as those posed by climate disruption and rising inequalities of risk, income, and wealth, they have clearly fallen short in galvanizing equitable and effective emergency responses to the global COVID-19 pandemic. The history of international relations dominated by American and European IR theorizing is seemingly due, if not overdue, for revision.

Histories, however, are only incidentally *records* of events past. More substantively and significantly, they serve as forward-looking *rehearsals* of the meanings of events still in the process of unfolding—a kind of narrative infrastructure for the materialization of certain convictions about what matters. Over the past two decades, efforts have been underway to explore the "All-under-Heaven World System" (*tianxia tixi* 天下体系) as an alternative infrastructure for theorizing international relations and global justice—an infrastructure that draws on Chinese political history and Confucian philosophy to address the realities of a complexly changing world. In keeping with the venerable Chinese practice of rewriting histories to explain the practical and moral necessity of dynastic transition, *tianxia* theorizing is predicated on convictions that we are currently in an interregnum and that a "dynastic" transition is already underway. The only salient question now is what its character will be.

As might be expected given the Confucian aim of fostering "harmony and not sameness" (*he'er butong* 和而不同), *tianxia* theorizing is not uniform.[1] It does, however, revolve around certain core principles or pattern-generating sources of coherence (*li* 理). The most distinctive of these, perhaps, is commitment to centering international relations and justice concerns on the quality of relational dynamics rather than on a balance among individual interests.[2] As we will see, this is consistent with Buddhist thought.

Yet a second unifying feature is to imagine changing the course of world history based on coordinates drawn exclusively from Chinese culture and its political past—a trajectory along which global dynamics would be carried into increasing alignment with values contrary to many of those that have informed Western theories of justice and international relations, including individual autonomy, equality, freedom (most fundamentally of choice), and rationality (most fundamentally in the pursuit of self-interest). Such a change of course may well be necessary. It is not entirely clear, however, that coordinates derived from Chinese culture, the values they evince, and the historical trajectories they support imagining, can or should be globalized.

On one hand, this is a matter of disciplinary definition. IR scholars have for decades argued for regional diversity in theory production and identified ethnocentrism as a central flaw of the discipline.[3] More substantively, however, a strong case can be made that the defining global challenges of the next several decades—including climate change and the impacts of artificial intelligence— will not be problems amenable to purely technical solutions through the discovery of new means to existing ends. Instead, they will be predicaments revealing conflicts among ends and interests that can only be resolved ethically by developing new, priority-structuring constellations of values. Granted this and the fact that every ethical system has blind spots, it can reasonably be argued that global predicament resolution will depend on realizing an "ethical ecosystem"—a system to the dynamics of which many different ethical approaches make distinctive contributions.[4] IR theorizing, I will argue, should be similarly diverse.

In what follows, I aim to clarify the nature of globally focused (rather than state-centric) international relations practice by considering an alternative, Buddhist position from which to contribute to the emergence of a theoretical ecology that is dynamically aligned with materializing two of the governing insights underpinning *tianxia* theorizing: (1) that relationality is ontologically more basic than individuality and (2) that effectively engaging and reorienting global social realities requires a sharp methodological turn away from balancing risks against desired outcomes, and a resolute turn toward embodying commitments to sharing the risks and responsibilities involved in fostering conditions for the progressive emergence of inclusively welcomed opportunity. Concisely stated, I want to envision reorienting international relations by subverting the ontological commitments tacitly endorsed by realist, neoliberal institutionalist, and constructivist theories of international relations; decentering the role of security / stability as a goal for international relations practice; and fostering diversity-enriching and equity-enhancing ethical improvisation.

The Middle Way (*Zhongdao* 中道) Is Not Compromising

Given the traditional description of Buddhist practice as a "middle path," a Buddhist vision of changing the course of international relations theorizing might be supposed to rest on a strategy of interpolation—adopting a compromise position, for example, between opposing Western and Chinese approaches—or on forwarding compromise as the methodological core of IR practice. That will not be the case. As I present it, the therapeutic strategy of the Buddhist middle path is to move perpendicularly or obliquely to any given spectrum of conflict-generating polarizations of positions and perspectives, thus expanding the spatial-temporal-causal context of relational negotiations. Methodologically, this involves *recognizing* the merits of opposing positions or perspectives, *resisting* their universalization or claims to sufficiency, and then *redirecting* relational dynamics at a tangent to their opposition to yield superlative or virtuosic (*kuśala*) outcomes and opportunities.

To briefly anticipate how this strategy applies to revising the dynamics of international relations, the proximal aim of engaging in international "relational therapy" is to maximize opportunities for mutual contribution to sustainably shared flourishing through consolidating convention-engendering commitments to relinquishing the horizons of relevance, responsibility, and readiness within which international relations are currently being negotiated. In practice this means dissolving the constraints on what international actors or relaters take to be relevant to their own welfare and flourishing; on what they will take a share of responsibility for; and on what they are ready to contribute toward realizing robustly shared values, intentions, and practices of the kind that yield superlatively equitable and liberating global outcomes and opportunities.

This method bears a strong family resemblance to Confucian-inspired *tianxia* "therapy." But Buddhism distinctively focuses less on the ideal of harmonious relations than on the reality of *healing* relations—realizing conditions for first acknowledging and redressing the historical wounds inflicted by national presumptions of independent existence and the rationality of self-interested sovereignty, and then strengthening capacities-for and commitments-to the shoulder-to-shoulder labor of expanding and enhancing opportunities for mutual contribution to sustainably shared welfare.

A Rationale for *Tianxia* Theorizing: Cosmology and Ontology Matter for Social Theory

All IR theories are rooted, implicitly or explicitly, in presuppositions about the nature of actors and agency, about the kind of world in which agency operates, and about the nature of causality. That is, IR theorizing invariably implies or enfolds specific ontological and cosmological commitments, even if these remain unspecified theoretically. From a *tianxia* perspective, Western IR theories are in a position very much like that of Newtonian physics and classical mechanics at the end of the nineteenth and early twentieth centuries when their assumptions about the basic natures of space, time, matter, and energy resulted in experimental designs that began producing empirical evidence for contradictory interpretations of the nature of light. Although realist, neoliberal institutionalist, and constructivist theorizing may have been adequate for explaining and managing international relations in a world of limited social, economic, and political complexity, the ontological and cosmological presuppositions embedded in them are proving inconsistent with key features of contemporary geopolitical and social realities. The failures of Western IR theories are foundational, not incidental.

This interpretation of contemporary geopolitical dynamics and the limitations of mainstream IR theory is not exclusively Chinese. Alexander Wendt, for example, has argued on physicalist—rather than Chinese culturalist—grounds that social sciences and IR theorizing have been conducted predominantly on the basis of outdated and deeply flawed, if not entirely false, ontological foundations, the cornerstones of which are commitments to engaging the world in deterministic, atomistic, and local / linear causal terms. His controversial claim is that the foundations of IR theory should be consistent with our best physical theories, taking into account the predictive power of quantum field theory and emerging work in quantum biology and decision theory, their experimental confirmation of phenomena like nonlocality and entanglement, and what this tells us about the ultimate nature of consciousness, causality, agency, and the dynamics of social reality.[5]

While the merits of Wendt's quantum turn are debatable, his critique is consistent with that of *tianxia* theorizing: conceptions of personhood, consciousness, mind-body relations, agency, and causality constitute the fundamental infrastructure of all social-scientific labor—including IR theorizing—and, if that labor is yielding conflicting or failed outcomes, then a change of infrastructure is in order. In classical Confucian thought, it is not autonomously individual human beings that are ontologically primary but rather relationally constituted human becomings.⁶ And, in contrast with Westphalian conceptions of states as discrete entities composed of similarly discrete individuals entering into free association for reasons of rational self-interest, classical Chinese cosmology and ontology favor seeing states as developing naturally through the thickening of relational dynamics—a process of congealing that results in progressively well-defined and refined behavioral patterns, rituals, and institutions (*li* 禮), ideally in alignment with the intrinsically dynamic cosmic order or *dao* (道). Thus, Chinese state formation can be seen as exemplifying the mutual and simultaneous construction of cosmology and culture on one hand and power and politics on the other, and the relational dynamics among states or nations are not best conceived as *inter*-actions among essentially independent agents, but rather as *intra*-actions or relational vortices within the natural and dynamically harmonious ordering of the cosmos as a whole.⁷

In keeping with Hobbesian assumptions about the "state of nature" being one of unconstrained and violent competition, Western IR theorizing has by and large been premised on the world order being anarchically ordered and fundamentally informed by the principle of state sovereignty and its corollary that interstate relations are necessarily external or contingent relations among equals. Nothing could be further from mainstream classical Chinese conceptions of the natural order of things. In the absence of a transcendental order premised on one-way dependence or causality, and premised instead on mutual dependence and intercausality, Chinese cosmological inquiry was not traditionally motivated by a search for an ultimate truth or principle with which to bring culture into agreement. Rather, it was guided by the pragmatic ideal of realizing increasingly refined relations within the human community and between it and the order of the cosmos as an intrinsically harmonious whole—a process, at once cultural and political, of realizing an inclusive harmony through "the intergenerational reauthorization of a moral orthodoxy."⁸

Social harmony might be understood as a horizontal relation among co-creative counterparts—an understanding according to which "Confucian harmony (*he* [和]) . . . is not expressible in the language of conformity, completion, perfection or closure" and is best understood as "a collaboration among the participating elements to make the most out of each situation."⁹ From at least the Han dynasty onward, this process of harmonization has been based on commentarial expansions of a shared discursive canon and on appeals to exemplary personal embodiments of ritual propriety rather than strict obedience to objective rules or laws. From this Confucian Chinese perspective, stable institutions and aptly enacted social and political roles are the necessary most reliable bulwark against anarchy or chaos (*luan* 亂) and the wholly "unnatural" demise of harmonious intra-actions.

This is a reasonably appealing vision. But it is also undeniable that the Confucian conception of social and political relations is resolutely hierarchic, even among presumed equals like friends. At the heart of *tianxia* theorizing is an acceptance of the "naturalness" of what Fei Xiaotong has described as *chaxu geju* (差序格局): a "differential pattern of association" or "order of stratified closeness" that can be visualized as a *radiating* pattern of concentric circles.[10] Given the one-world and thus nontranscendental assumptions underlying Chinese cosmology, Chinese conceptions of social and political order and power are conducive to seeing the *tianxia* world-system as "naturally" hierarchic in two dimensions: horizontally, as a practical order of relations between a dense relational center and increasingly distant and tenuously connected peripheries; and vertically, as a moral order of relations between superordinate exemplars of appropriate conduct and subordinate emulators thereof. Chaos or disorder can occur in either or both dimensions.[11]

Crucially, this conception of order did not develop along with the need to grapple with the practical realities of establishing and securing territorial limits to the reach of power. In fact, "the Confucian conception of *tianxia* refers to an ideal moral and political order admitting of no territorial boundary—the whole world to be governed by a sage according to principles of rites (*li* [禮]) and virtues (*de* 德)."[12] At least tacitly, the *tianxia* system was traditionally presumed to be morally homogenous. This marks an important difference between *tianxia* theorizing and other counters to substantialist presuppositions that individual things or entities pre-exist their interactions and are thus ontologically primitive.

Key *tianxia* theorists like Qin Yaqing draw, for example, on Emirbayer's manifesto for relational sociology and thus similarly oppose both the treatment of the international system, states, and state interests as immutably individual (whether in the context of neorealism or neoliberal institutionalism), and the conception of the agent in rational choice as motivated exclusively by self-interested cost-benefit maximization.[13] In fact, *tianxia* theorizing can in general be assimilated in good measure with recent turns in Western social science toward field theory, network analysis, and actor-network theory that variously emphasize position-defined practices and constitutive relationality.[14] But *tianxia* theorizing distinctively insists on being an irreducibly *moral* or *ethical relationalism*.[15] Although relational practices are admittedly able to be carried out in both expressive and instrumental modes, they nevertheless are seen as grounded in shared understandings of social norms and a Confucian morality that is held to be essentially different from and more effective in the context of international relations than the so-called Augustinian morality of individual responsibility that putatively prevails in the West.[16]

Thus, while contemporary Western practice theory and relationalism endorse the idea that "agency is . . . not an inherent feature of individuals but an effect of the differential distribution of power, knowledge, and recognition in social topographies," the *tianxia* world order is one in which these topographies are seen as once again (and rightly) becoming reconfigured such that they are both practically (horizontally) and morally (vertically) centered on China.[17] Thus, while the *tianxia* world-system is consistent with the widely recognized need to go beyond "methodological nationalism," it is conceived as a system centered resolutely on Chinese relational norms.[18]

Toward an Ecological Ethical Order: From Confucian Harmony to Buddhist Diversity

Given the size of its economy, China's practical centrality now and into the foreseeable future is an arguably value-neutral, empirical matter of fact. The centrality of China morally is not. To be sure, there is much that is appealing in regrounding IR theory and practice in an affirmation of the primacy of ethical relationality. There is also much that is appealing in Confucian critiques of individualism and constructions of relationalism that take the contemporary (not culturally Chinese) family as the natural source of ethical inspiration and innovation—a Confucianism directed toward realizing social justice as the result of virtuosic and irreducibly affective extensions of familial roles rather than as a product of abstract reasoning about human rights and responsibilities.[19] But endorsing the centrality of the moral or ethical relationality in IR theory need not be equivalent to either presuming or promoting the centrality of any particular moral or ethical system. It is far from clear that a combination of centralizing and hierarchic relational dynamics are—or should be—the "natural" basis for realizing a more just and equitable world order and fostering the kind of ethical improvisation required to resolve global predicaments rather than reducing them to the status of merely practical problems that can either be solved technically or dissolved politically.

On the contrary, we have good reasons to be wary of co-locating moral and political authority or presuming that they either naturally or ideally have a common origin. This is arguably the purpose of traditional birth narratives of the historical Buddha in which a seer predicts that he will become *either* a world-conquering political leader or an ego-conquering spiritual leader, not both. A secular logic for such a disjunction is neatly articulated by Jean-Luc Nancy in his critical distinction between the *shared* and the *common*.[20] It is a condition of shared cultures, morals, and socioaffective norms that they emerge and evolve through the distinctive participatory contributions of all involved. In contrast, having a common culture, morality, or set of socioaffective norms implies that any differences among us are inessential; ultimately, we are all equivalently parts of an organic and natural whole. In effect, assertions of a common culture or norms invariably carry coercive or disciplinary force—a truth that was made tragically evident in Nazi Germany. If putting common norms into practice is analogous to choreographed marching, putting shared norms into practice is like improvised dancing.

The core premise of an ethical ecosystem approach to addressing global predicaments is that differences in how we think, for example, about personhood, the good life, and social justice can be important ethical resources. The diversity of ethical perspectives is as crucial to the health and resilience of an ethical ecosystem as species diversity is to the vitality and resilience of a natural ecosystem. Reframing international relations practice in terms of ecological ethical relationality is not, however, just a matter of ensuring the conditions for cultural and ethical pluralism. The presence of plurality or *variety* is quantitative fact and entails nothing more than bare coexistence. *Diversity* is a qualitative index of the degree to which difference becomes a medium of mutual contribution to sustainably shared flourishing and thus implies coordination-enriching *interdependence*.[21] That is, diversity entails not just differing-from others but also meaningfully differing-for them. An ethical ecosystem is therefore predicated on ethical adaptation—a readiness to differentiate responsibly in the open-ended evaluation and improvisation of shared value systems.

Buddhism aligns with the premise of Confucianism and *tianxia* theorizing that "the logic of relationality has priority over both the logic of instrumental rationality (consequences) and the logic of normative rationality (appropriateness)."[22] It also shares with Confucianism the stance of granting philosophical primacy to ethics rather than either metaphysics or epistemology. Buddhism differs, however, in its cosmological premises, in emphasizing the critical importance of intentionality, and in its determination of what matters most relationally. These differences have significant implications for international relations.

Buddhism is a response to an essentially ethical, therapeutic question: how can conflict, trouble, and suffering be sustainably ended? Its answer is rooted in two insights. First, there are ultimately no independent existents or basic units of reality. Apparently individual entities and properties come into being through disambiguating acts of value- and intention-expressing abstraction or exclusion. Strongly stated, relationality is more basic than things related; all things are empty (*śunya*) of any essential and abiding self-nature; interdependence entails interpenetration; and each thing ultimately *is* what it *means* for all others. Second, our personal and social realities evolve through the confluence of linear and nonlinear causalities such that the quality of our life experiences and our environmental contexts are functions of our karma: the ongoing and dynamic entanglement that obtains among sustained patterns of values-intentions-actions and consonant patterns of relational outcomes-and-opportunities. Ultimately, there is no ontological gap between the "space of intentions (reasons)" and the "space of causes." Reality implies responsibility.

The presumption of traditional Chinese thought was that moral self-cultivation is a matter of aligning our conduct with already existing orders—emulating the human / social order manifest in the conduct of historical exemplars and according, as they did, with the *dao* or the celestial / natural order. Material and societal well-being were regarded as the results of aptly discerning and continuously fulfilling the "celestial mandate" (*tianming*). Thus, although Confucius declared that humans extend the *dao* rather than the *dao* extending the human (*Analects* 15:29), and although the celestial and the human were conceived as coming together as one (*tianren heyi* 天人合一), exemplary human conduct was nevertheless understood to be patterned on the comprehensive coherences (*li* 理) that govern all natural processes, from the movements of heavenly bodies to the passing of seasons and the life cycles of all living things.

This is not the case in Buddhist thought. As might be expected of a tradition that has persisted for over 2,500 years, Buddhism is not philosophically uniform. But it is generally accurate to say that what matters most in resolving conflicts, troubles, and suffering from Buddhist perspectives is consciousness or qualities of sentient, relational presence. Most basically, Buddhism conceives of consciousness (*vijñāna,* literally "differential knowing") as the value-articulating and dynamically coherent differentiation of sensed and sensing presences. Or differently stated, *matter* is the definition of a point of view, the determination of a perspective on *what matters*. Our material and social circumstances are *materializations* of what has consistently mattered to us, personally and communally, and any conflict, trouble, and suffering occurring therein can only be substantially resolved by redirecting and reconfiguring the values and intentions that have been informing our patterns of attention and conduct. Because present experiences are the results of past complexions of values, intentions, and actions, simply emulating the conduct of past exemplars cannot be a route to conflict resolution. Neither can emulating natural patterns, since the evolution of sensed presences cannot be separated from that of sensing presences. Ending conflict, trouble, and suffering involves changing the way things are and have been changing.

Crucially for rethinking IR, Buddhism insists that the causes of conflict, trouble, and suffering are never unilateral. Responsibilities for the occurrence of conflict, trouble, and suffering are always shared. The proximate aim of Buddhist practice is to cultivate the moral clarity (*śīla*), attentive mastery (*samādhi*), and wisdom (*prajñā*) needed to attend, think, speak, and act in ways that bring about superlative or virtuosic (*kuśala*) relational dynamics, while ceasing to attend, think, speak, and act in ways that are without-virtuosity (*akuśala*). Just as virtuosic musical performances set new standards of musicianship, *kuśala* conduct sets new standards of ethical excellence. Buddhist ethical practice involves finding ways of going beyond whatever is now deemed bad and mediocre conduct, but also beyond what is currently deemed good. It consists, in other words, in the recursively creative and improvisatory art of relationally liberating course correction.

The Buddhist cosmos, not unlike the cosmos as envisioned in traditional Chinese thought, is temporally open, without a beginning or a predetermined end. But the Buddhist cosmos is structured karmically, a cosmos in which intentions and values matter intrinsically. Sentient bodies and the environments with which they coevolve are *materializations* of effortful and temporally extended processes of making differences that make persisting differences. And the distinctive karmic insight is that the dynamics of negentropic, order-engendering materialization cannot be fully accounted for in terms of linear causal sequences. Very much like the entanglements central to quantum theory, karmic connections are nonlinear and nonlocal, and they have effects that are necessarily both material and phenomenal. In a karmic cosmos, time is two-dimensional, with causality manifesting in one dimension as linear *sequences* of material events and in the other as nonlinear patterns of *significance*. In such a cosmos, the presence of conflict, trouble, and suffering indicates the persistence of unresolved values conflicts and contrary intentions—a persistence in which we each necessarily have a share of enactive responsibility.

The operation of karma means that we cannot avoid being the patients of our own actions. Harm done to others is ultimately also harm done to ourselves. Given this, the successes of realist pursuits of competitive advantage and control are necessarily ironic. To get better at controlling situational outcomes, it is necessary to see our situation as continuously and increasingly in need of still further control. Karmically, this sets us on a trajectory for materializing environments at increasing risk of getting out of control. Our entire technoindustrial approach to development is a testament to the historical dynamics of control karma: the progressive realization of ever more controlled and controlling environments.

Yet, it is also not enough to shift from the rationality of finite game-playing, win-loss competition to that of still-finite game-playing win-win cooperation. From a karmic perspective, what matters most is what "winning" means. The neoliberal adage that a rising economic tide raises all boats points to a win-win scenario, but as widening gaps of income, wealth, and risk over the last several decades have made painfully obvious, absolute gains being realized by all do not necessarily prevent dramatic increases in relative inequality. Two investors, each realizing 10 percent returns, will have doubled the value of their investments in seven years. But that may mean earning a billion dollars for one investor and only a thousand dollars for the other. In short, win-win dynamics can still result in dramatically increasing inequalities not only of wealth, income, and risk, but of power and prestige. *Inequality is ultimately relational harm.*

Realizing this calls ethically into question both the hierarchic relationality that is assumed to be natural by many *tianxia* theorists, and their construction of the logic of relationality as one of managing "expressive" ties epitomized by relations among family members, "instrumental" ties typically involving relations among strangers, and "mixed" ties combining these relational modes and occurring mainly among nonstrangers.[23] As already noted, the Confucian logic of relationality implies a landscape of graded concern that is often visualized as a series of concentric circles, such that the interests of those who begin as strangers become morally considerable to the extent that they are able to pass centripetally through relational contexts governed by merely instrumental considerations into contexts where first mixed and then eventually expressive or affective considerations dominate. The logic here is that it is only once someone has begun mattering to us that we are obliged to consider how we might better matter for them. An ostensibly pragmatic rationale for such graded concern is the fact of resource scarcity. Putting concern into practice means investing resources that are necessarily in limited supply. If one is intent on investing resources in a way that will make difference relationally, it stands to reason that it is better to give one hundred dollars to a single relative than to give one dollar to each of one hundred strangers. Although often rhetorically softened, this is the basic mathematics of *guanxi* 關係 or favor-mediated and necessarily hierarchic relations of mutual loyalty.

The Mahayana Buddhist personal ideal of the bodhisattva compassionately committed to helping all sentient beings realize increasingly liberating relational dynamics stands in sharp contrast with the implicitly self-interested ideal of exercising "naturally" differential concern for the welfare of others. Compassion has been increasingly invoked as a "social emotion" that motivates us to build institutions designed to mitigate conditions that stifle "human dignity and the capacity for action" or that create "social hierarchy and economic deprivation."[24] To function thus as a political virtue, however, compassion must consist in something other than one-to-one acts of charity, since it is possible to proximally help those in conflict, trouble, and suffering without being motivated to identify and responsibly address the structure or institutional causes of their relational conditions. Thus, the compassion of the bodhisattva must be understood as consisting in the practice of intentionally suffusing one's entire situation with ever-deepening awareness of the presence of conflicts, trouble, and suffering; with ever-expanding understanding of the patterns of causes and conditions resulting in them; and with ever more skillfully enacted commitment to embodying the meanings-of and means-to the dissolution of those patterns.

Practicing compassion is not just a matter of caring about and caring for others. It involves realizing capabilities-for and commitments-to making improvisational use of situationally available resources to realize freedom-enhancing and predicament-resolving relational dynamics. The Buddhist method of doing so can be described as an ongoing process of relinquishing horizons of relevance, responsibility, and readiness—that is, taking progressively "higher" points of view to consider an ever-wider compass of things to take as relevant to resolving a relational predicament; to recognize to an ever-greater extent one's own implication in the predicament; and to anticipate and carry through on making ever more inclusively productive course changes.

This strategy does not imply the impossibility of strenuous resistance or forceful redirection. Recognizing that predicaments necessarily have complexly interdependent sets of causes does not preclude clear-eyed recognition, in addition, that responsibility is not equally distributed in all cases. The karmic insistence on shared responsibility points to the fact that in any given situation, we are implicated deeply enough to be able to make a difference in how things change. It is precisely because compassionate intervention can be unsettling for those involved, calling into question habits of thought, speech, and action around which identities have congealed, that the bodhisattva ideal pairs compassion with wisdom—the ability to discern the currents of meaning shaping relational dynamics and to know whether, when, and how best to intervene. It was not incidental that Chinese Chan master Linji Yixuan 臨濟義玄 (d. 866) described the bodhisattva path as often being one of "facing the world, going crosswise." That is not always immediately appreciated. Prejudices become institutionalized; narrow self-interest becomes an entitled habit. Compassion can be disruptive. But, if wisely offered, it will prove its value in resolving conflict, trouble, and suffering. It is wisdom—born of virtuosic appreciation of the interdependence and ultimate interpenetration of all things—being paired with compassion that undermines presumptive justifications of instrumental relationality.

An Appreciative Caution: Shared Responsibility for Relational Quality

Instrumental relations may be an ineradicable part of the human experience despite the best of Buddhist—or for that matter, Kantian—intuitions and intentions. But acquiescing to that fact should nevertheless be strenuously resisted. The existence and persistence of essentially instrumental relations with those positioned outside our circles of loyalty-mediated intimacy cannot be justified morally on the grounds of a doubly hierarchic "naturalism" that presumes the propriety of a single culture, people, or set of norms enjoying ultimate centrality and prominence.

Tianxia theorizing can be celebrated for rightly taking a holist, planetary realist perspective on global dynamics and for insisting on the primacy of relationality and the importance of human feeling (*renqing* 人情) in international relations. But it must be kept in mind that, in addition to meaning "emotion," *renqing* can also mean "favor," and an emphasis on it can easily devolve into potentials for corruption and coercion if not qualified by something like Buddhist compassion and a commitment to realizing relational dynamics that engender both greater diversity and universally heightening equity or qualities of inclusion. As Zhao Tingyang has stated with admirable clarity, Chinese political philosophy believes that "an institution is good if and only if it can be applied on all political levels, from the most basic to the highest, and from local to worldwide dimensions, thereby leading to a universal political system," and the foundation of any *tianxia* world-system must be "a worldwide institution reflecting the universally-accepted feelings of all peoples."[25] Yet, as he also makes clear, "Our supposed world is still a non-world.... The world exists only when people want it to."[26] The mandate of a *tianxia* approach to international relations is to realize the conditions needed for that wish to be embraced planetwide.

The conduct of the People's Republic of China over the late 2010s and early 2020s, both intranationally and internationally, has been in considerable tension with the Confucian aim of leading through humility and modesty (謙遜 *qianxun*), tirelessly enacting commitments to put others first and give credit where credit is due (*Analects* 13:1). Indeed, the Chinese government has often assumed a paternalistic stance domestically and a realist / instrumentalist stance internationally, placing the sovereign interests of the state above those of the people whose relational aspirations and creativity are its original source of strength. A true "world" may only be possible when all people wish it into existence, but valuing diversity entails allowing them to come to this on their own and in their own ways.

Qin Yaqing is certainly correct, from a Buddhist perspective, to argue that the logic of relationality precludes abstract individual rationality and the ideal of agency devoted solely to the pursuit of self-interest. And he is pragmatically justified in seeing rules-based governance as insufficient for enhancing relational quality. Affectively guided improvisation is necessary. Yet, in spite of astutely musing that perhaps "rules should be particularly stressed in a more communitarian society and relations taken into serious consideration in a more individualistic society," Qin somewhat ambivalently remarks that "the totality of relations is very much like an intangible hand that orients an actor toward a certain action."[27]

One cannot help but think here of Adam Smith's "invisible hand" and—contrary to Smith's own moral rationale for the market economy—the way that it has been algorithmically programmed to do the bidding of predatory capital. The efficacy of surveillance capitalism raises moral questions about our personal rights to futures of our own imagining.[28] The expanding reach and efficacy of smart governance raises equally moral worries about whether a world system hierarchically structured and organically centered on the values of harmony and stability might naturalize the use of artificial intelligence to proactively shape the "totality of relations" through the curatorial and progressively tailored nudging of choices at each personal node in the network of social relations. Could the forfeiture or foreclosure of both individual and collective rights-to-differ be warranted as a morally justified means to the end of universal harmony?

Qin is careful to acknowledge in his vision of relational governance and moral-political leadership the necessity of societies being "structured around differential relationships (*chaxugeju* 差序格局), peopled by profound persons (*junzi* 君子)."[29] Including the compassionate commitment and wisely virtuosic responsiveness of the bodhisattva ideal in our conceptions of "profound persons" is, I believe, an important qualifier—one that insists on the exceptionless intimacy of the means-to and meanings-of "profoundly" and ethically realized human becoming.

This suggests a significant Buddhist qualification of the *tianxia* cosmology. Like the cosmos imagined in traditional Confucian thought, the early Buddhist conception of the cosmos was organized concentrically around Mount Meru, as well as vertically in terms of qualities of sentient presence. With the rise of Mahayana Buddhism and the personal ideal of the bodhisattva, an imaginative transformation occurred such that the cosmos came to be seen as encompassing many different "Buddha-realms," each supporting distinctive means to realizing liberating patterns of relationality—an ecological world-system in which an unlimited number of different realizations of compassionately wise virtuosity are materialized. Harmony is, indeed, not predicated on sameness. But centrality can be realized in a distributed manner rather than a concentrated one. For stability to not become stultifying, it must be dynamic, a steadily evolving product of artful flexibility. For consonance to not become sterile, it must be open to dissonance. The harmonic possibilities of ancient Confucian court music or nineteenth-century European chamber music are not exhaustive. The South American chili pepper was initially at odds with the traditional Chinese palate, but it has become integral to the cuisines of Sichuan and Hunan. The great challenge, always and everywhere, is to differ coherently. The compassionately wise Buddhist aim of centering harmonically (*zhonghe* 中和) on the values of diversity and equity points toward a truly ecological world order, one committed to creatively and ethically expanding the compass of human-with-planetary virtuosity.

Notes

1. For a brief history and discussion of the multiplicity of *tianxia* approaches, see Hun Joon Kim, "Will IR Theory with Chinese Characteristics Be a Powerful Alternative?," *Chinese Journal of International Politics* 9, no. 1 (Spring 2016): 59–79.

2. See, for example, Qin Yaqing, "A Relational Theory of World Politics," *International Studies Review* 18, no. 1 (March 2016): 33–47.

3. See, for example, Ole Waever, "The Sociology of a Not So International Discipline: American and European Developments in International Relations," *International Organization* 52, no. 4 (1998): 687–727; Amitav Acharya, "Ethnocentrism and Emancipatory IR Theory," in *Displacing Security,* ed. Samantha Arnold and J. Marshall Biers. (Toronto: Centre for International and Security Studies, York University, 2000), pp. 1–18.

4. Peter D. Hershock, *Buddhism and Intelligent Technology: Toward a More Humane Future* (London: Bloomsbury Academic, 2021).

5. Alexander Wendt, *Quantum Mind and Social Science: Unifying Physical and Social Ontology* (New York: Cambridge University Press, 2015).

6. Roger T. Ames, *Human Becomings: Theorizing Persons for Confucian Role Ethics* (Albany: State University of New York Press, 2021).

7. Aihe Wang, *Cosmology and Political Culture in Early China* (New York: Cambridge University Press, 2000). On the ontological / epistemological distinction of *inter*-action and *intra*-action, see Karen Barad, *Meeting the Universe Halfway: Quantum Physics and the Entanglement of Matter and Meaning* (Durham, NC: Duke University Press, 2007), pp. 139–141.

8. Roger T. Ames, *Confucian Role Ethics: A Vocabulary* (Honolulu: University of Hawai'i Press, 2011), p. 16.

9. Ames, *Confucian Role Ethics,* p. 84.

10. Fei Xiaotong, *From the Soil: The Foundations of Chinese Society* (Berkeley: University of California Press, 1992).

11. Recognition of hierarchy in interstate relations is relatively underdeveloped in comparison with the reigning presumption of international anarchy. However, for an overview, see Ayse Zarakol, ed., *Hierarchies in World Politics* (New York: Cambridge University Press, 2017).

12. Joseph Chan, "Territorial Boundaries and Confucianism," in *Confucian Political Ethics,* ed. Daniel A. Bell (Princeton, NJ: Princeton University Press, 2008), pp. 61–84.

13. Qin Yaqing, "Rule, Rules and Relations: Towards a Synthetic Approach to Governance," *Chinese Journal of International Politics* 4, no. 2 (Summer 2011): 117–145; Mustafa Emirbayer, "Manifesto for a Relational Sociology," *American Journal of Sociology* 104, no. 2 (September 1997): 281–317.

14. For a concise discussion of these approaches, see David M. McCourt, "Practice Theory and Relationalism as the New Constructivism," *International Studies Quarterly* 60, no. 3 (September 2016): 475–485.

15. See Qin, "Rule, Rules, and Relations"; Feng Zhang, *Chinese Hegemony: Grand Strategy and International Institutions in East Asian History* (Stanford, CA: Stanford University Press, 2015).

16. Qin, "Relational Theory"; Zhang, *Chinese Hegemony*. See, e.g., Qin, "Rule, Rules, and Relations," pp. 125–137.

17. McCourt, "Practice Theory," p. 481.

18. Fiona B. Adamson, "Spaces of Global Security: Beyond Methodological Nationalism," *Journal of Global Security Studies* 1, no. 1 (February 2016): 19–35. The possibility of delinking *tianxia* theory from China-centered norms and values is explored by Salvatore Babones in *American Tianxia: Chinese Money, American Power, and the End of History* (Bristol, UK: Policy Press, 2017).

19. Henry Rosemont Jr., *Against Individualism: A Confucian Rethinking of the Foundation of Morality, Politics, Family, and Religion* (Lanham, MD: Lexington Books, 2015).

20. Jean-Luc Nancy, *Being Singular Plural*, trans. Robert Richardson and Anne O'Bryne (Stanford, CA: Stanford University Press, 2000).

21. This contrast can be illustrated by the difference between the species diversity found in healthy ecosystems and the species variety found in even the best-funded and best-stocked zoos, where the different species on exhibit are incapable of making any difference for each other.

22. Qin, "Relational Theory," p. 38.

23. Qin, "Relational Theory," pp. 37–38.

24. Martha Nussbaum, *Upheavals of Thought: The Intelligence of Emotions* (Cambridge: Cambridge University Press, 2001), pp. 413–414.

25. Zhao Tingyang, "A Political World Philosophy in Terms of All-under-Heaven (*Tian-xia*)," *Diogenes* 56, no. 1 (2009): 5–18; Zhao, "Political World Philosophy," p. 9.

26. Zhao, "Political World Philosophy," pp. 5–6.

27. Qin, "Rule, Rules, and Relations," p. 145; Qin, "Relational Theory," p. 38.

28. Shoshanna Zuboff, *The Age of Surveillance Capitalism: The Fight for a Human Future at the New Frontier of Power* (New York: PublicAffairs, 2019).

29. Qin, "Rule, Rules, and Relations," p. 137.

PART III

A Minimalist Morality for Solidarity and Mutual Critique

CHAPTER 12

Spheres of Global Justice and *Tianxia* Theory

Binfan WANG

IN THE LAST fifty years, globalization has profoundly changed many aspects of our world. For the beneficiaries of this wave, the entire world has never been so closely connected. With more and more issued visas, it is much easier for visitors from different countries to travel around the world, and immigrants have created several typical multicultural societies such as Australia and Canada. With the investment of global capital, people are enjoying products from everywhere, and the necessity of exportation has become the main reason for the huge development of countries such as Japan, Korea, Singapore in the 1970s, and China and India after the 1980s. With the establishment of various nongovernmental organizations (NGOs) and international organizations—and especially with the progress of regional integration, as seen in the establishment of the European Union—states enjoy more platforms to cooperate with each other, and potential conflicts might be reduced via mutual communication or global governance. To some extent, a world village is on its way.[1] However, the dark side of globalization is also apparent to its victims. Poverty is still a severe problem in many areas of the world, threatening the basic life of millions of people; moreover, the development of the world economy makes the gap between the rich and the poor wider, because developed states have limited interest in donating enough of their gross domestic product to help. The emission of carbon dioxide, mainly by large and developed states, exacerbates the global warming crisis, which might destroy the future for all human beings, and the appeal to address this issue from small island countries like Tuvalu was rejected at the 2015 United Nations Climate Change Conference in Paris. The abuse of democratization causes civil wars in states like Syria and Libya, and the chaos of society provides an opportunity for

269

terrorism (incited by organizations like Islamic State in Syria [ISIS]) to increase, which, ultimately, impacts almost all developed states, including the United States, Great Britain, France, and Germany. The wave of refugees caused by civil war and terrorism rushes into Western Europe and brings about a humanitarian crisis, and the lack of trust between the states in that region makes this severe dilemma unsolvable for the long term. Poor medical conditions in Latin America and Africa make infections, such as Ebola and COVID-19, a global issue. Consequently, more and more people are questioning the outcome or direction of globalization, and many have already suffered from radical reactions, such as Great Britain's exit from the European Union, the rise of the extreme rightists in Europe, and Donald Trump's victory in the 2016 US presidential election. It is true that we have underestimated the negative influence of globalization for a long time, as Dani Rodrik has warned that "globalization will contribute to social disintegration, as nations are split along the lines of economic status, mobility, region, or social norms."[2] Such a protectionist backlash under the name of nationalism or even racism will ruin the achievements we have made and currently enjoy.

As both the reflection and guidance of political reality, political theory has to face this globalizing world. Thus, as a concept, cosmopolitanism is more often discussed because it reveals the empirical changes, and some theorists have tried to articulate normative principles to help us understand this growing tendency.[3] Other scholars deal with current problems worldwide, such as world poverty, refugees, and terrorism, arguing that the current global order should be revised to cope with these phenomena. These types of studies are generally called "global justice" studies.[4] We understand them as theories of justice because they focus on the normative principles of political and social order, which both classical and contemporary political theorists have discussed for centuries, and we add "global" as the distinguishing feature because they have to cover the global context that transcends any single state. This topic includes traditional concerns in political theory, such as democracy, institutional design, and distributive rules, as well as new issues, such as environmental protection, immigration, and world poverty. No matter where we live in the world, we need global justice theories to provide some guidance.

Lessons from Walzer's *Spheres of Justice*

This scenario reminds us of the 1970s and early 1980s, when the discussion of justice raised by John Rawls was thriving among scholars. In 1983, Michael Walzer introduced an insightful argument that was different from most criticisms. In his book *Spheres of Justice,* Walzer warned that although the discussion of justice had lasted for centuries, all theories had the same problem: "The deepest assumption of most of the philosophers who have written about justice, from Plato onward, is that there is one, and only one, distributive system that philosophy can rightly encompass."[5] For Walzer, this assumption ignored the different backgrounds of political communities in which theories of justice were put into practice, and it simplified the lives of the people who grew up in diverse cultures as abstract rational individuals who might have reached consensus on the basic principles of an abstract society. To promote his argument, Walzer claimed that "Justice is a human construction, and it is doubtful that it can be made in only one way.... The questions posed by the theory of distributive justice admit of a range of answers, and there is room within the range for cultural diversity and political choice."[6]

Therefore, if we would like to pursue equality as the just principle of distribution in a society, the principle should be complex, not simple—the rule to distribute the basic needs should be different from the rule to distribute educational resources.[7] Later on, scholars such as David Miller and Joseph Carens developed Walzer's theory, shifting the focus from distribution or equality to the cultural background of political theories. As Miller argued, "A theory of justice needs a sociology to go with it—an account of how social relations must be constituted so as to make the theory feasible—and that multiculturalism must make us rethink that sociology."[8] Thus, before we discuss complex principles like equality, we should realize that the social or cultural background determines the complexity in theory.

Since we are engaged in the discussion about global justice, what should we learn from Walzer's warning, made in the early 1980s? There is no doubt that global justice is also a theory of justice, so we should keep an eye on the "sphere" and cautiously remind ourselves to take cultural diversity seriously rather than abstract the concept of a comprehensive globalized world into a single dimension.

There are three approaches to articulating a global justice theory—cosmopolitanism, statism, and a middle-way approach that reconciles the two.[9] This classification has nothing to do with cultural diversity; it only represents different attitudes toward states when thinking about global justice. Cosmopolitanism would like to embrace the discussion on domestic justice and apply it to the global scope with limited revisions, because the primary moral concerns being discussed remain similar. Statism argues that the basic context in which to discuss global justice is different from the context for domestic justice, because in the global society the subject is the state rather than the individual, so global justice is mainly about the relationships among states. To reconcile the disagreement between these two approaches, and to deal with complex topics other than individual goodness and the state, some theories choose the middle-way approach and construct new theories with different frameworks.[10] However, despite the fruitful insights from many theories of global justice, we have to realize that almost all theories do not take Walzer's warning seriously enough. Let us briefly go through the problem of three approaches, one by one.

For anyone who studies cosmopolitanism, Thomas Pogge's definition is very popular:

> Three elements are shared by all cosmopolitan positions. First, individualism: the ultimate units of concern are human beings, or persons—rather than, say, family lines, tribes, ethnic, cultural, or religious communities, nations, or states. The latter may be units of concern only indirectly, in virtue of their individual members or citizens. Second, universality: the status of ultimate unit of concern attaches to every living human being equally—not merely to some subset, such as men, aristocrats, Aryans, whites, or Muslims. Third, generality: this special status has global force. Persons are ultimate units of concern for everyone—not only for their compatriots, fellow religionists, or suchlike.[11]

Although advocates of different cosmopolitan theories usually argue against each other, these three elements have seldom been challenged. Consequently, although scholars articulate cosmopolitan theories differently, all of them start with the discussion of individual goodness, reveal why the current global order fails to protect the basic goodness of individuals around the world, and then suggest how to fix it. It is certainly not that these theories fail to recognize people who live in different cultures globally, but that they insist it is possible to find a general or universal argument about individual goodness or human dignity, while factors such as culture should be understood as accidental or irrelevant. While there is no doubt that such theories are cosmopolitan, is it possible to find a cosmopolitan theory that does not share all three elements?

We have reason to doubt Pogge's definition because cosmopolitanism literally only means that all human beings are (or should be) members of the world as a single community. The word "cosmopolitan" is derived from the ancient Greek word *kosmopolites,* which means "citizen of the world." Therefore, it does not stipulate that any cosmopolitan theory should be based on individualism; it does not even stipulate that the status of the ultimate units of concern should be totally equal. In fact, Pogge's definition represents the approach of microarticulation, which is widely shared by liberalism and utilitarianism. However, if we take it for granted, it narrows our thinking about other possibilities. Therefore, there should be other approaches that do not start with individualism but still construct cosmopolitan theories. For such theories, the ultimate unit of concern might be something else, and individuals may only indirectly be the units of concern. Moreover, it is true that the status of the ultimate unit should have global force, but the relationship among human beings might not necessarily be equal, which is against the principle of "universality" in Pogge's definition. All in all, current studies of cosmopolitanism are strongly influenced by the liberal tradition.

Unfortunately, we find a similar defect in the theories of statism, although they do not embrace individualism as the premise of discussion. Rawls's *The Law of Peoples* is a typical and influential theory of statism.[12] In his introduction on five types of domestic societies (peoples), the first and best type is liberal peoples, which honors human rights. The other four types are not ideal, or they are even bad, because they do not fulfill some principles of the liberal tradition, for example not honoring human rights in the full sense or accepting some form of hierarchy.[13] Rawls's theory is the development of Immanuel Kant's *Perpetual Peace* in the contemporary context, which is undoubtedly representative of the liberal tradition.

The middle-way approach tries to avoid some of the inadequacies of the other two approaches, but it does not pay enough attention to cultural diversity. Mathias Risse named his theory "pluralist internationalism" to emphasize that we should adopt different principles of justice in different contexts. However, Risse does not interpret the "context" as culture; rather, he views it as a vertical framework from the state to the world. The merit of his theory is to "acknowledge that normative peculiarity of the state" and "recognize multiple grounds" simultaneously, but his main concern is still the list of human rights that basically come from liberal society. He also "assumes that the principles of justice that apply domestically are Rawls's two principles."[14] If we are concerned about the cultural sphere, theories that choose the middle-way approach are not better than the others.

I have no intention to deny that these theories have made significant contributions to global justice, and I would like to emphasize that the classification itself is not the product of the liberal tradition. However, I have no doubt that Walzer would not be satisfied with most theories, as they paid very little attention to the sphere or cultural diversity during their construction. As Walzer has noted, no matter how we articulate a theory of global justice, we should not forget that the sphere it covers contains various cultures that deeply influence the lives and thinking of people throughout the world. Thus, there is one core weakness shared by all current theories: they all follow the logic of Western liberal thought after the Enlightenment. Seldom have such theories been rooted in other traditions in East Asia, India, Africa, the Muslim world, and so on.[15] That causes some problems: states such as China, India, and Iran, as well as those in Africa and Latin America, have very different histories and political cultures than states in Western society, but current theories of global justice ignore their traditions. In reality, these non-Western states are major contributors to or victims of global governance, and they usually complain about the order led by Western society. Therefore, we have no reason to be optimistic that theories of global justice strongly rooted in liberalism could be easily accepted and supported by them, as their cultural traditions may have different philosophical foundations for thinking about global justice or have different understandings of related concepts. If we neglect the severity of such a concern and abruptly regard Western theories as universal, theories of global justice face the danger of becoming "culturally biased, ontologically faulty, phenomenologically-monologic, and politically Modern."[16] Although this is not the fault of Western scholars who care about global justice, we should realize that our studies of global justice are a long way from "global." The ignorance of cultural diversity has become the barrier to further discussion, and something needs to be done.

The Possibility of Global Justice and the Shortage of Multiculturalism

Before continuing, we need to consider one question: If we pay careful attention to the spheres of justice or cultural diversity throughout the world, is global justice still possible? This worry is real, especially after my criticism about the current theories. No matter how any particular theory is articulated, it is impossible to completely ignore the influence of specific traditions (e.g., Western liberal, Chinese, Indian, African, Muslim). As Walzer says, "There is no single standard. But there are standards (roughly knowable even when they are also controversial) for every social good and every distributive sphere in every particular society."[17] In terms of global justice, the difficulty lies in the fact that we discuss a single society—the world—which contains various cultures, each regarded as the essence of one particular society. Consequently, it seems that the cultural root of every theory can be questioned. Similar to how I criticize mainstream studies on global justice, William Callahan also sharply points out that the *tianxia* theory formulated by Zhao Tingyang almost entirely excludes "the West" and seems to present a new hegemony where imperial China's hierarchical governance is updated for the twenty-first century.[18]

This refers to the debate between universalism and relativism, and I think it is necessary to clarify both the misunderstanding of Walzer's theory and my criticism of the Western-centeredness of current theories of global justice. Regardless of the extent to which we highlight Walzer's emphasis on the spheres of justice, it would be misleading to think that Walzer's theory is about relativism or that Walzer denies the possibility of any universal values. He reminds us that we cannot ignore the effect of culture when talking about justice; he does not say that there is no possibility for the various spheres to coincide or interact with each other and thus find some shared principles. As Joseph Carens points out, "It is descriptively inaccurate and conceptually misleading to suggest that every morality is a local morality or that the only morality shared beyond borders is a thin, minimal morality, itself the reiterated by-product of the distinct, thick moralities constructed in particular societies."[19]

Later on, Walzer developed his theories and argued that there are thick and thin theories of justice, and if we just focus on "negative injunctions, most likely, rules against murder, deceit, torture, oppression, and tyranny," we should be able to achieve some sense of universalism.[20] Regarding the discussion of global justice, my criticism of current studies is to voice a concern about the overwhelming influence of liberalism, which may narrow our thinking of global justice (for example, the three elements of cosmopolitanism noted by Thomas Pogge), and not to argue that any of the principles from current theories cannot be universally accepted simply because they come from the liberal tradition. It is not a problem for scholars to articulate a theory of global justice rooted in any specific tradition, as long as they are cautious about how universally the theory can be treated and as long as they are open to engaging in a cross-cultural conversation.

We have reason to be optimistic about the possibility of global justice, both empirically and theoretically. Empirically, globalization is proof that people and states from different cultural traditions can communicate to promote cultural exchange and even integration. Canada is a good example of a state where people whose races and cultural backgrounds are diverse can live together happily, where the state can regard multiculturalism as its official ideology. More and more international institutions and NGOs are leading global governance in the global arena and are, in part, taking on the role of traditional states.[21] Although they are encountering some difficulties, the number of immigrants worldwide has increased, not to mention the number of people who regularly experience international travel. To some extent, we are already living in a world village.

Theoretically, throughout history, we can observe that people from different traditions have achieved some basic consensus, and that people adopt values from other traditions either directly or by interpreting and revising them. For example, the Golden Rule, which means treating others as one wishes to be treated, is a basic moral principle expressed by traditions in ancient Egypt, China, India, Greece, the Near East, and Rome. Some typical liberal concepts, such as human rights and democracy, can also be accepted by non-Western traditions, such as Confucianism, with a revised interpretation and alternative names. For example, *minquan* 民權(people's right) is a concept close to human rights, and it has been widely used in Chinese discourse at least since the nineteenth century.[22] Democracy is one of the official values advocated by the Chinese government, with the revised meaning of "for the people" (or serving the people) rather than "by the people."[23] Thus, as long as we keep an open mind in the cross-cultural conversation, we can expect to see more and more consensus rather than conflict. Theories of global justice can be constructed with different starting points, and the more accounts like this that we know of, the better they might be accepted and supported by people from all over the world.

However, we should also admit that we are still far from making the context of political theory culturally diverse enough. In particular, we must realize that the contributions made by studies of multiculturalism are insufficient to respond to the criticisms I have raised above. It is helpful to clarify this point further because the liberal tradition has taken cultural diversity seriously. At least theoretically, people in the liberal tradition respect others in the same political community with very different cultural backgrounds. Studies on multiculturalism remind us of the significance of the "societal culture" that "provides its members with meaningful ways of life across the full range of human activities, including social, educational, religious, and economic life, encompassing both public and private spheres."[24] However, compared to the global scale of cultural diversity, the huge difference in objects and purposes demonstrates that it is difficult to apply multiculturalism theories and practices to global justice. According to Will Kymlicka, the five typical models of multiculturalism are national minorities, immigrant groups, isolationist ethnoreligious groups, metics, and African Americans.[25] In a liberal society, pursuing multiculturalism aims to ensure that "all national groups have the opportunity to maintain themselves as a distinct culture, if they so choose" and that "there is equality between groups, and freedom and equality within groups."[26] Current studies of multiculturalism mainly deal with the protection of the minority culture, which might relate to different living habits, cultural ceremonies, or local laws, but such protection will be strictly bounded in limited communities and will not influence the dominant society, which embraces political liberalism. In other words, multiculturalism usually focuses on the diverse spheres at local levels in a liberal society and it tries to ensure that their voices are not ignored. Under such conditions, political liberalism can tolerate and protect unique traditions in minority communities as long as those traditions do not threaten political liberalism as the official ideology. We see no indigenous or immigrant groups asking for changes in political institutions, ideology, or social structure for the whole society based on their own culture. Even if the case is as difficult as those of African Americans in the United States or French-speaking Canadians in Quebec, what they want is to have more say in the dominant culture, and their values are never in opposition to liberal democracy.

In contrast, the context of global justice is very different. Just look at our world village for which we would like to articulate a theory of global justice. It contains numerous groups of people with different levels of development, different memories of history, different lifestyle habits, different ideologies, different religious beliefs, different attitudes toward strangers, and even different expectations about the future. Furthermore, we cannot find any single tradition that can be regarded as the dominant one—diverse political cultures and social arrangements develop from different traditions, and they might even conflict with each other. Since the majority of people in the world today do not regard political liberalism as the only political ideology, theories of multiculturalism cannot solve the complex problem of global justice. Any theoretical claims concerning global justice based entirely on Western traditions face such challenges, because people in non-Western societies might either reject or fail to acknowledge the basic normative premises (such as individual goodness as the starting point of discussion) shared by almost all current studies. Only after taking cultural differences seriously can the principles raised by global justice studies be accepted by most people around the world. In order for human beings to live together as one world community, it is essential to connect diverse intellectual and cultural traditions in some ways.

Therefore, to achieve global justice, we have to go a step further. Studies on multiculturalism remind us of the existence of different minority traditions, and at the global level, we need to glean different ideas about global justice from both Western and non-Western traditions and promote cross-cultural conversations. We need to accept the complexity of culture, while simultaneously trying to be optimistic about the future of cultural communication. As Carens has argued:

> I assume that cultures evolve and change over time; that cultures are influenced, directly and indirectly, by other cultures; that cultures contain conflicting elements; that cultures are subject to many different, often conflicting interpretations, by both members and outsiders; that the extent to which a particular culture provides value and meaning to the lives of the people who participate in it may vary among the members of the culture and may itself be a topic of interpretive dispute; and that members of one culture may be exposed to, have access to, and even participate as members in one or more other cultures.[27]

If we would like to overcome the core weakness of current studies, we need more non-Western voices on global justice as the first step to make further debate, communication, and connections possible. As Leigh Jenco has argued, "In a deeply interconnected, multipolar world, the rigorous self-explanations of ethnic groups other than Anglo-Europeans should have their place in structuring legitimate social inquiry."[28] These studies utilize comparative political theory, which has been thriving in recent years. The comparison does not aim to demolish current arguments about global justice made by the proponents of liberal thought; rather, it seeks to identify more possibilities that can originate from different cultures providing a better understanding of the existing diverse sociological context for global justice. If attempts like this work, theories of global justice will follow Walzer's reminder of the spheres and be applicable to the global context that is culturally diverse.

In his theory of cosmopolitanism, Kwame Appiah argues that the task of cosmopolitanism consists of "debate and conversation across nations," and that "we must rely on the ability to listen and to talk to people whose commitments, beliefs and projects may seem distant from our own."[29] For Appiah, this conversation does not guarantee consensus, especially on rooted values, but it is still meaningful as "it helps people get used to one another."[30] Following the route mapped by Carens, Jenco, and Appiah, we need to be open to and curious about any theory of global justice from non-Western cultures, whether the source is ancient or modern and no matter how different it is from liberal thought. After listening to various stories about what a global order should look like, people from different cultures can become accustomed to and communicate with each other. Then, we can expect to look for better universal principles that are widely accepted for global justice. In Fred Dallmayr's words, "cross-cultural comparative theorists are genuine, even better, universalists" because they prevent the danger of monopolizing universalism by excluding all others from the monopoly.[31] This process might take generations to complete, but that is the only right way to find theories of global justice that can respond to Walzer's reminder and be accepted by most people around the world.

Inspiration from *Tianxia* Theory: Taking the Western Zhou Dynasty as an Example

I want to introduce the ancient Chinese tradition of *tianxia,* a theory that can be used to promote cross-cultural conversation. Leading scholars working on *tianxia* theory include Zhao Tingyang, Gan Chunsong, Bai Tongdong, and Qin Yaqing; however, their work mostly refers to ancient Chinese thought in general rather than focusing on specific theorists or dynasties.[32] Unlike the approaches used by those scholars, in this chapter I take the Western Zhou dynasty (1046 BCE–771 BCE) as an example to explore the old ideal *tianxia* system to discuss how different this ancient cosmopolitan theory with Chinese characteristics is from current theories of global justice, and what inspiration we can cull from it.

Ancient China is widely known as an enduring empire with a very different but comprehensive political culture in comparison to Europe. However, to seek the origin of this political culture, the target should be the Western Zhou dynasty, a dynasty that lasted for 275 years. The Western Zhou dynasty enjoys a special status in history, especially considering Confucianism and ancient China's political culture. As Edward Shaughnessy has argued, "Throughout China's long history, the Western Zhou has served as its guiding paradigm for governmental, intellectual, and social developments."[33] As the founder of Confucianism, Confucius treated the Western Zhou dynasty as a model of ideal governance, especially when the sage kings were in power, saying, for instance, "The Zhou gazes down upon the two dynasties that preceded it. How brilliant in culture it is! I follow the Zhou," and "The Virtue of the Zhou—surely it can be said to represent ultimate Virtue?"[34] Such an evaluation has remained very persistent throughout history, from scholars in different dynasties, even when people have more knowledge about other dynasties before and after the Western Zhou dynasty. Scholars who reconstruct *tianxia* as a theory of global justice will not deny the importance of the Western Zhou dynasty as a milestone and the foundation of the theory.[35] So why is this dynasty so unique and vital for *tianxia* theory?

In China, a period was named a dynasty when enough textual and physical evidence was found to prove the existence of a political authority that governed an ample space for some period of time. Based on this standard, the Western Zhou was not the first dynasty in Chinese history; it was preceded by two dynasties: Xia (2070 BCE–1600 BCE) and Shang (1600 BCE–1046 BCE). Historical studies also proved the existence of other small political authorities in these two dynasties that may or may not have interacted with each other. However, when studying ancient *tianxia* theory, we must note that it originated in the Western Zhou dynasty. When this dynasty was established, the relationship between the central authority (Zhou) and other small authorities changed. Unlike the Shang dynasty, which let other regional authorities remain independent, the Western Zhou dynasty decided to govern all of the territories it discovered. In other words, we can understand the Shang dynasty as one of the regional authorities that was most influential, while the Western Zhou dynasty tried to establish a united political authority with some regional authorities subordinate to it.[36] To some extent, the overall space discovered was governed by the principles made by Zhou. At that time, people used different names—*guo* 國 (state) for the region directly governed by Zhou and *ye* 野 (field) for the area governed by other authorities—to describe different areas based on their distance from the central state (i.e., Zhou).[37] These changes indicate that, for the first time, *tianxia,* as a concept as well as a political reality, is worth studying in Chinese history, which is why the Western Zhou dynasty is usually treated as the first model of *tianxia.*

Why did Zhou as a state intend to seek unity, and how could it maintain the *tianxia* system for 275 years? To understand the characteristics of the Western Zhou dynasty, we need to explore two perspectives: the meaning of *tian* 天 ("Heaven" or "god") and the so-called feudal system. As a concept, *tian* existed in the Shang dynasty, but at that time, the so-called god in the Shang dynasty acted as the patron saint of the Shang tribe only. However, in the Zhou dynasty, *tian* as a concept was universalized in three perspectives: scope, time span, and political significance. For the scope, *tian* as a concept overcame any single state and became the universalized protector of or judge for everyone.[38] In terms of time span, the coverage of "Heaven" also transcended one generation and included ancestor worship, which created an extensive lineage system for everyone in the world.[39] Therefore, combining the change of scope and time span, everyone living in the world and their past and future generations could be understood as living in a single *tianxia* and would be influenced by the "mandate of Heaven." For political significance, in the Western Zhou dynasty, humanistic morals replaced religious worship and set a precedent for the later Confucian political philosophy.[40] To be explicit, in the Western Zhou dynasty, the mandate of Heaven set three principles for kings to follow: (1) the king should restrict his private desire and strengthen morality; (2) from the perspective of governance, the king should try to civilize rather than dominate his people; and (3) the king should always be cautious about punishment.[41] Thus, *tianxia* as a concept not only connects everyone in the world literally, but also represents a political system and establishes some moral principles for its maintenance, including the prototype of benevolent governance emphasized by Confucius and Mencius later on.

In addition to the meaning of "Heaven," which tried to establish uniform principles to govern the world, the institutional design in the Western Zhou dynasty is also worth mentioning. Scholars usually use "feudalism" to describe the overall picture of governance at that time, but as Li Feng has pointed out, "feudal fief" is an inadequate term for characterizing those authorities.[42] Compared to the traditional "lord-vassal relationship" that is private in feudalism, the relationship between the central state (Zhou) and regional states should be understood as a "ruler-subject relationship" that is public and demands unconditional submission. Moreover, the medieval fief "was a form of stipend and was a property with limited rights but more contracted obligations," while the regional state in the Western Zhou dynasty "was essentially a form of government that had responsibility for civil administration, justice, and the military, and was considered necessary by the Zhou central court in accordance with the grand strategy of the Western Zhou state."[43] Therefore, for a more accurate description, those regional states should be called "settlement-based states that were founded on delegatory rules."[44]

There were complicated tensions between the central state (Zhou) and other states. The central state had substantial control over other states, as the king of Zhou could nominate the ministers of the military and judiciary and even lead military actions that required those powers and minority groups to follow him.[45] The king of Zhou also controlled sacrificial rituals in all other states, guaranteeing his leadership in politics and culture.⁴⁶ Confucius described such a relationship as follows: "ritual, music, punitive expeditions. and attacks against foreign powers issue from and the Son of Heaven," thus representing an ideal status of overall governance.⁴⁷ The regional state "constituted an autonomous geopolitical entity located in a specific area, and was equipped with a small but complete government that enjoyed the combined right of civil administration, legal punishment, and military authority."⁴⁸ This sense of independence was well respected in Chinese history as we find almost no evidence that "the central court had ever attempted to interfere in the domestic affairs of the regional states, except in matters of succession to regional rulership that could well concern the interests of the Zhou king."⁴⁹

The *Book of Rites* describes how kingly governance should rely on and respect the climate, geography, and customs of different regions while also unifying the way of governance.⁵⁰ Under such a relationship, regional states are represented as a part of the united spirit of the Chinese cultural community on the one hand and as diverse local cultures and customs on the other. While taking care of their own governance, the regional states were also "active participants in the political life of the Western Zhou state," as "it must have been quite frequent for the regional rulers, especially newly established ones, to pay visits to the Zhou king in his capital in the Wei River valley. Moreover, the bronze inscriptions also show that the Zhou king stationed royal inspectors in the regional states, a practice that continued through the entire Western Zhou period."⁵¹ Therefore, the tension between the central state and the regional states remained healthy, as the sense of unity was stable enough, and the independence of the regional power and the diversity of the local culture were also well respected.

There is a famous description of the Western Zhou dynasty in the *Classic of Poetry*: "Zhou is an old state, but its mandate is ever renewing." It is an old state because, as a political authority, it already existed during the Xia dynasty and the Shang dynasty, but it is ever renewing because its institutional system and its political culture had far-reaching influence and, to some extent, even "shaped the spirit of Chinese culture."⁵² As the first dynasty to establish the *tianxia* system and maintain it, the Western Zhou dynasty left two significant legacies.

First, after the Western Zhou dynasty, unity became the overwhelming goal for almost all other dynasties, so the change of dynasties did not affect the ongoing status of the *tianxia* system. The Western Zhou dynasty understood itself to be the governor of "All-under-Heaven" rather than just a large state, and the leader of a united political and cultural community rather than just a strong political authority; most later generations inherited that intention. In the Western Zhou dynasty, China as a concept already included the Xia dynasty's and Shang dynasty's descendants and many other tribal groups, creating a new and comprehensive cultural identity for China.[53] Even though the territory of the *tianxia* expanded, the grand ideal to govern the entire area that was discovered and the practice of the central-local institutional system always made China a political and cultural community that included various tribal identities. Moreover, the Western Zhou dynasty developed the idea of the legitimacy of dynastic change. Rather than naming itself as the origin of a new history, the Western Zhou dynasty chose to accept the legitimacy of dynastic changes in the past and even the potential handover of power through dynasty changes led by the mandate of Heaven in the future. This choice reveals that the mandate of Heaven would last forever, while any political community that governed *tianxia* could only be one part of that history rather than its entirety. This understanding created the possibility for China to be an enduring empire represented by many dynasties throughout history. Although there were many different dynasties after the Western Zhou dynasty, they mostly followed Zhou's choice to regard themselves as the latest period in the process of dynastic changes rather than as a new beginning of history. That is why ancient China has complete and continuous historical records—a history used to govern *tianxia* made by different political authorities in different dynasties.

Second, the success of the Western Zhou dynasty, especially its strong mandate to govern All-under-Heaven, was understood as the result of the practice of virtue, highlighting the significance of benevolence. As one of the most crucial concepts in Confucianism, benevolence has many interpretations. In the context of the *tianxia* system, it mainly focuses on peace, respect, and the pursuit of morality. Zhou regarded the collapse of the Shang dynasty as the outcome of overemphasizing power that led to the change of the mandate of Heaven; to avoid repeating the same mistake, the law in the Western Zhou dynasty was tightly bound by virtue and reflected in the practice of rituals.[54] It is not easy for people nowadays to imagine that the sense of unity remained solid and stable when Zhou, as the central state, was not powerful in terms of military might or large in terms of its scope, and regional states had full control of their own military power. As the first model of *tianxia* theory, it revealed the interesting relationship between power and virtue and how benevolent governance, as well as the practice of rituals, could overcome the logic of realism. The emphasis on virtue before power strongly influenced the subsequent thought of Confucius and Mencius. For example, Mencius always highlighted that for a state, the size of the territory and the strength of the military are not as important as the practice of benevolent governance, and that small states could not only survive but also succeed in the interstate competition as long as they followed the Western Zhou dynasty as a good model.[55]

I have no intention of avoiding the topic of the vulnerability of this type of system, especially considering the historical reality. Just as Li Feng has pointed out, it is a question of whether the institutional methods the central state used to control the regional states "could stand the test of time."[56] When the regional states no longer respected the status of the central state, the *tianxia* system in the Western Zhou dynasty collapsed, and Chinese history entered the Spring and Autumn and Warring States periods when many regional states competed to become the dominant power. However, almost all the political communities that successfully united China and created new dynasties inherited the Western Zhou dynasty's legacy to seek the unity of *tianxia,* and most of them also chose to practice benevolence as the virtue of governance.[57] Starting from the Western Zhou dynasty, the *tianxia* system lasted throughout ancient China's history until the early twentieth century, with more and more regions included in the united political community.

Conclusion

Scholars such as Zhao have argued that *tianxia* theory represents a better approach to thinking about global politics as it can overcome the struggle for power and the endless competition among states.[58] I have no interest in identifying the best theory of global justice, as I only want to introduce more non-Western theories of global justice that might contribute to the cross-cultural conversation. We need various new theories to enrich the content of the discussion rather than trying to determine the best theory for the world today. Therefore, for people who would like to explore global justice, what innovation can we find from the *tianxia* system in the Western Zhou dynasty? In my opinion, three points that are very different from the liberal tradition can be regarded as the contribution from ancient Chinese thought.

First, the *tianxia* theory emphasizes the normative sense of unity, requiring us to think from the perspective of the world as a political unit.[59] Advocates of globalization have been trying to view the fragmented world as one community, but the lack of normative foundation to think of the world as a whole diminishes that attempt, resulting in the need to overcome the inevitable disadvantages. Radical cosmopolitan thinkers like Peter Singer would support a world government, but it would not be possible to imagine how to justify its legitimacy without the normative thinking of unity. Macroconstruction rather than microarticulation is one of the core features of Chinese political culture, which helps us overcome individualism as the foundation for thinking about a cosmopolitan world. Unlike the liberal tradition, which guarantees individual goodness first, in *tianxia* theory, the more the order of unity is maintained, the better able we will be to ensure that humans will flourish.

Second, it is possible to maintain a healthy tension between global justice and local justice, between unity and cultural diversity. The concept of unity requires that the whole world share some universal principles, but the practice in the Western Zhou dynasty shows that we can also leave enough space for regional culture and political governance. Taking the Western Zhou dynasty as an example, we can see that it is not necessary to institute a world government to apply *tianxia* theory to the contemporary world, as the ideal order can be achieved within the basic framework of a collection of states. However, *tianxia* theory does not follow the logic of the Westphalian system, which takes independence and noninterference as its priority, as it requires every subject of the global community to participate in activities guided by some normative principles beyond the states. Therefore, in comparison to studies of multiculturalism, which highlight the significance of respect and the protection of local cultures, *tianxia* theory goes one step further to consider how these diverse local traditions could contribute to a better world community.

Third, *tianxia* theory shows the possibility of reconsidering equality as an unchallengeable principle of global justice. We have no reason to deny the value of equality, as antidomination is always a task for global justice. This chapter has challenged the dominant position of liberalism in the academic context, and contemporary republican thought has convinced us of the value of antidomination to fight against institutional injustice.[60] However, just as republicanism tries to distinguish antidomination from equality, *tianxia* theory reveals an interesting tension between equality and hierarchy. In the case of the Western Zhou dynasty, although the regional states varied in size and power, they were treated equally in the eyes of the central state, and strong states were prohibited from invading weak ones at will. The equality of the regional states provided the foundation to protect cultural diversity. However, the *tianxia* system also embraces the spirit of just hierarchy, which behaved as the central-local relationship and the famous *hua–yi* 華-夷 (Sino-Barbarian) distinction. Although every tribe or political authority is part of *tianxia,* the *hua–yi* distinction sets a basic standard to push every subject in the world system to accept the basic benefits of civilization (such as benevolent governance) and prevent barbarous and antivirtuous actions. Thus, it improves the overall governance levels for all states while simultaneously strengthening the sense of unity.

In 1990, Fei Xiaotong, the famous Chinese sociologist, introduced an inspiring motto for the ideal of global justice: "Appreciate the unique beauty of one's own and cherish the beauty of others with openness; when beauties integrate with each other, great unity shines on the world" (*Gemeiqimei, meirenzhimei, meimeiyugong, tianxiadatong* 各美其美, 美人之美, 美美與共, 天下大同).[61] Taking *tianxia* theory as a model, we can see three features in this motto: we need to realize and accept the existence of cultural diversity as the first step; after understanding different traditions as "beauties," we should expect to see more cross-cultural conversations, rather than just take different traditions for granted and struggle at sharp disagreements; and, finally, great unity is always the ultimate ideal for the world. It is interesting to see that this motto could also support my approach for studying global justice following Walzer's reminder: we should appreciate the unique beauty of theories from different cultural backgrounds to think about the world-system and try our best to integrate them to find consensus and establish universal principles as a theory of justice that is sufficiently global. The road to achieving this motto is certainly long and winding, but this is the lifelong mission of all theorists who care about global justice.

Notes

1. Among all theorists, Peter Singer might be the one who is most optimistic about such a picture. In his book *One World*, Singer argues that we will observe one atmosphere, one economy, one law, and one community in the near future. See Peter Singer, *One World: The Ethics of Globalization* (New Haven, CT: Yale University Press, 2002).

2. Dani Rodrik, *Has Globalization Gone Too Far?* (Washington, DC: Institute for International Economics, 1997), p. 69.

3. As Fred Dallmayr argues, cosmopolitanism as a concept is used in two different ways. Sometimes it mainly acts as the description of "ongoing, empirically observable processes of border-crossing and hybridization"; other times it represents a moral vision that can be used to formulate the global order. Political theorists are usually concerned about the latter. See Fred Dallmayr, *Being in the World: Dialogue and Cosmopolis* (Lexington: University Press of Kentucky, 2013), p. 31.

4. For a good summary of recent studies on global justice, see Mathias Risse, *Global Political Philosophy* (Basingstoke, UK: Palgrave Macmillan, 2012).

5. Michael Walzer, *Spheres of Justice: A Defense of Pluralism and Equality* (Oxford: Robertson, 1983), p. 5.

6. Walzer, *Spheres of Justice*, p. 5.

7. Although Walzer refers to cultural diversity to justify his argument about the spheres, culture (especially the difference between Western and non-Western cultures) was not the focus of his argument in 1983. For him, the principle of equality should be complex mainly because of diverse social situations rather than cultural backgrounds.

8. David Miller, *Justice for Earthlings: Essays in Political Philosophy* (Cambridge: Cambridge University Press, 2012), p. 91.

9. Mathias Risse uses the terms "globalists," "statists," and "nonrelationists" (supporters of cosmopolitanism) in his book to classify studies of global justice. Scholars choose different dimensions to understand these theories, but the core concern is always the role of state in global justice. See Mathias Risse, *On Global Justice* (Princeton, NJ: Princeton University Press, 2012).

10. Considering the large number of theories, in this chapter I can only choose several typical and influential studies from each approach to analyze. For cosmopolitanism, typical theories include Singer, *One World;* Thomas Pogge, *World Poverty and Human Rights* (Cambridge: Polity Press, 2008); Simon Caney, *Justice beyond Borders* (New York: Oxford

University Press, 2005); and Martha Nussbaum, *Frontiers of Justice* (Cambridge, MA: Harvard University Press, 2006). For statism, typical theories include John Rawls, *The Law of Peoples* (Cambridge, MA: Harvard University Press, 1999); and David Miller, *National Responsibility and Global Justice* (New York: Oxford University Press, 2007). For the middle-way approach, typical theories include Risse, *On Global Justice;* and Philip Pettit, *Just Freedom* (New York: W. W. Norton, 2014).

11. Pogge, *World Poverty and Human Rights,* p. 175.

12. Rawls uses the term "peoples" instead of "states" in his theory to highlight that traditional sovereignty, which is essential for states, might be harmful to liberal principles and should be excluded from his theory. However, if we focus on the classification of studies on global justice, Rawls' theory is certainly a theory of statism, rather than cosmopolitanism or the middle-way approach.

13. See Rawls, *Law of Peoples,* pp. 4–5. I am just showing how Rawls' discussion on five types of peoples closely follows the logic of liberalism, not arguing that this part of his theory is wrong or incoherent.

14. Risse, *Global Political Philosophy,* pp. 109, 108.

15. I need to emphasize that I am criticizing the overall picture of studies on global justice, and it is unfair to claim that it is any single theorist or theory's fault that this is happening. After all, liberalism is important and influential in the world, and it is unbelievable that studies of global justice are not guided by liberal thought at all. However, since the voice of liberalism is absolutely strong recently, that is also problematic.

16. Kathleen G. Roberts, *The Limits of Cosmopolis: Ethics and Provinciality in the Dialogue of Cultures* (New York: Peter Lang, 2014), p. 6.

17. Walzer, *Spheres of Justice,* p. 10.

18. See William A. Callaghan, "Chinese Visions of World Order: Post-hegemonic or a New Hegemony?," *International Studies Review* 10, no. 4 (December 2008): 749–761.

19. Joseph H. Carens, *Culture, Citizenship, and Community: A Contextual Exploration of Justice as Evenhandedness* (New York: Oxford University Press, 2000), p. 27.

20. Michael Walzer, *Thick and Thin: Moral Arguments at Home and Abroad* (Notre Dame, IN: University of Notre Dame Press, 1994), p. 10.

21. The role of these nonstate organizations has been becoming more and more important. For example, the World Bank has contributed much to help the poorest population in the world, and under the threat of the COVID-19 pandemic recently, we have strongly relied on the World Health Organization to manage the distribution of vaccines, especially for states in Africa.

22. See Stephen C. Angle, *Human Rights and Chinese Thought: A Cross-Cultural Inquiry* (New York: Cambridge University Press, 2002).

23. Daniel A. Bell, *The China Model: Political Meritocracy and the Limits of Democracy* (Princeton, NJ: Princeton University Press, 2015), p. 138.

24. Will Kymlicka, *Multicultural Citizenship: A Liberal Theory of Minority Rights* (New York: Oxford University Press, 1995), p. 76.

25. See Will Kymlicka, *Contemporary Political Philosophy: An Introduction* (Oxford: Oxford University Press, 2002), pp. 348–365.

26. Kymlicka, *Multicultural Citizenship,* pp. 113, 194.

27. Carens, *Culture, Citizenship, and Community*, p. 15.

28. Leigh Jenco, ed., *Chinese Thought as Global Theory: Diversifying Knowledge Production in the Social Sciences and Humanities* (Albany: State University of New York Press, 2016), p. 1.

29. Kwame A. Appiah, *The Ethics of Identity* (Princeton, NJ: Princeton University Press, 2005), p. 246.

30. Kwame A. Appiah, *Cosmopolitanism: Ethics in a World of Strangers* (New York: W. W. Norton, 2006), p. 85.

31. Fred Dallmayr, "Beyond Monologue: For a Comparative Political Theory," *Perspectives on Politics* 2, no. 2 (2004): 253.

32. See Zhao Tingyang, *The Tianxia System—An Introduction to the Philosophy of World Institution* (Beijing: China Renmin University Press, 2011); Gan Chunsong, *Back to Wangdao—Confucianism and the World Order* (Shanghai: East Normal University Press, 2012); Bai Tongdong, *Against Political Equality: The Confucian Case* (Princeton, NJ: Princeton University Press, 2020); Qin Yaqing, *A Relational Theory of World Politics* (Cambridge: Cambridge University Press, 2018).

33. Edward Shaughnessy, "Western Zhou History," in *The Cambridge History of Ancient China: From the Origins of Civilization to 221 B.C.*, ed. Michael Loewe and Edward Shaughnessy (Cambridge: Cambridge University Press, 1999), p. 292.

34. Confucius, *Analects*, trans. Edward Slingerland (Indianapolis, IN: Hackett, 2003), pp. 23, 85.

35. Due to space limitations, I will not explain the discussions on the Western Zhou dynasty in several *tianxia* theories in detail. All in all, scholars like Zhao Tingyang, Gan Chunsong, and Bai Tongdong all pay special attention to the Western Zhou dynasty when they introduce their understandings of *tianxia* theories.

36. David N. Keightley, *The Ancestral Landscape: Time, Space and Community in Late Shang China, ca. 1200–1045 B.C.* (Berkeley: University of California, Berkeley, Institute of East Asian Studies, 2000), pp. 56–57.

37. Zhang Guangzhi, *History and Civilization of Western Zhou Dynasty* (Shanghai: Shanghai Scientific and Technological Literature Press, 2012), p. 181.

38. Xu Zhuoyun, *The History of Western Zhou Dynasty* (Beijing: SDX Joint Publishing Company, 1994), p. 100.

39. Chen Yun, *Ritual Propriety of Zhou and the Kingly Governance of Tianxia as / by a Family: Focusing on the Political System of Yin & Zhou* (Beijing: China Renmin University Press, 2019), p. 277.

40. Xu Zhuoyun, *History of Western Zhou Dynasty*, p. 109.

41. Zhang Guangzhi, *History and Civilization*, p 222.

42. Li Feng, *Bureaucracy and the State in Early China: Governing the Western Zhou* (Cambridge: Cambridge University Press, 2008), pp. 288–290.

43. Li Feng, *Bureaucracy and the State*, p. 290.

44. Li Feng, *Early China: A Social and Cultural History* (Cambridge: Cambridge University Press, 2013), p. 153.

45. Yang Kuan, *History of Western Zhou Dynasty* (Shanghai: Shanghai People's Publishing House, 2003), p. 394.

46. Chen Yun, *Ritual Propriety of Zhou*, p. 336.

47. Confucius, *Analects,* p. 193.

48. Li Feng, *Landscape and Power in Early China: The Crisis and Fall of the Western Zhou 1045–771 BC* (Cambridge: Cambridge University Press, 2006), p. 111.

49. Li Feng, *Early China,* pp. 131–132.

50. Chen Yun, *Ritual Propriety of Zhou,* pp. 341–344.

51. Li Feng, *Early China,* pp. 131–132.

52. Chen Lai, *Ancient Religion and Ethics: The Origin of Confucian Thought* (Beijing: SDX Joint Publishing Company, 2009), p. 196.

53. Li Feng, *The Collapse of Western Zhou Dynasty* (Shanghai: Shanghai Classics Publishing House, 2007), pp. 330–331.

54. Zhang Guangzhi, *History and Civilization,* p. 217.

55. Mencius claimed that "With King Wen as a model, he will, in five years, if his state is large, or in seven years, if his state is small, be sure to govern *Tianxia*" (4A7); and "There are cases of a ruthless man gaining possession of a state, but it has never happened that such a man gained possession of *Tianxia*" (7B13). To be explicit, Mencius admits that the global order is not always that ideal, but in the long term, benevolent governance will be better than power domination. For discussion in detail, see Wang Binfan, "A Confucian 'Law of Peoples': Mencius's Thought on Global Justice," In *Global Justice in East Asia,* ed. Hugo El Kholi and Jun-Hyeok Kawk (New York: Routledge, 2019), pp. 141–157.

56. Li Feng, *Landscape and Power,* p. 115.

57. As the first dynasty of China as an empire, the Qin dynasty (221 BCE–206 BCE) did not embrace benevolent governance as the principle. However, since it collapsed in fifteen years, it is usually regarded as a counterexample. Following Qin, the Han dynasty treated Confucianism as the official ideology and from then on, all dynasties afterward highlighted the practice of benevolent governance at least superficially.

58. See Zhao, *Tianxia System.*

59. This point is first raised by Zhao, who quoted chapter 54 of the *Laozi:* "thinking world from the world." See Zhao Tingyang, *A Possible World of the All-under-Heaven System* (Beijing: CITIC Publishing Group, 2016), p. 3.

60. See Pettit, *Just Freedom,* pp. 109–149.

61. Fei Xiaotong, *Gaining Knowledge from Practice* (Beijing: Peking University Press, 1998), p. 435.

CHAPTER 13

Tianxia and Global Distributive Justice

Sor-hoon TAN

SINCE ZHAO TINGYANG suggested the "*tianxia* system" as an alternative to the prevailing Westphalian model of international relations (IR) in the first years of the twenty-first century as a better way to address problems of world politics, global problems have grown more pressing and the world has become ever more chaotic. More and more people have lost confidence in the current international system as the realpolitik among nation-states seems to be creating more problems than it solves for the world. The problems of global distributive justice— that some populations are starving in an era of unprecedented level of material production and wealth, and income and wealth disparities are worsening within and across national boundaries—are among those problems that the current international system, despite various international aid programs, has not made very significant progress in solving. As early as 1972, the philosopher Peter Singer responded to the Bengal famine of the previous year with a utilitarian argument that affluent persons in developed countries have a moral obligation to help the less fortunate, even beyond their national boundaries.[1] Since then, a lively discourse has grown with competing theories of global justice, as well as arguments over the conceptual coherence of global justice and the practical viability of any proposed scheme of just global (re)distribution.[2]

Although discussions about the topic of global distributive justice are relatively sparse in contemporary Confucian political philosophy, it is worth exploring what would be a Confucian position on this important issue and what kind of solutions it might propose or favor when it comes to whether and how to help citizens of foreign countries. It is an issue that gains in relevance as the People's Republic of China (PRC) moves into the ranks of affluent countries. And if we understand global justice more broadly as imposing obligations not only on nation-states but also on individuals, a Confucian theory of global justice could provide ethical guidance for affluent citizens of other East Asian countries with Confucian cultural legacies. At both levels, it may have even wider impact if Confucianism succeeds in becoming a world philosophy. Insofar as the *tianxia* concept is being offered as a "Chinese," and more specifically a "Confucian" concept of global order, what would it contribute to solving global distributive problems? Zhao's latest English publication on the topic, *Redefining a Philosophy for World Governance* (2019), does not claim that his theory is Confucian, but he acknowledges Confucian inspiration in one key aspect of his conception of the *tianxia* system, which has implications for problems of global distributive justice. Rather than elaborating his theory to construct a Confucian approach or solutions to global justice problems, I shall argue that Zhao's *tianxia* philosophy has some serious problems and furthermore is incompatible with the ethical emphasis of Confucianism, which render his *tianxia* concept unsuitable for framing any Confucian theory of global distributive justice. In contrast to Zhao's philosophy, some Confucian scholars have offered their own Confucian *tianxia* theories, which could provide the basis for tackling global distributive problems. However, the theoretical work these *tianxia* concepts are supposed to do in any Confucian conception of global distributive justice needs further scrutiny and elaboration. I propose an approach that goes beyond the policies of governments in international relations.

The Scope of *Tianxia*

Over the years, debates about the concept of *tianxia*, what it means, and its implications in contemporary discourses about global order and world politics have attracted more and more participants with different interests and expertise and therefore widely varied perspectives. Among the issues being debated is the connection between the contemporary concept and the concept as it occurs in premodern Chinese texts, in other words, whether the contemporary concept can lay claim to being part of Chinese "tradition" and any international relations (IR) theory based on the concept could consequently be considered a *Chinese* IR theory or an IR theory with Chinese characteristics. While the two concepts need not be exactly the same, there must be significant overlap or continuity in meaning. Another is the implication of the concept for the PRC's global role. Some use the concept to counter or balance nationalism in order to set out a peaceful Chinese path to global leadership. Others focus on contrasting Chinese global leadership with that of the United States or on proposing an ideal model of global leadership. Critics question the cultural authenticity of the concept and the viability of the model, and the harshest criticisms see the theory as an apology for Chinese global domination.³

Most scholars recognize that *tianxia* 天下 has multiple and different meanings depending on textual and historical contexts. As a term of political geography, during the Western Zhou period, it certainly does not refer to the entire world as we know it, but only to the area directly governed by the Zhou ruler and those areas recognizing the authority of the Zhou ruler through a system of ritual obligations.⁴ Even with the erosion of that authority during the Warring States period, the *Mencius* retains that meaning in its discussion of how *tianxia* "could be settled through unity," that is, by ending the struggle for power among the various states that used to recognize the authority of the Zhou ruler (1A6). The *Mencius* also has passages that include in the scope of *tianxia* the lands of the *yi* 夷 and *di* 狄, neighboring tribes with very different customs and beyond Zhou's political authority.⁵ From the Han to the Tang dynasty, the term acquired three layers of meanings: (1) China—the area under the reigning emperor in what is vaguely known as the "Central Plains," the residents of which claimed to be descendants of *huaxia* 華夏, the "glorious Xia" dynasty; (2) China and those outside the *huaxia* cultural area who paid tribute to the Chinese emperor, including various parts of today's East Asia; and (3) in addition to the first two areas, it also includes the "extreme territories" (*jueyu* 絕域), that is, the faraway lands of the Han dynasty's westward explorations.⁶ The first meaning is both political and cultural: when referring to only China as the descendant polity and civilization of the "glorious Xia," *tianxia* implies the *yi–xia* distinction, which distinguishes the Chinese as not only culturally different from but also more civilized than other peoples. Yet there is also a tension between *tianxia* and the *yi–xia* distinction, as increasingly what was not yet brought under the suzerainty of the Chinese ruler was viewed as potentially a part of his *tianxia,* which could and should be brought under his cultural influence, if not his political control. While the increasing geographical scope of the *tianxia* concept over time lends weight to the contemporary move to use the term to refer to the whole world, its entanglement with the Chinese traditional idea of the *yi–xia* distinction raises the red flags of imperialism and cultural hegemony.⁷

D. C. Lau's translation of the *Mencius* translates *tianxia* as "Empire." This seems reasonable in discussions of the realpolitik of Mencius's time or general cases of power struggle, but perhaps misleading in ethical discussions praising ethical exemplars. If the "great man" (*da zhangfu* 大丈夫) is an ethical exemplar, then the "great way" he practices surely is for the world rather than merely "the empire" (*Mencius* 3B2). Similarly, the example set by the sage king Shun "worthy of being handed down to posterity" should be "for the world" (4B28). The translation of "the world" also seems reasonable in the *Analects*' ethical discussions of conducting oneself in relation to *tianxia*, with appropriateness (*yi* 義) (4.10) and humaneness (*ren* 仁) (17.6), that is, how *tianxia* responds to ritual propriety (*li* 禮) and *ren* (12.1). Even if the reference the authors of early Confucian texts had in mind when employing that term was only the Zhou empire due to their limited political-geographical horizon, insofar as we recognize them as engaging in ethical discourse it would be more appropriate to translate the term as "the world." When Mencius discusses *liangzhi* 良知, "what one knows without having to reflect on it," as being nothing but extending humaneness and appropriateness to *tianxia*, whether one translates *tianxia* as "the empire" or "the world" determines the extent to which we believe Confucian ethical excellence could be extended. Similarly, to understand the Zhou *tianxia* system as a world-system implies that what applies to a limited empire in the past could be extended to the world today. It is often not easy to separate the normative from the descriptive meanings and both are present in some uses of the term in early Chinese texts, especially when historical persons, practices, or institutions are explicitly or implicitly held up as exemplars. The resulting ambiguity may obscure the problem of universalizing what was not intended to be universalized, or what might not be universalizable.[8]

Normative Relevance of Historical "Experiments"

Whatever the difference between the world as known to or considered significant by the Chinese of earlier times on the one hand and the world today on the other hand, the connection required for a contemporary *tianxia* theory to lay claim to being part of Chinese tradition rests on whether the ancients' practice and institutions—how they acted toward *tianxia* or in it, and how they perceived the actual and ideal relations among the different components of *tianxia*—could and should serve as a model for our actions and institutions in today's world. Alternatively, one might seek this connection by turning away from historical practice and institutions, and constructing the contemporary theory from traditional textual resources interpreted as transcending time and place, as Zhao Tingyang's latest refinement of his theory does by giving the *tianxia* system an ontological underpinning that links the concept of *tianxia* with the concept of the three powers (*sancai* 三才), that is, Heaven-earth-human. As such, it becomes "a trinity of three worlds," encompassing the whole physical world, a sociological-psychological world of heartfelt support from (identification with?) "all people's hearts," and a political world defined by a world-system that is an infinitely open network, wherein "local structure replicates the whole structure," characterized by voluntary cooperation, with the aim of "turning enemies into friends, not to distinguish enemies from friends."[9] What the ontological foundation provides is a transcendental reason "to acknowledge diversity in the world and its cooperative and peaceful relationship and to reject unilateral universalism or cultural imperialism."[10]

Zhao's redefinition of *tianxia* philosophy for world governance, however, does not detach the concept from historical practice. Central to his theory is the invention or "political experiment" of the Zhou dynasty, the historical *tianxia* system that enabled a small state to establish its governance over the *tianxia* of "ten thousand states" for nearly eight hundred years. According to Zhao, the Zhou dynasty's politics was world politics, and not merely state or interstate politics, and its *tianxia* system has universal significance insofar as the relations among the states in this system could apply to contemporary international relations. The "basic properties that are essential for a shared world system are: (1) the *tianxia* system must guarantee that the benefits of joining will outweigh those of staying outside, thus making all states willing to recognize it and join; (2) it must ensure that all states are interdependent in interests and that their relationship is mutually beneficial so as to secure a world order with universal safety and lasting peace; (3) it must be able to develop public interest, shared interest and public enterprise beneficial for all states, so as to ensure the system is universally beneficial."[11]

While the concept of *tianxia* has been present throughout Chinese history, the political experiment Zhao identifies as the Zhou *tianxia* system ended with the Qin unification, which implemented instead a "grand unity system of central governance" (*dayitong* 大一統).[12] Zhao distinguishes an external and an internal application of the *tianxia* methodology after the collapse of the Zhou *tianxia* system. The former is the tributary tradition from the Han dynasty to the Qing dynasty, which has been the focus of attention of historians studying China's past foreign relations policies and behavior. Some of those studies have concluded that, historically, China had been an imperialistic world power in the past while others present more benign portrayals of China's relations with tributary states. In IR and Confucian discourses, some argue for a "Chinese-style" global order by turning to the tributary system as the application of the *tianxia* concept; but Zhao dismisses this external application of the *tianxia* methodology, as it "has promised very little substantive power" compared to the Zhou tributary system.[13]

Focusing on Zhao's earlier publications (2009–2015), Jun-Hyeok Kwak sees no difference between Zhao's *tianxia* concept and those scholars who interpret the concept with the tributary systems of the Ming and Qing dynasties. Kwak criticizes their *tianxia* concept for driving a Chinese-style cosmopolitanism, which advocates a hierarchical global order that is culturally parochial and moreover would probably degenerate into domination as it "displays a pervasive negligence of voices from peripheral states against the hegemonic state in the China-led tributary system throughout the history of East Asia."[14] He demonstrates how Korean and Japanese scholars' views of the relations between imperial China and its tributary states differ significantly from the all-embracing and compatible relations of Zhao's own idealized *tianxia* system. Kwak turns to an alternative *tianxia* concept in the work of an eighteenth-century Korean Practical Learning (*Silhak* 實學) scholar, Hong Daeyong 洪大容 (1731–1783), who argued that all countries in *tianxia* are equal, and adopted an "ethics of difference" based on Zhuangzi's relativism. By bringing Hong's views in his *Dialogue on Mount Uisan* (*Uisanmundap* 醫山問答) into conversation with contemporary neo-Roman Republicanism, Kwak argues that Hong's *tianxia* concept offers an "antihierarchical non-centrism," in which "reciprocal non-domination" serves as "a regulative principle that guides different ethical justifications to the requirements of peaceful coexistence by constraining all states against the possible excess of domination in the asymmetrical relationship between them."[15]

In *Redefining a Philosophy for World Governance* (2019), Zhao explicitly eschews the Chinese tributary system as a model for his *tianxia* world-system and argues instead that the "political gene" of the *tianxia* concept, which supported and maximized the development of the Chinese civilization, is more evident and stable in the internal application of the *tianxia* concept's infinitely open, all-inclusive, compatible, and relationally rational political methodology, "to create a world-pattern state that is neither an empire nor a nation-state."[16] "Since grand unity China encompasses a world structure, its political intention is to unify all states under its governance, include all peoples in one family and put *tianxia*'s ideals into practice in one country, thereby defining a political form in which a country, limited in its territory, expresses the all-inclusiveness concept of *tianxia*."[17]

The internal application of the *tianxia* concept enabled the "grand unity system of central governance" of the Han dynasty onwards to "expand its territory into a super-sized country without being an expansionary empire."[18] Beyond material wealth, the Central Plains developed a "spiritual world that was universally open so that all peoples could utilize it to construct and expand their political power.[19] Ancient China grew territorially and became more diverse internally by being open to hitherto non-Chinese polities engaging in a political game of capturing the authority of *tianxia*. Zhao calls this the "whirlpool" formula of growth. It made China into "a collective reconstruction of a common order of existence by many cultures," and Chinese culture became "an enriched and commonly shared culture, among which various cultures are so infused that they are no longer traceable individually."[20] To forestall criticisms of ethnocentrism and cultural imperialism, he emphasizes that, within this process of growth, "all ethnic groups are coinventors, rather than mere receivers of the culture of the Central

Plains."²¹ Zhao also paves the way to extend the internal application of *tianxia* concept into a model of world politics by arguing that China "is a methodology, not a limited concept." "The openness of the whirlpool gaming—thanks to the concept of *tianxia*—determined that China is a concept that is continuously and even endlessly growing; a concept that continuously approaches the magnitude of *tianxia*. It also means that *tianxia* belongs more and more to the world, not merely to China."²²

While I am sympathetic to Zhao's account of cultural interactions, it is important that we do not confuse this cultural process with the political system that structures the potential and actual use of coercive power. It is also misleading to treat the "whirlpool gaming" as a purely peaceful open process of cultural engagement and change. We should not forget that this same process, which includes "capturing the authority of *tianxia*," understood metaphorically as "deer hunting in the Central Plains" (*zhulu zhongyuan* 逐鹿中原) in the Chinese tradition, was a process of struggle for power, which was often violent and bloody. The cultural mixing that resulted, usually after considerable time, does not make the political struggle peaceful or benign. Instead of the evidence of multidirectional flows of cultural exchanges between the Chinese and other civilizations, which are abundant but often have not been acknowledged by the Han majority in its account of Chinese cultural development, more historical studies of specific policies and government actions with impact on different ethnic and cultural groups are needed to establish that past Chinese governments have handled internal diversities in ways that could serve as models for us.²³

Zhao's discussion of the model of "one country, multiple systems" as inspired by the *tianxia* system, and implemented from the Han dynasty onward, is more pertinent to the political question. This is an innovative solution to the problem of integration and distinctiveness that became more problematic in the grand unity system. Its mature version in the Tang dynasty is described as a flexible control system over many ethnic groups with a political core, but it was "void of any sense of cultural center. It was a political system based on cultural equality."²⁴ Furthermore, "the system in the controlled provinces was adapted to the customary practices of the locals, who enjoyed a high degree of autonomous governance."²⁵ For Zhao, this internal structure of one country with multiple systems, as an application of the concept of *tianxia* with its all-inclusiveness and compatibility, is a development of the "political gene" of the Chinese civilization. Comparison of Zhao's "one country, multiple systems" model with the PRC's current implementation of the "one country, two systems" model in Hong Kong is inevitable. Even before the popular protests of 2019–2020 and their aftermath, Hong Kong's post-1997 political and social changes probably would make many observers hesitate in accepting a global order associated with any policy of "one country, multiple systems" presided over by the PRC. Either the PRC has not inherited the "political gene" of inclusiveness and compatibility that allows local systems a high degree of autonomy, or the Chinese "political gene" is quite different in character from Zhao's benign description.

Many critics disagree with Zhao's reading of Chinese history. For example, Guo Yi compares Zhou rulers' relations with the *yi* 夷 with colonization.[26] Hu Jian argues that, for the Zhou, *tianxia* was a cultural imagery that refers to the cultural order of the politically decentralized feudal system and not to political order; it certainly did not include any "world institution" responsible for everyone's well-being.[27] While the concept acquired a political meaning and institutional content with Qin unification, it does not transcend the monarchical state or empire. As the ideology that legitimizes the "grand unity" *tianxia,* Confucian "peace under Heaven" is understood since the Qin as requiring military conquest of "barbarian" territories to bring them under the political rule of the Chinese state / empire, as well as the transformation of the tribes living in those territories with Confucian culture.[28] Zhao's "philosophical renewal" appears to be bringing together contradictory meanings of the concept that prevailed under radically different historical circumstances. These contradictory meanings not only challenge the claim that past Chinese political institutions and practices could provide normative guidance today, but also raise doubt as to the likelihood that a new global order presided over by the PRC would be an improvement on the present status quo, even for those who consider the status quo nothing more than US-dominated chaos.

If it was true that the Zhou did not dominate other states in its *tianxia* system and there was therefore genuinely voluntary cooperation among its states, it was probably due to the suzerain being a small state. In our current world, could a small state become world suzerain? It is very doubtful if larger and more powerful states would consider joining such a world-system more beneficial than being part of a system it could dominate. It is also unlikely that any state capable of world dominance could be trusted to restrain itself from exercising that power. If the PRC gains sufficient power to transform the world, does China's history reassure us that the new resulting global order would live up to the promises of Zhao's idealized *tianxia* model? For those who worry about the risks of imperialism and hegemony by powerful states in the current situation of unequal state power, and more specifically whether the PRC will turn out to be another global hegemon if it has the chance of realizing its own vision of global order, the basic properties of the Zhou *tianxia* system outlined by Zhao offer insufficient reassurance. Unequal power means that a system with those properties could still be unjust unless the world suzerain is a just power that does not favor itself above others; otherwise the system would still not give every state its due, even if all states benefit to some extent. While some benefits may be shared but the alternative is no benefit at all, the notion of "voluntary cooperation" hides the unjust reality of less powerful states having little or no say in which benefits should be shared and how they should be distributed, which renders the voluntariness of their choice suspect.

Zhao's use of the metaphor of "genes of civilization" when comparing the ancient Chinese *tianxia* with the ancient Greek *polis* seems to imply that the PRC has a special advantage when it comes to realizing a modern-day *tianxia* system that is infinitely open and all-embracing.[29] This is a common assumption among advocates of *tianxia* theories, and it sometimes leads to claims about the PRC as a political actor that are filtered through rosy glasses, such as this conclusion of a recent monograph, *Tianxia, the World and the State: The History of the Development of Modern China's Concept of Foreign Relations:* "Even during the difficult war times, China never forgot for an instant the greater goal of all human beings living together in peace and harmony. The ideal of great commonality for All-under-Heaven not only ensures that China will never have expansionary ambitions, but it also ensures that the Chinese people will find it difficult to have deep-rooted national consciousness."[30]

At the very least, evidence of strong nationalistic sentiments in the PRC in recent decades casts doubt on the above view. Zhao's redefinition of "China" as a "methodology" could be used to distinguish Chinese cultural resources from the state power of the PRC. Despite the civilizational genes metaphor, Zhao's theory provides independent criteria for a new *tianxia* system that avoid presuming that the PRC will or should be the world suzerain of such a system. To fill that position, the PRC or any other global power would have to be able to solve global problems to maximize benefits for all nation-states and not just for itself by (1) adopting the all-inclusive perspective that "internalizes" the whole world; (2) employing relational rationality to balance individual rationality in order to give priority to mutual safety and security, to shared interests instead of exclusive interests; (3) operationalizing relational rationality into a strategy aimed at maximization of reciprocal interests; and (4) subscribing to compatible universalism, wherein "any value that can be defined by symmetrical relations is a universal value."[31] Zhao insists that he does not envisage the new *tianxia* system as having a single state as a suzerain but rather sees power residing in the "network" of nation-states.[32] This could be a new line of thinking or the next stage of Zhao's *tianxia* theory, perhaps following the turn to practice and relations in IR scholarship.[33]

Tianxia in Confucian Discourse

While Zhao's *tianxia* theory is clearly normative in recommending a model to guide changes in international relations and in acknowledging the Zhou's *tianxia* system as "an ideal political concept," Zhao seems to eschew the ethical when he denies that "government by virtue" is a doctrine of ethics for the Zhou and interprets it as a "concept of political economics" meaning "fairness in benefit distribution."[34] A theory of global justice based on his *tianxia* philosophy would be antithetical to the primacy of the ethical in Confucianism, despite the fact that the norm for benefit distribution in that system, the maximization of reciprocal interest, is a "Confucian improvement" that Zhao explicitly derives from *Analects* 6.30: "established iff [if and only if] let established; improved iff let improved."[35] The cited passage is Confucius's explication of "the method of humaneness (*ren*)," and no Confucian scholar would accept stripping it of ethical significance. Even for those who want to argue that political philosophy constitutes an important or even the most important part of Confucianism, it would be difficult to deny the importance of the ethical, let alone its relevance.[36]

Accepting the importance of the ethical in Confucianism does not mean that one has to reduce the political to the ethical. Gan Chunsong, whose work on "institutional Confucianism" is highly critical of interpretations of Confucianism centered on heart-mind and human nature (*xinxing ruxue* 心性儒學)—new Confucianism premised on a form of moral metaphysics—for its neglect of political institutions, nevertheless highlights the ethical aim of the Confucian *tianxia* concept. This ethical aim is central to its political meaning of a harmonious order transcending region and race. Confucian *tianxia* theories need to balance this ethical concern with attention to political institutions: the theoretical presupposition of universal good human nature supports a universalizable ethical principle, which enables Confucians to adopt a critical stance toward de facto institutions and practices throughout Chinese history. From a Confucian ethical-political perspective, criticisms of historical inaccuracies or romanticization of Chinese imperial politics miss the point of applying the *tianxia* concept to contemporary global politics. According to Gan, for Confucians, *tianxia* is primarily about an ideal realm (*jingjie* 境界), which might not be realizable, and need not be realizable in concrete details (which are seldom if ever provided); but it serves as a model for actual politics and should guide the construction and operation of institutions at all levels.[37] In terms of institutions, Gan separates the ideal, in which nothing lies outside the scope of a *tianxia* government, from the reality of territorial limits and the historical emphasis on cultural superiority resulting from differences between inner and outer regions and the *yi-xia* distinction in traditional Chinese thought. Gan observes that, while Shang and Zhou historical narratives tend to employ the concept of *tianxia* in discussions of territorial division and cultural differences, the Confucian texts of the school of Zisi and Mencius focus on internal ethical emotions, which are as relevant to the concept of *tianxia* as they are to personal cultivation.[38] The process of building a harmonious world containing well-governed states, ordered families, and cultivated persons requires ethical treatment of distant others on the basis of those others' needs and desires.[39]

Central to Confucian teachings is a relational ethics that is applicable in all situations in which humans interact. The primary ethically significant relationships in Confucian ethics are those between persons, not those between nation-states or other groups, for the simple reason that only human persons have feelings and therefore are capable of empathy, which is the basis of reciprocity in relationships. This does not mean that political systems and social institutions are unimportant, for they structure the interactions of the people involved, whether voluntary or not. What it does mean is that the diagnoses of flaws in existing institutions and proposals of reforms must be based on an understanding of the kinds of human relations Confucians believe to be ethical. While Confucians should not neglect political institutions in Chinese history, which were "experiments" to put into practice Confucian ethical teachings, the complex motivations and constraints inevitably rendered the results less than ideal, so that any "Confucian model" those institutions could offer is always open to debate and requires justification by the ethical ideals. Institutions, policies, and actions must be evaluated on the basis of what kinds of human relations are being initiated and sustained. How should we relate to those who do not belong to the same nation-states as ourselves in order to achieve a peaceful world? A world-system that aims to turn enemies into friends rather than distinguish between enemies and friends would certainly be compatible with a Confucian ethical vision, but who would establish such a system if global political leaders lack the virtues that enable friendship and the treatment of others humanely and justly, regardless of national or any other group or institutional boundaries?

Contemporary *tianxia* theories all aspire to offer better ways to solve global problems. Can the concept offer any new perspectives on the problem of global distributive justice, in contrast to the prevailing utilitarian or Kantian approaches in Anglophone political philosophy discourse? How would Confucians answer the question of what we owe to one another in the world at large beyond the confines of our country? A 2014 article by Shi Yongzhi addresses the topic of global justice with the *tianxia* concept. Shi argues that the "China dream" is organically related to the "world dream" in which human beings enjoy a world "without wars and killings, starvation and poverty, with habitable environment. Achieving global justice is a basic requirement for this."[40] In his view, the popular theories of international justice rooted in Western culture lack a stable ethical foundation. Through criticizing Rawls's *The Law of Peoples,* he suggests that Chinese *tianxia* thinking could overcome three obstacles to global justice. *Tianxia* justice would eliminate the divide between oneself and others, us and them, so that everyone would be treated equally as an individual rather than differently according to membership of various groups, be it of their nations or races. It would reject all military conquests or interventions. It would adopt as its basis a thin version of Confucian humaneness (*ren* 仁), understood as "loving others." The concept of humaneness does not offer a unique distributive principle or way to resolve conflicts of interests. According to Shi, it would support the principles of Rawls's theory of justice being applied globally (although Rawls himself rejected that possibility in the *The Law of Peoples*). However, *ren* explains the source of our sense of justice.[41] Shi's *tianxia* conception of global justice endorses rather than challenges the substance of most Western cosmopolitan justice, while insisting that Chinese culture be allowed to make its distinctive and necessary contribution to the theorizing of global justice. If Mencius is right that all humans have the "sprout" of humaneness, and Confucian personal cultivation offers a way to realize that humaneness in people, then Confucianism could answer the motivation question better than most cosmopolitan theories of justice, which tend to neglect this in their almost exclusive focus on determining the distributive principles. What this implies is that, rather than abstractly thinking of the world as *tianxia,* cultivation of Confucian virtues, at least the "thin" form of *ren,* is necessary to motivate people to support and implement principles of justice on a global scale.

Given the importance of humaneness in Confucian ethics, it is uncontroversial to take it as the starting point for a Confucian theory of global distributive justice. The inspiration for Zhao's principle of Confucian improvement of maximization of reciprocal interests is the "method of *ren*" in *Analects* 6.30. Tu Wei-ming had previously cited this passage as the basis of "global core values," which other scholars have also recognized as a Confucian contribution to traditional Chinese *tianxia* thinking.[42] For Tu, the *Analects* passage pertains to individual ethical actions leading to *ren,* the primary disposition of an exemplary person, but could be extended into a principle for collective action. This passage and *Analects* 15.24, "Do not impose on others what you yourself do not want," elucidate the "principles of reciprocity and human flourishing," which Tu argued could help solve global distributive problems. Instead of invoking self-interest and security of individuals, they demand "a transfer of assets from the 'haves' to the 'have-nots' simply because of blatant inequality." Despite the self-other relation in these passages being nonspecific, it would be a mistake to think, as Shi seems to do, that Confucianism could be enlisted to support universal egalitarianism, which would mean that our ethical responsibilities to inhabitants of faraway lands are no different from our ethical responsibilities to our fellow citizens or even our family members. While reciprocity applies in all relationships and we have the responsibility to contribute to others' flourishing whenever it is possible to do so, different people have different claims on us, depending on their specific relationships with us; love or concern for others is gradated, justifiably stronger and more extensive for those closer to us. Such gradated love and concern are attentive to the particularity of others and their specific relationships to oneself even as they extend Confucian ethical responsibility to the global level and all humans (or even beyond the species boundary to animals and the environment). A Confucian conception of global distributive justice would probably be contextualist, that is, which scheme of distribution is justified would depend on cultural and other contexts, and what we owe our fellow citizens as a matter of justice would differ from what we owe other human beings.[43]

Tianxia as a Relational World

Translated as "the world," *tianxia* is a spatial concept defining or expanding the scope of Confucian ethical approaches to human relations. As such, its theoretical role in debates over global order is trivial, as the Confucian alternatives do not differ from Western cosmopolitan theories in spatial scope but in the nature of what constitutes global order and how it could be brought about. Confucian *tianxia* alternatives to global order as a moral or "just hierarchy" and critics targeting their hegemonic character focus on the structures of equality or inequality. In my view, Confucianism is not fixated on particular social or global structures, just as it is flexible about institutional arrangements. For Confucians, global order is constituted by harmonious relations among people at the global level. As Qin Yaqing (chapter 9 in this volume) argues, *tianxia* should not be merely a spatial concept; it should offer a different understanding of the world as constituted by human relations.

Qin argues that mainstream IR theories—structural realism, neoliberal institutionalism, and structural constructivism—share the culturally embedded assumptions of ontological individualism and epistemological rationalism.[44] Without denying the contribution of this worldview to intellectual inquiry and academic progress, Qin proposes an alternative Confucian worldview with relationality as its fundamental assumption. This relational world is "composed of continuous events and ongoing relations rather than substantial objects and discrete entities."[45] Its logic of human action is a logic of relationality, which contrasts with the logic of consequences and the logic of appropriateness based on instrumental or normative rationality.

In other words, the logic of relationality holds that an actor makes judgments and decisions according to their relationships to specific others, with the totality of their relational circles or contexts as the background. In any social setting, what action an actor is to take depends very much on their relationships with specific others and their relations with the relational contexts in which they are embedded. In other words, their interests, desires, and preferences, which motivate their actions, are not fixed. Rather they change as the nature of a relationship changes.[46]

In Qin's view, "*Tianxia* is thus a totality of relations in motion."[47] Qin's Confucian understanding of *tianxia* draws on the *yin–yang* dialectics of the *Zhongyong* to present a view of relations as fundamentally nonconflictual and harmonious, "supporting the belief that harmony is not only desirable, but also reachable, for it is the state where the world is in and of its true self."[48] This *tianxia* concept can ground a theory of global governance as relational governance to complement rule-based governance, in order to define or redefine interests of various kinds to promote cooperation instead of conflict.

While Qin does not touch on distributive justice, his conception of *tianxia* complements what I consider a Confucian approach to the problems of distribution and poverty addressed by Western theories of justice. I have argued that, instead of focusing on evaluating and guiding actions in terms of how to divide benefits and burdens, Confucians view distribution problems as ethical failures in relating to others, emphasizing the interactive processes that constitute human relationships, with the aim of improving those relationships. Instead of individuals conceived as separate units, relationships, particularly family relationships, are prominent in Confucian ethical discussions. Instead of deciding who should own what—determining the right division as a solution to individuals' competing claims to goods and resources—there is a preference for sharing, for working together to try to fulfill the needs of all. Dividing burdens and benefits is only one among many different considerations in how each person relates to others in a variety of relationships that constitute their social life. The central question of theories of distributive justice, "Who gets what?," is not the central question of Confucian social life. When distribution cannot be avoided, a particular distribution is acceptable, not because there is anything inherently right about one way of dividing goods and resources over others, but because it serves better in a specific context to nurture a thriving family or a harmonious community. Confucian solutions to distribution problems—which may or may not involve dividing benefits and burdens among individuals or groups—should promote the flourishing of an entire network of relationships that constitute a community.[49]

A Confucian response to the global problems of poverty and undesirable inequalities would begin with an understanding of the ethically appropriate relationship between rich and poor citizens of different countries. Rather than asserting the moral significance of common humanity or a priori human equality in the abstract to ground the obligation of the rich to give some of their wealth to the poor, regardless of nationality, Confucians would draw on the common human emotions of our attachment to those close to us, which motivate us to care for them, and extend the social relations that constitute our ethical selves beyond the intimate ties of family and kin. "All you have to do is take this very heart here and apply it to what is over there. Hence one who extends his bounty can tend those within the Four Seas; one who does not cannot tend even his own family" (*Mencius* 1A7).

Just as we could not bear our loved ones starving and suffering from poverty and would do everything in our power to prevent that, we should act to prevent others from suffering a similar fate. This follows from Confucius's teaching of reciprocity cited by Tu Wei-ming and others. The "ethical extension" of a person's relational network, which gives meaning to life and both offers opportunities to and constrains action, needs to adapt to a more complex globalizing world. Thinking in terms of concentric circles of family, state, and the world is too simplistic. Families today can be international in both spatial distribution and nationalities of members. Friends abroad are not necessarily less close in terms of attachment compared to people who happen to live next door. Some of us have neighbors of varied nationalities. However, "ethical extension" remains the Confucian relational ethics' answer to why and how one should help those less affluent than and not closely related to oneself, including the citizens of other countries with whom one has no direct interaction.

One of the most eloquent passages in the *Mencius* is his condemnation of King Hui of Liang for living in luxury while people under his rule starved: "There is fat meat in your kitchen and there are well-fed horses in your stables, yet the people look hungry, and in the outskirts of cities men drop dead from starvation. This is to lead the animals in the devouring of men" (*Mencius* 1A4). This rejection of inequalities with inhumane results has more general application. Any rich person who ignores the plight of the global poor is also guilty of "leading the animals in the devouring of men." Just as there is no difference between "killing a person with a knife and killing him with misrule" in the case of King Hui, Mencius would see no difference between allowing others to die by refusing to share one's wealth and killing them with a weapon. For the same reason, Confucians should oppose inequalities that deny a decent human life to the global poor, although Confucianism does not assume that human beings have equal moral worth that makes equality an intrinsic value and a universal ideal.

From a Confucian perspective, not only do governments have the responsibility to ensure those they govern have enough for physical survival and ethical life, but this responsibility must be extended to citizens of other countries so that good governance in one's state can extend to bringing "peace to All-under-Heaven." As that process described in the *Great Learning* begins with personal cultivation, which applies to everyone, each of us, and not just governments, has the responsibility of ensuring that those living in foreign countries, and not just our family members and fellow citizens, are not denied the chance to live ethically; only then can there be real peace for all. No one has enough resources or the capacity to ensure this for everyone in the world, but all of us can try our best to do this for as many people as possible, beginning with those we come into daily contact with, but insofar as we have the resources or influence over the use of our country's resources, we extend this support to others even beyond national and other boundaries.

International aid programs are common means to help the global poor in the current system. Unfortunately, they are often inefficient and sometimes ineffective in helping those who really need assistance because of political wrangling and selfish greed. For example, some countries have refused to contribute the share required of them by international aid agencies on the grounds that others are not contributing their fair share. While richer populations should bear correspondingly more of the costs of international aid, Confucians would not waste time quarrelling over the exact amount each party should pay. The emphasis would be on the responsibility of every country (just as it is for every person) doing what it can to help, because it is the ethical thing to do; not doing so is to lack the moral excellences of *ren* and *yi*. Others failing to do the right thing is never an excuse for one's own ethical failure, as Confucian teachings of personal cultivation require one to emulate exemplary conduct and examine oneself when confronted with unethical conduct to ensure that one is not guilty of the same (*Analects* 4.17). Nor should aid to the global poor primarily be carried out as transactions between governments. Indeed, experience has shown that high administrative costs and sometimes corruption can significantly diminish the effectiveness of such aid and willingness to contribute to such programs. Transnational networks could be established to facilitate more direct actions by nongovernmental groups (not necessarily established NGOs, which can be as bureaucratic as national governments) and enable private individuals to engage in direct assistance to those in need and to undertake projects that would lift people out of poverty in sustainable ways.

This relational ethical response to global distributive problems has implications for our reflections on global order. It emphasizes that, while political institutions need to change, our current dilemma requires a deeper cultural transformation that must involve every person's cultivation of humaneness. Beyond that, global order will need the strengthening of interdependence across national boundaries by building relationships embedded in ordinary people's daily lives. Such relationships will not give special consideration to nationality but attend instead to the specific activities and the responsibilities they generate for various participants. Rather than establishing some kind of world government, or some suzerain that could restrain itself from dominating other nation-states, this approach implies decentralization of both activities and power in the global arena and empowerment of ordinary people in activities of all kinds, not just overtly political actions.

Reflections on global order, whether Confucian or not, cannot ignore institutional problems. Current international institutions are very much in need of reform, as they seldom encourage the growth, in various contexts and at various levels, of transnational relational networks with Confucian ethical characteristics to replace or at least balance the hostilely competitive relationships that seem to be taking over people's lives in global capitalism as well as the realpolitik of international relations. Wholesale replacement of the international system is not likely to happen under current circumstances. Any attempt to do so is likely to involve coercion and, if successful, the outcome could be maintained probably only through hegemonic domination. One could try to bring about institutional reforms more gradually through more cooperative means, but the more important work for Confucians is to bring about the cultural transformation that will sustain harmonious social relationships across all boundaries. While the cultural transformation is no easier than the wholesale replacement or piecemeal reform of the international system, it is something that ordinary persons could contribute to in their own way, one project at a time. Only that cultural transformation could thoroughly transform world politics.

Notes

1. Peter Singer, "Famine, Affluence and Morality," *Philosophy and Public Affairs* 1, no. 3 (1972): 229–243.

2. Kok-Chor Tan provides a good philosophical introduction to the topic in *What Is This Thing Called Global Justice?* (New York: Routledge, 2017). For an overview of various theories and debates in the global justice discourse, see Thomas Pogge and Darrel Moellendorf, eds., *Global Justice: Seminal Essays*, 2 vols. (St. Paul, MN: Paragon House, 2008). See also Gillian Brock, "Global Justice," in the *Stanford Encyclopedia of Philosophy*, last updated Summer 2022, https://plato.stanford.edu/entries/justice-global/#Aca; and the journal *Global Justice: Theory Practice Rhetoric,* https://www.theglobaljusticenetwork.org/index.php/gjn.

3. William A. Callahan, "Tianxia, Empire, and the World," in *China Orders the World: Normative Soft Power and Foreign Policy,* ed. William A. Callahan and Elena Barabantseva (Washington, DC: Woodrow Wilson Center Press, 2011); Itty Abraham, "Tianxia: A Distinctly Chinese Vision of Global Hegemony," *Economic and Political Weekly,* June 20, 2015, https://www.epw.in/journal/2015/25/stratrgic-affairs/tianxia-distinctly-chinese-vision-global-hegemony.html.

4. Chun-shu Chang, *The Rise of the Chinese Empire* (Ann Arbor: University of Michigan Press, 2007), p. 34.

5. Mencius, *Mencius,* trans. D. C. Lau (Harmondsworth, UK: Penguin, 1970), 2A6, 3B5, and 4A6.

6. Wang Yongping 王永平, 從 '天下' 到 '世界': 漢唐時期的中國與世界 (From *"tianxia"* to "world": China and the world during Han and Tang dynasties) (Beijing: China Social Sciences Press, 2015), p. 7.

7. Apart from actual practice, the works of Confucian thinkers also are not completely free from ethnocentrism, although Confucian philosophy also has resources to question and resist it. See Sor-hoon Tan, "Cultural Crossings against Ethnocentric Currents: Toward a Confucian Ethics of Communicative Virtues," *International Philosophical Quarterly* 45, no. 4 (2005): 433–445; Sor-hoon Tan, "Cosmopolitan Confucian Cultures: Suggestions for Future Research and Practice," *Journal of International Communication of Chinese Culture* 2, no. 3 (2015): 159–180.

8. For a more detailed discussion of the problem arising from the mixing of normative and descriptive meanings of *tianxia*, see Sor-hoon Tan, "Nationalistic Guo, Cosmopolitan Tianxia?," in *Reimagining Nation and Nationalism in Multicultural East Asia*, ed. Sungmoon Kim and Hsin-wen Lee (New York: Routledge, 2017), pp. 65–66.

9. Tingyang Zhao, *Redefining a Philosophy for World Governance* (Singapore: Springer, 2019), pp. 9–14.

10. Zhao, *Redefining a Philosophy*, p. 18.

11. Zhao, *Redefining a Philosophy*, pp. 6–7.

12. Zhao, *Redefining a Philosophy*, p. 17.

13. Zhao, *Redefining a Philosophy*, p. 41. Cf. Feng Zhang, *Chinese Hegemony* (Stanford, CA: Stanford University Press, 2015); David Kang, *East Asia before the Rest* (New York: Columbia University Press, 2012); Daniel A. Bell and Pei Wang, *Just Hierarchy* (Princeton, NJ: Princeton University Press, 2020).

14. Jun-Hyeok Kwak, "Global Justice without Self-centrism: *Tianxia* in *Dialogue on Mount Uisan*," *Dao* 20, no. 2 (2021): 292.

15. Kwak, "Global Justice," p. 304.

16. Zhao, *Redefining a Philosophy*, p. 41.

17. Zhao, *Redefining a Philosophy*, p. 24.

18. Zhao, *Redefining a Philosophy*, p. 23.

19. Zhao, *Redefining a Philosophy*, p. 29.

20. Zhao, *Redefining a Philosophy*, p. 33.

21. Zhao, *Redefining a Philosophy*, p. 34.

22. Zhao, *Redefining a Philosophy*, p. 32.

23. For an example of recent studies of cultural exchanges between the Chinese and other civilizations, see Wang, 從'天下'到'世界' (From "tianxia" to "world").

24. Zhao, *Redefining a Philosophy*, p. 38.

25. Zhao, *Redefining a Philosophy*, p. 39.

26. Guo Yi 郭沂, 從古代中國的天下一體看當代全球化趨勢 (Contemporary globalization trends from the perspective of ancient Chinese All-under-Heaven as one entity), 哲學動態 (*Philosophical Trends*), no. 9 (2006): 22.

27. Hu Jian 胡鍵, 天下秩序：一種文化意象 (*Tianxia* order: A kind of cultural imagery), 社會科學文摘 (*Social Science Digest*), no. 12 (2017): 22.

28. Hu, 天下秩序 (*Tianxia* order), p. 24. For a balanced account of different dynasties' complex and debated handling of frontier relations, see Rosita Dellios and R. James Ferguson, *China's Quest for Global Order: From Peaceful Rise to Harmonious World* (Lanham, MD: Lexington Books, 2013), chapter 3.

29. Zhao, *Redefining a Philosophy*, p. 2.

30. Chen Tingxiang 陳廷湘 and Zhou Ding 周鼎, 天下世界國家：近代中國對外觀念演變史論 (*Tianxia*, the world, and the state: The history of the development of modern China's concept of foreign relations) (Shanghai: Sanlian, 2008), p. 294 (author's translation).

31. Zhao, *Redefining a Philosophy*, pp. 58–60.

32. Zhao offered this clarification during the conference.

33. David M. McCourt, "Practice Theory and Relationalism as the New Constructivism," *International Studies Quarterly* 60, no. 3 (September 2016): 475–485.

34. Zhao, *Redefining a Philosophy*, pp. 8–9.

35. Zhao, *Redefining a Philosophy*, pp. 60–61. Cf. "Authoritative persons establish others in seeking to establish themselves and promote others in seeking to get there themselves." In Roger T. Ames and Henry Rosemont Jr., trans., *The Analects of Confucius: A Philosophical Translation* (New York: Ballantine, 1998).

36. At the conference, Zhao clarifies that his intention was not to reject the ethical, but to emphasize the need for political-economic changes in order to realize the Confucian ethical ideal, and that the political move is more fundamental, given disagreements over the ethical.

37. Gan Chunsong 干春松, "世界和諧之願景：中庸與儒家的天下觀念 (The aspiration of world harmony: *Doctrine of the Mean* and the Confucian concept of tianxia), 學術月刊 (*Academic Monthly*) 40, no. 9 (2008): 48. For Gan's study of the relationship between the Confucian ethical ideals in traditional texts and Chinese historical political institutions and social realities, and its lessons for contemporary times, see Gan Chunsong 干春松, 制度儒學 (Institutional Confucianism) (Shanghai: Shanghai People's Press, 2006).

38. Gan, 世界和諧之願景 (Aspiration of world harmony), p. 50.

39. Gan, 世界和諧之願景 (Aspiration of world harmony), p. 52.

40. Shi Yongzhi 石永之, "中國夢與世界夢：從天下正義到全球正義" (China dream and world dream: From *Tianxia* justice to global justice), 管子學刊 (*Guanzi Journal*), no. 2 (2014): 73.

41. Shi, "中國夢與世界夢" (China dream and world dream), p. 74.

42. Tu Wei-ming, "Core Values and the Possibility of a Fiduciary Global Community," in *Restructuring for World Peace: On the Threshold of the Twenty-First Century*, ed. Katharine Tehranian and Majid Tehranian (Cresskill, NJ: Hampton Press, 1992), pp. 333–345; Chen Hongyan 陳鴻燕 and Zhao Dan 趙丹, 中國人的世界觀：對天下觀念的思考 (Chinese worldview: Reflection on the *tianxia* concept), 大慶師範學院學報 (*Journal of Daqing Normal University*) 28, no. 4 (2007): 27.

43. Cf. David Miller, *National Responsibility and Global Justice* (Oxford: Oxford University Press, 2007).

44. Yaqing Qin, *A Relational Theory of World Politics* (New York: Cambridge University Press, 2018), chapter 4.

45. Qin, *Relational Theory*, p. 108.

46. Qin, *Relational Theory*, pp. 207–208.

47. See Qin Yaqing, "*Tianxia*: A Process of Relations," chapter 9 in this volume.

48. Qin, "*Tianxia*."

49. Sor-hoon Tan, "The Concept of *Yi* (義) in the *Mencius* and Problems of Distributive Justice," *Australasian Journal of Philosophy* 92, no. 3 (2014): 489–505.

CHAPTER 14

Heavenly Governing All-under-Heaven

Reconceptualizing the Confucian *Daren* 大人 Idea for the *Tianxia* 天下 Leadership

Xinfeng KONG

1

What was first described by Samuel Huntington in the 1990s as the "clash of civilizations" seems to have become a prophecy of the "new normal" of international politics in the post–Cold War period as the politics of identity is profoundly reshaping the epistemic accounts of how modern politics approach different groups.[1] As Harold R. Isaacs comments, "the more global our science and technology, the more tribal our politics . . . the closer we get to other planets, the less able we become to lead a tolerable existence on our own."[2] It is of great realistic importance for modern thinkers to return to the classical world of the Axial Age, and even the pre-Axial Age, and to revisit the wisdom of the ancient philosophers on the governance of the "world." As Zheng Kai 鄭開 observes, "Reflecting on the great spiritual creation of the ancient sages thousands of years ago, and the possibility of genocide and extermination existing in the so-called 'civilized world' today, we can't help but feel ashamed: can't the spiritual creation of the ancient people continue to serve as the source of the political wisdom that has been almost exhausted today?"[3]

An example of such an effort is the proposal of a *tianxia* system in the early years of the twenty-first century when Zhao Tingyang 趙汀陽 first proposed the theory.[4] It has since received increasing academic attention and enrichment from the fields of China studies and international relations. This chapter is a similar effort to fill some theoretical and methodological gaps in the current academic discussions of the *tianxia* (All-under-Heaven) theories. On the one hand, what is often missing from such discussions is the identity and qualification (the source of "natural leadership") of the governor and leader of *tianxia*; in other words, who should be governing the *tianxia* system? On the other hand, the current discussion of *tianxia* is often constrained by a reductionist view of the term itself, which calls for a philosophical reconceptualization of several pre-Qin Confucian concepts that are relevant to *tianxia*, including *tian* 天, *de* 德, *junzi* / *daren* 君子 / 大人, and *tianxia* itself, in their original historical context with special attention paid to the earlier periods and of the Hundred Schools of Thought.

2

Before delving into the idea of *tianxia*, it is necessary to explore the concept of *tian* / Heaven. According to Feng Youlan's 馮友蘭 classical analysis, *tian* / Heaven could be conceptualized at five different levels: the Heaven as nature 自然之天, the Heaven as material 物質之天, the Heaven as destiny 運命之天, the Heaven as domination 主宰之天, and the Heaven as righteousness 義理之天.[5] According to the discourses in the *Shang Shu* (尚書), the two concepts that have the most profound impact on the Confucian idea of *daren* are the Heaven as domination and the Heaven as righteousness. After the House of Zhou 周朝 continued to secularize and rationalize their governance, they transformed the abstract idea of Heaven as domination into the ultimate source of political legitimacy in the secular sense, meanwhile gradually stripping away the dominant role of Heaven and elevating the role of secular men in political life.

Chinese philosophy in the pre-Qin period witnessed a transformation from the "Order of the *di*" 帝令觀 in the Shang dynasty to the "Order of the *tian*" 天命觀 in the Western Zhou dynasty. In his examination of the evidence from oracle bone script, Herlee Creel found that the term *di* 帝 obviously refers to the supreme god for Shang people as well as an important deity to whom they offered sacrifice; in comparison, the term *tian* is rarely mentioned in the Shang script and has nothing to do with the sacrifice practice. For the peripheral Zhou people, however, *tian* / Heaven was initially the supreme god whom they worshipped. Both the term *tian* and the term *di* appear in the Chinese characters on bronze inscriptions in the Zhou dynasty, with the former appearing far more frequently than the latter.[6]

It should be noted that the *di* of the Shang people has been determined to be their "clan deity," namely the ancestor of their own group. The *tian* of the Zhou people, however, was a much more detached and broader concept that transcended the boundaries among different clans. The scope of the perception of supreme gods, in this sense, highlights a significant difference in the religious traditions of the Shang and Zhou dynasties.[7] The belief of the people in the concept of *tianxia* is indeed derived from the process of "degodification" or disenchantment of *tian* / Heaven and the elevation of the role of secular men in the governance of *tianxia*. Philologists have shown that Heaven (*tian* 天) and greatness (*da* 大) were interchangeable Chinese characters in ancient times. In addition, abundant evidence can be found in several pre-Qin Confucian classical texts that *daren* had come to reference *tianren* 天人 / *tianmin* 天民 / the heavenly human beings, who are by definition those most capable of performing the heavenly virtues. Therefore, the concepts of *daren* (the great human) and *tianren* (the heavenly human beings) are interchangeable in the original discussion of *tianxia* governance in Confucian classics.[8]

In this respect, pre-Qin Confucian philosophy developed a holistic discourse that unifies the Heaven and human with the concept of *de* 德. In this discourse, those capable of governing with heavenly *de* / *aretē* are identified as the governors of *tianxia*, who in Confucian terminology are conceptualized as *tianren* or *daren*. The core logic of this discourse can be summarized as follows: (1) a conceptualization of *de* is the epistemological foundation of the idea of Heaven; (2) a commonly understood concept of Heaven is the basis of any discussion on *tianxia*; (3) the recognition and adoption of *de* constitutes the defining feature of *daren*; and (4) being able to govern with heavenly *de* serves as the very source of the legitimacy for *daren* to bring peace to All-under-Heaven.

If we return to the ideal of *tianxia* governance in Confucian theories, we can find in-depth and profound discussions on the relevance of the idea of *daren* to the governance of *tianxia*. What is believed to be one of the oldest classical statements in history comes from the *Book of Changes* (易經):

> The great man (*daren*) is he who is in harmony, in his attributes (*de*), with heaven and earth; in his brightness, with the sun and moon; in his orderly procedure, with the four seasons; and in his relation to what is fortunate and what is calamitous, in harmony with the spirit-like operations (of Providence). He may precede Heaven, and Heaven will not act in opposition to him; he may follow Heaven, but will act (only) as Heaven at the time would do. If Heaven will not act in opposition to him, how much less will men! how much less will the spirit-like operation (of Providence)![9]

The "sixteen-character spiritual legacy of sage kings" (*shiliuzixinchuan* 十六字心傳) believed to be passed down between the sage kings (first from Yao to Shun, then from Shun to Yu) as a "political testament" recorded in the *Shang Shu* was indeed another testimony to the ideal qualities owned by the *daren*: "The mind of man is restless, prone to err; its affinity to what is right is small. Be discriminating, be uniform in the pursuit of what is right, that you may sincerely hold fast to the Mean."[10] Similar to the previous quotation from the *Book of Changes*, Xunzi defines *daren* as follows: "Brightness comparable to the Sun and Moon; greatness filling the Eight Poles—such a person is truly what is meant by 'Great Man.'"[11]

Wang Yangming 王陽明, a master of Neo-Confucianism in the Ming dynasty, also made a classic definition of *daren* in his elucidation of *daren*'s defining trait of "illustrating the illustrious virtue" (*mingmingde* 明明德): "Somebody humbly asked: 'Could you please tell me why the *Great Learning* lies in "to illustrate illustrious virtue"?' Master Yangming answered: 'The Great Man is whoever takes everything in Heaven and Earth as one body, regards All-under-Heaven as one family, and the Central Kingdom as one man.'"[12]

Another concept that is often viewed as synonymous with *daren* yet is discussed far more frequently in academia is the idea of *junzi* 君子. In this chapter, I would adopt the opinion of Zhang Yaonan 张耀南 on the relationship between *daren* and *junzi* that these are essentially interchangeable concepts: "The personality of *junzi* is in essence the same as the personality of *daren*, which is the antonym of *xiaoren* 小人; the fundamental meaning of *junzi* is 'greatness.'"[13] Another convincing perspective on this issue is that although both *daren* and *junzi* describe the quality and state of life of the sages in the Confucian discourse, the idea of *junzi* puts an emphasis on gentleness and tolerance, whereas the idea of *daren* highlights the greatness and loftiness of their lives.[14]

Before Confucius made the great ideological reform of "matching one's *de* with his position" (*yidepeiwei* 以德配位) and even "qualifying one's position based on his *de*" (*yidezhiwei* 以德致位), the pre-Qin China philosophers mostly associated *daren* with sage kings and *junzi*, who we defined at that time as people of noble blood (*junzi* had been once understood literally as "sons of nobles") and were therefore qualified for political positions under the *fengjian* 封建 system. It was not until the Eastern Han dynasty that the term *junzi* was ultimately defined by the imperial court as "a moral name" (*daodezhicheng* 道德之稱).[15] Throughout the history of imperial China, the element of "political position" has always been retained in the conceptualization of *daren*, but it is not necessarily limited to the high-ranking officials and the nobles. Rather, *daren* in theory should feature several virtues including ambition, self-discipline, respect for the political order, integrity, and courage, and it is the idea that unifies elements of political position, education, virtue, and political practice. The greatness of *daren* lies in the fact that *daren* transcends the boundaries of the self, the bloodline, and even the race, but rather assumes the political responsibility of governing plural groups under the unity of mutually shared virtues.

3

The previous section offers a brief outline of the Confucian idea of *daren;* at its core, *daren* (which has a singular quality but can apply to multiple persons) is defined as those most capable of governing with heavenly *aretē / de*. Thus, there is a dual relationship between the *tianxia* / All-under-Heaven and the *daren*. First, *daren* should prioritize *tianxia* over their own being, their family, their hometown, and their country; they should assume the political responsibility to "extend the way and illustrate illustrious virtue to the whole world" (*mingmingdeyutianxia* 明明德于天下). Second, being able to govern with heavenly *aretē / de* serves as the very source of the legitimacy for *daren* to bring peace to All-under-Heaven (*pingzhitianxia* 平治天下). As the concept of *aretē / de* constitutes the key component of the holistic theory of *daren*, it is extremely necessary for us to revisit the original meanings and implications of *aretē / de* in the context of the pre-Qin Confucianism.

After exhausting most relevant research on the conceptualization of *de,* I choose to incorporate the viewpoints of Zou Xiaodong 鄒曉東 and Si Weizhi 斯維至 as well as adopt the approach taken by Zheng Kai in his above-mentioned research on political thought prior to the Hundred Schools of Thought period, and I identify two possible ancient meanings of the Chinese term *de* in the pre-Axial Age:

1. *de* as "to seek / strive for" (verb);
2. *de* as "life / nature / clan name" (noun).

Both meanings stand in stark contrast to the modern understandings of *de,* which often refer to concepts including morality, ethics, and mentality. They are also different from the interpretations of *de* during the Axial Age when *de* is frequently used as a key concept in theories of classical virtues. Nevertheless, tracing the conceptualization of *de* back to its earliest meanings—which have been obscured by historical and semantic changes over thousands of years—would significantly inspire our discussion on *tianxia* today.

Chinese historian Wang Guowei 王國維 famously claimed that "the rise and fall of the Yin and Zhou dynasties constituted the most significant change that ever happened to Chinese politics and culture."[16] The core of such a revolution, Wang argued, was the institutionalization of a ritual system during the Western Zhou period as an expression of *de*. The Zhou ritual system, with *de* as its ethos, directly laid the conceptual foundation for a grand unification that unified different groups along the hierarchy, from the emperor to the commoners, into a community with moral identity, and therefore became a fundamental component of the civilizing process of *junzi*.[17] Under such an effort at unification, the "virtue-based community" is in essence some kind of political and cultural community, as the institutionalization of the ritual system during the Western Zhou dynasty established the political tradition of "governing by virtue" also known as "the Kingly Way" (*wangdao* 王道) in later generations.[18]

However, although scholars have earnestly endeavored to find the exact meaning of the ancient Chinese character *de* in the oracle bone script and bronze inscriptions during the past one hundred or more years, "philological materials and methods are not yet enough to illustrate the earliest meanings of *de*."[19] It can be said that the concept of *de* in the pre-Axial-Age China has become a major issue in the academic circles of contemporary Sinology. According to Zheng Kai, *de* as ethos played a central role and became the "collective thought" in pre-Axial-Age China. In order to make it easier for modern people to understand the concept of *de* in Yin and Zhou China, Zheng Kai put it together with the ancient Greek word *aretē* (in Latin: *virtus*), believing that the two are "very similar to each other, and their fate in the history of thought is also the same." "Most people believe that the Chinese phrase *dexing* 德性 is quite properly used to translate the ancient Greek philosophical concept *aretē*."[20] In this regard, "The pre-Qin Chinese and ancient Greek philosophers were very similar in their treatments of *de* and *aretē*."[21] The ancient Greeks called the performance and specialty of things *aretē*, which vaguely encapsulated the meanings of "essence / nature" and "good." When we talk about ancient virtues today, we tend intuitively to keep only the sense of "goodness," or even to understand them simply as virtues or moralities, while largely forgetting the "essence / nature" meaning of *de* and *aretē*.

Therefore, we must have a sound understanding of what the ancient *de* meant. Taiwanese historian Huang Mingchong 黃銘崇 points out that "the concept of *de*, according to the context of the bronze inscriptions analysis, ... is something that has been passed down in clans and families through the ages."[22] According to another modern Chinese historian, Li Zongtong 李宗侗, the earliest concept of *de* refers to "clan / family names," or *mana*: "In fact *mana* is what Chinese people understand as *xing* 性, and *xing* 姓 as well."[23] Si Weizhi further determined the earliest meaning of *de* to be "life" (*sheng* 生).[24] In this way, we can better understand why there are so many sayings in pre-Qin classics such as "the greatest *de* (attribute / virtue) of Heaven and Earth is called *sheng*" and "those who have great *de* (attributes / virtues) definitely will achieve great success and fulfillment." Another Taiwanese historian, Wang Jianwen 王健文, has made a detailed analysis of the word *de* in classical Chinese politics. Wang thinks that its original meaning is the "holy nature of a certain clan / tribe" and that the specific content can be explained through "ethnic tradition," "ancestral clan *nomos*," "a dynasty's founding spirit," and so on. Those who have *de* as a "sacred attribute" can rightfully own land, people, and authority. But since the Spring and Autumn period, *de* has most often been used in the context of morality and goodness. Wang named the former usage as *dexing* 德性 or *de* as essence or nature, and the latter as *dexing* 德行 or *de* as good manners and morality.[25] The creators or founders of some certain political order or dynasty earned their supremacy by the possession and implementation of *dexing* 德性 (*de* as essence or nature) while the successors to them should maintain their supremacy by the loyal inheritance and imitation of the *de* of their ancestors, which is called *dexing* 德行 (*de* as good manners and morality). The "virtuous" deeds of the founders were initially carried out in history and gradually became governing doctrines or constitutional laws for their descendants, and this phenomenon in turn created the Chinese *jingshi* 經史 tradition of classical canons and historical records—the unification and transformity of the history of the founding fathers with the governing philosophies of the descendants.[26]

Zou Xiaodong of Shandong University further revisits the historical and social context of the ancient *de* in detailed studies of some of the inscriptions discovered on the oracle bones, and he illustrates effectively the process or dynamic meaning of *de* as "to seek / to strive for" during the Shang dynasty. He believes the character *de* on the bronze inscriptions inherited the same meaning as the character *de* on the oracle bone inscriptions and in the ancient texts that have been preserved and handed down to the present.[27]

4

As discussed above, the original meanings of the ancient Chinese character *de* could be both "life / nature / clan name" and "to seek / to strive for." Thus, the essential *de* of *tian* (heavenly *aretē*) is "life" and "to let live," or as the *Book of Changes* states: "The great attribute of heaven and earth is the giving and maintaining life. What is most precious for the sage is to get the highest place (in which he can be the human representative of heaven and earth). What will guard this position for him? Men. How shall he collect a large population round him? By the power of his wealth. The right administration of that wealth, correct instructions to the people, and prohibitions against wrongdoing; all of these constitute his righteousness."[28]

Therefore, the utmost *aretē* for the heavenly virtuous *daren* with the highest place is nothing else but selflessness, which Confucius elaborated upon as the so-called three selflessnesses (*sanwusi* 三無私) of the Heaven, the Earth, and the Sun and Moon.[29] Thus, a *daren* should model himself on the Way and obey the Law of the Heaven. In his answer to Duke Ai of Kingdom Lu, Confucius listed several attributes of the Heaven, such as perpetuity (*buyi* 不已), openness (*bubi* 不閉), spontaneity (*wuwei* 無為), and accessibility (*yichenger-*

ming 已成而明). As the famous opening sentences of *Focusing the Familiar* or *Doctrine of the Great Mean* (*Zhongyong* 中庸) state:

> What *tian* commands is called natural tendencies; drawing out these tendencies is called the proper way 道; improving upon this way is called education.[30]

Toward this end, the Confucian *daren* or *junzi* may attain the goal of governing *tianxia* via the following route:

> Thus, the proper way of this ruler is rooted in his own person, is corroborated by the ordinary people, and is compared with the way of the Three Legendary Sage Kings so there is no mistake. Established between the heavens and the earth, this way does not run contrary to their operations. Confirmed before the gods and spirits, no doubts attend it. Having waited one hundred generations for the appearance of the sage, there are no second thoughts. Confirming this way before the gods and spirits so there is no doubt about it, is to know *tian;* having waited one hundred generations for the appearance of the sage so there are no second thoughts, is to know the human. It is for this reason that this ruler moves and generations take his conduct as a way for the world, acts and generations take his actions as a model for the world, speaks and generations take what he says as the norm for the world. Those at a distance look to him in expectation; those close by never weary of him.[31]

The Way of the Heaven is not far from the human. The thoughts and actions of the *daren* mentioned above in chapter 29 of *Focusing the Familiar* (or *Doctrine of the Mean*) have a two-way process. Firstly, these thoughts and actions are "rooted in his own person," which means *daren* are those people who have proved to be good students of Heaven by taking good care of and actualizing their own innate human nature blessed by the Heaven. Secondly, all of their deeds and actions are for the people All-under-Heaven and naturally get the support and loyalty of the people, with the *daren* themselves becoming not only the governors but also the tutors of the people. What is more, the ancient meaning of *de* as "to seek / to strive for" and "holy innate nature" is quite similar to the *aretē* of the ancient Greek philosophers in being an epistemic theory, emphasizing the prudential or *phronesis* aspect of the *tianxia* governance. "Governing *tianxia*" is not something purely and vainly idealistic but is based on solid, realistic political considerations.

So far I have reconceptualized the Confucian *daren* heavenly governing of All-under-Heaven. However, I have to add something more with an invitation to my readers to revisit the historical context of the fall of the House of Shang and the rise of the Western Zhou dynasty (*YinZhouzhibian* 殷周之變) in order to find something valuable for contemporary discussions on the governance of *tianxia*.

If we adopt the ancient meaning of *de* and interpret it as "life / nature / clan name," then virtue should be a natural attribute owned by each and every entity and ethnic group over the world; in other words, the most important aspect of virtue is the *de* of creating and maintaining life (*shengshengzhide* 生生之德). Therefore, although a *daren* is born as having various identities by nature, he is also transcendental in nature because the notion of All-under-Heaven itself acknowledges the multicultural attribute of the world. This acknowledgment is well manifested in the traditional Confucian classics and can again be traced back to the early history of the rise of Zhou. Western Zhou was a peripheral city-state, small in size and marginalized in terms of the broader civilization. Therefore, upon the conquest of the Shang dynasty, the new regime inevitably faced the challenge of governing the vast land and heterogeneous people, and it had to find a viable way to include all the various groups under Heaven in order to overthrow the existing order and to establish a new one. As pointed out by Huang Mingchong,

> Facing the enemy much bigger in size over a long time, the Zhou people had to unite with all non-Shang groups to fight against the Shang. Consequently, although the valiant Zhou army was certainly cruel to the enemy during the war (as can be seen from the number of deaths of the enemy in the battles), the Zhou regime was fairly lenient and generous towards its ally states. The army did not treat the prisoners of war with violence. Compared with the Shang Dynasty . . . the Zhou people were magnanimous. Under such circumstances, the Zhou people had developed the idea of ethnic equality, and adopted a quite tolerant and respectful mentality towards the long-existing clans residing in the Yellow River area [the so-called virtue of respect for others: *jingde* 敬德].[32]

Political elites in the Zhou dynasty managed to transform their own specific political and cultural attributes—namely using heavenly *de* as the basis for governance—into a more universal political discourse that allowed them to not only unite allies in war but also establish legitimacy in peace. At the core of this discourse was the construction of a set of heavenly virtues under the patriarchal and feudal systems. The ruling house instituted both systems to establish a hierarchy while successfully preserving the openness and mobility of the order of *tianxia*. As the *Commentary of Zuo* (左傳) depicts vividly:

> When the Son of Heaven would ennoble the virtuous, he gives them surnames from their birthplaces [or the birthplaces of their ancestors]; he rewards them with territory, and the name of it becomes their clan-name. The princes again confer the clan-name from the designation of the grandfather, or from his honorary title. Or when merit has been displayed in one office by members of the same family for generations, the name of that office may become the clan-name, or the name of the city held by the family may become so.³³

Another account in the *Commentary of Zuo* reports on the significance of both systems as follows:

> I have heard that in the setting up of States and clans, in order to the security of the parent State, while its root is large, the branches must be small. Therefore, the Son of Heaven establishes States; princes of States establish clans. Heads of clans establish collateral families; great officers have their secondary branches; officers have their sons and younger brothers as their servants; and the common people, mechanics and traders, have their different relative of various degrees. In this way the people serve their superiors, and inferiors cherish no ambitious designs.³⁴

Upon the conquest of the Shang dynasty, the House of Zhou was famous for its philosophy of governance in seeking "to illustrate *de* and be careful in the use of punishments" (*mingdeshenfa* 明德慎罰), a philosophy of great practical significance in the context of *tianxia*. As pointed out by Si Weizhi, the polarity of punishment-based and *de*-based governance in fact marks the ethnic division between the "in-group" and the "out-group." *De* is only applied to people of the same identity as the ruler, whereas punishment applies to people of other identity groups. Therefore, a ruler will rule by virtue if a member of his own ethnic group commits a crime but will punish the people of other ethnic groups with brutal corporal punishment or even wage war.³⁵ This was just as Isocrates appealed to the king of Macedonia to bring together the Greeks by means of persuasive and rhetorical devices but to coerce the barbarians with force: "It is through *de* the people of the Central States are cherished; it is through severity that the wild tribes around are awed (*deyirouzhongguo, xingyiweisiyi* 德以柔中國, 刑以威四夷)."³⁶

By contrast, the House of Zhou did not wipe out all remnants of their former enemy—the Yin people of the Shang dynasty—but rather appeased them with the *fengjian* 封建 institutions. This initiative not only ensured the longevity of the Zhou dynasty but also introduced the Chinese political traditions of "cherishing men from afar" (*huairouyuanren* 懷柔遠人) and divide and rule. This unusual strategy of statecraft, as Zheng Kai puts it, reflects the maturity of the political philosophy and the superb quality of the political institutions in Western Zhou.[37]

Another inspiring philosophy of governance of the House of Zhou in its early days was its effort to allow the survival of the House of Yin and other former lords of *tianxia*'s descendants (*cunwangxujue* 存亡續絕). The political impact of this decision on the Zhou dynasty has been remembered in the *Analects* of Confucius: "He revived states that had been extinguished, restored families whose line of succession had been broken, and called to office those who had retired into obscurity, so that throughout the kingdom the hearts of the people turned towards him."[38] With the winner of the war putting an end to the other regime but not eliminating the loser's bloodline, and the loser of the war vacating merely his power but retaining his offspring, this initiative could be seen as a moderate distinction between the political-military concept of the state and the cultural-religious concept of the nation based on a political humanitarianism. In addition, it also constituted an important source of secular rationalism in ancient China and thus laid the foundation for the highly inclusive and cohesive "Chinese civilization" and the widely accepted "consensus as the ideal of *tianxia*." The historical significance of this initiative, in the words of Zheng Kai, lies in its ability to

> win the hearts of the people politically and continue the theory of the *de*-based Mandate of Heaven. As a result, the political rationality of the Western Zhou Dynasty was brought into being, and a mode of *de*-oriented rather than power-oriented philosophies and patterns of governance was incubated. Its political rationality and model of governance enabled the Western Zhou Dynasty to continuously expand its political territory and to promote national integration that led to the prototype of the Chinese nation. It was the building block of the formation of "Chinese consciousness" and the Chinese nation, as well as the foundation of the ideological and cultural tradition formed in the pre-Axial Age and that prospered in the Axial Age. This type of political and cultural tradition is still relevant today.[39]

The idea and practice of governing with heavenly *aretē* established the characteristics of civilization, peace, tolerance, and resilience of "Chineseness" as its political identity. Japanese-Chinese scholar Wang Ke 王柯 once put forward a theory of the "triple dichotomies of *tianxia*," identifying it as the origin of the perception of China as a unified multiethnic state. The so-called triple dichotomies of *tianxia* refer to the dichotomies between the ideal and realistic *tianxia* ("within the Four Seas" vs. "Nine Grand Islands"), between the "internal clan" and "extended families" (the foundation of *tianxia* as a hierarchy), and between the "Middle Kingdom" and the "Four Barbarians" (*tianxia* as the Sinicization process of Chinese civilization).[40] Wang points out that an in-depth reading of the idea of *tianxia* helps to explain why throughout history, the Chinese have always been seeking for the establishment of a multiethnic nation-state, and why they have always believed that the only acceptable form of *tianxia* would be a multiethnic one.[41]

Since the Western Zhou, the history of China is a history in which *tianxia* as an idea has expanded in size, in space, and in the plurality of group identity. "China" is not merely a concept of spatial geography but is also a highly civilized concept of subjectivity and a people's self-awareness of living in such space. All who live in this space, who share the idea of "China," and who identify themselves through a minimal ideal of a civilizational-political order, can be identified as Chinese. By the same logic, the modern world as a community with a shared future for mankind can also be understood as a historical subject that has been shaped through the unity of pluralism developed in history, with the pluralism under the unity of globally shared virtues and values transcending the boundaries of race and bloodline.

What is more, one corollary thesis that has not been yet fully expressed concerning the meaning of "*tianxia*" governance is the awakening of humanism and the replacement of "religion" (*zongjiao* 宗教) by "education" (*jiaoyu* 教育) in the Yin–Zhou transition. Moving from religion to education is the way to extend *tianxia* and avoid violent interethnic conflict, and this is also the way to cultivate *daren* who govern *tianxia*. Huang Mingchong points out that the cultural dissemination of the Shang dynasty was mainly achieved on the basis of the exchange of goods, while the Western Zhou dynasty achieved its purpose of cultural dissemination through education. One of the significant achievements of the Yin–Zhou transition was the replacement of ancient religion and shamanism by the new education. In other words, the original order of "Politics-Religion-Economy" in the Shang dynasty was replaced by "Politics-Education-Economy" in the Western Zhou dynasty. It can be said that as early as three thousand years ago, if we take Mesopotamia and the Mediterranean area of the Western world as models, China had already developed a quite "modern" model in world history. Due to this early example of a "local modernity," the transition from Yin to Zhou has real significance in the history of the world and the history of human civilization that we must, definitely and with some urgency, revisit.

To this end, I would like to summarize this chapter by citing the anthropologist and sociologist Fei Xiaotong 费孝通, who has famously said, "Cherish your own values, and respect the values of others; when both are respected and cherished, the world will become one harmonized and unified *Tianxia*" (*Gemeiqimei, meirenzhimei, meimeiyugong, tianxiadatong* 各美其美，美人之美，美美

與共，天下大同). These words perfectly echo the conceptualization of *tianxia* in the pre-Qin period and show that the Confucian-based discourse can still shed some light on global governance in the modern world.

Notes

1. Samuel P. Huntington, "The Clash of Civilizations?," *Foreign Affairs* 72, no. 3 (Summer 1993): 22–49.

2. Harold R. Isaacs, *Idols of the Tribe: Group Identity and Political Change* (New York: Harper and Row, 1975), p. 2.

3. Zheng Kai, *Between Virtue and Li: The History of Thought in the Period of the Former Masters* (Beijing: SDX Joint Publishing Company, 2009), p. 109: "遙想數千年以前古代聖賢的偉大精神創造，反觀今日'文明世界'里仍然存在著種族屠殺與滅絕的危險，我們不禁深自愧嘆：難道古代先民的精神創造不能給今天已趨於枯竭的政治智慧掘開源頭活水麼？"

4. Zhao Tingyang 趙汀陽, "天下體系：帝國與世界制度" (*Tianxia* system: Empire and the world system), 世界哲學 (*World Philosophy*), no. 5 (2003): 2–33.

5. Feng Youlan, *New Edition of the History of Chinese Philosophy* (Beijing: People's Publishing House, 2001), p. 103.

6. Herlee Creel, *The Birth of China: A Study of the Formative Period of Chinese Civilization*, 4th ed. (New York: Frederick Ungar, 1961).

7. Zheng, *Between Virtue and Li*, p. 82.

8. Si Weizhi, *Ancient Chinese Social Culture Draft* (Taipei: Yun Chen Cultural Publishing Company, 1997), p. 372.

9. *Book of Changes*, "Qian-Wen Yan," translated by James Legge: "夫大人者，與天地合其德，與日月合其明，與四時合其序，與鬼神合其吉凶。先天而天弗違，後天而奉天時。天且弗違，而況於人乎？況於鬼神乎？"

10. *Shang Shu*, "Counsels of the Great Yu," translated by James Legge: "人心惟危，道心惟微，惟精惟一，允執厥中。"

11. *Xunzi*, "Dissolving Partiality," translated by John Knoblock: "明參日月，大滿八極，夫是之謂大人。"

12. Wang Yangming, *On the Great Learning*, translated by author: "敢問：大人之學，何以在於明明德乎？陽明子曰：大人者，以天地萬物為一體者也，其視天下猶一家，中國猶一人焉。"

13. Zhang Yaonan, *On Daren: The Ideal Personality of Chinese Tradition* (Beijing: Peking University Press, 2005), p. 8.

14. Pan Lin, *General Discussions on The Great Learning* (Shanghai: Fudan University Press, 2015), p. 18.

15. Yu Yingshi, *The Ideal of Junzi: Modern Interpretation of Chinese Traditions of Thought* (Taipei: Linjing Publishing Company, 2022).

16. Wang Guowei, *On the System of Yin and Zhou Dynasties, Guang Tang Ji Lin*, vol. 10: "中國政治與文化之變革，莫劇於殷周之際。"

17. Zheng, *Between Virtue and Li*, p. 84.

18. Yu Dunkang, "History of Thought during the Spring and Autumn Period," *New Philosophy* 1 (2003); Zheng, *Between Virtue and Li*, p. 89.

19. Zheng, *Between Virtue and Li*, p. 42.

20. Zheng Kai, *A Survey on Daoist Political Philosophy* (Beijing: Peking University Press, 2019), p. 110.

21. Zheng, *Between Virtue and Li*, p. 391.

22. Huang Mingchong, *New Volume: History of Chinese: The Formation of Ancient Civilization* (Taipei: Linking Publishing Company, 2016), p. 331.

23. Li Zongtong, *New Research on Ancient Chinese Society* (Shanghai: Kaiming Bookstore, 1948), p. 184.

24. Si, *Ancient Chinese Social Culture Draft*, p. 372.

25. Wang Jianwen, *By the Grace of God: The Concept of "State" in Ancient China and the Foundation of Its Legitimacy* (Taipei: Dongda Book Publishing Co., 1995), pp. 65–95.

26. Wang Jianwen, *By the Grace of God*, pp. 97–133.

27. Zou Xiaodong Zou, *Will and True Knowledge: The Difference between Da Xue and Zhongyong* (Jinan: Qilu Publishing House, 2018), pp. 266–310.

28. *Book of Changes*, "Xici" II.

29. *Book of Rites*, "Confucius at Home at Leisure," in *The Notes and Commentaries of the Book of Rites* 禮記正義 (Beijing: Peking University Press, 2000), p. 1630 (author's translation).

30. *Focusing the Familiar: A New Interpretation and New Translation of "Zhongyong,"* trans. Roger T. Ames and David L. Hall (Beijing: China Social Sciences Press, 2011), p. 109: "天命之謂性，率性之謂道，修道之謂教."

31. *Focusing the Familiar*, pp. 138–139: "故君子之道，本諸身，徵諸庶民，考諸三王而不繆，建諸天地而不悖，質諸鬼神而無疑，百世以俟聖人而不惑。質諸鬼神而無疑，知天也；百世以俟聖人而不惑，知人也。是故君子動而世為天下道，行而世為天下法，言而世為天下則。遠之則有望，近之則不厭."

32. Huang, *Formation of Ancient Civilization*, p. 349.

33. *Commentary of Zuo*, trans. James Legge: "天子建德，因生以賜姓，胙之土而命之氏。諸侯以字為諡，因以為族。官有世功，則有官族，邑亦如之."

34. *Commentary of Zuo*, trans. James Legge: "吾聞國家之立也，本大而末小，是以能固，故天子建國，諸侯立家，卿置側室，大夫有貳宗，士有隸子弟，庶人工商，各有分親，皆有等衰，是以民服事其上，而下無覬覦."

35. Si, *Ancient Chinese Social Culture Draft*, pp. 365–395.

36. *Commentary of Zuo*, Duke Xi, year 25.

37. Zheng, *Between Virtue and Li*, p. 105.

38. Confucius, *Analects*, "Yao Yue," trans. James Legge: "興滅國，繼絕世，舉逸民，天下之民歸心焉."

39. Zheng, *Between Virtue and Li*, p. 109.

40. Wang Ke, *China: From "Tianxia" to Nation-State* (Taipei: Chengchi University Press, 2014), pp. 1–26.

41. Wang, *China*, p. 50.

CHAPTER 15

Without War or Conquest
The Idea of a Global Political Order in Asoka's *Dhamma*

Rajeev BHARGAVA

IN THIS CHAPTER, I outline a model of global ethical leadership found in the inscriptions of the third-century-BCE emperor Asoka, who introduced a strong moral dimension to the idea of a global order. Physical conquest and warfare were the principal constituents of the royal political ethic in the past. It was the duty of a good king to exhibit military prowess and physical courage on the battlefield, to covet ever more territories, and eventually, a little later in time, to have a large empire. This must be true everywhere in the world, but it was certainly the case in the fifth to sixth centuries BCE in India, precisely the period of empire formation. Though he inherited the warrior ethic of military prowess and territorial expansion from his ancestors and followed it during his early rule, over time, Asoka began to see the futility of warfare and the human cost of territorial conquest. As a result, he proposed that rulership should be based on and guided by a new political morality for which he used the Indic term "*dhamma.*" Both ruler and subjects were to submit to this higher ethic. In order that political violence and conquest be minimized, kings had to rule less by force and more by persuasion. Officials were to be appointed to instruct people and to spread *dhamma* not only within the territory of the king but globally as a moral minimum that was compatible with different forms of ethical life. Physical conquest was to be replaced by moral conquest, brute power, and domination by moral hegemony. Thus, Asoka envisaged a new global order grounded largely in nonviolence and noninjury toward others.

This chapter explores Asoka's ideas on such an ethically global order in greater depth and detail. It delineates the politico-moral ethic, called *dhamma,* that undergirds this order and explains how precisely this political morality minimizes violent conquest and war and emphasizes instead moral and intellectual leadership, both within the king's own territory and beyond it. It shows that one of the central aspirations of Asoka's *dhamma* is a form of universalism, to shape the global order by sending emissaries all over the world.

The main source of knowledge about Asoka comes from his inscriptions or edicts that lie scattered in more than thirty places throughout India, Nepal, Bangladesh, Pakistan, and Afghanistan.[1] Most of them are written in Brahmi script, from which all Indian scripts and many of those used in Southeast Asia later developed. The language of the edicts in the eastern part of the subcontinent is Prakrit, associated with the people of Magadh; in the edicts of western India the language is closer to Sanskrit, written in the Kharoshthi script; one extract of Edict 13 is in Greek; and one bilingual edict in Kandahar, Afghanistan, is written in Greek and Aramaic. Asoka's edicts, the earliest decipherable corpus of written documents from India, have survived throughout the centuries because they are written on rocks, cave walls, and stone pillars. These edicts appear to be in Asoka's own words rather than in the more formal language in which royal edicts or proclamations in the ancient world were usually written.

Asoka's *Dhamma* as Civic Religion

At the core of Asoka's conception of *dhamma* lies a set of precepts about how to lead a good individual and collective life. *Dhamma* is generally understood in the India's scholarly tradition to mean law. But Romila Thapar has used the term "social ethic" and Patrick Olivelle has proposed that *dhamma* be reconceived as "civic religion," a term revived by Robert Bellah after Jean-Jacques Rousseau first coined it in his classic work *The Social Contract.*[2] I wish to argue that Asoka's *dhamma* is a comprehensive political ethic. It is an ethic because it tells both the ruler and ruled how to live their lives and what makes life worth living. It is political not only because in the last instance it is to be inculcated by the political ruler but because, apart from a personal and social dimension, it has a strong political component.

Dhamma as Personal and Social Morality

Asokan inscriptions are most explicit about *dhamma* as personal morality—having more to do with the cultivation of personal and religious virtues, spiritual growth, and development of moral character than with obedience to civil and criminal law. Rock Edicts 2 and 3 testify to this. *Dhamma* consists in "obedience to mother and father. Giving to friends and acquaintances and relatives, to *Brāhmaṇas* and *Śramaṇa*. Showing kindness and abstaining from killing living beings." Other virtues include "spending little and storing little" and "speaking the truth." Both Rock Edicts 9 and 11 and Pillar Edict 7 add that "proper regard to slaves and servants" is morally important.

In Pillar Edict 2, *dhamma* is related to "having few faults and doing many good deeds (*Kalyāna*), compassion (*Dayā*), charity (*Dāna*), truthfulness and purity (*sochaye*)." Later two other virtues are added: self-control (*samyāma*) and purity of mind (*bhāvaśuddhi*). *Dhamma,* without discrimination, is applicable to all regardless of social station, economic status, gender, or ethnicity. Its aspiration, like the Buddha's, is universal.[3]

But *dhamma* is not to be equated with personal or individualistic morality. To reject the idea that *dhamma* is obedience to law does not entail that it is to do entirely with personal moral injunctions. True, force and coercion are not part of the moral and political lexicon of the epigraphs.[4] Asoka relies on persuasion (*nijhati*) rather than legislation, but it does not follow that this is identical to personal morality. Individual morality is not the only alternative to law. As important for Asoka is collective or intergroup morality—what we owe each other as members of religio-philosophical groups. In this social dimension, *dhamma* consists of a specific form of *samyāma,* that is, *vācāgutti* (restraint of speech).

Society in Asokan times had deep religio-philosophical diversity. Members of different religio-philosophical groups (*pāṣaṇḍas*) jostled with one another. Given this diversity, profound disagreements and conflicts were commonplace between ritual-oriented Vedic Brahmins, philosophically minded Brahmins, and antiritualists such as Ajivikas, Jains, and Buddhists who also differed from one another on issues of ontology and morality. Space limitations do not allow me to go into the details of these differences, but it is clear that for a ruler with imperial ambitions, it was important to find a way to enable all *pāṣaṇḍas* to live together.[5] What, despite profound differences in worldviews, could the basis of such coexistence be? For Asoka, such coexistence is impossible without shared values, what he called "the essentials (*saara*) that constitute the common ground of these conflicting conceptions."[6]

What then are these essentials? What then is the social component of *dhamma*? The fundamental principle of *dhamma* in its social dimension is *vācāgutti,* variously interpreted as "restraint of speech" or "control of tongue." Why give such importance to speech? Asokan inscriptions themselves do not give an answer to this question, nor is evidence of verbal battles of that period available, but the edicts imply that word wars during this time were intense and brutal. They simply had to be reined in. And what kind of speech must be curbed? Edict 12 says speech that without reason disparages other *pāṣaṇḍas* must be restrained. Speech critical of others may be freely enunciated only if we have good reasons to do so.[7] However, even when we have good reasons to be critical, one may do so only on appropriate occasions and even when the occasion is appropriate, one must never be immoderate. Critique should never belittle or humiliate others. Thus, there is a deep, complex, and layered restraint on one's verbal speech against others; let us call it other-related self-restraint. However, the edicts do not stop at this. They go on to say that one must not eulogize one's own *pāṣaṇḍa*. Undue praise of one's own *pāṣaṇḍa*, without good reason, is as morally objectionable as unmerited criticism of the faith of others. Moreover, the edicts add that even when there is good reason to praise one's own *pāṣaṇḍa*, it too should be done only on appropriate occasions and even on those occasions, never immoderately. As bad as blaming other *pāṣaṇḍas* out of devotion to one's own *pāṣaṇḍa* is undue or excessive self-glorification. This is a way to make others feel small; besides, unreflective, uncritical, effulgent self-praise damages one's own *pāṣaṇḍa* too. By offending and thereby estranging others, one's capacity for mutual interaction and possible influence is undermined. Thus, there must equally be multitextured, ever-deepening restraint for oneself. Let this be self-related self-restraint.

In Edict 7, Asoka emphasizes the need not only for *samyāma* (self-restraint) but also *bhāvaśuddhi* (purity of mind), again a self-oriented act.[8] But in my view, *bhāvaśuddhi* too has an another-oriented connotation. It includes cleansing oneself of ill will toward others. Self-restraint and self-purification are not just matters of etiquette or prudence but are morally salient.

For Asoka, hate speech and self-glorification produce discord and dogma. He wishes instead to advance mutual understanding and mutual appreciation, for which it is better to have concourse (*Samavāya*), an assembly of *pāṣaṇḍas* where representatives of each one can hear one another out and communicate with one another. This may not always generate agreement, but it certainly makes each one a *Bahuśruta,* that is, one who listens to all, the perfect listener, or one who hears or has heard the many, and thereby has become open-minded. This way *pāṣaṇḍas* get an opportunity to tease out the impurities and imperfections from their own collective ethical self-understanding. This is the only path to *Ātma pāṣaṇḍa vāddhi* (an enhancement of ethical self-understanding) of one's own *pāṣaṇḍa* and to *par pāṣaṇḍa vāddhi* (growth in the ethical self-understanding of others). It also advances the essentials of all (*saravadhi*). The edicts here imply that the ethical self-understanding of *pāṣaṇḍa* is not static but constantly evolving and that such progress is crucially dependent on mutual conversation and dialogue. Censuring others without good reason or immoderately interrupts this process and, apart from damaging *dhamma,* diminishes mutual growth of a *pāṣaṇḍa*. In another passage, Asoka says that those seeking improvement in their own ethical views should not only communicate with others with different ethical perspectives in order to learn from them, but even follow their precepts and "obey" them. Thinking as if you were in someone else's shoes may not on occasions be sufficient; you have to act with their shoes on. This form of practical engagement introduces an ethically charged experiential dimension.

Vācāgutti and *samovāya* are social virtues irreducible to personal or individual virtues because they involve a set of dispositions and comportment not only concerning one's own self—the particular beliefs and practices that are dear to one—but also involving other selves. Like civility and openness, they are associated with individuals but are irreducibly interindividual or relational. They are therefore best viewed as attributes of whole societies. We may legitimately speak of a civil (with *samyāma* and *vācāgutti*) society, an open society, and a harmonious rather than an acrimonious society. Asoka himself conveys strongly that he has in mind "harmony" as an attribute of social life.[9] The social dimension of *dhamma* requires that each group act in a manner that generates harmony in society. Thus *samyāma, vācāgutti,* and *samovāya* are best included as key values of *dhamma* in its social dimension.

Dhamma as Political Ethic

It is, however, in the third, political dimension of *dhamma* that Asoka seeks a revolution. In this crucial political component of *dhamma* he attempts to outline how political power is to be used for ethical purposes, what ethical relation there must be between the ruler and the ruled, and what is expected of royal officials. Here Asoka seeks a profound change in the very idea of kingship he had inherited from his ancestors. Political rule was to be delinked from the prevailing warrior ethic. *Dhamma* in this third political dimension not only challenges what constitutes heroic virtues but also changes our understanding of what the ruler owes to people not directly his subjects. In short, he wishes to transform the prevailing views on interstate relationships or what ethical principles shape the global order. True, these are not present explicitly in the list of virtues or norms associated with *dhamma* but nor, I would argue, is *dhamma* conceivable without it. In the remaining part of this chapter, I elaborate this new, political dimension of *dhamma,* which is somewhat less emphasized by scholars on Asoka.

A brief quasi-phenomenological account of the pre-Asokan period, based partly on Vedic texts but in part also speculative, is in order if we are to grasp the depth and scope of Asoka's ethical ambition.[10] The Rig Veda, the oldest text of the pre-Asokan period, is a very valuable resource to get an idea of the ancient warrior ethic. In the Rig Veda, the most important god and the ultimate exemplar to all humans is Indra, the god of sky, rain, and thunder, who being violent, strong, and hypermasculine, is also the god of war. Indeed, Vedic cosmogony depends on Indra's immense and powerful physique. He is able, through sheer brawn, to push apart the world into two halves, Heaven and Earth, release primordial waters, and split open the cosmic mountain so as to free imprisoned sunlight and cattle.

The language used to glorify Indra is extremely masculine and violent. With his *ojas,* a Sanskrit term signifying both physical strength and the power of rulership and domination, Indra smashes and pulverizes rivals. He destroys, crushes, splits apart, slays, and breaks an enemy's rage. Rig Vedic poets portray Indra's terrifying demeanor and unbridled, brute force by way of sexually charged metaphors involving male dominance and female subservience. Indra's physical act of forcing enemies down corresponds to a political act of subjugation and deference. Ritual practitioners direct Indra to conquer the universe and to conduct cattle raids and open warfare for profit.

Rig Vedic poet-priests clearly propagate a violent masculine ideology—a Rig Vedic warrior ethic—wherein all males, whether young or old, become real men by participating in the ritual tradition and by being strong, tough, and dominant. Bravery, toughness, and brute strength are celebrated as core components of manhood and men who flex their muscles in cattle-raiding expeditions and open warfare are praised and honored. The ideal men, who accept Indra as their role model, are called by the name of *śū́ra* ("big / strong man; champion"), signifying one with an expert martial and political role. The real heroes of early Vedic ritual culture embody menacing and hypermasculine identities and use their own bodies in powerful and intimidating ways. Men who embody specialized male roles (*śū́ra, rā́jan*) are glorified, and skill in horse and chariot combat is selected for special praise. While they do not represent the only values of Aryan men, migratory conquest, martial expertise, and manliness are dominant motifs in the Rig Veda, just as virile powers and qualities are widely seen as the primary virtues of a man.

Seasonal skirmishes and open warfare are central to the ideology and life of Rig Vedic culture. The need for food and water leads to cattle raiding and competition for natural resources (such as access to grazing grounds and waterways), which escalates into open warfare and claims to chieftainship and sovereignty. This is seen as the natural condition of humankind. The image projected by the Rig Vedic poets of themselves and of their community is shot through with notions of conflict and competition for resources. Rig Vedic poet-priests promote various ways that men can prove their masculinity, but the dominant role is that of man as warrior. Poets expect that men defined by the terms *vīr* and *śū́ra* will acquire wealth from violent excursions and will distribute the spoils among clansmen in the ritual arena. They must have been aware of the horrific consequences of war. Here is a passage from the *Mahabharata,* composed in fragments much earlier but written between the first century BCE and the first century CE, that captures the atrocities of wars in the early Vedic period and any era:

> As Arjuna showers arrows on his adversaries, a terrible river starts flowing on the battlefield. Its water was blood from the wounds of weapons on men's bodies, its foam human fat; broad in current, it flowed very swiftly, terrible to see and to hear. Corpses of elephants and horses formed its banks, the entrails, marrow and flesh of men its mud. Ghosts and great throngs of demons lined its banks. Its waterweed was hair attached to human skulls, its billows severed pieces of armour, as it bore along thousands of bodies in heaps. Fragments of the bones of men, horses and elephants formed the gravel of that fearful, destructive, hellish river; crows, jackals, vultures and storks, and throngs of carrion beasts and hyenas were approaching its banks from every direction.[11]

That this ethic is gloriously amoral, exalts ruthlessness, brooks no conception of justice, and permits the use of any means to achieve selfish goals hardly needs underscoring. And that this warrior ethic was around in Asokan times and survived him is demonstrated in several subsequent inscriptions and manuscripts. To take just one example, in the *Mahabharata,* Bhishma, the elder statesman, admonishes Yudhishtra, who wishes to follow an Asoka-like ethic: "Nothing great can be achieved through pure compassion [*ānṛśaṁsya*]. Further, people do not hold you in much respect for being gentle, self-controlled and excessively noble and righteous, a compassionate and righteous eunuch. . . . The behavior you want to follow is not the behavior of kings."[12]

Dhamma above the Ruler and the Ruled

Asoka's *dhamma,* I argue here, is a courageous repudiation of this warrior ethic. Three points must be kept in mind before I further elaborate the political dimension of *dhamma*. First, Buddha's teachings opened up the possibility of the radical sociopolitical restructuring of the world and the self by politico-moral action from above. Buddha's ethic included the pivotal importance of moral action. Once one stands outside the whole cosmos and is able to see its limitations, and once the transcendental point from which one examines the cosmos is viewed as emanating a moral vision, it becomes possible to imagine a profound restructuring of society and polity in accordance with that vision. D. D. Kosambi is imaginatively on to this point when he says that more than a personal conversion of the emperor, there appears to have taken place in Ashokan times a deeper conversion of the whole previous state apparatus. The king not only preaches a new morality but is able to launch radically new political and administrative measures that include public morality as an essential ingredient and provide a framework within which radically differing ethics can coexist and nourish one another.[13] Indeed, Asoka never tires of saying that he is breaking away from the past, that he is inaugurating a new order, something unlike any of his predecessors has done. His is a radically new vision of kingship.[14]

Second, also emerging at this time in India is the idea of what later came to be called the *cakravartin,* the wheel turner. The wheel that these great rulers turn is the wheel of *dhamma.* Whereas the Buddha turned the wheel of the *dhamma* in the religio-philosophical sphere, the *cakravartin* turns it in the political sphere. The *cakravartin* represents the Buddhist political ideal of the just ruler, who brings peace and prosperity to his subjects. The normative king, it seems, is intrinsic to the social and moral order of the world.

Third, with the birth of the idea of a moral ruler or the "normative king," Asoka's *dhamma* is seen in a new light.[15] Before Asoka, right and wrong actions were possibly determined by the king himself. The law must not have been applied in a consistent or legitimate manner but in a highly personal and arbitrary one. Thus, rajas are often depicted as rewarding or punishing according to the way their personal interests are served.[16] By fashioning the idea of *dhamma,* Asoka attempts to tame the institution of kingship itself and to contain the absolute exercise of power by the king. Indeed, the reconceptualization of *dhamma* may also be viewed as an attempt to transform power into authority by infusing it with certain norms. It is also, as far as possible, to place strategic considerations secondary to the moral vision of *dhamma.*[17] *Dhamma* is a fundamental moral principle above even the *cakravartin.*

What then does *dhamma* require of the subjects? What subjects owe to the king and his officials is obedience to his commands. They must follow *dhamma.* Yet, Pillar Edict 7 makes it clear that this compliance must arise from persuasion (*nijhati*), not law (*niyāma*). Everyone must follow *dhamma* out of an inner disposition to comply: one's conscience, as it were.

This does not exhaust the political dimension of *dhamma,* however. For it must also include what the king owes his subjects. The politico-moral order stands above the king, at least partially. Just as the head of the family is as much part of the family as his wife and children are, just so, the king is part of the political order as much as his subjects are. And just as all members of the family owe something, though not the same, to each other, just so, the king owes something to his subjects, though it is qualitatively different from what the subjects owe him. Pillar Edict 6 clarifies what this is: *sarvajña, sarvaloka hitá* (welfare of all living beings in this world and hereafter), or *sukhā* (happiness) in this world and *swarga* (Heaven) in the other. Asoka declares that even those condemned to death must have the possibility of attaining *swarga.*

The Transformative Moment: Rock Inscription 13

Buddha's teachings certainly played a role in Asoka's vision. But the turning point in his life came in the eighth year of his rule after the war waged on Kalinga.[18] The scale of wanton destruction at Kalinga left Asoka distraught and changed his perspective on war. The edicts mention the displacement and deportation of 150,000 people and the death of at least 100,000. They speak of "many more who perished unknown." The slaughter, death, and deportation has "caused immense grief to the beloved of the gods and weighs heavily on his mind." The war, he discovered, had tragic consequences not only for those who directly suffered violence but for practically every resident of Kalinga, for even those who were fortunate to have escaped its direct impact suffered from the misfortunes of their friends, acquaintances, colleagues, and relatives. No one then is unaffected by the horrors of war, no one does not undergo suffering. After all, it is the survivors of war who are left to grieve. Romila Thapar rightly notes that "the regret and remorse at the suffering in Kalinga is not the regret of a man moved by a passing emotion, but the meaningful contrition of a man who was consciously aware of the sorrow he had caused."[19]

The realization that those who suffered were followers of *dhamma* made things worse. Ordinary people living in his territory, those who were not themselves warriors but *Brāhmaṇas, Śramaṇa,* followers of other *pāṣaṇḍas,* householders, all followed *dhamma* when they obeyed their mothers, fathers, and teachers and behaved well and devotedly toward their friends, acquaintances, colleagues, relatives, slaves, and servants. The thought of what happened to such dhammic people during the Kalinga war weighed heavily on Asoka's mind and, at the time of inscribing Edict 13, he writes, "If even a thousandth of that were to occur now, he would be filled with horror." It has been said that it was easy for Asoka to renounce war after he had already established a large empire. But imperial ambitions have no limit and at whatever stage this was done, it must be seen as a significant self-limitation. Indeed, Asoka not only began to discourage war but publicly denounced the very idea of glorifying continuous conquest.

In other words, Asoka made a valiant attempt to move away from the warrior ethic, that is, the ethics of physical courage and manly prowess, particularly on the battlefield. He firmly refused to play war games, dismissing the idea that fame and glory are goods in themselves. The only kind of fame and glory he wishes is one that is achieved by obeying and following the *dhamma.* Alternatively, he can be seen to be changing the very idea of what counts as glory; dhammic glory is achieved by getting rid of all evil tendencies that give us only demerit.[20] Indeed, there is glory and dignity in siding with victims of plunder and conquest, with the poor and the downtrodden rather than with the heroic chieftains. It also lies in elevating life-sustaining goods of ordinary persons well above power, conquest and glory. To secure material welfare for his subjects is central to the king's *dhamma*.

Material Welfare of Subjects

The ruler's commitment to provide material welfare to his subjects in Asokan inscriptions is echoed elsewhere in Buddhist texts. "After the *cakkavattī* had brought the entire universe under his umbrella, he must proceed to ensure that his people live in comparative comfort, in a world where destitution has been wiped out."[21] Asoka takes it upon himself to take care for the sick and the aged, plant mango groves, dig wells, build rest houses along main routes, and grow banyan trees along the roads in order to provide shade to both humans and animals.[22] Thus, Asoka speaks of providing two kinds of medical services, medicinal herbs for humans and plants for animals, neither of which were available earlier.[23] The inclusion of animals is extremely interesting. With respect to many life-sustaining goods, there is no real distinction between humans and animals. Animals and humans alike need drinking water, food, protection from the sun, and also medical treatment. Fulfilment of basic needs is crucial to not just humans but also animals. This commits Asoka to not just human universalism but a universalism across species.

The king owes a modicum of material welfare to his people and the subjects know that the king has these obligations to them. The provision of life-sustaining goods is neither excluded from *dhamma* nor reduced to it. Not that a concern for material well-being was entirely absent from the plans of earlier rulers. "But I have done these things in order that my people might conform to Dhamma," Asoka says.[24] I suppose this means that all these acts are part of a larger moral vision that he explicitly formulated. It is part of Asoka's *dhamma,* his moral vision that people live and travel in comfort, be happy, and enjoy material benefits. War, conquest, and the pursuit of glory upset both the physical security of humans and their valid pursuit of life-goods. They violate *dhamma*. Therefore, they must be eschewed.

The masculine Kshatriya culture is also relentlessly un-self-critical and unforgiving. For Asoka, however, the ruler is required to develop two further virtues. First is the ability to self-correct. Since a leader learns from his followers and his mistakes, he must be ready to own them up. This is already demonstrated in Edict 13. But this self-reflective, self-critical tone is present in other inscriptions too. For instance, in Edict 14, he says, "In some places there are inaccuracies, some passages have been omitted or the engraver has made some errors and in acknowledging them, he is acknowledging inadequacies in his edicts." Second, as far as possible one who does wrong should be forgiven. One must reconcile with adversaries. He says this in the context of forest dwellers. He says that "he wants to reconcile with the forest dwellers, he doesn't want to have any kind of hostility with them." Yet, reconciliation cannot happen under any condition, at any cost. Asoka warns forest dwellers that while he feels remorseful and is prepared to atone, "He still has power and can use it against them."[25] This shows his concern for those who are not yet part of his political order but also that there are limits to political toleration. The tribes must repent for the wrongs they have done and show their allegiance to *dhamma,* or else they may face coercion.

Thus, by formulating *dhamma* and elaborating how it is to be realized, Asoka attempts to reshape the entire Brahmana-Kshatriya culture. What Buddha appears to have done to the Brāhmaṇas and their ideology, Asoka appears to be doing to the Kshatriyas and their ideology. The introduction of the idea of civility too must be understood in this context. Asoka wants a change not only in the warrior ethic but in what might be called the word-warrior ethic, in the reckless display of manliness in verbal fighting, in hostility conveyed through words, in attempts at braggadocio and using language to humiliate others. By advising against violence (*hiṃsā*) through speech (*vāchā*), he shows that he is as keen to inhibit any assault on human dignity as to prevent killing.

Thus, Asoka considered only one victory to be important: the victory of *dhamma.* The only form of conquest that mattered to him was moral conquest. He had transformed himself from a defender of the warrior ethic of physical conquest to a defender of the political ethic of moral hegemony. In the past, he says, there were war drums and a spectacle of arms and weaponry. Now he wishes a moral spectacle, wishing through these festivities to stoke the moral imagination of the people. Likewise, in the past, people conquered territories and built kingdoms in order to enhance their own pleasure. They worked for their own good, for their own benefit, but Asoka says that he has changed all that. He thinks that all his descendants should also be like him and get all their pleasure and delight from following *dhamma* rather than vanquishing other people's territories, which only brings suffering to everyone and torture to all moral beings. The purpose of kingship, of state building, Asoka claims, is not to benefit the king himself but to benefit everybody, to bring happiness to everybody, illuminated by *dhamma.*[26] This, he acknowledges, earns the king spiritual revenue (merit).[27]

Further evidence of the disavowal of the warrior ethic comes from his views on hunting. In Rock Edict 8, he speaks once again of a break with the past when it was mandatory for kings to go on pleasure tours for hunting and other amusements. The king, he says, continues to tour, but these tours from then on are purely dhammic. On such travel, he meets Brāhmaṇas and Śramaṇa and bestows them with gifts. Indeed, he does something more important: he gives instructions in *dhamma* to others. He conducts moral assemblies and discussions. He arranges deliberations, conversations, dialogues, and question-and-answer sessions on ethics, on what is good and bad, on how to do the right thing, all of which gives him great pleasure. The pleasure derived from doing and discussing the ethically significant is qualitatively different from the pleasures of self-seeking. In short, Asoka wishes to have moral education as an important component of his politics. He wishes to embody this morality in his person and to educate others by his own example. When he leads by example, he gives spiritual insight (*cakhu-dāne*) with which to lead the good life.[28]

The idea that political morality can be taught by instruction and example is what really distinguishes Asoka from all his predecessors. Some kings in the past had probably glimpsed the idea of *dhamma*, he says.[29] They may even have genuinely searched for ways by which to foster *dhamma*, to make it a part of everyday life and popular consciousness. But they did not succeed in getting people to respond to their calls, to ensure an enduring relationship with *dhamma*. For Asoka, this lacuna was to be filled by formal education. Inculcation, teaching, and instruction help people to devote themselves to *dhamma*. There is an element of formality here. Initiation in customary practices seems to Asoka to be insufficient. A whole discourse on *dhamma* is required, which in turn needs specialists, a new class of intellectuals employed and trained by the ruler's administration. These intellectuals are responsible for teaching *dhamma*, to make its content explicit and to explain it in moral assemblies. Besides, it is not enough to know *dhamma*. One has to be moved by the love (*kāmātaya*) of it and have the energy to realize it.[30] This intense love generates conviction and commitment. *Dhamma* requires that it be taught by educators who love and are committed to it and can communicate both to all subjects. Inculcating this enduring commitment is as important as careful examination, obedience, and the fear of committing wrong or sin.[31]

It is important for Asoka that *dhamma* grows. But this growth is of two kinds. First, there is a deepening of its meaning, as when its content is enriched in mutual encounters between different *pāṣaṇḍas*. Second, growth also refers to its spread among the people. *Dhamma* needs moral and intellectual refinement but also a vertical spread. Asoka seems to have a universal aspiration for *dhamma*. He wishes that its moral appeal not be restricted to elites but also inspire ordinary folks. It must become part of their common sense, must penetrate the popular imagination, and must take hold of the entire social imaginary. *Dhamma* is a sociopolitical project, a kind of mission to transform popular consciousness. This means that moral educators and intellectuals must take *dhamma* everywhere within the kingdom to help raise popular ethical awareness. Engraving and inscribing *dhamma* is one way to realize this mission, but the message also needs to travel to other countries and get to far-off places. For this traveling, messengers are required. Asoka arranged for such travel. Indeed, he believed that *dhamma* was continuously growing in his own time due to his own love of morality, through instruction and education, and by the effort of messengers—the moral educators and frontier officials.

Expansive Hegemony

It is this idea that rulers must be committed to impart *dhamma* through pedagogical techniques such as public meetings, discussions, and question-and-answer sessions that underscore the fact that Asoka's political project aimed at rule by persuasion and consent. Elsewhere I have argued that we might here deploy the idea of "expansive hegemony," a concept developed two millennia later by the Italian philosopher Antonio Gramsci.[32] Hegemonic rule is different from two other, more common forms of rule.[33] First, there is rule by violent conquest and brute force. This form of rule is discussed by Kautilya's *Arthā śāstra,* which, though not a text about imperial rule, encourages rulers to be desirous of conquests (*Vijigīṣu*) and to have as their ultimate goal "conquest in all four directions."[34] Second, there are rulers who seize power by violent conquest of an alien territory and then rule by compelling the conquered to assimilate to their own worldview. This is rule by domination. Here, the focus is on the identification of ways by which countries ideologically opposed to the conqueror are neutralized. This too is discussed extensively in the *Arthā śāstra*. As Patrick Olivelle puts it, "A king's success hinged to a great extent on his ability to 'outwit' his foreign rivals. The *Arthā śāstra* has a technical term for this, *atisaṃdhā*—the 'outwitting' or 'overreaching' of rivals. Whether through diplomacy, intimidation, supplication, or open hostility, a king always sought some kind of advantage against ally and enemy alike."[35] In this form of rule, other populations are made to acquiesce to the conqueror, even if it means getting them to lose their identity, merging it in the cultural identity of the conqueror. However, here, since a king's rule also depends on ideas and not on brute force alone, the ruling ideas must be the conqueror's own. But Asoka provides a third, alternative mode of rule, without brute force or cultural domination. Here, the ruler provides ethical education to his subjects and takes active measures to arrive at a consensus. This is rule by hegemony. This is done by leaving untouched a country's and its people's conception of the good, their distinctive ethic and individuality, but emphasizing some elements already present in their views and building upon them. A common ground is discovered from within so that the basic objectives of all rulers are no longer in conflict. Indeed, at some level there is some unity or active consensus on values. This is strikingly similar to some points made by Xunzi. "His majesty ... wins the allegiance of others ... without having to wage war, of gaining his objectives without resort to force, and of the world submitting to him without his armies exerting themselves."[36]

When a ruler is morally hegemonic in this sense, he manages to arrive at a new ethic that coalesces the multiple ethical perspectives of all the groups in his society. Expansive hegemony is entirely consistent with maintaining diversity and endorsing pluralism. This new ethic provides a social cement to rule within as well as beyond the boundary of his own territory. Therefore, this ethic spreads beyond the territorial boundary of the hegemon's rule. This establishes the basis of a new kind of imperial order where brute force and domination are replaced by the intellectual and moral leadership of the hegemon that shows the way and inspires and improves upon the status quo. The ruler of one country is then able to provide intellectual leadership and moral direction to others in such a way that those who are led feel their own lives enriched. This is achieved pedagogically, by moral education. The *cakravartin* conquers other kingdoms not by physical force but by moral appeal.[37] Wherever he travels he is welcomed and people voluntarily "submit" to his rule out of respect for his adherence to the principles of *dhamma*.

Asoka claims that his efforts at education in and about *dhamma* and all other practices and ceremonies that surround these pedagogic efforts have borne fruit. The hard work by him and his officials has achieved at least two things. One, certain moral virtues have grown such as mercy, truthfulness, purity, gentleness, charity, and liberality as well as a better quality of social relations, both interpersonal and interpasandic. There is greater obedience to mothers and fathers and to teachers. There is deference to people who are aged. There is greater regard for *Brāhmaṇas* and *Śramaṇa* (these two classes exist everywhere, to Asoka, except for Greece), for the wretched and the poor, the slaves and servants. And two, there is harmony between *pāṣaṇḍas*. This respectful coexistence has increased as never before in the past. Besides, this is not just something occurring in his own time, but something that will continue in the future. This royal conviction results from his belief that his good work will be carried forward by his sons, grandsons, and great-grandsons, all of whom have committed themselves to the practice and instruction of *dhamma*.

If the hegemon is interested not only in gaining the affection and consent of his own people but also of people of other countries, he must give up an instrumental attitude toward them. He must also be moved by a commitment to their identity and welfare. The idea is to provide transformational leadership in which leaders and "followers" have a reciprocal relationship that raises everyone to higher levels of motivation and morality, alongside or perhaps beyond the life-goods. Though Asoka does not explicitly mention this, he seems to abandon the view presupposed by the old warrior ethic that interstate relations are anarchic, a view held by many and formulated later by Kautilya, for whom the origin or basis of kingship is not to be found in transcendent moral principles or a social contract but solely in the staff (*daṇḍā*) or coercive political power.[38] This is so because Kautilya's principal motivation is *arthā* or worldly success. The importance of every moral principle, if recognized, is secondary. Olivelle sums up his political ideology succinctly: "Ultimately, Kauṭilya's focus on *daṇḍa* does not reduce the king to a naked tyrant.... It is simply that he measures all things in the end according to how well they support the material power of the king." While the king is quite happy to conform to the traditions of kingship and Brāhmaṇism, at heart, Olivelle says, Kauṭilya's true faith lies in power, and he does not hesitate to subvert these traditions if it will further the king's interests. For Kautilya "the fruitfulness of all human activities—many of which are quite worthwhile—relies ultimately on effective governance."[39]

In contrast, Asoka wants to rule by *dhamma,* by persuasion rather than force. This is not easy. For a start, the ruler must educate others by his own example. He must follow each and every aspect of *dhamma*. To illustrate this point: for Asoka, no living thing must be sacrificed and no festival for this purpose be permitted. He says that there was a time when in his kitchen hundreds of thousands of living animals were killed every day for meat but now, he admits with embarrassment, that only three animals are killed: two peacocks and one deer, and the deer is not killed every day. He then resolves that even these animals shall not be killed in the future.

Asoka leads by example also by devoting all his time to the material and spiritual welfare of everyone. The ruler, he says, must play a crucial role in day-to-day governance.[40] Rock Edict 6 indicates that the primary duty of the ruler is to rule for his subjects. Official matters in the past, it says, were not dispatched quickly and reports were neither composed nor received by the king at all times. Political administration was inefficient, everything was done leisurely, and the king did not devote enough time to this task. Pre-Asokan kings were rarely involved in day-to-day administration, for there was no real interest in ensuring the welfare of the subjects. But now, in Asoka's own time, by his conduct, things have transformed because anybody can approach him at all times and is allowed to interrupt him while he is dining, in his own apartment or in the apartments of his women, in his carriage or in the cattle shed. Information is being fed to him all the time; reports are given of what is happening in the country, on the basis of which he can act and transact public business. When he gives a verbal instruction to his officers concerning, say, a donation or a proclamation, and if there is any ambiguity, difference of opinion, or dispute over what it means and if as a result there is any deliberation or discussion over it among the officers, then it is reported to Asoka immediately. He adds, "But simply hard work and efficiency in doing things, in dispatching business is not enough, you have to get the results."[41] The main result he wishes to have is the happiness and welfare in this world and in Heaven. The other crucial quality is the attitude and motive with which the ruler acts. Any good deed of great significance or consequence that he has performed and for which he is known, he has done only to discharge his debt to all beings.

Asoka acknowledges that it is easy to commit sins, to do wrong, but far more difficult to do good or follow the right, to do what is morally correct. Those who want to do the right thing follow a difficult path in their life and they are not always allowed to do this. Circumstances do not always permit it. There is something boastful about these edicts. There is a clear sense of purpose in his thought and action; there is a sense of self-confidence that he will be able to realize *dhamma* and realize it well. He also claims that he is the first person to appoint officers of *dhamma* who are working among servants and nobles, Brāhmaṇas and wealthy householders, among the poor and the aged, and that it is not easy to ensure that these officers work tirelessly for *dhamma*.

Asoka believes that no king can rule on his own but needs a team of committed officials. Rock Edict 5 tells us that state officials are crucial for *dhamma*. These officials must work for all sections, among the servants and among the nobles, among the poor and the aged, among the wealthy householders, and in women's residences.[42] They must work with all classes of people and all *pāṣaṇḍas*. They must even be committed to promoting the welfare of prisoners, releasing those who have children or who are sick or aged. They must ensure that *dhamma* be practiced not only by everybody, but everywhere, regardless of age, gender, wealth, or social status.

The king must appoint different categories of officers to perform different functions. These officers, who increase the glory of *dhamma* throughout the world, act on behalf not only of him but of his queens, his sons, and other princes.[43] Yet the king must play a direct, active role in ensuring that officials follow *dhamma*. In the Separate Edict 1, he gives instructions directed at officers and city magistrates: "If I (morally) approve of something, I desire it. And anything I desire I seek to achieve by taking appropriate action." It follows that only a ruler who himself follows *dhamma* has the ability to appoint the best person suited for this job. He tells his officers that "they can influence the many thousands of living beings under their charge, only if they gain their affection." But personal affection does not come in the way of performing dhammic functions. Impersonality is not a condition of impartiality. These officials are expected to be impartial, to conduct judicial proceedings, and to reward and punish impartially (*viyohālasamtā* and *daṇḍ samtā*).[44] Besides, only if the ruler leaves the offer of rewards and punishments to the discretion of the officials will they exhibit responsibility and confidently and fearlessly discharge their duties.

It follows that obedience to *dhamma* does not entail a spurious universalism in which each person, at all times, in all contexts, and regardless of their role, is required to follow the same moral precepts. Undoubtedly, some moral precepts are to be followed by everyone, but there are parts of *dhamma* meant for one section in relation to another section. What one section does, the other does not have to do. For example, the precepts for the educator or the instructor cannot be the same as for the instructed or the educated. But the point is that these precepts are relevant for everybody and must be known to everybody. Furthermore, another quality or virtue is expected of the king and all his officials: impartiality in the legal-procedural domain (*viyohala samatva*) and impartiality in the domain of retributive punishment (*daṇḍā samatva*).

Conclusion

I will conclude by briefly making four points. First, for Asoka, the content of *dhamma* is not determined by what the ruler wills or desires. Rather, the ruler is as bound to and by it as are his subjects and follows, whatever action *dhamma* implores him to do. Though objective, this good is not to be equated with any particular thick, substantive conception of the good of a specific *pāṣaṇḍa*. Instead, the good it promotes is common to all *pāṣaṇḍas* and deliberately thin in content. To follow *dhamma* is to avoid evil—vices such as cruelty, envy, arrogance, fierceness, and wrath—and cultivate virtues such as compassion, truthfulness, purity of mind, self-restraint, open-mindedness, and harmony. None of these dictate any particular thick idea of the good life.

Second, Asoka's *dhamma* takes a stand against the violent warrior ethic and promotes any ethic that abjures a violent culture of glory and vainglory. What makes it paternalistic is that the ruler views himself as the father and his subjects as his own children, and he puts the entire apparatus of rule into effect to realize what is objectively considered to be good for them.[45] He sees it as his personal and direct responsibility to do so. If and when the subjects go against *dhamma,* it becomes his duty to intervene in their lives, not coercively but largely through education and persuasion.

To break away from this warrior ethic, Asoka underscores the moral significance of nonviolence and noninjury to others. He strongly discourages ill treatment of the aged, servants, and even slaves. Asoka had seen this warrior ethic creep into intellectual life. While elites viewed themselves as rival warriors, at the more popular level, people acted as word warriors, living in a culture of verbal abuse and mutual humiliation. There was hate speech around with people doing violence to each other through words, saying all the wrong things on the wrong occasion. Asoka addresses this problem of verbal violence, particularly among *pāṣaṇḍas,* and through a variety of self-restraints wishes a change in this culture by bringing in the idea of general moral concern and dignity.

Third, Asoka wanted to launch a new, sustainable global moral order. He tries to offer a new paradigm for kingship specifying how power is to be ethically wielded. He tries to specify what it is to be a proper king and to be an exemplar of good rule. This ethical perspective is meant potentially for the entire world, to foster the formation of a new global order with qualitatively different interstate relations, one guided by principles of *dhamma*. As he says, "The Beloved of the Gods considers the victory by Dhamma to be of foremost significance." In Rock Edict 13, he claims that

> in this moral endeavor, he has gained victory on all frontiers to a distance of six hundred *yojanas* [about 1,500 miles], where reigns the Greek king named Antiochus, and beyond the realm of that Antiochus in the lands of the four kings named Ptolemy, Antigonus, Magas, and Alexander, and in the south over the Colas and Pandyas as far as Sri Lanka. Likewise, here in the imperial territories among the Greeks and the Kambojas, Nabhakas and Nabhapanktis, Bhojas and Pitmikas, Andhras and Parindas, everywhere the people follow the Beloved of the Gods' instructions on Dhamma. Even where the envoys of the Beloved of the Gods have not gone, people hear of his conduct according to Dhamma, his precepts and his instruction in Dhamma, and they follow Dhamma and will continue to follow it.[46]

Fourth, ancient, premodern, predemocracy rulers and their states can be classified into three kinds. First, there are those rulers who conquer territories and rule people by brute force and elaborate surveillance. They enslave them, treat them as subhumans, subject them to arbitrary power, and tyrannize them. Second, there are those who seize power in the territory that they inhabit or conquer other territories but then form alliances with subsidiary rulers, neutralize opposition, impose authority, and compel others to accept their worldview. This is rule by domination. In such states, the elementary needs of people may be met but their conception of the good life is utterly disregarded. Political domination is accompanied by cultural domination. Third, and finally, there exists another kind of ruler who rules neither by brute force nor by domination. Instead, he provides political, cultural, and intellectual leadership. He wishes to arrive at a political ethic that accommodates the worldview of his subjects and where multiple conceptions of the good life exist, and seeks to find a common ground and to integrate these conceptions into his political ethic. In short, he encourages discussion among different groups within his territory and once a common political ethic is identified, he becomes its guardian. He leads by example, doing everything within his power to provide ethical education to his subjects. Though formulated in an entirely different era and context, the modern Italian philosopher Antonio Gramsci coined the term "expansive hegemony," which is deployable for such rule. When a ruler is morally hegemonic in this sense, he manages to arrive at a new ethic that coalesces the multiple ethical perspectives of all the groups in his society. Expansive hegemony is entirely consistent with pluralism. This new ethic provides a social cement to his rule within the territory and can be equally valuable to rulers and subjects beyond the boundaries of its originator. Therefore, this ethic may not only take root within the territorial boundary of the hegemon's rule but spread beyond it. This diffusion does not happen automatically but is undertaken by suitably trained moral educators. Asoka is probably the first leader to have conceived the idea of something closely resembling expansive hegemony.

Modern European imperialism was different from all historical empires. Though all expansionist states extended their power by territorial acquisition or by political and economic domination over other peoples, most premodern empires did not aim to create an interconnected global order by constructing their world as infinitely expandable. But globality was a defining feature of modern European imperialism. The internal dynamics of these states made their aspirations global, and they tried to achieve this order by means of conquest, trade, religious conversion, and cynical diplomacy. European global order either eliminates or co-opts non-European ways of life, transforming them so that they reinforce the global order. In such an order, European and in particular Anglo-American ideological presumptions have been transcribed into formal rules of the game, to which individual states must commit themselves or risk becoming economic and political pariahs.[47]

The Asokan inscriptions sow the seeds of an entirely new kind of global non-imperial order where brute force and domination are replaced by intellectual and moral leadership of the hegemon. Word is spread not just by traveling trained officials of the state but by the ruler himself, who leads by example. Although others have challenged the very idea of an imperial global order, Asokan inscriptions are the first to have conceive this possibility.

The twentieth-century futurologist and social critic H. G. Wells remarked that "amidst the tens of thousands of names of monarchs that crowd the columns of history, their majesties and graciousnesses and serenities and royal highnesses and the like, the name of Ashoka shines, and shines, almost alone, as a star."[48] He was right. Asoka's insight that we can find an alternative to the violent chaotic world order in a moral vision that is common to all countries and can bind them together into a harmonious world order is what makes him a fascinating figure even in our own times. In *Glimpses of World History,* Jawaharlal Nehru, India's first prime minister, writes:

> Men of religion have seldom, very seldom, been as tolerant as Ashoka. In order to convert people to their own faith they have seldom scrupled to use force and terrorism and fraud. The whole of history is full of religious persecution and religious wars, and in the name of religion and of Gods

perhaps more blood has been shed than in any other name. It is good therefore to remember how a great son of India, intensely religious, and the head of a powerful empire, behaved in order to convert people to his ways of thought. It is strange that any one should be so foolish as to think that religion and faith can be thrust down a person's throat at the point of the sword or a bayonet.[49]

In the mythology of India's secular nationalism, Asoka is the tolerant and wise king par excellence, one who rules by moral persuasion rather than by force or domination. He acknowledges substantive religio-philosophical differences but proposes that through self-restraint and mutual discursive encounters, each society can live with these differences, learning from and enriching each other. What we need more than anything else today is peace and solidarity to meet the challenges of climate change and global diseases, rather than new forms of colonization and imperial conquest. By outlining an ideological vision that incorporates substantive differences within each society and between societies, and by seeking harmonious coexistence, Asoka develops a model of intellectual leadership and hegemonic global order that continues to have contemporary relevance.

Notes

1. I do not wish to read ancient texts as a mirror in which I see my own socially embedded self. On the contrary, I wish to acknowledge their radical otherness, their remoteness from us. I begin with the presumption that they would appear to us strange and puzzling. I hope to be surprised by their resemblance to us. In short, I wish to first discover what these ideas meant in their own time and place before raising the question of their relevance to us. I hope these texts would challenge some of our deeply cherished assumptions, both those taken for granted in contemporary India and those presupposed by mainstream Western epistemic frameworks. To give ideas of an ancient text the power to change our own thoughts, it is crucial that we be familiar with the social history of these ideas.

2. Romila Thapar, "Is Secularism Alien to Indian Civilization?," in *The Future of Secularism*, ed. T. N. Srinivasan (Delhi: Oxford University Press, 2007), pp. 83–108; Patrick Olivelle, "Asokan Inscriptions as Text and Ideology," in *Reimagining Asoka*, ed. Patrick Olivelle et al. (Delhi: Oxford University Press, 2012), pp. 170–183.

3. Olivelle, "Asokan Inscriptions," p. 172.

4. The similarities with Confucius are striking, for he too argued against relying exclusively or strongly on law to effect social harmony or ethical development. See Joel Kupperman, "Tradition and Community: Formation of the Self," in *Confucian Ethics: A Comparative Study of Self, Autonomy and Community*, ed. Kwong-Loi Shun and David B. Wong (Cambridge: Cambridge University Press, 2004).

5. For a detailed account of interpasandic differences, see Rajeev Bhargava, "Beyond Toleration: Civility and Principled Co-existence in Ashokan Edicts," in *The Boundaries of*

Toleration, ed. Alfred Stepan and Charles Taylor (New York: Columbia University Press, 2014).

6. See Heinrich Zimmer, *Philosophies of India,* ed. Joseph Campbell (Delhi: Motilal Banarsidas, 2000 [1951]), pp. 469–470. "Asoka, rather than trying to uphold one view or the other—and thereby identifying himself with one school or the other—sought to emphasize what he held to be the 'essence' common to all sects and schools. Doing otherwise would have been to encourage a more vociferous conflict of ideas and practices among these sects and schools, thereby compromising the concord and cohesion he was trying to build up within his kingdom."

7. "There should not be condemnation of others without any ground. Such slighting (*lahuka,* from *laghu*) should be for specified grounds only." See Radhakumud Mookerji, *Asoka* (London: Macmillan, 1928), p. 159.

8. E. Hultzsch, *Inscriptions of Asoka* (Oxford: Clarendon Press, 1925).

9. Both K. R. Norman, "Buddhism and Asoka," in *The Philological Approach to Buddhism* (Oxford: The Pali Text Society, 2008), pp. 147–169, and Patrick Olivelle in "Asokan Inscriptions," have used the term "harmony" for Asoka's normative ideal for society.

10. Upinder Singh, *Political Violence in India* (Cambridge, MA: Harvard University Press, 2017); Jarrod Whitaker, *Strong Arms and Drinking Strength: Masculinity, Violence, and the Body in Ancient India* (New York: Oxford University Press, 2011).

11. Singh, *Political Violence in India,* p. 317.

12. Singh, *Political Violence in India,* p. 93.

13. D. D. Kosambi, *An Introduction to the Study of Indian History* (Bombay: Popular Prakashan, 1985 [1956]), pp. 200–203. Finally, the rules governing ordinary people and the ruler himself stemmed from the same moral source. This was quite unlike the statecraft recommended by Chanakya, in which an entirely amoral ruler committing all kinds of crimes against subjects and neighbors reigned over a morally regulated population.

14. See for instance Rock Edicts 4, 6, and 8 in Hultzsch, *Inscriptions of Asoka,* pp. 5–8, 11–13, 14–15.

15. This normative king, one who rules by a moral vision is, as Xunzi puts it, a True King. The similarities between the two are striking.

16. *Samyutta Nikaya,* III, pp. 301–303, quoted in Uma Chakravarty, *Social Dimensions of Early Buddhism* (Delhi: Munshiram Manoharlal, 1996).

17. Here there may be a marginal difference in the views of Xunzi and Asoka.

18. Asoka's views on the adverse impact of war seem similar to those of Xunzi, but with a crucial difference. Xunzi appears to think of the political consequences of war that will eventually threaten the king's rule. Asoka is concerned more about the social and moral consequences of war.

19. R. Thapar, *Asoka and the Decline of Mauryas* (Delhi: Oxford University Press, 1961), p. 36.

20. But it is very difficult to achieve this, both for low-placed and for high-placed men, but it is more difficult for high-placed men because they have too many things that distract them from achieving *swarga.* They are more inclined to do something that is morally wrong. To do the right thing, you have to undergo extreme effort. You have to renounce everything else to achieve it, and this is difficult.

21. The ideal king Maha Sudassana, for instance, establishes a perpetual grant (*evarupang danang patthapeyyang*) to provide food for the hungry, drink for the thirsty, gold for the poor, and money for those in want, as well as wives for those who require them. *Digha Nikaya*, II, p. 137; *Dialogues of the Buddha*, II, p. 211; Thomas W. Rhys Davids and Caroline A. F. Rhys Davids, *The Dialogues of the Buddha*, 3rd ed. (London: Luzac, 1951). This *dhammiko dhammaraja* "patronizes *samanas* and *brahmanas* who are worthy, providing them with all the things necessary to pursue their goals." *Digha Nikaya*, II, p. 141; *Dialogues of the Buddha*, II, p. 217.

22. Hultzsch, *Inscriptions of Asoka,* Pillar Edict 7, pp. 130–137.

23. Hultzsch, *Inscriptions of Asoka,* Rock Edict 2, pp. 2–3.

24. Romila Thapar's translation of Pillar Edict 7, in *Asoka and the Decline of Mauryas,* p. 265.

25. Hultzsch, *Inscriptions of Asoka,* Rock Edict 13, pp. 22–25.

26. The contrast with the tradition of thinking articulated later by Kautilya could not have been sharper. For Kautilya, the king's rule is explained in the last instance by the ambitions of the king and animated by the king's unique capacity to coerce and compel others.

27. Hultzsch, *Inscriptions of Asoka,* Rock Edict 8, p. 14–15.

28. Hultzsch, *Inscriptions of Asoka,* Delhi-Topra Pillar Edict 2, pp. 120–121.

29. Hultzsch, *Inscriptions of Asoka,* Delhi-Topra Pillar Edict 7, p. 134.

30. Hultzsch, *Inscriptions of Asoka,* Delhi-Topra Pillar Edict 1, pp. 119–120.

31. Hultzsch, *Inscriptions of Asoka,* Delhi-Topra Pillar Edict 3, pp. 121–122. The sins mentioned here include fierceness, cruelty, anger, pride, and envy. Sinful actions are motivated by these negative passions.

32. In Rajeev Bhargava, "Asoka's *Dhamma* as a Project of Expansive Moral Hegemony," in *Bridging Two Worlds: Comparing Classical Political Thought and Statecraft in China and India,* ed. Amitav Acharya et al. (Oakland: University of California Press, 2023). For a discussion of the idea of expansive hegemony in Gramsci, see Chantal Mouffe, "Hegemony and Ideology," in *Gramsci and Marxist Theory,* ed. C. Mouffe (London: Routledge, 1979), pp. 168–203.

33. Yan Xuetong shows that Xunzi too divides leading powers into three types: *wang* (the true king or the humane authority), *ba* (the lord-protector / hegemony), and *qiang* (the powerful / tyranny). Xunzi says, "The True King tries to win men; the lord-protector to acquire allies; the powerful to capture land." This threefold classification is similar to mine, except that I use the term "hegemony" in a different Gramscian sense.

34. Patrick Olivelle and Mark McClish, "Introduction," in *The Arthaśāstra,* ed. and trans. Olivelle and McClish (Indianapolis, IN: Hackett, 2012), p. lxxi.

35. Olivelle and Maclish, "Introduction," p. lvi.

36. "On the Regulation of a King," in *Xunzi: A Translation and Study of the Complete Works,* ed. John Knoblock, vol. 2 (Stanford, CA: Stanford University Press, 1988), p. 227.

37. The reference to conquerors by physical force is to those who perform the Brahmanical *asvamedha* rite. In contrast to the *asvemedhi,* rival kings welcome and submit to the *cakravartin* and ask him to teach them (*anusasa maharajati*).

38. Yan Xuetong, "Xunzi's and Kautilya's Thoughts on Interstate Politics," in Acharya et al., *Bridging Two Worlds;* Olivelle and McClish, "Introduction."

39. Olivelle and McClish, "Introduction," p. lv.
40. See Yan, "Xunzi's and Kautilya's Thoughts."
41. Hultzsch, *Inscriptions of Asoka,* Rock Edict 6, pp. 11–13.
42. Hultzsch, *Inscriptions of Asoka,* Delhi-Topra Pillar Edict 7, p. 134. "The rajukas are appointed for hundreds of thousands of people who are supposed to instruct the people to follow the *dhamma*."
43. Yan, "Xunzi's and Kautilya's Thoughts."
44. Hultzsch, *Inscriptions of Asoka,* Delhi-Topra Pillar Edict 4, pp. 124–125.
45. He presents himself as a father figure and says that "just as I would desire welfare and happiness in this world and the next for my children, just so, I desire the same for all men."
46. Romila Thapar's translation of Rock Edict 13 in *Asoka and the Decline of the Mauryas,* p. 256.
47. On the global order constructed by European imperialism, see for instance Walter C. Opello Jr. and Stephen J. Rosow, *The Nation-State and Global Order: A Historical Introduction to Contemporary Politics* (Boulder, CO: Lynne Rienner, 1999).
48. H. G. Wells, *The Outline of History* (New York: Macmillan, 1920), pp. 426–432.
49. J. L. Nehru, *Glimpses of World History* (New Delhi: Oxford University Press, 1989), pp. 62–63.

CHAPTER 16

From John Dewey to the Confucian "Idea" of Internationalism

Roger T. AMES

IN THIS CHAPTER, I want to explore the Confucian tradition as a resource we might draw upon for a possible planetary order. My starting point is that "family reverence" (*xiao* 孝) has served and continues to serve as the prime moral imperative within this culture. I will argue that family feeling as "morality close to the bone" has been the root and the substance of a Confucian vision of the social, political, and global order. When we think at a planetary scale, we must allow that the institution of family has always been indispensable in providing a basic level of social welfare and security in all dimensions of the human experience that can never be provided by the nation-state or other such formal entities. In spite of the fact that family relations have in some degree been subordinated to individual autonomy within liberal culture, I would argue that these basic feelings still exert a strong hold on most people regardless. Indeed, with family carrying with it the wisdom of interdependence, it is perhaps the model of human organization that can most effectively challenge the prevailing ideology of individualism and the pernicious effects of justified self-interest that prevail at both a local and a global scale.

The Argument

1. John Dewey makes a distinction between the "idea" of democracy and the political "forms" that come to constitute it, arguing that we must constantly return to this "idea" in order to reform those political forms that will never reform themselves.

2. In Dewey's formulation of this idea of democracy, he rejects those familiar liberal values ascribed to persons of individual autonomy and simple equality in favor of relational equity and an achieved diversity among them.
3. To capture his alternative conception of persons, Dewey introduces the neologism "individuality" to describe the emergence of consummate persons whose achieved identities within the social organism are due to the quality of the relations they have been able to cultivate with others in family and community.
4. Dewey wants to differentiate this qualitative conception of a relationally achieved individuality from what in his time had become the pernicious fiction of discrete individuals who in pursuit of their own pecuniary interests had become responsible for a social anarchy—everyone for themselves.
5. Such unique individuality pursued through relational equity and productive of an achieved diversity transforms mere association into the shared flourishing of the Great Community.
6. Turning from discrete individuals to nation-states, for Dewey, the Westphalian conception of the sovereign state is a scaled-up version at the political level of the fiction of individual autonomy and simple equality. This modern state system still prevailing today results in an international version of anarchy with every state acting on behalf of its own exclusive interests and out for itself.
7. For Dewey, more fundamental than this notion of the formal nation-state is the shared lives of the world's people, imbricated as they are in all of their various interpenetrating activities: politics, economics, culture, technologies, environment, religion, security, health, and so on.
8. Dewey's idea of internationalism thus challenges the persistent form of national sovereignty and can be appealed to in rejecting the Westphalian values of political autonomy and equality in favor of an inclusive relational equity and achieved diversity scaled up to a global level.
9. Dewey uses the example of China to contest the recently developed conception of the nation-state. He argues that China does not fit when shoehorned into this Western category; indeed, in many ways China is "a world of its own."
10. Based upon his own personal observations on political China, Dewey avers that one clear discrepancy lies in the fact that while Western liberals tend to look to the national government to guarantee personal rights, social stability, and procedural justice, there seems to be a profound indifference among Chinese people broadly toward their own politics and institutions.

11. I would suggest that what Dewey takes to be an erstwhile political apathy among the Chinese people might raise an important question, not only about Dewey's perception of China, but also regarding his own conception of the idea of internationalism. The question is: In the Confucian alternative to a nation-state, what is the conception of the political? And given this Confucian conception of the political as a perceived isomorphism between family and state (*jiaguotonggou* 家國同構), how does this understanding of the political factor into a Confucian vision of internationalism?
12. Dewey, while philosophically revolutionary in many ways, is still himself representative of a philosophical tradition that has not regarded family with its partial relationships as a relevant model for its regulative institutions or as a paradigmatic source of social and political order.
13. At the same time, the example of Confucian China, with the centrality of the institution of family functioning as the ultimate source and substance of social and political order, strengthens in a profound way Dewey's argument that societal forces more fundamental than the formal state constitute the idea of democracy within nation-states and the idea of internationalism that would obtain among them.
14. While Dewey appeals to relational equity and achieved diversity as alternatives to the values of autonomy and equality to ground his idea of both democracy and internationalism, he simply ignores the fact that it is the institution of family alone that can serve as the root and the ultimate guarantee of these same values.
15. Dewey's failure to discern the centrality of family and state isomorphism in Chinese political culture as a world of its own is just one example of the broader and persistent problem of Western politicians and the Western media either overlooking or ignoring the Chinese perspective on contemporary issues.
16. Again, with family-centered values rather than liberalism being the dominant norm among most of the world's cultures, we have to resist our own common sense in any discourse on a new geopolitical order that would either ignore the institution of family or set it aside as a special case.
17. In a changing world cultural order, will the Confucian values of equity and diversity grounded in the institution of family challenge dominant liberal values as a resource for real democracy and for the quality of internationalism needed to respond effectively to our shared human predicament: global warming, environmental degradation, income inequities, international terrorism, food and water shortages, pandemics, and so on?

18. As a concrete example of how these Confucian values make a difference in addressing the human predicament, we might look at the response of the various East Asian nations to the COVID-19 pandemic. The response of these nations, all with very different "forms" of governance and yet with the shared Confucian "idea" of family, has been relatively successful, while the response of the Western liberal nations has been nothing less than catastrophic.
19. Perhaps just such an asymmetry at the international level might make the argument that if our wisdom does not appreciate the implications of social and political order being rooted in and ultimately derived from the institution of family, perhaps necessity itself will recommend it.

John Dewey and the Idea of Democracy

John Dewey's conception of democracy and the Great Community it produces is nothing more or less than advocacy for an inclusive, morally consummate, and indeed spiritual way of living. In pursuit of this end, Dewey begins from his seminal distinction between the "idea" (and sometimes "ideal") of democracy, and democracy as political "forms." Dewey is keenly aware that form, political or otherwise, is recalcitrant and does not reform itself. Thus, for reformist Dewey in order to resist what in his time he perceives to be an unfortunate tendency in the evolution of the American liberal democracy to drift away from the secure moorings of its defining premises, there is a clear need for him to articulate the idea of democracy and to advocate that this idea be invoked regularly and consistently as a way of evaluating, criticizing, and retrofitting the persistent forms of democracy.

In *The Public and Its Problems,* Dewey provides an explicit definition of this idea of democracy in the following terms: "From the standpoint of the individual, it consists in having a responsible share according to capacity in forming and directing the activities of the groups to which one belongs and in participating according to need in the values which the groups sustain. From the standpoint of the groups, it demands liberation of the potentialities of members of a group in harmony with the interests and goods which are common."[1] We must be careful here because Dewey's language if misunderstood—and it frequently has been—can betray his deeper meaning. For Dewey, the "individual" and the "group" are neither separate nor separable entities. On the contrary, given Dewey's empirical commitment to the wholeness of experience as the starting point of all philosophical reflection, situation has priority over the abstraction of agency, and relationality has priority over the abstraction of individuation. For Dewey, "liberty and equality isolated from communal life are hopeless abstractions" because "equality then becomes a creed of mechanical identity which is false to facts and impossible of realization. . . . Liberty is then thought of as independent of social ties, and ends in dissolution and anarchy."[2] Disposing of the familiar perceived contest between individuals and society, Dewey sees persons not as discrete individuals but as vital, holographic configurations of relationships within the communal ecology. Comparing this social organism with the animal body, Dewey insists that "human society represents a more perfect organism. The whole lives truly in every member, and there is no longer the appearance of physical aggregation, or continuity. The organism manifests itself as what it truly is, an ideal or spiritual life, a unity of *will*. If then, society and the individual are really organic to each other, then the individual is society concentrated. He is not merely its image or mirror. He is the localized manifestation of its life . . . its vital embodiment."[3] Dewey's insight is simple: we do not "come into" relationships but are constituted holographically in our associations, and thus we function in medias res as radically embedded within a communal ecology.

The familiar institutionalized forms of democracy—a constitution, the office of the president, the polling station, the ballot box, the nation-state itself—if left unreformed by frequent appeal to the idea of democracy, far from being a guarantee of political flourishing, can on the contrary become a source of oppression, violence, and coercion. Formal institutions, while certainly necessary, are often historical carryovers from dynastic forms of government endorsed by traditions that have not only failed to embody the idea of democracy in their own hour, but in their inertia, stand the danger over time of further retarding if not even threatening the necessarily historicist and emergent "idea" of democracy itself. Witness the flawless constitution of the genocidal Stalinist Soviet Union, the Jim Crow laws of the American South, or the ostensive right of a well-regulated civilian militia to bear arms as the Second Amendment to the US Constitution. Such examples are familiar forms of democracy that fail utterly to embody the animating idea of democracy, an ideal that in its definition requires that forms of governance be inclusive and liberating for the entire community.

Such political forms are by their very nature conservative, and their "re-form" must wait upon the living and liberating idea of democracy as it circulates through the structures of the would-be thriving community. Given Dewey's radical empiricism, the idea of democracy must be prospective in the affordance it gives to the uniqueness of each person and each situation, and thus it requires of any political form that it be open to the requisite reformulations and adjustments necessary to accommodate the continuing emergence of difference. Such an understanding of democracy acknowledges a continuing Apollonian and Dionysian tension between form and the vital fluidity of the idea itself. This same reformist dynamic is also captured in the basic Confucian cosmological postulate of the inseparability of "forming and functioning" (*tiyong* 體用).

But Dewey's idea of democracy goes well beyond its service as a strategy for perpetual political reform. For him, given that everything we do as human beings, physically, intellectually, and culturally, is in our associations with others, and given that nothing and no one does anything by itself, the underlying assumption of a discrete individual is a fiction. Already in Dewey's time, individualism had become a pernicious fiction. In reconceiving democracy, he goes beyond its political implications to develop its cosmological if not even religious implications. Such a capacious understanding of democracy can be used as a touchstone in his efforts to make the most of the creative possibilities of the human experience for everyone involved—what we might call the ideal of an unbounded, optimizing symbiosis.

For Dewey the idea of democracy, then, is the answer to this question: how do we grow these initially inchoate, constitutive relations of persons-in-community in the way that will best optimize their productivity? What Dewey has done in defining the idea of democracy is to first reject the liberal values of individual autonomy and simple equality, and then to argue that they must be replaced with the values of relational equity and achieved diversity. These alternative values promise unique persons they will get what they need for personal realization from their community at the same time as they return the dividends from this relational equity to the Great Community as its achieved diversity.

Dewey on an Achieved Individuality

How then do we achieve this optimizing symbiosis in the human experience? In his *Individualism Old and New,* Dewey lays out a blueprint for how human beings are to realize this idea of democracy by moving from mere association to cultivate a quality of relations that would elevate them through relational equity and an achieved diversity to become the Great Community. He worries over the growth of an aberrant form of individualism in his own time that had broken with Emerson's promise to conjure forth for us a nonconformist and self-reliant American soul. For Dewey, real "individuality" as "the most characteristic activity of a self" is the Emersonian project of each of us aspiring after the highest quality of our own personal uniqueness. Such unique persons certainly have their own integrity, but such integrity does not acquire its moral meaning and aesthetic value exclusive of personal relations. Indeed, these same persons as constituted by their relations can only achieve their individuality by activating the ways in which they differ *from* each other to enhance what they mean *for* each other and *for* the community as a whole.

Dewey rues the fact that the notion of the individual had degenerated into a then prevailing creed of a self-interested and contentious "individualism."[4] Such a new individualism is little more than a crass, zero-sum mercantile culture of winners and losers. For Dewey, with this new individualism, "the spiritual factor of our tradition, equal opportunity and free association and intercommunication, is obscured and crowded out. Instead of the development of individualities which it prophetically set forth, there is a perversion of the whole ideal of individualism to conform to the practices of a pecuniary culture. It has become the source and justification of inequalities and oppressions."[5] Setting up a sharp distinction between his own neologism "individuality" and this decadent "individualism," Dewey goes on to exhort philosophers in their search for the Great Community to step up to the challenge of formulating a new conception of persons that embodies the very idea of democracy as a personal, social, political, and ultimately religious ideal. For Dewey, "the problem of constructing a new individuality consonant with the objective conditions under which we live is the deepest problem of our time."[6] We need to aspire to an individuality in which the social confluence of such achieved individualities becomes the optimal communal flourishing that is coterminous with them. The fictions of individual autonomy and simple equality have to be abandoned in favor of relational equity and achieved diversity as the grounding values (what Charles Taylor calls the "hypergoods") of the Great Community.[7] Dewey is explicit in offering a more complex understanding of both liberty and equality as these ideas are transformed to foster equity and diversity within the life of the community: "Liberty is that secure release and fulfillment of personal potentialities which take place only in rich and manifold association with others: the power to be an individualized self making a distinctive contribution and enjoying in its own way the fruits of association. Equality denotes the unhampered share which each individual member of the community has in the consequences of associated action. It is equitable because it is measured only by need and capacity to utilize, not by extraneous factors which deprive one in order that another may take and have."[8] Dewey is particularly emphatic on wanting to clarify this profoundly different understanding of equality. For him, equality is not some simple presocial quantitative given but a diversity achieved through relational equity that gives full affordance to difference as these values come to define the Great Community: "Equality does not signify that kind of mathematical or physical equivalence in virtue of which any one element may be substituted for another. It denotes effective regard for whatever is distinctive and unique in each, irrespective of physical and psychological inequalities. It is not a natural possession but is a fruit of the community when its action is directed by its character as a community."[9]

Individuality as the Source of Equity and Diversity

Dewey's idea of democracy in its aspiration to enable all persons to achieve their unique individuality as a shared communal goal is not one possible option for associated living that exists among other alternatives. Indeed, as Dewey insists, the idea of democracy "is the idea of community life itself."[10] This idea is the never-to-be-realized or completed social, political, and ultimately religious ideal of consummate relatedness. It is the sustained quality of the "doings and undergoings" of each and every person in this Great Community that for Dewey transforms what are mere shared patterns of association into real democracy. It is the attainment of the optimizing, virtuosic relationality of focal, holographic individuals as each of them uniquely and cooperatively shapes and is shaped by the emerging groups and communities to which they belong. This notion of individuality is for Dewey the ultimate source of relational equity and achieved diversity in community, aspiring as it does to a sustained optimizing symbiosis as its end-in-view.

Such achieved individuality as the source and substance of the Great Community is Dewey's alternative to the cluster of terms we associate with liberal individualism: individual autonomy, equality, rationality, freedom, individual choice, and so on. There is for Dewey a simple logic here. Since we are constituted by our relations, it follows that if our friends and neighbors do better, we do better. The idea of democracy then, is a moral, aesthetic, and religious aspiration. Positively stated, democracy is a fundamentally aesthetic strategy for getting the most out of the relations that constitute a community in the sense that this strategy is both holistic and inclusive—every detail is relevant to the totality of the effect. And negatively stated, it is a recognition that any lethargy or coercion in these same relationships is a diminution in their creative possibilities. Taken as a religious ideal, democracy is the felt worth persons acquire in making the most of themselves through the cultivation of their relations in community. Dewey becomes harshly critical in contrasting this real "religiousness" with those institutionalized religions that would inflict the violence of an imposed uniformity upon their followers:

> Religion as a sense of the whole is the most individualized of all things, the most spontaneous, undefinable and varied. For individuality signifies unique connections in the whole. Yet it has been perverted into something uniform and immutable. It has been formulated into fixed and defined beliefs expressed in required acts and ceremonies. Instead of marking the freedom and peace of the individual as a member of an infinite whole, it has been petrified into a slavery of thought and sentiment, an intolerant superiority on the part of the few and an intolerable burden on the part of the many.[11]

Peter Hershock in his monograph *Valuing Diversity* draws upon the Buddhist tradition to theorize his version of the values of relational equity and achieved diversity, a formulation that can be useful in bringing further clarity to Dewey's notion of individuality as the ground of the Great Community.[12] In Hershock's language, relational equity is the heightened realization of dynamically shared well-being, and achieved diversity is the conserving and coordinating of differences for the full appreciation of the creative possibilities of any situation. Hershock's reasoning is as follows. The values of both individual autonomy and simple equality are grounded in a doctrine of external relations that subordinates our relations with others to our individual selves. A doctrine of external relations prioritizes our integrity over our interdependence with each other, and the ostensive sameness that obtains among us—our "equality"—over our many differences. Thus, the notions of autonomy and equality as they attach to individuals give us a sense of differences as mere "variety"—differences that do not make much of a difference. We certainly have differences among us that we do well to register and tolerate, but such differences are in some important degree mitigated by the assumption that we as individuals are still to be treated as equals. And as persons that would assert their individual autonomy, the relations they enter into are perceived to be external and contingent rather than intrinsic and constitutive.

While comparative equality and individual autonomy guarantee that difference can only be variations among basically similar people (variety), the pursuit of relational equity and an achieved diversity allows for the continuing diversification of qualities and propensities that grow our differences into resources for mutual enrichment (diversity). Variety among equals stands in contrast to the diversity that can only be achieved by fully activating and appreciating the important differences we have from each other. That is, we not only need to acknowledge that we differ *from* each other (variety) but must in fact be able to actively differ *for* each other and, in so doing, allow our differences to really make a difference (diversity). This is what Hershock, Wang Ban, and Qin Yaqing in their essays in this volume describe in different terms as an "ethical ecology." For them the global human condition can only be addressed by promoting an ethical ecology in which differences in ethical perspectives (*side* 私德) can be activated in the global commons to contribute to realizing globally shared values (*gongde* 公德).

For Hershock, there are two important corollaries to this valorization of equity and diversity we might note. First, equity and diversity cannot be engineered by individual agents (who do not exist); they must emerge as a function of the coordinated activity among relationally constituted members of family and community. And second, the values of equity and diversity extend beyond any narrowly conceived communal locus to guarantee the mutual implication and inseparability of ethical, economic, and ecological considerations and, as we shall see, offer a conception of the political as an alternative to the Westphalian notion of the sovereign state.

Internationalizing Dewey's "Great Community"

Westphalian sovereignty is the principle of international law that emerged out of the Peace of Westphalia (1648) ending the Thirty Years' War. According to this formulation of international relations that today still undergirds our modern state system, each nation-state regardless of size has an equal right to sovereignty over its own territory. In many respects, this concept of national sovereignty can be read as the values of autonomy and simple equality scaled up from the individual to the level of the sovereign nation-state. And just as with the concept of the discrete individual, this notion of the individual sovereign state is again a fiction. In Dewey's essay "[John] Austin's Theory of Sovereignty," he argues that Austin fails to recognize that the formal institutions of state sovereignty are in fact themselves only secondary constructions of the more primary and thus sovereign social forces that give them expression: "In every existing civilized state governmental power is in the hands of a certain body of persons, capable of more or less accurate assignment and thus Austin's conception seems to agree fairly with facts. But ... take away the forces which are behind governments—which have made them what they are, and the existence and character of these governments is an accident, likely to be changed at any moment. Admit these forces, and, since they determine the government, they are sovereign."[13]

Dewey anticipates Alfred North Whitehead's fallacies of "simple location" and "misplaced concreteness" but in political guise—that is, the attribution of exclusive sovereignty to the formal institution of the state itself while ignoring the underlying processual transitivity of the vital social forces to which governments owe their very existence.[14] For Dewey, this doctrine of the sovereign nation-state, far from serving the values of equity and diversity among states, produces a kind of international, "everyone for themselves" anarchy that allows for a "denial on the part of a political state of either legal or moral responsibility." He avers that "it is a direct proclamation of the unlimited and unquestionable right of a political state to do what it wants to do in respect to other nations and to do it as and when it pleases. It is a doctrine of international anarchy; and as a rule those who are most energetic in condemning anarchy as a domestic and internal principle are foremost in asserting anarchic irresponsibility in relations between nations."[15] It is not lost on Dewey that the reality of European international relations in the more than three and a half centuries since the rights of equal and sovereign states were ushered in by the Peace of Westphalia has amounted to little more than perpetual war, "for *right* is here only a polite way of saying power. It was usual during the World War to accuse Germany of acting upon the notion that Might makes Right. But every state that cultivates and acts upon the notion of National Sovereignty is guilty of the same crime."[16]

Dewey himself as a self-declared internationalist in scaling up his idea of democracy and the Great Community to the idea of internationalism at a global level wants nothing less than to transform international relations and the world's geopolitical order. Dewey begins from the wholeness of experience as the grounding cosmological assumption of his pragmatism in extending this idea of democracy from the social to the political, and from the nation-state to his internationalism. For Dewey, the formal nation-state is just one more political form. It is not itself a final end, and indeed it must always be understood as subordinate to the quality of the more primary social forces that sustain and continue to shape it. Dewey asks if the state

> is not just an instrumentality for promoting and protecting other and more voluntary forms of association, rather than a supreme end in itself.... The state remains highly important—but its importance consists more and more in its power to foster and coordinate the activities of voluntary groupings. Only nominally is it in any modern community the end for the sake of which all the other societies and organizations exist. Groupings for promoting the diversity of goods that men share have become the real social units. They occupy the place which traditional theory has claimed either for mere isolated individuals or for the supreme and single political organization.[17]

For Dewey, to think in terms of the sovereign state like the "new pecuniary individualism" he reviles is yet another example of our inveterate pattern of substance thinking that must be overcome. It is a clear illustration of a failure to distinguish between a noun and a gerund, a thing and an event, a leg and the activity of walking, a body and the eventfulness of embodied living. Simply put, we need to include both form and function as two aspects of any human activity. In his essay "The Emancipation of the International Spirit," Dewey insists that it is the geopolitical interdependence characteristic of internationalism that is the fact, and that the sovereign nation-state is only a second-order abstraction from what are fundamentally organic, *intra*-national (rather than *inter*-national) relations:[18]

> While economic forces have brought about the present world internationalism, the results extend far beyond industry and commerce. They extend beyond the political area, whether diplomatic or military. It is a commonplace that the discoveries of science and the fruitions of art now quickly become the possession of the whole world, and that the nations are sharers in a noble emulation.... It is matter of utilizing for good the economic interdependence of the peoples who inhabit the earth, and of making it possible for an international mind to function effectively in the control of the world's practical affairs.[19]

Our penchant for giving primacy to national sovereignty is anathema to and is belied by the growth in "trans-national interests" that follows from thinking internationally. Clearly, opines Dewey, "the weal and woe of any modern state is bound up with that of others. Weakness, disorder, false principles on the part of any state are not confined within its boundaries. They spread and infect other states. The same is true of economic, artistic and scientific advances. Moreover the voluntary associations just spoken of do not coincide with political boundaries. Associations of mathematicians, chemists, astronomers; business corporations, labor organizations, churches are trans-national because the interests they represent are worldwide."[20] Reflecting on the unwarranted prominence given the nation-state, Dewey rues the fact that "it is the vogue of this doctrine, or dogma, that presents the strongest barrier to the effective formation of an international mind." His conclusion, then, is that "internationalism is not an aspiration but a fact, not a sentimental ideal but a force." And when achieved, internationalism gives the lie to "the traditional dogma of exclusive national sovereignty."[21]

It is the enriching possibilities made available to local communal life by appreciating the fact that political boundaries conjoin as well as divide us that inspired Dewey's internationalism and made him a citizen of the world.[22] In his reflections on local communal life, Dewey insists that "while local, it will not be isolated. Its larger relationships will provide an inexhaustible and flowing fund of meanings upon which to draw with assurance that its drafts will be honored. Territorial states and political boundaries will persist; but they will not be barriers which impoverish experience by cutting man off from his fellows; they will not be hard and fast divisions whereby external separation is converted into inner jealousy, fear, suspicion and hostility."[23]

Dewey announces explicitly that "we must make the accident of our internal composition into an idea, an idea upon which we may conduct our foreign as well as our domestic policy."[24] For Dewey it is clear that, if we aspire to a true internationalism, we need to articulate an idea of internationalism at a more fundamental level than the fragmenting of what is a continuous humanity into discrete, formal, and abstract nation-states. A truly robust notion of internationalism will require us to give primacy to those interdependent organic forces that operate at a much deeper and pervasive level than the epiphenomenon of the nation-state. Otherwise, worries Dewey, we must accept the inevitable fact that "an international judicial tribunal will break in the end upon the principle of national sovereignty," and that all of our best efforts at internationalism will fail as a consequence.[25]

Dewey and the "China" Exception to the Nation-State

Dewey takes the perceived tension between nationalism and his internationalism a step further in asking, "When did nations begin to be anyway? How long has France been a compact and homogeneous nation? Italy? Germany? What forces made them nations?"[26] Dewey when asking about the future of internationalism is particularly interested in the anomaly that China represents when the geopolitical order of the world is construed in terms of nation-states. In an essay entitled explicitly "Is China a Nation?" Dewey observes that "our whole concept of nation is of such recent origin that it is not surprising that it does not fit in any exact way into Chinese conditions."[27] With its population of more people than the entire continent of Africa, and with almost twice the population of a combined Eastern and Western Europe, China is not a "country": it is not an Italy, a Vietnam, or an Argentina. Dewey resists the uncritical assumption of most of our political philosophers today that this continental civilization called China can be shoehorned comfortably into our category of a nation-state. For Dewey, an understanding of China must be pursued within an evolving global context, where "one must repeat that China is changing rapidly; and that it is as foolish to go on thinking of it in terms of old dynastic China—as Mr. Bland for example insists we must do—as it is to interpret it by pigeon-holing its facts in western conceptions. China *is* another world politically and economically speaking, a large and persistent world, and a world bound no one knows just where. It is the combination of these facts that give it its overpowering intellectual interest for an observer of the affairs of humanity."[28]

China and an Alternative Model of Social and Political Order

As one way of arguing that China is a world of its own, Dewey, in offering his interpretation of prevailing political attitudes within China and how the Chinese people themselves perceive governance, distinguishes himself as an astute observer as well as a curious and self-critical cultural pluralist. Dewey anticipates present-day China's argument that the Western model of development is only one among many, and that it should not be taken to be some universal template suitable for all cultural traditions. For Dewey, the familiar European ethnocentrism of his time was one more dogmatism that we can do without. He observes that "we have taken European political development as a necessary standard of normal political evolution. We have made ourselves believe that all development from savagery to civilization must follow a like course and pass through similar stages. When we find societies that do not agree with this standard, we blandly dismiss them as abnormalities, as survivals of backward states, or as manifestations of lack of political capacity."[29] Dewey was personally familiar with at least one alternative model of governance he saw in the phenomenon of China itself. Having spent his sojourn of more than two years traveling and lecturing throughout this vast country, Dewey was keenly aware of the attitude of the Chinese population in general as it is captured in the popular refrain "Heaven is high and the emperor is far away" (*tiangaohuangdiyuan* 天高皇帝遠).

From his own on-site observations, Dewey avers that Chinese citizens are largely apathetic in their relation to their political institutions, choosing to live instead under the conditions of a peculiarly Chinese version of an anarchism of indifference. Dewey is persuaded that "the central factor in the Chinese historic political psychology is its profound indifference to everything that we associate with the state, with government."[30] Dewey goes further with this description of Chinese society. While the usual formal apparatus of governance for us is vitally important in guaranteeing personal rights, social stability, and procedural justice, it has only marginal relevance to the seemingly tranquil and untroubled lives of the Chinese people: "We take for granted the existence of government as an agency for enforcing justice between men and for protecting personal rights. We depend upon regular and orderly legal and judicial procedure to settle disputes as we take for granted the atmosphere we breathe. In China life goes on practically without such support and guarantees. And yet in the ordinary life of the people peace and order reign."[31]

I think Dewey's interpretation of this erstwhile political apathy might reveal a blind spot in his understanding of Chinese governance and, perhaps more importantly, in his own formulation of the idea of internationalism. I do not believe that Dewey is wrong in his observations on what seems to be Chinese apathy except to say that the difference between the keen sense of civic responsibility in liberal democracy and a perceived Confucian lack of interest in the operations of the state might have a better explanation. We might have to ask the following questions: What is the Confucian conception of the political? What does this tradition take to be the source and the institutions of proper governance?

In the big picture, thinking through the real source of governance in China might serve us as a corrective to the continuing perception promoted by G. W. F. Hegel that political apathy among the Chinese people is best explained by China being a first-order "oriental despotism." On Hegel's reading, all power lies exclusively in the hands of the emperor while everyone else blindly does his bidding. Hegel reports that in this Chinese world "moral distinctions and requirements are expressed as Laws, but so that the subjective will is governed by these Laws as by an external force. Nothing subjective in the shape of disposition, Conscience, formal Freedom, is recognized.... While *we* obey, because what we are required to do is confirmed by an *internal* sanction, there the Law is regarded as inherently and absolutely valid without a sense of the want of this subjective confirmation."[32] Hegel's perception of Chinese totalitarian governance is still alive and well today in the anti-China hysteria of Western politicians broadly and the media through which they speak.

Again, clarifying the Confucian alternative understanding of the political is important because it reinforces Dewey's own insight that in assessing the role of the nation-state, we must see it as a second-order abstraction from the more primary social forces that lie beneath it. The difference is that while Dewey identifies these forces as the more fundamental and fluid "voluntary associations" and "groupings" that flow across political boundaries, the Confucian tradition would insist that it is the institution of family that must be the root and source of proper governance.

The Confucian Institution of Family as the Root and Source of Proper Governance

Dewey, like most contemporary political philosophers, is all but overlooking the central role that the complex institution of family has played historically and still plays today as the primary source of the Confucian social and political order. And if Confucian politics is importantly defined by family, then the Chinese are anything but apathetic. We might begin from the *Analects* to argue it is family that is traditionally taken to be the ultimate source of governance. Confucius himself is making an astute observation when he asserts that within this cultural tradition, the proper functioning of the institution of family is integral to the production of the sociopolitical order of the state: "Someone asked Confucius, 'Why are you not employed in government?' The Master replied, 'The *Book of Documents* says: "It all lies in family reverence. Being filial to your parents and finding fraternity with your brothers is in fact carrying out the work of governing." In doing these things I am participating in governing. Why must I be employed in government?'"[33]

More recently, but in the same vein, the distinguished late-Qing scholar Yan Fu 嚴復 (1854–1921), who translated and introduced Western liberalism into the Chinese academy through the works of Adam Smith, T. H. Huxley, John Stuart Mill, Herbert Spencer, and others, once remarked that if we ask after the source of social and political order in imperial China over the past two millennia, 30 percent can be attributed to the emperor and 70 percent to family lineage.[34] Yan Fu is remarking here on the fact that almost all aspects of the human experience in pre-Republican China—economic, political, ethical, religious, and so on—took place within the life of distinctive, extended family and clan lineages (*jiazu* 家族 or *shizu* 氏族).[35]

This dependence upon the institution of family as the primary source of social and political order has not been given full shrift except by a few of our most perceptive observers. Today as we anticipate the continuing rise of Chinese economic, political, and cultural influence, we might remember that centuries ago, Gottfried Wilhelm Leibniz, a comparative philosopher in an earlier age, attempted to make productive sense of Confucian China for the Europe of his own time and place. Comparing China with Europe, Leibniz asks, "who would have believed that there is on earth a people who, though we are in our view so very advanced in every branch of behavior, still surpass us in comprehending the precepts of civil life . . . the precepts of ethics and politics adapted to the present life and use of mortals."[36]

Leibniz goes on in this comparison to express, in language that would seem to be a stern repudiation of Hegel's caricature of top-down, unilateral imposition, the idea that social and political order emerges importantly from within. In the words Leibniz chooses we can hear clear reverberations of the specific Confucian moral imperatives of "family reverence" (*xiao* 孝) and "ritual propriety" (*li* 禮):

> In a vast multitude of men they have virtually accomplished more than the founders of religious orders among us have achieved within their own narrow ranks. So great is obedience toward superiors and reverence toward elders, so religious, almost, is the relation of children toward parents, that for children to contrive anything violent against their parents, even by word, is almost unheard of. . . . Moreover, there is among equals, or those having little obligation to one another, a marvelous respect, and an established order of duties. . . . Neighbors and even members of a family are so held back by a hedge of custom that they are able to maintain a kind of perpetual courtesy.[37]

In advancing his own generalizations about European and Chinese cultures, Leibniz saw a clear contrast between the value invested in those abstract, theoretical disciplines in the European academy that are in search of axiomatic-deductive demonstration, and the more aesthetic and pragmatic applications of the Chinese tradition—a distinction that broadly distinguishes a European confidence in the disciplining dividends of the rational sciences and formal institutions from those alternative rewards that can be derived from virtuosity in the art of living within the forces of family and community life.

Family as the Ultimate Source of Relational Equity and Achieved Diversity

I have argued elsewhere that the Confucian religious life is human- and family-centered, seeking to "bind tightly" (L. *religare*) within family and community without any reference to a conception of an external Abrahamic God.[38] There is an analogy here between Confucian religiousness and its vision of the political life; both are family focused, and only then, by radial expansion, do they extend to the world beyond. The traditional Confucian way of life does not embrace what Aristotle with his *Politics* (*Politikà*), being understood as "the affairs of state," would take as the asymmetrical distinction between *oikos* and *polis*, between family / household and the realm of politics. Instead, witnessing a persistent isomorphism between family and state (*jiaguotonggou* 家國同構) throughout the early Confucian canons, we come to understand that the perceived primary source of both social and political order in this tradition is the institution of family as it is rooted in the prime moral imperatives of "family reverence" (*xiao* 孝) and its complement, "an achieved propriety in one's roles and relations" (*li* 禮). While Confucian texts certainly regard the abstract rule of law and the application of punishments as necessary ancillary institutions, at the same time they construe appeal to law as a clear admission of communal failure. There is a passage in the *Analects* that sets up a rather stark contrast between the efficacy of formal legal instruments and that of the tensile communal bonds woven out of robust family relations, with the expectation that family and community through a cultivated sense of shame can become self-governing: "The Master said: 'Lead the people with administrative injunctions and keep them orderly with penal law, and they will avoid punishments but will not develop a sense of shame. Lead them with moral virtuosity and keep them orderly through aspiring to propriety in their roles and relations, and they will develop a sense of shame, and moreover, will order themselves.'"[39]

Moral virtuosity in the person of the ruler is certainly perceived as an important factor in good governance, but this morally suasive role model, as the erstwhile parent of the people, is most effective when such rulership can take the form of "reigning" rather than "ruling," with the people properly ordering themselves.[40] At its most fundamental level, it is the proper functioning of roles in family and community and the commensurate sense of shame such roles produce within ritually choreographed relations that serve as the primary source of social and political order. A dynamic *li*-structured family and community is a concrete and powerful guarantee of social solidarity, while abstract laws and policies can at best serve as no more than secondary injunctions.

Dewey personally had a singularly strong devotion to family, was committed to many of the values that are the substance of family-based feminist care ethics, and was a pioneer in early childhood education. Even so, what leads me to think that Dewey might not have fully appreciated the Chinese investment in family as the primary source of political order is the fact that family as an institution has not been a significant inspiration for institutionalized order within the broad sweep of Western philosophy and culture. We would be hard-pressed to find any family-centered philosophical notion that is in any way comparable to or has had the vital importance that "familial reverence" (*xiao* 孝) serves in its role as the prime moral imperative for Confucian philosophy. If we rehearse the contributions of our principal philosophers, few indeed have invoked family as a productive model for organizing the human experience. Plato's rejection of the family in the *Republic* and Aristotle's denigration of the "household" (*oikos*) as a source of privation are fairly representative. And even Dewey, who would allow that democracy "accords with the historic spirit of the Chinese race," is true to the mainstream of his own tradition (with perhaps additional encouragement from the May Fourth reformers) when he avers that China will have to get past the traditional family system as a precondition for any process of modernization and democratization.[41] Bertrand Russell's visit to China overlapped with Dewey's, and reflecting back on this intense experience, he expressed a similar reservation with respect to the institution of family: "Filial piety, and the strength of the family generally, are perhaps the weakest point in Confucian ethics, the only point where the system departs seriously from common sense. Family feeling has militated against public spirit, and the authority of the old has increased the tyranny of ancient custom."[42]

Perhaps within the Western narrative, for those philosophers who would look to moral reasoning as the ultimate source of adjudication, this sustained disinterest in the always partial relations that emerge from family feeling might be due to the perceived centrality of impartial principles as a necessary condition for ethical conduct. In any case, it explains in some degree why we fail to register the importance of family when we reflect upon the Chinese model of political order. Such a lack of interest in family as a source and measure of order in our own philosophical narrative contrasts starkly with the Confucian worldview, in which family is *the* governing metaphor, and in which in fact *all* relationships are ultimately perceived as familial. The signature of Confucianism is that morality as it is cultivated through the commitment to "consummate conduct in one's roles and relations" (*ren* 仁) is an extension and expression of immediate family feeling. In the *Analects* we read the following: "Exemplary persons concentrate their efforts on the root, for the root having been properly set, the vision of the moral life will grow therefrom. As for family reverence and fraternal deference, they are I suspect, the root of consummate conduct (*ren* 仁)."[43]

Family is the root of moral growth because it is the single human institution to which persons are most inclined to give themselves utterly and without remainder: time, money, a body part, their very lives. A positive sense of shame expressed as a commitment to the family and to the extended community guarantees that relations are prosocial and thus preemptive in their minimizing antisocial behaviors. Family is the entry point for the growth in relations that is the substance of Confucian morality, and as these vital relations expand outward radially into the community, they have the primary role not only of transforming mere association into the Great Community but of transforming the Great Community itself into the Great Family.

The contemporary philosopher Zhao Tingyang 趙汀陽 reflects on how first setting the root and then on that basis pursuing growth is the beginning and the projected end in the Confucian way of becoming consummately human: "The primary issue for the human way is that of generation and regeneration, and the first step herein is growth. This is the starting point for the evolutionary thread of Chinese thought. The 'doing' of growth must seek what a thing relies upon to be 'deeply rooted and firmly planted' in its growth. Therefore, growth first of all requires putting down roots. The two metaphors of growth and putting down roots set out the path for Chinese thought."[44]

In the Confucian canons, it is the family as the ultimate source and the indispensable medium for an achieved propriety (*li* 禮) that promises us an "optimizing harmony" (*he* 和) in all of our roles and relations. The *Analects* insists that "an optimizing harmony (*he*) is the most valuable function of achieving propriety in our roles and relations (*li*). In the ways of the Former Kings, the sustaining of this quality of harmony through achieving propriety in their roles and relations made them elegant, and was a guiding standard in all things large and small. But when things are not going well, to realize harmony just for its own sake without regulating the situation through an achieved propriety in roles and relations, will not work."[45] If a superlative harmony achieved through relational equity and an achieved diversity is the desired goal, it is the underlying judgment in this Confucian tradition that it is the institution of family that is a necessary condition in achieving this end.

Confucian Family and a New World Cultural Order

Shifting our attention from nuclear to extended families, and from the community and the state to the "global village" the world is supposedly becoming, there is yet another sociopolitical factor we might bear in mind. There is nothing perhaps more familiar than family; after all, the words "familiar" and "family" share the same root (L. *famulus*). Everyone has a family. Consequently, family reverence as a moral imperative provides us the broadest possible basis for developing appropriate ethical feelings, where such feelings are more primordial and comprehensive than the more cognitive activities of thinking or reasoning. Indeed, family plays a key role in producing moral persons. If we learn to love by being loved, ethics everywhere relies in an important degree upon family feeling.

In this way we can come to appreciate that the idea of family, while rooted in the most immediate of family feelings, needs to be extended far beyond it. This is an important point, for one recurrent criticism of Confucian thought has been that however useful it may be for local interactions with blood relatives, it is less helpful for providing guidelines on how to deal with strangers, or even how to care enough about strangers to *want* to deal with them in a humane manner.⁴⁶ The challenge for Confucian philosophy—and it has been a formidable one— has always been to overcome any inclination to an exclusionary nepotism and parochialism and to function holistically and inclusively in serving the interests of all concerned. The Confucian tradition has long been aware that there are many important dimensions of the human experience that require impartiality, transparency, and objective regulative ideals. Beginning with the distinction made between an inclusive "optimal appropriateness" (*yi* 義) and an exclusive "personal advantage" (*li* 利) that we find as early as the *Analects* and the *Mencius*, Confucianism has struggled with this seemingly necessary relationship between ethical conduct and a sense of impartiality.⁴⁷ But rather than equating morality with objectivity, Confucian philosophy is holistic in seeing an important role for both particular and more general considerations, both equity and diversity. That is, rather than invoking some transcendental moral standard or some faculty of impersonal reason as the single warrant for claiming such impartiality—a strategy that is necessarily hobbled by the contingencies of always specific circumstances— the Confucian tradition in developing its understanding of impartiality has remained true to its commitment to holism. Even in the distinction made between subjective and objective perspectives, impartiality is served practically by extending one's range of concern from "the master-eye view" (*zhuguan* 主觀) that might possibly be limited by some self-serving personal advantage (*li* 利) to "the guest-eye view" (*keguan* 客觀) that seeks what is most appropriate for all concerned (*yi* 義), including the interests of the master. The point is that Confucian moral thinking is holistic, where real justice can only be achieved by giving full affordance to both partiality and impartiality rather than choosing between them.⁴⁸

The Confucian texts in general make it clear that family is the entry point for moral competence, and that one must learn to extend family reverence beyond the immediate family circle to ripple out in ever-widening radial circles, until ideally one embraces, and feels at one with, the world at large. Family is the governing metaphor in the Confucian worldview precisely because it serves as a deliberate strategy for optimizing the creative possibilities of equity and diversity available to persons through their relationships. The ethical importance of the idea of family, as the texts make clear, lies in understanding that it is only through the many and loving interactions with our own Grandmother that we learn to correlate such feelings with other grandmothers regardless of the language they happen to speak, the color of their skin, or their religious beliefs. The Confucian emphasis is on the holographic correlation between the person "Grandmother" and the role of "grandmother." Given that the term "grandmother" as opposed to the proper name "Grandmother" can be read as an abstraction, it is difficult at times to appreciate fully the strong focus on specificity in early Confucianism. But even so, the difference between "grandmother" and "individual," "self," or "person" should be fairly clear. To see this difference another way, when we focus on specific family roles like grandmother that are familiar to us, the ignoring of others is more difficult to countenance and the hatred of others is more difficult to sustain. Although there is no essential grandmother, there are sufficient family resemblances among and between grandmothers the world over that when we attend to them in that role instead of dwelling on their physical and cultural differences, our empathetic association makes seeing them as wholly other almost impossible. This is the import of the passage in the *Classic of Family Reverence* when Confucius says: "Exemplary persons (*junzi*) in their teachings (*jiao*) on family reverence (*xiao*) do not travel daily from one family to the next to meet with each of them individually. Their teaching of family reverence is their way to show respect (*jing*) for every father in the empire; their teaching of fraternal deference (*ti*) is their way to show respect for every elder brother in the empire; their teaching of ministerial deference is their way to show respect for every lord in the empire."[49]

Certainly, many of the citizens of the developed nations as well as the urban elites in those that are less developed subscribe more or less to the liberal model of society and government based upon the Enlightenment understanding of human beings as free, rational, and autonomous individuals. But the great majority of the rest of the world's peoples in Africa, Asia, and the Middle East do not seem to define themselves fundamentally as free and autonomous individuals. Their self-understanding is they are embedded in a social ecology of daughters and sons, mothers and fathers, spouses, siblings, cousins, neighbors, and members of clans—all with close ties to specific geographic areas—and communities, religious and secular. Except for the Westernized urban elites in such areas, most of the peoples there would define themselves in a much more relational, "Confucian" language than in Enlightenment and modern liberal terms. Thus, if in looking for resources for a changing geopolitical order we seriously desire to engage in an inclusive cross-cultural dialogue rather than a polemic, the familial terms must be allowed into the discourse even if they do not come to dominate it.

Again, this tendency of Western theorists to overlook the centrality of family in the construction of traditional Confucian social and political order is a symptom of a much larger problem. In the current political discourse, whether the topic is Hong Kong, the South China Sea, or the Belt and Road Initiative, there is little if any attempt to frame these global issues by thinking through and including a Chinese perspective, whatever that might be. Said another way, the Chinese perspective when expressed from within is dismissed outright as China's excuse for tyranny, and any external voice that would have the temerity to say anything positive about China is accused of either naïveté or the coddling of dictators, or both. This is not to say that a Chinese perspective on any of the contemporary issues is going to win the day or even be persuasive, but intelligence in the discourse requires the capaciousness to entertain different, usually imperfect, and sometimes irreconcilable perspectives at the same time.

Development generally, and the global impact of China's own growth more specifically, is producing a range of changing economic and political patterns that are relatively easy to track. But with China now as an increasingly dominant player that is here to stay, what about cultural change? What difference will this wholesale reconfiguration of economic and political dominance make for the elite world cultural order that has long been dominated by a powerful liberalism? And what will be the role of traditional Confucian values in the evolution of a new world order as China quite properly insists that its culture should have its place at the table? Will these family-centered Confucian values under the rapidly evolving conditions in evidence today contribute to a new cultural world order?

When Dewey, with his cosmological understanding of democracy as a social, political, and religious ideal, demands from it the optimizing of the available human resources, Confucian philosophy would argue vociferously that the only institution that can achieve real democracy as it is being promoted in this Deweyan sense of relational equity and achieved diversity is the family. Acknowledging Dewey's insistence that there are social forces more fundamental than the concept of nation-states, will a Confucian ethic that locates moral conduct within a thick and richly textured pattern of family, community, and political relations not only change the international culture but provide the substance needed for Dewey's idea of internationalism to become a widely shared value?

Over a single generation, the rise of Confucian Asia and particularly China has precipitated a sea change in the prevailing economic and political order of the world. This recent and dramatic geopolitical reorientation has remained largely entrained within the troubling dynamics of a "perfect storm": global warming, pandemics, food and water shortages, environmental degradation, massive species extinction, international terrorism, income inequities, proxy wars, nuclear proliferation, and the list goes on. When we look for the cultural resources necessary to respond to this global predicament, we must anticipate the need for a critical shift in our values, intentions, and practices in which priority must be given to those dispositions that, in anticipation of coordinated flourishing across national, ethnic, and religious boundaries, will support replacing the familiar competitive pattern of sovereign nations as single actors pursing their own self-interest, with the model of a world family of nations strengthening relations to collaborate on addressing our increasingly complex problems.

If there ever was a clear example of how the family-centered values of Confucianism can make a concrete difference in responding to these pressing issues of our times, we need look no further than the COVID-19 pandemic the world has endured and will continue to endure. In the early 2020s we have in America become inured to if not numbed by the spiraling numbers posted daily of the legions of victims who on ventilators have died alone. With some 80 percent of the persons dying being over sixty-five years old and thus many of them being grandmothers, when on any day's media account of the pandemic, a cold number becomes a human face, this grandmother is usually pictured and remembered first as a loved one within her own particular family, and then by extension, as a person who has contributed in one way or another to the well-being of her community. For Confucians in this very basic sense, when you have loved one grandmother you can love them all.

It can be fairly argued that the East Asian Confucian countries all with very different forms of government have been enabled by the idea of family to manage the pandemic with a relatively low number of casualties.[50] Their experience stands in stark contrast to the devastating experience suffered by the Indo-European cultures where the numbers lost have been staggering. Even though this obvious asymmetry in response still persists, from the very outset there was little inclination on the part of Western countries to either learn or benefit from their Asian counterparts. Perhaps in the decades ahead as humanity continues to ride out the perfect storm, it will be necessity itself rather than human wisdom that will challenge a continuing Western commitment to individualism with the Confucian idea of family.

Notes

1. John Dewey, *The Later Works, 1925–1953*, ed. Jo Ann Boydston, 17 vols. (Carbondale: Southern Illinois University Press, 1981–1990), vol. 2, p. 327.

2. Dewey, *Later Works*, vol. 2, p. 329.

3. John Dewey, *The Early Works, 1882–1898*, ed. Jo Ann Boydston, 5 vols. (Carbondale: Southern Illinois University Press, 1967–1972), vol. 1, p. 237.

4. Dewey, *Later Works*, vol. 7, p. 286.

5. Dewey, *Later Works*, vol. 5, p. 49.

6. Dewey, *Later Works*, vol. 5, p. 56.

7. "Hypergoods" is a useful neologism introduced by Charles Taylor in his *Sources of the Self: The Making of the Modern Identity* (Cambridge, MA: Harvard University Press, 1989), pp. 62–63: "Most of us not only live with many goods but find that we have to rank them, and in some cases, this ranking makes one of them of supreme importance relative to the others. . . . Let me call higher-order goods of this kind 'hypergoods,' i.e., goods which not only are incomparably more important than others but provide the standpoint from which these must be weighed, judged, decided about."

8. Dewey, *Later Works*, vol. 2, p. 329.

9. Dewey, *Later Works*, vol. 2, pp. 329–330.

10. Dewey, *Later Works*, vol. 2, p. 328.

11. John Dewey, *The Middle Works, 1899–1924*, ed. Jo Ann Boydston, 15 vols. (Carbondale: Southern Illinois University Press, 1976–1983), vol. 14, pp. 226–227.

12. Peter D. Hershock, *Valuing Diversity: Buddhist Reflection on Realizing a More Equitable Global Future* (Albany: State University of New York Press, 2012).

13. Dewey, *Early Works*, vol. 4, p. 80.

14. See A. N. Whitehead, *Process and Reality: An Essay in Cosmology*, corrected edition, ed. David Ray Griffin and Donald W. Sherbourne (New York: Free Press, 1978), p. 10.

15. Dewey, *Later Works*, vol. 3, p. 156.

16. Dewey, *Later Works*, vol. 3, p. 157.

17. Dewey, *Middle Works*, vol. 12, pp. 196–197.

18. We commonly use the prefix "*inter-*" to suggest a joint, external, and open relationship that conjoins two or more separate and, in some sense, comparable entities: we use our "personal" computers to access the "internet" ("inter" + "network") and to get onto "the web," where the web is the conjoining of a matrix of independent nodes each with its own secured integrity. By way of contrast, "*intra-*"—meaning "on the inside," "within"—references internal and constitutive relations contained within a given entity itself. *Intra*- has immediate organic, ecological implications—an inside without an outside. It references a radical contextuality—the inseparability of the holographic one and many (*yiduobufen* 多不分)—where global order is the always provisional, emergent, and resolutely unsummed totality of all orders without any single privileged and dominant order among them.

19. Dewey, *Later Works*, vol. 3, pp. 349–350.

20. Dewey, *Middle Works*, vol. 12, p. 197.

21. Dewey, *Middle Works*, vol. 12, pp. 196–197.

22. Whenever a Deweyan term seems abstract and vacuous—"social intelligence" or "citizens of the world"—we need only to turn to Dewey's own biography to fill out its concrete content. Dewey lived such terms.

23. Dewey, *Later Works*, vol. 2, p. 370.

24. Dewey, *Middle Works*, vol. 8, p. 203.

25. Dewey, *Middle Works*, vol. 8, p. 203.

26. Dewey, *Middle Works*, vol. 13, p. 73.

27. Dewey, *Middle Works*, vol. 13, p. 73.

28. Dewey, *Middle Works*, vol. 13, p. 75. The reference is to J. O. P. Bland's *China, Japan, and Korea* (New York: Charles Scribner's Sons, 1921).

29. Dewey, *Middle Works*, vol. 11, p. 215.

30. Dewey, *Middle Works*, vol. 11, p. 216.

31. Dewey, *Middle Works*, vol. 12, p. 41.

32. G. W. F. Hegel, *Philosophy of History*, trans. J. Sibree (New York: Dover, 1956), pp. 111–112.

33. *Analects* 2.21: 或謂孔子曰:「子奚不為政?」子曰:「《書》云:『孝乎惟孝、友于兄弟,施於有政。』是亦為政,奚其為為政?」

34. Zhou Yiqun cites Yan Fu as claiming that social and political order in the two millennia of imperial China was from its beginnings "seventy percent a lineage organization and thirty percent an empire." Yiqun Zhou, *Festival, Feasts, and Gender Relations in Ancient China and Greece* (New York: Cambridge University Press, 2010), p. 19n55.

35. The Chinese sense of the political might prompt us to ask ourselves whether the center of our own political lives lies in those thick relations closer to home in our neighborhoods, classrooms, and workplaces rather than in our relation to some distant potentate.

36. See G. W. Leibniz, *Writings on China,* trans. Daniel J. Cook and Henry Rosemont Jr. (La Salle, IL: Open Court, 1998), p. 46. See also Franklin Perkins, *Leibniz and China* (Cambridge: Cambridge University Press, 2004).

37. Leibniz, *Writings on China,* pp. 47–48.

38. Roger T. Ames, *Human Becomings: Theorizing Persons for Confucian Role Ethics* (Albany: State University of New York Press, 2021), pp. 255–258.

39. *Analects* 2.3:子曰:「道之以政,齊之以刑,民免而無恥;道之以德,齊之以禮,有恥且格。」

40. See *Analects* 8.18:子曰:「巍巍乎!舜禹之有天下也,而不與焉。」"The Master said, 'How majestic they were, Yao and Shun, who reigned over the world but did not rule it.'" And again, at 15.5:子曰:「無為而治者,其舜也與?夫何為哉,恭己正南面而已矣。」"The Master said, 'If anyone could be said to have effected proper order while remaining noncoercive in his actions (*wuwei*), surely it was the legendary sage-ruler Shun. What did he do? He simply assumed an air of reverence and faced due south.'"

41. Dewey, *Middle Works,* vol. 11, p. 197; Dewey, *Middle Works,* vol. 13, p. 103: "The notion that, by the mere introduction of western economy, China can be 'saved,' while it retains the old morality, the old set of ideas, the old Confucianism—or what genuine Confucianism had been petrified into—and the old family system, is the most utopian of sentimental idealisms." And at p. 230: "There is an enormous interest in making over the traditional family system, in overthrowing militarism, in extension of local self-government, but always the discussion comes back to education, to teachers and students, as the central agency in promoting other reforms."

42. Bertrand Russell, *The Problem of China* (London: George Allen & Unwin, 1922), p. 5.

43. *Analects* 1.2:「君子務本,本立而道生。孝弟也者,其为仁之本与。」

44. Zhao Tingyang 趙汀陽, 惠此中國 (The making and becoming of China: Its way of historicity) (Beijing: CITIC Press, 2016), pp. 148–149: 人道問題首先正是"生生,"而"生生"的第一步便是生長,這正是中國思想演化線索的始發點。生長之事,必求生長之物"深根固柢"而使存在獲得生長的依據,因此生長首先要扎根。"生長"和"扎根"這兩個隱喻表示了中國思想的行徑。

45. *Analects* 1.12:「禮之用,和為貴。先王之道斯為美,小大由之。有所不行,知和而和,不以禮節之,亦不可行也。」See also 12.1 and 12.15.

46. The sociologist Ambrose King (Jin Yaoji 金耀基) explains that while Confucian persons are defined in terms of their particular relations with each other (*lun* 倫), they lack the conceptual and practical resources for relating effectively to the "group" (*qun* 群) more broadly construed. For King, the greatest limitation of Confucian ethics lies in its failure to provide the structural resources for particular persons to become fully social beings. See Am-

brose King, "The Individual and the Group in Confucianism: A Relational Perspective," in *Individualism and Holism: Studies in Confucian and Taoist Values,* ed. Donald Munro (Ann Arbor: University of Michigan Press, 1985), pp. 62–65.

47. See, for example, *Analects* 4.16, 14.12, 14.13, 16.10, and 19.1, and *Mencius* 1A1, 2A2, 7A33, 7A34, 7B31. The Confucian formula of "putting oneself in the other's place" (*shu* 恕) and then "doing one's best" (*zhong* 忠) is another variation on this deferential attempt to keep one's range of concern open and inclusive in determining the moral thing to do.

48. The spirit of the "capabilities approach" developed for the economics of welfare by Nobel laureate Amartya Sen in the mid-1980s shares this same concern that real justice must respect particularity. Amartya Sen, *The Idea of Justice* (Cambridge, MA: Harvard University Press, 2009).

49. Henry Rosemont Jr. and Roger T. Ames, *The Chinese Classic of Family Reverence: A Philosophical Translations of the* Xiaojing (Honolulu: University of Hawai'i Press, 2009), pp. 112–113.

50. The figures available as of March 31, 2021, on the COVID-19 Dashboard by the Center for Systems Science and Engineering at Johns Hopkins University, provide the following numbers of deaths from COVID-19: China 4,841, Japan 9,155, South Korea 1,731, Vietnam 35, Taiwan 10, Singapore 30. See https://gisanddata.maps.arcgis.com/apps/opsdashboard/index.html?fbclid=IwAR3gpd96foNID6ATcrvexEpvPLvJ8w8r8AXVU3cncMxAjkwY6VIpzveWFgA#/bda7594740fd40299423467b48e9ecf6.

Contributors

ROGER T. AMES is Humanities Chair Professor at Peking University, Senior Academic Advisor of the Peking University Berggruen Research Center, and Professor Emeritus of Philosophy at the University of Hawai'i. He is former editor of *Philosophy East and West* and founding editor of *China Review International*. Ames has authored several interpretative studies of Chinese philosophy and culture, and his publications also include translations of the Chinese philosophical classics. His most recent monograph is *Human Becomings: Theorizing Persons for Confucian Role Ethics* (2021). He has most recently compiled the new *Sourcebook in Classical Confucian Philosophy* (2023) and its companion, *A Conceptual Lexicon for Classical Confucian Philosophy* (2021).

RAJEEV BHARGAVA is an Honorary Fellow at CSDS. He was the Centre's Director from 2007 to 2014 and is currently the Director of its Parekh Institute of Indian Thought. He has been a Professor at the Jawaharlal Nehru University and the University of Delhi. He is also an Honorary Fellow at Balliol College, Oxford. Bhargava has been a Fellow at Harvard University; at the Institute of Advanced Studies, Jerusalem; at the Wissenschaftskolleg, Berlin; and at IWM, Vienna, as well as a Berggruen Fellow at Stanford University, Tsinghua University, and New York University, and a Professorial Fellow at the Institute of Social Justice, ACU, Sydney. Bhargava's publications include *Individualism in Social Science* (1992); *What Is Political Theory and Why Do We Need It?* (2010); and *The Promise of India's Secular Democracy* (2010). His edited works include *Secularism and Its Critics* (1998); *Politics and Ethics of the Indian Constitution* (2008); and *Politics, Ethics and the Self: Re-reading Gandhi's* Hind Swaraj (2022) His latest publication, *Between Hope and Despair: 100 Ethical reflections on Contemporary India* (2023), is written for a wider public.

PETER D. HERSHOCK is Director of the Asian Studies Development Program and Coordinator of the Humane AI Initiative at the East-West Center in

Honolulu. He was a Berggruen Institute China Center fellow in 2017–2018. His philosophical work makes use of Buddhist conceptual resources to address contemporary issues of global concern. He has authored or edited more than a dozen books, including *Reinventing the Wheel: A Buddhist Response to the Information Age* (1999); *Buddhism in the Public Sphere: Reorienting Global Interdependence* (2006); *Valuing Diversity: Buddhist Reflection on Realizing a More Equitable Global Future* (2012); *Public Zen, Personal Zen: A Buddhist Introduction* (2014); *Human Beings or Human Becomings? A Conversation with Confucianism on the Concept of Person* (edited, 2021); and *Buddhism and Intelligent Technology: Toward a More Humane Future* (2021).

LIAM C. KELLEY is Associate Professor of Southeast Asian Studies in the Institute of Asian Studies (IAS) at Universiti Brunei Darussalam (UBD). Primarily a historian of premodern Vietnam, he has published on a variety of topics, from the culture of premodern Sino-Vietnamese diplomatic relations, to the medieval construction of Vietnamese antiquity, to the impact of globalization and the digital revolution on area studies. Beyond those topics, Professor Kelley is currently re-examining the Chinese sources on early Southeast Asian history, and in 2022 published the first installment of a two-part article on "Srivijaya." Finally, together with Senior Professor Phan Le Ha of the Sultan Hassanal Bolkiah Institute of Education (SHBIE) at UBD, Professor Kelley organizes an annual conference called Engaging with Vietnam: An Interdisciplinary Dialogue (engagingwithvietnam.org).

XINFENG KONG was born in Qufu City of Shandong Province in 1980, and he is one of Confucius' seventy-sixth-generation lineal descendants. He studied the history of Western political thought and political theory in the School of Government of Peking University from 1998 to 2009 and received his PhD there with a doctoral dissertation on Thomas Hobbes' political theory on man and citizen. His main research fields include the history of Chinese and Western political thought, contemporary Chinese state governance, and the Sinicization of Marxism. He has published several books and dozens of academic papers, and in recent years has been focusing on the study on Confucian virtue politics and Chinese political theory. He serves as Dean of the School of Marxism at Minzu University of China in Beijing. In 2021, he was appointed a Mount Ni Scholar in Confucianism by his hometown municipal authority.

JUN-HYEOK KWAK is Professor of Philosophy (Zhuhai) at Sun Yat-sen University. He received his PhD from the University of Chicago in 2002. His research interests lie at the crossroads of political philosophy from Socrates to Machiavelli, contemporary sociopolitical theories, and comparative philosophy. He has published numerous articles and books on political philosophy, comparative philosophy, and global justice in various languages, including "Confucian Role-Ethics with Non-Domination: Civil Compliance in Times of Crisis" (*Ethical Theory and Moral Practice,* 2022) and "Deliberation with Persuasion: the 'Political' in Aristotle's *Politics*" (*Australian Journal of Political Science,* 2021). Currently, he is serving as general editor of the Routledge series Political Theories in East Asian Context and coeditor of *Journal of Social and Political Philosophy.*

VIREN MURTHY teaches transnational Asian history at the University of Wisconsin–Madison and researches Chinese, Japanese, and Indian intellectual history. He is the author of *The Political Philosophy of Zhang Taiyan: The Resistance of Consciousness* (2011), *The Politics of Time in China and Japan* (2022), and *Pan-Asianism and the Legacy of the Chinese Revolution* (2023). He is coeditor with Prasenjit Duara and Andrew Sartori of *A Companion to Global Historical Thought* (2014); with Joyce Liu of *East Asian Marxisms and Their Trajectories* (2017); and with Max Ward and Fabian Schäfer of *Confronting Capital and Empire: Rethinking Kyoto School Philosophy* (2017). He has published articles in *Modern Intellectual History, Modern China, Frontiers of History in China, positions: east asia cultures critique, Jewish Social Studies, Critical Historical Studies,* and *Journal of Labor and Society.*

TAKAHIRO NAKAJIMA is Director of the Institute for Advanced Studies on Asia, University of Tokyo, and former Director of the East Asian Academy for New Liberal Arts. He is currently interested in Chinese philosophy and Japanese philosophy from the viewpoint of world philosophy. His publications include *History of Chinese Philosophy* (2022); *Philosophy in Crisis: Discourses of Imagination* (2021); *History of World Philosophy* (edited with Kunitake Ito, Shiro Yamauchi, and Noburu Notimi, 2020); *Zhuangzi and the Happy Fish* (edited with Roger T. Ames, 2015); *Praxis of Co-existence: State and Religion* (2011); and *The Reverberation of Chinese Philosophy: Language and Politics* (2007).

MUSTAPHA KAMAL PASHA is Personal Chair in International Politics at Aberystwyth University in Wales. He was Sixth Century Chair and Head of International Relations at the University of Aberdeen between 2006 and 2013, and previously taught at the School of International Service, American University, from 1993 to 2006. He is the author and editor of several books, including *Globalization, Difference, and Human Security* (2013); *International Relations and the New Inequality* (with Craig Murphy, 2002); and *Colonial Political Economy* (1998). His recent work *Islam and International Relations: Fractured Worlds* (2017) explores the confluence of international relations theory and Islam. A recipient of numerous awards, including research fellowships from the Japan Society of the Promotion of Science (JSPS), he served as vice president of the International Studies Association in 2012–2013.

QIN YAQING is Distinguished Chair Professor at Shandong University and Professor of International Studies at China Foreign Affairs University. He is an associate member of the Royal Academy of Belgium. His academic research focuses on international relations theory and global governance, and his recent publications include *Globalizing IR Theory: Critical Engagement* (2020); *Reconstruction of Order in a Multiplex World* (2019); *A Relational Theory of World Politics* (2018); and *Global Governance: Reconstruction of Order in a Multiplex World* (2019).

MOGOBE B. RAMOSE is a Research Professor in the Sefako Makgatho Health Sciences University, Department of Clinical Psychology, Ga-Rankuwa, South Africa. He obtained the doctor of philosophy (Philosophy) degree from the Catholic University of Louvain (KUL) in Belgium. He holds the master of science degree in international relations from the London School of Economics and Political Science at the University of London. His special areas of interest are ethics, African philosophy, and philosophy of law. He is a member of the Steering Committee of the International Federation of Philosophical Societies. His book *African Philosophy through Ubuntu* has been translated into Dutch. He has published many articles in peer-reviewed journals and as chapters in books. He is a widely quoted author.

SOR-HOON TAN is Professor of Philosophy at Singapore Management University. Her research focuses on comparative studies of Confucianism and John Dewey's Pragmatism. She is author of *Confucian Democracy: A Deweyan Reconstruction*. She has edited the *Bloomsbury Research Handbook on Chinese Philosophy Methodologies* and *Challenging Citizenship: Group Membership and Cultural Identity in a Global Age*. She is coeditor of *Filial Piety in Chinese History and Thought; The Moral Circle and the Self: Chinese and Western Perspectives; Democracy as Culture: Deweyan Pragmatism in a Globalizing World;* and *Feminist Encounters with Confucius*. Her works have appeared in *Philosophy East and West; Dao: A Journal of Comparative Philosophy; Journal of Chinese Philosophy; Australasian Journal of Philosophy; Journal of Value Inquiry; Transactions of the Charles S. Peirce Society; Contemporary Pragmatism;* and other academic journals.

CONTRIBUTORS

CHRISTIAN UHL is Associate Professor for Japanese Studies at the University of Ghent, Belgium. He obtained his PhD in Japanese and modern Chinese studies at the University of Heidelberg, Germany, and publishes on modern Japanese and Chinese intellectual history and philosophy. His publications include "Fukuzawa Yukichi and Miyazaki Tōten: A Double Portrait in Black and White of an Odd Couple in the Age of Globalizing Capitalism" (2014); "Translation and Time: A Memento of the Curvature of the Poststructuralist Plane" (2012); and "Displacing Japan: Takeuchi Yoshimi's Lu Xun in Light of Nishida's Philosophy—and Vice Versa" (2009).

BAN WANG is the William Haas Professor in Chinese Studies in the departments of East Asian Languages and Cultures and Comparative Literature at Stanford University. His major publications include *At Home in Nature: Technology, Labor, and Critical Ecology* (2023); *China in the World: Culture, Politics, and World Vision* (2022); *History and Memory* (2004); *Illuminations from the Past* (2004); and *The Sublime Figure of History* (1997). He has edited or coedited eight books in the fields of Chinese and comparative studies, including *Chinese Visions of World Order: Tianxia, Culture, and World Politics* (2017); *Words and Their Stories* (2011); and *Trauma and Cinema* (2004). He has taught at the State University of New York–Stony Brook, Harvard University, Rutgers University, East China Normal University, Yonsei University, and Seoul National University.

BINFAN WANG is a PhD candidate in the Department of Political Science, University of Toronto. Wang's research interests include the comparison between Chinese thought and contemporary Western political theory, especially on global justice, meritocracy, and nationalism. He has published an article in *Philosophy East and West* and presented several papers at the annual meetings of the American Political Science Association. He is writing a dissertation titled "All-under-Heaven: A Confucian Theory of Global Justice."

QINGXIN K. WANG is a Professor in the School of Public Policy and Management, Tsinghua University, Beijing, China. His specialization includes East Asian politics and international relations, political philosophy, and Confucian political thought. He received a master's degree in Western philosophy from Columbia University and a PhD in political science from the State University of New York at Buffalo. He taught at the University of Hong Kong and the National University of Singapore for many years before joining Tsinghua University.

STEVEN Y. H. YANG is the "Tianxia" Project Consultant at the Berggruen China Center. His interest in the topic of *tianxia* began during his time as a Yenching Scholar at the Yenching Academy of Peking University. He interviewed Zhao Tingyang in spring 2020 for his research paper "Global Governance with Chinese Characteristics—Analyzing the Concepts of *Tianxia* as a Chinese Alternative." He is grateful for the many great opportunities to learn from a diverse range of distinguished scholars in this project.

Index

Adorno, Theodor, 106
"All-under-Heaven" theory. See *tianxia* 天下 All-under-Heaven theory
Ames, Roger T., 15–16, 224
Annan, Kofi, 229
Appiah, Kwame, 278
Aquinas, Thomas, 176–177, 184
Aristotle, 361–362
Arkoun, Mohammed, 208
Arthā śāstra, 334
ASEAN (Association of Southeast Asian Nations), 232
Asoka, 15, 322–344
Augustine, Saint, 176–177, 255
Austin, John, 354

Bai, Tongdong, 278
Baik, Young-Seo, 238
Bell, Daniel, 23, 137
Bellah, Robert, 101, 323
Belt and Road Initiative, 146, 365
Benedict XVI (pope), 103
Bentham, Jeremy, 177
Berggruen Research Center, Peking University, 2
Bhargava, Rajeev, 15
Bidet, Jacques, 119, 120, 138, 145–147, 151
Bodin, Jean, 176
Book of Changes, 3, 310–311, 314
Book of Rites, 281
Buddha, 328–332
Buddhism, 13, 105, 109, 111, 248, 352–353; and bodhisattva, 260–261, 263; and diversity, 256–261; and international relations, 250–265

buren 不忍 ("a heart that cannot bear suffering"), 9, 89–91
Burke, Edmund, 157, 161

Cai Yong, 41
Callahan, William, 274
capitalism, global, 9, 10, 11, 68–96, 97–117, 118–151; morality of, 75–76; Pope Francis on, 76–77
Carens, Joseph, 271, 274–275, 277–278
Chan, Sin-yee, 137
Ch'en Ku-ying [Chen Guying], 127
Chu Sinan, 204
Clemenceau, Georges, 155
Confucianism, 14, 27, 119, 147, 226, 252–254, 282; and the concept of the human, 212–216; and the concept of the political, 347, 357–359; criticism of, 140–141; and a critique of Zhao Tingyang, 289–307; and education, 15; and ethics, 14–15, 15–16, 100–102, 112, 142–143, 156–157, 184–187, 192, 289–307; and familyhood, 33–34; and "family reverence" (*xiao*), 345, 359–367; and harmony, 256–261; Hong Daeyong's transvaluation of, 27–31; and internationalism, 345–370; and Islam, 198–220; and leadership, 308–321; Leibniz on, 360; political philosophy of, 155–171; on public (*gongde* 公德) and private (*side* 私德) morality, 160–168; and a relational ontology, 203–204, 212, 221–235; and the *tianxia* discourse, 297–301
Confucius, 28, 56, 89, 118, 132, 137, 141, 147, 231, 258, 281, 283, 314, 341

Conrad, Sebastian, 101
"continuity in change" (*biantong* 變通), 7
cosmopolitanism, 8, 11, 155, 271–274, 285; and anticosmopolitanism, 39–67; Chinese-style, 24–27, 35–36, 204, 293–294; defined, 272; Islamic, 204–211, 214–216; and the League of Nations, 180; Liang Qichao on, 155–171; Sun Zhongshan on, 167–168; Zhao Tingyang's compatible, 23–27. *See also* internationalism
COVID-19 pandemic, 1, 16, 118, 230, 250, 270, 348, 367
Creel, Herlee, 309

Dallmayr, Fred, 278, 285
Daoism, 27, 119, 226
daren 大人 (the great man), 15, 308–321; in the *Book of Changes,* 310; and *junzi,* 311; Wang Yangming on, 311; in Xunzi, 311
Darwin, Charles, 107, 110
de 德 (life, nature, clan, name) (conventionally, "virtue"), 312–317
"Declaration of the Rights of Man and Citizen," 74
decoloniality studies, 9, 40, 236
Deng, Xiaoping, 98, 141
de Tejada, F. E., 87–88
Dewey, John, 128, 345–370; on China, 357–359; and the Great Community, 346, 351–356, 363; and the "idea" of democracy, 345–346, 348–350; and "individuality," 346, 350–351; and internationalism, 346
dhamma (politico-moral ethic), 15, 322–344; as a civil religion, 323; and expansive hegemony, 334–338; and material welfare of subjects, 331–334; as personal and social morality, 323–326; as a political ethic, 326–328; above the ruler and the ruled, 328–331
di 帝, as Shang deity, 309–310
Dialogue on Mount Uisan 醫山問答, 8, 23, 27–36, 294
diversity, achieved, 250–265, 346, 347, 351–353; and the family, 360–364
Djamson, E. C., 73–74
Don Quixote, 103
Dryer, June Teufel, 110
Dương, Bá Trạc, 61–62, 64

Eagleton, Terry, 164
El Baradei, Mohamed, 80

Emerson, Ralph Waldo, 350
Emirbayer, Mustafa, 222–223
Enright, D. J., 80–81
equity, relational, 250–265, 346, 347, 351–353; and the family, 360–364
"ethical ecology," 13, 251, 256–261, 353

"family reverence" (*xiao* 孝), 15–16, 345
Fei, Xiaotong, 14, 255, 284–285, 319–320
Ferguson, Niall, 98
Fieldhouse, D. K., 73–74
Francis (pope), 76–77
Fukuyama, Francis, 162
Fukuzawa, Yukichi, 131–134, 149
Fung, Yu-lan (Feng Youlan), 91, 309

Gabriel, Markus, 238–239
Gan, Chunsong, 22, 141, 144, 278, 288–299
Gan, Yang, 141
Gentili, Alberico, 177
George, David Lloyd, 155
Gia Long, 43–47, 51–52
Gindin, Sam, 139
God, monotheistic, 198, 208, 237, 242–244
Gramsci, Antonio, 143, 334, 339
Great Learning, 28, 33, 303, 311
Grotius, Hugo, 177
guanxi 關係 (relations), 224, 260

Habermas, Jürgen, 182, 238
hakkō ichi'u ("the world under one roof"), 10, 107–108
Hall, David L., 224
Hardt, Michael, 138
Haug, W. F., 98–99, 111
Hegel, G. W. F., 10, 104, 106–107, 111, 119, 123–129, 140–141, 143, 148, 149, 358–360
hegemony, 21–38, 39–67
Heidegger, Martin, 104
Held, David, 182
Heraclitus, 110
Hershock, Peter D., 13, 352–353
Hồ, Chí Minh, 64
Hobbes, Thomas, 203, 225, 254
Hong, Daeyong 洪大容, 8, 21, 23, 27–36, 294; and an alternative understanding of *tianxia,* 31–36; and familyhood, 33–34; and harmony,

254; and the transvaluation of Confucianism, 27–31
Hong Kong, 295–296, 365
Hu, Shi, 120
hua 華 (civilized) and *yi* 夷 (uncivilized) distinction, 24, 215, 237 248, 284, 296; Vietnamese version of, 47–65
Huang, Mingchong, 313, 316, 319
Huang, Zongxi, 131–133
Hughes, Christopher, 121–122
Huh, Bong, 26
Humboldt, Alexander von, 242
Huntington, Samuel, 308
Huxley, T. H., 359

internationalism, 345–370. *See also* cosmopolitanism
international order, the evolution of modern, 176–182
international relations (IR) theory, 22–23, 221–235, 354–356; a Buddhist revisioning of, 250–265; and governance by relations, 230–233; the middle way as a Buddhist methodology, 252–253; and neoliberal institutionalism, 229–230
intra-national relations, 3–4, 254–356, 368
Isaacs, Harold R., 308
Ishimoda, Shō, 139
Islam, 11–12; and Confucianism, 198–220; cosmology of, 204–208, 216; and the concept of the human, 212–216; and *Tawhid* (Islamic principle of Oneness), 205–211; and *Ummah* as the human community, 208–211

Jackson, Patrick, 223
Jenco, Leigh, 277–278
John XXIII (pope), 69
justice, global, 13–14, 21–38, 212–213, 269–288, 289–307; epistemic, 70, 74–77

Kang, David, 23
Kang, Youwei, 134–135, 141, 155, 157, 161, 168
Kant, Immanuel, 92, 104, 110–111, 178, 221, 237–238, 243, 262, 273
Karatani, Kojin, 105, 138
Kautilya, 334–336
Kelley, Liam, 9
Kennedy, John F., 81–83

Keohane, Robert, 229
Kesley, Jane, 77
Kindleberger, Charles, 229
King, Ambrose, 369–370
Kobayashi, Toshiaki, 110
Kong, Xinfeng, 15
Konoe, Fumimarō, 108
Kōsaka, Masa'aki, 104
Kosambi, D. D., 328
Koselleck, Reinhart, 236
Kotoku, Shusui, 139
Kropotkin, Pyotr, 168–169
Kwak, Jun-Hyeok, 8, 10, 293–294
Kymlicka, Will, 276

Lange, H. M., 72–73
Laozi, 26, 119, 123–129, 145
Lau, D. C., 291
League of Nations, 107, 155, 166, 178, 180
Leibniz, G. W., 105–106, 110, 360; and possible worlds, 239–240
Lenin, Vladimir, 143
Levenson, Joseph R., 170–171
Levinas, Emmanuel, 124, 239
Li, Dazhao, 157, 168
Li, Feng, 282–283
Li, Minqi, 111
Li, Zehou, 147
Li, Zongtong, 313
Liang, Qichao, 11, 132–133, 139, 155–171, 202–203; on public (*gongde* 公德) and private (*side* 私德) morality, 160–166
Lin, Qun, 120, 140–143
Linji, Yixuan, 261
Liu Bang, 240–242
Lu, Buwei, 132
Lumumba, Patrice, 79
Luo, Mengce, 157
Lương, Trúc Đàm, 62–63

Mahabharata, 327–328
Mahbubani, Kishore, 232
Mao, Zedong, 11, 120, 138, 141, 143, 157, 158, 159, 168–170
Maruyama, Masao, 108–109, 149
Marx, Karl, 101–103, 119, 126, 128
Marxism, 10–11, 118–120, 140–142
McArthur, Douglas, 180

Meiji Restoration, 135
Mencius, 17, 56, 89, 137, 142–145, 186, 283, 288, 291–292, 303, 364
Mill, J. S., 359
Miller, David, 271
Minh Mạng, 47–59
Mizoguchi, Yūzō, 133, 166, 168
Moore, Thomas, 225
morality, minimalist, 13, 15, 16, 270–275
Mori, Atsushi, 124, 237, 244–248
Mozi, 29–31
Muhammad, Prophet, 208
multiculturalism, 274–278
Murthy, Viren, 10–11

Nakajima, Takahiro, 12, 13, 124
nationalism, Chinese, 120–123, 137–140; Sun Zhongshan on, 166–168
nation-state, 10–11, 155–173, 345, 346, 347, 354–356; China exception to the, 357–359; and relationality, 12
Negri, Antonio, 138, 143–144
Nehru, Jawaharlal, 340–341
Nesbitt, Nick, 144
New World Order, 118–147; and Confucian family, 363–367; as the "Greater East-Asian co-prosperity sphere," 108; Japanese, 107–112, 119–120, 236–237
Nexon, Daniel, 223
Ngô, Giáp Dậu, 60–62
Nishida, Kitarō, 10, 103, 104–112; and the dialectical universal, 104–107; political philosophy of, 107–112, 131
Nishitani, Keiji, 104
Nomura, Yasunori, 249
"no outside" (*wuwai* 無外), 3, 40, 222–223
Nowack, Martin, 233
Nui, Onoue ("the Dark Lady of Osaka"), 102

Obama, Barack, 229
Olivelle, Patrick, 323, 334
ontology, of relations, 203–204, 212, 221–235
Owen, Wilfred, 80

Palmer, H. W., 70
Panitch, Leo, 139
pāṣaṇḍas (religio-philosophical groups), 324–325, 333, 338

Pascal, Blaise, 243–244, 248
Pasha, Mustapha Kamal, 11–12
Pax Americana, 5–6, 102, 229
Pax Britannica, 229
Pax Sinica, 5–6
Piketty, Thomas, 71–83, 138
Plato, 14, 362
Poe, Edgar Allan, 241–244, 248
Pogge, Thomas, 272–273, 275
Postone, Moishe, 120, 143–144, 151
predicament, human, 1–2, 13; history of, 70–83
Purdue, Peter, 111
Pye, Lucian, 135

Qin, Yaqing, 12, 13, 111, 255, 262–263, 278, 301–302, 353
Quốc, Thụy, 64–65
Qur'an, 206, 209

Ramose, Mogobe B., 9
Rawls, John, 25, 192, 270, 273, 299–300
Reagan, Ronald, 98
relationality, 12, 13; and a Buddhist revisioning of international relations, 250–265; as a Chinese ontology, 203–204, 212, 221–235; hierarchical, 21–38; and the *tianxia* world, 301–305; and *yinyang* as the meta-relationship, 225–228; and *zhongyong* dialectics, 225–228, 302
rheomode (the language of *ubu-ntu*), 86–89
Rig Veda, 326–328
Risse, Mathias, 273
Rodrik, Dani, 270
Rousseau, Jean-Jacques, 128, 164, 323
Russell, Bertrand, 92, 362

Schuessler, John M., 81
Schularick, Moritz, 98
Schupp, Karl-Heinz, 107, 110
Schwartz, Benjamin, 196
Schwarzkopf, Norman, 181
sekai shinchitsujo ("new world order"), 10
Shaughnessy, Edward, 278–279
Shi, Yongzhi, 299–300
Shiji (The Record of the Grand Historian), 240–242; as human astronomy, 241
Shimizu, Kōsuke, 103, 109, 111
Si, Weizhi, 312, 313, 317

Sima, Qian, 240–242
Singer, Peter, 283, 289
Smedley, Agnes, 170
Smith, Adam, 110, 262, 359
social Darwinism, in Vietnam, 60–65
Spencer, Herbert, 359
Spinoza, Baruch, 246
Sun, Yat-sen (Sun Zhongshan), 11, 157, 158, 162, 169, 170; on nationalism, 166–168
Suzuki, Shigetaka, 104

Takeda, Taijun, 124, 237; and parallel worlds, 240–242
Takeuchi, Yoshimi, 241–242
Tan, Sor-hoon, 14, 15, 120, 137–138, 142
Tanaka, Chigaku, 108
Tang, Junyi 唐君毅, 3
Tawhid (Islamic principle of Oneness), 205–211
Taylor, Charles, 351
Tennō (emperor) system, 108–110, 131
Terreblanche, Sampie, 71–83
Thapar, Romila, 323, 330
Thatcher, Margaret, 98
Thiệu Trị, 58–59
tian 天, as Zhou deity, 309–310
tianxia 天下 All-under-Heaven theory: American, 111; as anticosmopolitan and protoracial, 39–67; as Chinese cosmopolitanism, 23–27; compared with UN order, 174–197; and the concept of the human, 212–216; in Confucian discourse, 297–301; as a cosmological order, 202–204, 216; defined, 221–224; as *dhamma*, 322–344; as East Asian civilization, 237–238, 248; as family, 41–42; Gan Chunsong on, 22; and global justice, 269–288, 289–307; Hong Daeyong's interpretation of, 31–36; and Islam, 11–12, 198–220; and just war, 188–189; as lacking in universality, 237–238; and leadership, 308–321; maintenance of order, 187–194; as a model for a new global order, 97–117; as a moral community, 211–216; and the nation-state, 155–173; ontology of, 123–128, 221–235, 253–256; as parallel worlds, 240–242; as praxis, 12, 248; and principles of international cooperation and mutual assistance, 191–192; public (*gongde* 公德) and private (*side* 私德) morality, 160–166, 353; as a relational world, 301–305; scope of, 290–292; and self-defense, 189–191; territorial integrity and proportionality of punitive force, 193–194; and the *Ummah*, 199–201; universalizing in the East Asian context, 236–249; Vietnamese conception of, 9, 39–67; Zhou dynasty model of, 11, 14
tianxia system 天下體系, 2–3, 39–42, 157, 250
tiyong 體用 ("forming and functioning"), 4, 349
traditional Chinese medicine (TCM), 224
transcendence and immanence, 198–199, 210–211, 213–216, 224, 239
tributary system, Chinese, 23, 35–36, 111, 196, 293–294
Trump, Donald, 270
Tu, Wei-ming, 300–301, 303

ubu-ntu ("humaneness"), 9; philosophy of, 83–88
Uhl, Christian, 9, 120
Ummah ("the community of the faithful"), 12, 204–206; as the human community, 208–211; as a moral community, 211–214; and *tianxia*, 199–201
United Nations (UN), 11; compared with *tianxia* order, 174–197; and UN Charter, 178–180, 187, 192, 194–195, 229
Universal Declaration of Human Rights, 14, 74–75, 179, 187

Vandevelde, Toon, 79
Vattel, Emer de, 177
Vietnam, and possessing *tianxia*, 42–65

Wakeman, Frederic, 163
Walzer, Michael, 13–14, 15, 270–275, 278, 285
Wang, Ban, 5, 10–11, 139, 353
Wang, Binfan, 14
Wang, Guowei, 312
Wang, Jianwen, 313–314
Wang, Ke, 318–319
Wang, Mingming, 202–203
Wang, Pei, 23
Wang, Qingxin K., 11
Wang, Yangming, 233, 311
wangdao 王道 (the Kingly Way of government), 90–91, 165, 313
Weber, Max, 101, 103
weiqi 圍棋 (*go*), 224, 231

Wells, H. G., 340
Wendt, Alexander, 253–254
Westphalian order, 1, 8, 12, 23, 24, 39, 109, 174, 176, 199, 202, 203, 204, 205, 209, 210, 211, 212, 214, 215, 222, 254, 289, 346, 353, 354
Whitehead, Alfred North, 223, 354
Wilhelm, Hellmut, 227
Wilson, Woodrow, 107, 155, 166
Wong, Kan Seng, 232
Wu, Emperor of the Han, 241

Xi, Jinping, 100, 112
Xiang Yu, 240–242
xiao 孝. See "family reverence" (*xiao* 孝)
Xu, Jilin, 238
Xunzi, 163, 311, 342, 343

Yan, Fu, 359
Yan, Xuetong, 343
Yeltsin, Boris, 121
yiduobufen 一多不分 (one is many, many one), 3–4
Yijing. See *Book of Changes*
yin–yang meta-relationship, 225–228

Zhang, Taiyan, 139
Zhang, Wenmu, 122–123
Zhang Feng, 23
Zhang Yaonan, 311
Zhao, Tingyang, 2–3, 22, 39–42, 56, 65, 110–111, 119–120, 123–128, 157, 238, 262, 274, 278, 283, 289–290, 292–298, 308, 363; and compatible cosmopolitanism, 23–27; Marxist critique of, 140–146; objections to his *tianxia* theory, 5–11, 13, 23–27; and relational rationality, 25; and the whirlpool model of world order, 4–5; and worlding the world, 128–147
zhongyong 中庸 dialectic, 225–228, 232–233, 302; and harmony, 227–228
Zheng, Kai, 308, 312–313, 318
Zhou dynasty *tianxia* model, 11, 14, 28–30, 159–160, 278–284, 309, 315–320; compared with UN model, 174–187; nature of, 182–185; rites compared with international law, 175
Zhouli (*Book of Zhou Rites*), 185, 195
Zhuangzi, 29, 31–34
Zhu Xi, 28–29, 33
Zou, Xiaodong, 312, 314
Zuozhuan, on Confucian morality, 184–185, 187–194, 316–317

Printed in the United States
by Baker & Taylor Publisher Services